Rapidex®
SELF LETTER DRAFTING COURSE

INSTANT LETTER PRODUCER

So fast — that it produces letters in minutes!
So simple — that even a below average person can use it!

Step 1 : Refer to the Index
Step 2 : Turn to the relevant page
Step 3 : Select the desired sentences
Step 4 : Arrange them in proper order

.....and your letter is ready! Shape and mould the letter the way you want it to be. Give it the right shade of meaning .... And have as many letters as you want on the same subject!

PUSTAK MAHAL®
Delhi•Bangalore•Mumbai•Patna•Hyderabad•London

Publishers
Pustak Mahal®, Delhi

J-3/16, Daryaganj, New Delhi-110002
☎ 23276539, 23272783, 23272784 • *Fax:* 011-23260518
E-mail: info@pustakmahal.com • *Website:* www.pustakmahal.com

London Office
51, Severn Crescents, Slough, Berkshire, SL 38 UU, England
E-mail: pustakmahaluk@pustakmahal.com

Sales Centre
10-B, Netaji Subhash Marg, Daryaganj, New Delhi-110002
☎ 23268292, 23268293, 23279900 • *Fax:* 011-23280567
E-mail: rapidexdelhi@indiatimes.com

Branch Offices
Bangalore: ☎ 22234025
E-mail: pmblr@sancharnet.in • pustak@sancharnet.in
Mumbai: ☎ 22010941
E-mail: rapidex@bom5.vsnl.net.in
Patna: ☎ 3294193 • *Telefax:* 0612-2302719
E-mail: rapidexptn@rediffmail.com
Hyderabad: *Telefax:* 040-24737290
E-mail: pustakmahalhyd@yahoo.co.in

© **Pustak Mahal, Delhi**

ISBN 978-81-223-0033-8

Edition : 2008

Printed at : Param Offsetters, Okhla, New Delhi-110020

INTRODUCTION

We all are required to write letters on one occasion or another. So, the aim of this book is to provide practical help to all those who feel handicapped in letter writing and are not confident of how to go about it. This volume is an encyclopaedia of letters for all occasions.

Letter writing is an art and the ability to write well is a pre-requisite for any profession. Flair for writing is a key to personal success too. Without letters, it would be difficult to place an order, merchandise, pay bills, borrow money, seek a job, accept invitations or even to communicate with one's near and dear ones. Thus, in a way, letter writing skill, especially for business, is as important in the present day business world, as food or fresh air for man to live.

A man's personality is often reflected in his letters. In nearly every walk of life, at every step, it often becomes vitally important to write one's own letters, and write them well. These help one to communicate with others which, in turn, also develop one's own personality. A good letter is, thus, enriching for both, the sender and receiver.

It is not difficult to write letters in a foreign language, here to say English, if one keeps certain guiding principles in mind. By just studying a few common examples one can be sure of oneself.

This book is intended as a concise and practical guide for writing correct and effective letters. It is also a handy manual for quick and convenient reference. To become proficient in letter writing, you just have to learn and then apply the fundamental principles and techniques presented in this book. Throughout the book you will find a number of sample letters. Get this book and study it. Keep it handy at office, home or school. Refer to it as often as necessary. It will surely help you write correct and effective letters – ideally suited to all occasions and requirements. Rare indeed is a person who can sit down and dish out a wonderful letter without giving it a second thought.

We have great pleasure in putting into your hands a thoroughly revised and enlarged edition of Self Letter Drafting Course. It is needless to stress that the revision has been extensive and done by professional experts in the field, tuning it to the changed present day world incorporating latest styles and trends. Many new sentences have been added and the existing sentences have been redrafted to make them more effective. Vocabularies have also been revised and made more useful in drafting personal, social and business letters.

We have attempted to give you more reading matter. An attractive type face has been used and the layout and get-up of the book speak for themselves. We are sure our readers shall find this edition improved a lot, convenient and highly useful.

Publishers

Contents

SECTION-I

Personal and Social Letters

SECTION-II

Job Applications

SECTION-III

Business Letters

6

Some Important Guidelines for Effective Letter Writing

Good skill in letter writing, especially in English, is an asset in today's world of growing competition. This skill comes in handy not only in business relations but also in personal relationships. Today, we require its help at almost every step in our life.

The basic purpose of a letter is communication. It takes a message across and expresses certain ideas. So, in more ways than one, letter writing is a creative exercise. Every letter calls for a particular style and economy of words. Clear, correct and simple English is the basis of good letters. And clear writing with a good style can emerge only from clear thinking.

Letter writing has been made absolutely simple and easy through this manual. From here ready-made letters can be used by making a little or no changes. Once the guiding principles given in this book are understood and followed properly, letter writing can be a pleasure. At the beginning of each chapter a short section has been devoted to the essential elements concerning the type of correspondence the chapter deals with. This is followed by a particular number of model letters which the reader can use as inspiration for his own writing.

In letter writing you must make sure that you are: **Timely and Natural**

I. **Be Timely** : A letter which aims at meeting a social obligation fails in its purpose if it arrives late. It can cause inconvenience and hurt the other's feelings.

II. **Be Natural** : While writing letters you should be as natural as possible. You should be able to visualize the reaction of the reader after reading your letter. So, the tastes, interests and preferences of the person you are writing to, must be kept in mind while addressing him in a social letter. One should write in such a style that one is talking to the reader. Such a letter is a genuine expression of one's feelings and ideas.

Other Principles of Letter Writing:

1. **Purpose and Content** : Let us first see what the guiding principles of a good letter writing are. Most important are the 'purpose' and 'content'. You must be very clear on why you are writing the letter and what is to be said. For instance, a letter of apology should merely apologize instead of repeating the details of offence. A letter of congratulations is different from a "letter of Greetings" or "Best Wishes" just as an order of goods should not dwindle into a letter of complaint about previous supplies etc. There should also not be any repetition of ideas.

2. **Paragraphing and Punctuation** : Whatever one has to convey must be arranged properly. Paragraphs and punctuation are the elements which give the letter a proper form and order. As a result, they are essential for a good letter.

   One should see to it that a group of similar ideas are expressed at one place only and a long letter with a lot of repetitions not properly paragraphed makes it monotonous to read. Earlier the paragraphs used to be indented, whereas, the latest trend is starting the paragraph from the margin itself. A new paragraph can be introduced for every new topic to be detailed in the letter. Particularly in commercial letters it is desirable to introduce paragraphs. Inside the paragraph, it is the punctuation that controls the flow. Long sentences without proper punctuation are clumsy and can even suggest wrong meaning.

3. **Language and Style** : Correct choice of words and expressions go a long way in making a letter lucid and readable. If one manages to develop a good style in English, it can be a valuable asset. However, in letter writing one should avoid unnecessary words and try to be as natural as one is in day-to-day conversation, in conveying the message.

4. **Who are you writing to?** : Another important principle of letter writing is to know who the letter is being written to. Whoever the addressee is, whether a relative or a pen friend, the manager of a hotel or the director of a Company, one must make sure that one's letter is correctly directed to that person only and to nobody else. Even if it is required in a business letter that a copy be marked to a second person or persons, take care that the information is not passed to anybody not concerned with the matter. That may adversely affect the interest of the sender. If you know about the receiver, you must keep his tastes, interests and preferences in mind and try to visualize his reaction upon receipt of your letter. Would he be bored or interested, offended or amused, alienated or attracted etc. are the points to be thought about while writing a letter. What overall impression it is going to make on the reader is very important.

5. **Tone** : The tone of letter can make a world of difference. In some cases, it is more important than the contents. So, it is essential to strike the right note from the very beginning. It, of-course, matters what one says, but what also matters a great deal is how it is expressed. Just as in conversation one can be ironic, friendly, cold, passionate or dignified, one can express such a tone in writing too. One should be more careful in regard to the tone while writing than speaking because the impact of a harsh tone in speaking can be immediately perceived and something can be instantly done about it. But a bad tone in writing can lead to irreparable damages. In personal letters, one has a variety of tones to choose from – one can be quizzical, ironic, circumspect, down-to-earth, hearty or coy, forthright or prudent. However, business letters call for greater care and caution. Since they have a bearing on the general business and have financial implications, they acquire added importance. Therefore, in style letters should aim at being friendly and polite, direct and correct.

6. **Length** : How long should a matter be? In fact there is no prescribed limit for any letter. It should be as long as its subject demands. Thus, its length can range from two lines to any number of pages. However, care should be taken to conclude the letter on a gentle note.

These are just a few basic rules of good letter writing. In the final analysis, letters, like life itself, break all rules. A good letter is one that moulds itself according to the dictates of time and occasion, and thus suits the particular situation. The model letters which follow in this book, therefore, should be regarded rather as examples than final.

One must keep in mind throughout that **personal letters express one's personality, formal letters say what one is supposed to say and business letters talk about business.** Thus, one may find letter writing as delightful as any other writing experience.

Personal and Social Letters

Characteristics of a Decent Letter

Personal Letters

Personal letters are those which are written between relatives and friends. At one time or the other, all of us are called upon to write such letters. These letters can be carriers of information, messenger of love and sympathy, promoters of harmony and harbingers of peace and tranquility. A good personal letter must appear natural.

Social Letters

These are usually written in the context of a social obligation. The occasion can be happy or unfortunate. These can also be written to make enquiries, lodge complaints and convey congratulations.

Some typical occasions are :

1. Greetings and Congratulations
2. Thanks
3. Invitations
4. Condolences
5. Sympathy
6. Educational matters
7. Office matters
8. Landlord and Tenant
9. Complaints
10. Between Couples
11. Apologies
12. Matrimonial Replies
13. Family Letters

Form and Arrangement :

The (From) Address: We begin a letter with a heading which is the address. In Britain, it is customary to write your full postal address at the top right-hand corner of the notepaper or letter-pad. The name or number of the house or building is followed by the name of the road or street, and then the name of the village, town or country. The date is written after that. Here are some typical styles of writing addresses:

> 4/45, SBP Buildings,
> Roop Nagar,
> Delhi-110007.
> April 2, 2000.

The address given at the top-right hand side of a letter is usually the one to which you wish replies to be sent. Thus, if you write from home but are going to stay at another place in the near future, you can mention this new address preceded by the word 'from'.

> From: Hotel Cortina,
> Napean Sea Road,
> Bombay-400 001.
> July 14, 2000.

If a person is staying at another person's house, the name of the owner is written above the address and is preceded by the letters 'C/o.' which denotes 'care of':

> C/o. Dr. P.C. Gupta,
> 4/40, Roop Nagar,
> Delhi-110007.
> March 20, 2000.

The Date :

There are four principal ways of writing the date on a letter:

1. Sunday, 10th September, 2000*
2. 10th September, 2000*
3. September 10, 2000
4. 10-09-2000**
5. 10/9/2000**

To Address or Inside Address

As for personal letters, the lay-out or style differs from person to person. However, there are some formal personal letters, almost like commercial correspondence, in which case the addressee's address is written in the letter itself on the left-hand side of the page below the Date and above the salutation. E.g.

10th September, 2000

M/s. Unicorn Books Pvt Ltd.,
F2/16, Ansari Road, Daryaganj
New Delhi-110 002

Dear Sirs,

M/s. is the short form of Messrs which is the plural form of Mr., and the last line of Inside Address is normally under-lined.

Example in case of personal letters:

Dr./ Mr./ Mrs./ Miss R N Gupta,
350, Civil Lines,
Srinagar,
Kashmir.

This address should be same as the one written on the envelope. In fact, sometimes in business letters, when 'window envelopes' are used, the letter is folded in such a way that the Inside address actually becomes the "To Address" on the Envelope, being visible through its window.

Yes, the letter becomes ready for despatch after signature and you have to put it in an envelope and write the "To Address" on the envelope. In case of Personal Letters, normally one can omit writing the "To Address" inside the letter. The letter can simply start with the salutation. Always write the address correctly and clearly.

(* These are the common styles of writing dates in India. ** In some foreign countries, these may be mistaken as October 9, 2000 because they write in the order of month-date –year)

Salutation :

Mostly letters begin with 'Dear....' written from the left-hand margin. This is called "salutation".

While addressing someone elder, one begins the letter using salutations such as 'Dear Father', 'Dear Aunt' etc. But while writing to a friend or so, 'Dear' is followed by the person's first name or even the nickname.

E.g.   Dear Sharada, or   Dear Charu,

(Sharada is the name and Charu is the nickname)

There must be a comma after the salutation. The text of the letter and the first word of salutation begin with capital letters:

Dear Ram,   Dear Rita,   Dear Tony,   Dear Johny,

As a rule, the text of the letter should begin leaving space for 5 alphabetical letters from the margin as in the case of starting a paragraph. (It may vary from place to place). E.g.

Dear Mala,

    What a long time...........

As one's relationship develops, the salutation can reflect various degrees of increasing cordiality, intimacy, friendship or love. E.g.

Dear Sonia,   My dear Naresh,   Dearest Sonia,

My dearest Sonia,   My dearest,   Darling, etc.

And thus such a letter becomes a very personal message; an instrument for exchange of love and affection between two persons.

While writing a personal letter to someone who is not a close friend or to someone who is treated with respect, the salutation begins as:

Dear Mr......,   Dear Mrs..........,   Dear Miss..........

followed by the person's surname. People are addressed in a letter as they are addressed in a conversation, especially in social letters.

But if the name is not known, it can start saying "Dear Sir" or "Dear Madam" etc.

When writing to a firm we use "Sirs" in place of "Sir". E.g. " Dear Sirs, "

Body of the Letter :

After salutation the body of the letter starts. This can be divided into three parts – (1) introduction, (2) Main message/ information or the descriptive middle portion (3) Conclusion. There are no strict rules regarding the body of letter of Personal Letters, which can be flexible and changeable according to the relation of the sender and receiver.

(i) Introduction :

Following are some examples that could be used to introduce the body of Business Letters. A few of them hold good in case of Personal Letters too.

1. Thank you for replying/ responding to my letter so promptly.

2. I have just received your letter.

3. Thank you for your prompt reply.

4. It was nice to hear from you after such a long time.

5. You will be glad/sorry to learn....

6. Thank you for your letter dated....

7. Trust this finds you in good health and cheers.

8. Thank you for your letter No....... dated....... regarding......

9. We thank you for your letter No....... dt........

10. Received your letter No....... dated....... on.......(subject)....

11. We have received......

12. We are in receipt of your letter No...... dated...... regarding......

13. This refers to your letter......

14. This has reference to your letter........

15. With reference to your letter.....

16. According to your letter......

17. Referring to your letter No....... dated....... regarding......., we would like to say that.....

18. This is with reference to your letter......

19. This is in response to your letter No........ dated........

20. This is in connection with your post-card dated.....

21. Please refer to your letter No...... dated....... on the subject of ....

22. We would like to inform you that........

23. This is to state that......

24. This is to inform you that.....

25. This is to request you that.....

26. We are pleased to ......

27. We have pleasure in informing you that.....

(ii) **Message or Descriptive Middle Portion :**

This is the main part of the letter. Here we answer the questions or supply the information asked for. In case of personal letters, we also try to include interesting and important things. No stereo typed text can be exemplified here as this differs from case to case and from time to time. Its size may be as big as two-three pages or as brief as a line or one paragraph. It is dependent on the message to be communicated but in case of business letters, it has to be brief and descriptive.

(iii) **Conclusion :**

The personal letter, usually, ends with a wish. Here are a few examples:

1. Please give my Best Wishes/ love/ regards to.......

2. I hope to see you soon (or hear from you soon)

3. Everyone here joins me in sending you love/ wishes.

4. Wishing you a quick and complete recovery and....

5. Thanks a lot and be in touch.
6. Please convey our regards and respects to all there.
7. Have a nice time.
8. Have an enjoyable vacation.
9. Cheers.
10. Take care.

In Business Situations :

11. Assuring you of the best of our attention at all times.
12. Awaiting to hear (hearing) from you.
13. Hope to have your early response.
14. We hope to hear from you.
15. Sorry for the inconvenience caused to you.
16. Thanking you.
17. An early reply is requested.
18. Hope the matter is clear now.
19. Awaiting your prompt action.

There are minor differences when these forms are used on each occasion and should be chosen according to the context.

The Complimentary Close :

Most of these close with the subscription "Yours......" and the 'Y' in 'Yours' must invariably be in Capital Letter.

When writing to friends, one can close a letter just as one likes – with expressions of deep affection or familiarity. The most common endings of personal letters are:

Yours,

Yours sincerely,

Yours very sincerely,

Yours affectionately,

Sincerely yours,

Affectionately yours,

Sincerely,

Love,

With love,

Complimentary Close is always followed by a 'comma' as in case of "Salutation"

The Signature :

Underneath the Complimentary Close, you put your signature. Always put your signature clearly. If the letter goes to known personal circle, an initialling will be enough instead of a full signature, whereas, if it is formally addressed to someone, your full signature and name will be necessary.

If the letter is typewritten, the writer's name will be typed leaving space for signature above. A woman could indicate whether she is married or not by writing 'Mrs' or 'Miss' with the name after her signature.

Post Scripts (P.S.) :

These are permissible when something important has been forgotten. These are put after the signatures, starting on the left-hand side of the paper. Generally, this should not exceed 2 or 3 lines.

Letters of Greetings and Congratulations

At one time or another all of us are required to write Letters of Greetings or congratulations to our friends, colleagues, acquaintances or relatives. The main purpose of these letters is to share the happiness of others making the social ties more cordial and everlasting. Thus, the less formal these letters are the better it is. One should express one's happiness is a simple and natural way. The important occasions which call for greetings/ congratulations are classified below:

Occasions for Greetings :

1. Birthday
2. New Year/ Anniversary
3. Engagement/ Marriage
4. Festivals
5. Birthdays of great men or Saints
6. Special occasions like the Independence Day, Republic Day etc.

Occasions for Congratulations :

1. Birthday
2. Engagement/ Marriage
3. Birth of a child
4. Success in examinations
5. Getting a job
6. Getting a promotion
7. Recovery from a long and serious illness
8. Getting a prize
9. Success in elections
10. Elevation to an important position
11. Getting some nomination or membership of some important organization
12. Surviving a serious accident
13. Release of work by some author
14. Winning some award or acclamation in the case of an artist/ scientist/ actor
15. Getting some academic degree.

Some model sentences suiting the above occasions have been given separately. These have been constructed keeping in view the occasion for writing a particular letter. A ready-made letter can be had by just properly arranging these sentences. A model letter has been given to help you draft a letter to suit the particular occasion.

Birthday Greetings

It is customary all over the world to send birthday greetings. Of course children's birthdays are celebrated with more gaiety and fun than that of adults. But even for adults and old people, it is ideal that we send Greetings on such occasions. Everyone wishes to be greeted on his/her birthday, and people do it to cement the mutual relations with the warmth of love, affection and cordiality.

Start the Sentence with an expression of happiness :

1. Thank you for your invitation to attend your birthday party/ function.
2. It was very nice of you to invite me/ us to your birthday party.....
3. What a pleasant surprise to know that the coming Monday is your birthday!
4. How delightful/ interesting it is to learn that you are celebrating your birthday next week!
5. I am desperately/ eagerly waiting to join you in your birthday party, next week.
6. Thanks a lot for inviting me to your birthday party next week. I like to share your joy of the occasion.
7. It will be a matter of great pleasure for me to attend your birthday party.
8. I express my joy and happiness on the eve of your birthday celebrations.
9. Accept my heartiest greetings on the eve of your birthday celebrations.
10. Thankyou thanks for your birthday invitation. It has given me immense pleasure.
11. Thank you for inviting me to your birthday party. I am looking forward to attending it.
12. I convey my heartiest congratulations and wish you many happy returns of the day.
13. Please accept my best wishes on this happy occasion.
14. I join all your friends and family members in wishing you a very happy birthday.

After congratulations, convey Good Wishes for future happiness :

15. I take this opportunity to wish you all success for the long life ahead.
16. May all happiness and prosperity be with you in the days to come.
17. May you live long to enjoy the fruits of all your labour.
18. I wish this birthday to be followed by many more such happy occasions in your life
19. May every day in future be like your birthday/ be as rosy as this happy day.

Expressing inability to join the birthday function :

20. It's really very kind of you to have invited me to your birthday party, but I'm sorry I won't be able to make it as I will be out of town that day.
21. It was very nice of you to invite me/ us to your Birthday party.
22. It was very kind of you to invite me/us to your birth-day celebrations.
23. It's a pleasure being invited to your birthday party, but, I am sorry I can't make it as I'm ill.
24. I, of course, wanted to join your birthday party, but, I am badly tied up with business affairs.
25. As my sister is leaving for the US on that day, I regret, I won't be able to attend it/ make it.
26. Had I not to go out on tour, I would certainly have been amongst your guests/ with you on this happy occasion.

27. I wish I could participate in/ attend the function and meet you all but due to unavoidable official commitments, I regret, I will not be able to make it.

Inform about sending some gift:

28. Very shortly, you will receive/ Through my brother I am sending a small gift from my side as a token of my love and affection for you.
29. I hope you would like the small gift I have sent to you today by post.
30. I've bought a nice gift for you which I will give you when I come down to Delhi next month.

Closing by summarizing the message:

31. Wishing you all success,
32. With all my felicitations,
33. Congratulations and Best Wishes,
34. Wishing you the best of luck.
35. Hope to hearing from you soon,
36. Thank you very much for remembering me

Sample Letter

My dear........,

What a pleasant surprise to know that the coming Monday is your birthday![3] It will be a matter of great pleasure for me to attend your birthday party.[7]

Please accept my best wishes on this happy occasion.[13] I wish this birthday to be followed by many more such happy occasions in your life.[18] It is really very kind of you to invite me to your birthday party, but, I am sorry I won't be able to join as I will be out of town on that day.

Very shortly you will receive a small gift from my side as a token of my love and affection.[28]

Wishing you the best of luck,[34]

With regards,

                                        Yours sincerely,

My dear........,

What a pleasant surprise to know that the coming Monday happens to be your birthday!

It is very kind of you to have invited me to your birthday party, but, I regret that I will not be able to join it as I will be out of town on that day.

I wish this birthday to be followed by many more such happy occasions in your life. My best wishes to you on this occasion.

You will, very shortly, receive a small gift from my side as a token of my love and affection.

Warm personal regards,

                                        Sincerely,

Congratulations on Engagement / Marriage

> While writing letter on someone's engagement/ marriage, express your feelings and sentiments as warmly as the occasion obviously warrants. If one is writing to someone close, its length cannot be prescribed.

At the very outset express your happiness:

1. How happy/excited I am to learn about your engagement/ marriage!
2. How excited I was when I received your wedding invitation card!
3. The other day, when Mohan brought the news of your marriage/ engagement, I was quite thrilled.
4. My happiness and joy knew no bounds when I came to know about your marriage.
5. I am truly overjoyed to learn about your daughter's wedding/ engagement.
6. The happy news of your engagement/ wedding has given tremendous pleasure to all of us here.
7. You don't know how eagerly I am looking forward to attend your wedding.
8. Thank you for your invitation to attend your marriage with Gita on (date)
9. Thank you for your kind invitation to the wedding of your son/ daughter with----- on (date).
10. It has been a pleasure to hear about the long awaited event/ most important event in your life, taking place on (date)

After expressing happiness, convey congratulations :

11. Please convey my best wishes and congratulations to your daughter/ son.
12. God bless you on this happy occasion.
13. With many thanks for the invitation, please accept my congratulations/ best wishes on this memorable occasion in your life.

In order to convey your special interest on the occasion, add one or two sentences in praise of the person/s fiancé/ fiancée:

14. I am happy to know that you are getting married to a girl of your own choice.
15. My sister, who once happened to be a college-mate of your fiancée, tells me that she is a remarkable girl.
16. Your fiancé, who is our family friend, is a very fine chap.
17. It is of great delight to know that your fiancée is a lecturer in a local college.
18. I must say that you really are very lucky to have him/ her as your life-partner.
19. I am certain that you two will make a happy married couple/ an ideal match/ couple.
20. Now with your daughter married off to such a good family, your worries are over.
21. I am pleased to learn that your daughter-in-law is not only sweet but highly educated too.
22. It is really great that your would-be son-in-law is such a senior executive at such a young age.
23. I know your fiancée well and I am convinced that she will make an ideal/ a good wife.

Marriage bestows a social privilege, but, it also means new responsibilities. It will not be out of place to mention about it. Preferably these sentences are written by elderly people to the youngsters:

24. With all my heart, I wish you a blissful conjugal life.
25. One thing you should not overlook is the fact that marriage means many compromises and adjustments.

26. You are committing yourself to a great responsibility and I wish you all success in sailing through it.
27. But, see to it that you act as a cementing factor in the new family.
28. I take this opportunity to wish both you and (the 'would be's name) a long and happy married life.

Enquiries about the date of marriage can be made, if the letter is being written on the occasion of engagement :

29. Please let me know when the marriage is going to be solemnized.
30. I hope it takes place as early as possible.
31. If I can be of any service during the wedding, please let me know.
32. It has been very thoughtful of you to have chosen October for wedding when the weather is going to be pleasant.

Close by summarizing the message :

33. Congratulations, and Best Wishes to the newly weds.
34. Please convey our best wishes to your son/ daughter for a long and happy married life.
35. Wish you/your ....(son/daughter/nephew/niece) a long and happy married life.
36. I am eagerly looking forward to joining you on this occasion.
37. Best of luck in life.
38. Hope you won't mind my absence in the functions, but don't forget to see us with your sweetheart when you are in Delhi.
39. I wish I could participate in/ attend the functions and see you all there, but, owing to prior engagements/ pre-occupation/ unavoidable official commitments/ being out of town, I regret I will not be able to make it.
40. I was holding back this reply on the hope that I would be able to make it, but, due to the last minute change in plans, I regret I will not be able to attend the functions.
41. As things stand now, I hope to be able to participate in the function unless some problem crops up at the last moment/ unless I happen to be out of town.
42. I am just waiting to arrange a gala party in honour of your marriage after the great event.
43. Congratulations and wish you a happy married life.

Sample Letter

Dear ....,

How excited I am to learn about your engagement![1] Congratulations and Best Wishes for a happy married life. I am happy to know that you are getting married to a girl of your own choice.[14] I am certain that you two will make an ideal couple.[19] You are now committing yourself to a great responsibility and I wish you all success in sailing through it.[26] Please let me know when the marriage is going to be solemnized.[29] Iv am eagerly looking forward to joining you on this occasion.[36]

Best of luck in life.[37]

With love and regards,

Sincerely Yours,

Congratulations on the Birth of a Child

A child's birth, commonly called "New Arrivals", has a unique importance in one's life. On this momentous occasion you can share the parents happiness by sending them a note of felicitations. The parents of the new born would be delighted to receive it. Normally the greetings should be addressed to the parents but sometimes it can be sent to the grand parents when the parental couple happens to be quite young. Greetings on such occasions make the social ties lasting too.

Start the letter by expressing your happiness on getting the good news:

1. I was very happy to know that you are now the mother of a lovely baby girl.
2. I am delighted to learn that you have now become the proud father of a pretty little boy/girl.
3. How excited I am to learn that somebody has arrived to fill the gap of loneliness in your life!
4. The new fills me with joy. I know how long you have waited for a child.
5. Everybody at my place/ at our end is quite thrilled to know that you have been blessed with a baby boy/ girl.

Convey your heart-felt congratulations after greeting the birth of the baby :

6. Hearty congratulations.
7. Congratulations to you both on becoming the proud parents.
8. Please accept my heartiest congratulations on this occasion.
9. My best wishes are with all three of you.
10. Best of Luck/ Wishing you all the Best.
11. Congratulations and I am very eager to see your cute baby.
12. Congratulations on becoming the proud parents / grand parents of a cute baby girl/ baby boy.
13. My wife joins me in sending you the best wishes.
14. Congratulations on being the proud parents.

A few sweet words about the child can add to the pleasure of the parents :

15. I join you to welcome the new member of your family.
16. I can well imagine how thrilled you are as you have always wished for a baby girl.
17. I am happy for Manisha also as she always wanted a little brother.
18. The baby, I am sure, will be a source of joy to both of you.
19. I can well imagine how thrilled you are by the birth of twins – (a boy and a girl)
20. The baby, I hope, is as pretty as the parents.
21. Hope he/she brings to you all luck and prosperity.
22. With a daughter and a son, now your family is happily/ ideally complete!
23. I know that the silence/loneliness in your life has, now, been broken by a naughty little boy/ girl.

Wish for parents' well being after writing about the newly born:

24. Your son must be quite excited at the feeling of becoming/ having become a proud father.
25. Wishing the baby good health and long life.

26. You must be quite excited at the feeling of having become a fathe

27. It is nice to learn that your daughter-in-law and grand-child are keeping good health.

28. I hope, both the mother and the child are keeping good health.

29. Hope the mother and the child are keeping well. Take care.

30. I am truly concerned about your wife's health. I hope everything will turn out well.

You can further show a personal concern by writing a few more things about the child:

31. Please inform me when the christening ceremony is going to take place.

32. Please inform us of the christening ceremony as it takes place.

33. Let me know when the name-giving ceremony is being held.

34. I hope you have consulted a good astrologer to cast the baby's horoscope.

35. I have a few good books on child care which I think you must read.

At the end, extend your good wishes and blessings to the baby:

36. We wish your new baby/ new born grand-child a long and healthier life.

37. I hope your child turns out to be a brilliant young man in the years to come.

38. The child is really lucky to have got such loving parents.

39. I am sure your child will be the shining star of your family.

Give an affectionate ending to your letter if you have shown your willingness to see the child:

40. I will be visiting you when you return from the maternity home.

41. I am dying to see you and your baby.

42. I will make it a point to see you and the baby when we come to Delhi next.

43. I shall pay a visit to you next time I am in Delhi.

44. There are occasions when I really curse myself for being in a foreign country, unable to see the dear ones.

45. Cheers.

Sample Letter

Dear ....,

I am delighted to learn that you have now become the proud father of a pretty little girl.[2] Please accept my heartiest congratulations on this occasion.[8] I can well imagine how thrilled you are as you always wished for a baby girl.[16] I hope, both the mother and the child are keeping good health.[28] Please inform me when the christening ceremony is going to take place.[31] I am dying to see you and your baby.[41]

With regards,

Sincerely yours,

Congratulations on Success in Examination

It is quite natural for anyone to feel proud of his success in an examination. On such occasions a word of praise goes a long way to inspire him/ her and boosts the morale. This would also help him improve his performance.

Convey your happiness:

1. How excited I was to find your roll number in the newspaper and know that you have passed your M.A. in first division!
2. It is thrilling to learn from Ramesh that you have passed the Higher Secondary Examination with flying colours.
3. I am very happy to know that you have passed your B.A. in first division.
4. We are thrilled to hear that your son has passed the Higher Secondary Examination with very good marks.
5. You can't imagine my excitement at the news of your becoming a doctor.
6. My heart is filled with joy to learn that you are now a full-fledged engineer.
7. This news came as a pleasant surprise that you/ your son/ your daughter have/ has passed B.Com degree exam with first rank.
8. It was great to know that you/ your son(daughter) have/has passed the BA Hons. Examination with distinction.

Congratulate in sweet words :

9. Accept my heartiest congratulations on your creditable success.
10. Congratulations. You have kept up the tradition of being always higher in the rank/ merit list.
11. You have held the dignity of our institution high and memorable.
12. Our congratulations to your son on his remarkable success.
13. Please convey our congratulations and love to your son/ daughter on his/ her remarkable/ brilliant success.
14. My wife joins me in congratulating you on your brilliant success.
15. Your success is an achievement which you can be proud of.
16. You must be thrilled at realizing your lifelong ambition of becoming an I.A.S. officer.
17. It's really a splendid achievement and we are all proud of your success.

Express good wishes for a bright future :

18. Now there is scarcely any doubt about your becoming a lecturer.
19. We hope that you get a cadre of your choice and are nearer to your home.
20. With your excellent academic record it will not be difficult for you to get a good job soon and share your father's responsibilities.
21. Have you made up your mind for the future plans?
22. What are the further plans of your son/ daughter?

23. I am quite sure you will be an asset to your profession.
24. Now you are well qualified to shoulder the responsibility of your father's business and make it more flourishing.

Making enquiries about his future plans shows your personal concern for the person:

25. What do you intend to do now?
26. Are you planning to go abroad for higher studies?
27. Do you plan to expand your father's business or go in for higher studies?
28. You must have started looking for a suitable job by now.
29. Why don't you drop in one of these days, so that we can discuss about your future plans?
30. As Sujata is a promising student, I hope you will encourage her to study further.

Due appreciation of a few other things can also be made:

31. Such good result is the outcome of your hard work.
32. There is, of course, no doubt that your success is the outcome of your hard work.
33. You have maintained and followed the splendid tradition of your family.
34. Why don't you try for the I.A.S./ Management / Engineering?
35. Its is all the more creditable that you have achieved such a brilliant success despite your recent illness.
36. It's really creditable for you to have done so well with a full time job.

In the end, you can wish again for the person's future glory:

37. I am sure you have a bright future.
38. (I) hope your future will be as bright as your present.
39. Please convey our blessings and good wishes to your son for a bright future.
40. I wish that you surpass all previous records in the years to come.
41. I wish that the field you have chosen offers you more satisfaction and successes in the coming years.
42. Best Wishes.

Sample Letter

Dear ....,

How excited I was to find your roll number in the newspaper yesterday and know that you have passed your M.A. in first division![2] Accept my heartiest congratulations on your creditable success.[9] Now there is scarcely any doubt about your becoming a lecturer.[18] Such good result is the outcome of your hard work.[31] Hope your future is as bright as your present.[38]

With love,

Yours sincerely,

Congratulations on Getting a Job

It is no joke getting a good job these days. Hence sending a message of congratulations makes sense, especially among close friends and relatives. Treat his happiness and relief as your own.

First show your happiness on getting the news:

1. How excited I am to know that you have been appointed a Sales Engineer/ Lecturer/ Doctor in a local firm/ college/ hospital!
2. We are extremely thrilled that you have got a fantastic offer from a firm in the United States.
3. I am extremely happy to learn about your appointment as an executive with TELCO.
4. It is a great relief to learn that finally you have managed to get a good job.
5. I am glad to know that finally you have got a good job.
6. It was nice to know that at last you got a better job of your choice.

Then, convey your congratulations:

7. Accept my heartiest congratulations on this happy occasion.
8. Hearty congratulations on this great achievement.
9. You are really lucky to have got a job of your choice.
10. At last all your financial problems are, now, going to be over.
11. Please convey my congratulations to your son on his first appointment.
12. My congratulations and good wishes on your new assignment in a foreign company.
13. Everyone at home joins me in congratulating you.
14. Please accept my felicitations on getting a responsible position at such a young age.
15. I am sure your mother must be quite thrilled at your achievement.
16. Congratulations on your success in your continuous effort.
17. Hearty congratulations on fulfilment of your dream. Now you owe a grand party to us.
18. It proves that every effort is paid sooner or later.

Making enquiries about the job will express your intimate concern for the person:

19. Does it require shift duties?
20. How is the beginning?
21. Is the work very taxing?
22. What kind of work does this job involve?
23. Will you be out of station quite frequently?
24. What all perks (perquisites) are you going to get?
25. For how long will you be on probation?
26. Do you find the job interesting?

27. How do you find the new office atmosphere?
28. Is your boss a nice person?
29. How is the beginning? You know that well begun is half done!
30. I hope it is a very challenging and enjoyable job.
31. Take it as a good beginning and discharge your duties with heart and soul.

Convey your expectations of the person's quick promotions :

32. I don't think it will be difficult for a person like you to rise in your career.
33. I am sure within 10-15 years you will be the General Manager of the Company.
34. There are very good prospects in this job and you will like it.
35. Though the job involves hard work, the prospects for promotions are good.
36. I am sure you will be able to make a wonderful career from this.
37. For a person of your back-ground, it is easy to ascend the peak of excellence.

Give due recognition to the person's merit on getting the job:

27. Bright young men like you are assets to any organisation.
28. I am sure you will come up to the expectations of your superiors.
29. If there are any departmental examinations in your cadre, make sure to appear in them.
30. I have another friend in your firm and he praises you for your splendid performance.

Close the letter with your good wishes:

30. I wish you all success in your new job.
31. I hope your new job will be rewarding and satisfactory.
32. Our good wishes are with your son who has made such a great start in life.
33. I wish you to create favourable impression on your seniors through your performacnce.
34. I hope, apart from the regular work, you are able to achieve something spectacular.
35. I am sure you will contribute something substantial to the healthy growth of the organisation.

Sample Letter

Dear........,

I am extremely happy to learn about your appointment as an executive with TELCO.[3] Accept my heartiest congratulations on this happy occasion.[7] What kind of work does this job involve?[22] I don't think it will be difficult for a person like you to rise.[32] I have another friend in your firm and he praises you for your splendid performance.[30] I hope that your new job will be rewarding and satisfactory.[31]

With good wishes,

Yours sincerely,

Congratulations on Promotion

> The promotion of a person in his job speaks of his talents and competence. Such an occasion calls for congratulations. It conveys the message that you find your happiness in his happiness.

First of all, convey the pleasure :

1. How delighted I am to know that you have become the Marketing Manager of your firm!
2. It was great to know that you..........
3. I am extremely happy to learn about your promotion to the post of Zonal Manager.
4. It was great to know about your promotion to the next rank.
5. It is good to know that you have finally accepted the promotion which you were evading because of the fear of a transfer.
6. It is very reassuring to know that the long awaited promotion has finally come through.
7. I was overjoyed to learn that you have been taken out of the typists' pool and promoted as the Private Secretary.
8. The news of your promotion has come as a great delight to all of us here.
9. We were highly delighted to know that you have become the............

Thereafter extend greetings :

10. Please accept my heartiest congratulations on your elevation to a higher post.
11. Hearty congratulations on your recognition.
12. Hearty congratulations on your deserving promotion.
13. Congratulations on your promotion which was already due.
14. Please accept my congratulations on this befitting recognition of your merits.
15. Please accept my felicitations on getting such a high rank/ post.
16. Our felicitations on your deserving recognition.
17. My wife joins me in congratulating you on this occasion/ your promotion.
18. Though a little late, your turn has come at last.

Give expression to your confidence in the person's capabilities to rise upto the expectations:

19. There is no doubt that you were the most deserving of all the candidates considered for promotion.
20. Greater responsibilities, of course, mean more work but I know you never shirk hard work.
21. Promotion means more accountabilities and I am sure you will be able to accomplish your tasks efficiently.
22. This promotion will, of course, mean additional responsibilities and I am sure you will discharge them efficiently.
23. You have, now, got what you deserve and I am sure you will still rise in your career.
24. It means that your organization has good faith in your capabilities and it expects more from you.
25. As you have been given a position where you have to take decisions, your responsibilities have increased, but I am confident of your abilities to shoulder them.

26. As this is a responsible post, you may have to work harder than before, but I have no doubt that you will meet the challenge and earn the admiration of your employers.

Wishing for a continued rise in the career :

27. I am sure you will continue to climb the ladder of success.
28. I wish you to add many more feathers to your cap.
29. However, take care that success does not go to your head.
30. It is just a beginning and many more are in the offing.

Talk of some bright aspects of the promotion :

31. Now, you will have to be more discreet in deciding things since so much depend upon them.
32. Your promotion has again proved that only the fittest can come up.
33. Your company has, of course, taken a very wise decision in promoting you to such a key position.
34. The Government has given due recognition to your performance by promoting you out of turn.
35. It is only a beginning and we are sure that you will keep on ascending in your career.
36. We are sure you will add more and more feathers to your cap.

Close the letter with your good wishes for the person's success in the new position :

37. Your promotion speaks itself about your capabilities.
38. This promotion was not only due, but you deserved it also.
39. I am sure you are able to meet the new challenges efficiently.
40. Wishing you the best of luck in your challenging task.
41. Hope, tolerance and foresightedness guide you while discharging new duties.
42. (I) hope you make a popular officer.
43. Our good wishes are always with you for further promotions in your career.
44. Good Luck for your future successes and keep in touch.

Sample Letter

Dear........,

The news of your promotion has delighted all of us here.[8] My wife joins me in congratulating you on this occasion.[17] There is no doubt that you were the most deserving of all the candidates considered for promotion.[19] However, take care that success does not go to your head.[29] I hope you are able to meet the new challenges efficiently.[39] Our good wishes are always with you for further promotions.[43]

With regards,

                                              Yours sincerely,

When you conclude a personal letter you could add usages like:
Good Luck,	Keep in touch	Take care
Bye/ Bi	Cheers	See you

Congratulations on Winning a Prize/ Successes/Awards etc.

> Winning a prize is a very satisfying experience. On such happy occasions one wants one's happiness to be shared. Thus, by sharing his/her happiness you can inspire the individual to win more laurels.

First of all, express your pleasure:

1. It's very exciting/delightful to learn that you've come in the merit list of the Higher Secondary Examination.
2. The exciting news that you've won the first prize in the competition organised by the Indian Literary Academy, has filled us with joy.
3. It's very thrilling to hear that your university has named you the 'Sportsman of the Year' and awarded you a gold medal.
4. How delighted I am to know that you've been awarded the scholarship for higher studies abroad !
5. It's difficult to express in words my joy at your getting first prize in the All India University Elocution Competition.
6. I'm as happy as you, if not more, at your coming first in the International Children's Painting Competition.
7. It was really great amazing to know that...........
8. We were proud to know/ hear that you won the first prize ....
9. Felicitations on your having won the first prize in the .... competition.
10. We were sure that you could make it happen.

Now give your heart-felt congratulations:

11. Please accept my heartiest congratulations on this glorious achievement.
12. Please convey to your son my hearty congratulations and blessings on his great achievement.
13. Please accept my hearty congratulations on securing a higher position in the merit list.
14. My wife/ mother joins me in congratulating you on this happy occasion.

Praise his merit for winning the prize:

15. In fact, your splendid performance and the subsequent reward haven't come as surprise, because I know that you are an ace debater/painter/athlete.
16. I was sure that a brilliant boy like your son could definitely top the list.
17. This recognition of your talents was, in fact, long overdue.
18. This is another well-deserved addition to the prizes you have already won
19. Your hard work and passion for perfection alone could bring such reward in hand.
20. It was heartening to see you rise unbeatably in the competitions.
21. You have made your parents and friends proud of your achievements.

Discuss the expected good results of winning the prize :

22. With a gold medal in hand it won't be difficult for you to manage a scholarship for higher studies abroad.

23. This award has, of course, confirmed your reputation as a writer.
24. These are the landmarks that will get counted in your long span of career.
25. Having won this high recognition, you can now make a name in the national as well as international competitions.
26. It's really fortunate of you/ You are really lucky to have won this scholarship as you will, now, be able to continue your studies without any financial difficulty.
27. With the help of the prize money/ award money, you will be able to go ahead with your creative writing without any financial problems.
28. With this excellence in debating, you might well turn out to be an important public speaker in future.

Make this occasion a source of happiness for everyone in the family :

29. Your parents must be feeling very proud of you./ You have made your parents really proud.
30. All your friends here are extremely proud of your distinguished achievement.
31. You must be feeling really proud of your son.
32. How we wish we were as talented as you!
33. My family is overjoyed at your impressive performance.

Once again, extend your good wishes at the end of the letter :

34. This is just the beginning and many such awards will follow you.
35. I wish you to add many more feathers to your cap.
36. I hope your very talented daughter achieves many such distinctions in life.
37. (I) hope you continuously strive to better your record.
38. Best Wishes for a distinguished and bright future.
39. Keep it up and you will reach the peak of fame.

Sample Letter

Dear ....,

It is very exciting to hear that your university has named you the 'Sportsman of the Year' and awarded you a gold medal.[3] Please accept my heartiest congratulations on this glorious achievement.[11] In fact your splendid performance and the subsequent reward have not come as a surprise because I know that you are an ace athlete.[15] Having won this high recognition you can, now, make a name in the national as well as international competitions.[25] Hope this is just the beginning and many such awards will follow you.[34]

My best wishes for a distinguished and bright future.[38]

With regards,

Yours sincerely,

When you write too personalised a letter, you could use a usage like one of the following according to the context:

Congratulations......   Fabulous......!   Great......!
Wonderful......!   Amazing......!   Fantastic......!
Terrific......!   Marvellous......!   Miraculous......!

Congratulations on Recovery from Illness

> A letter of good wishes on the recovery of a person from 'a long illness will make him happier. It shows a concern for the other person and a desire to share his/her happiness and suffering. It makes social ties more endearing and lasting.

Begin with a feeling of happiness over the recovery from illness:

1. I am delighted to know that the plasters on your thighs have been finally removed and you have been discharged from the hospital.
2. It is a great relief to hear that you are now back home and have recovered from your illness.
3. It is a great relief to know that you have at last recovered from your prolonged illness and have started walking.
4. I am very happy to hear that your son/ daughter/ brother/ sister has recovered from his/ her serious illness and is, now, back to a new life.
5. I am happy to know that your wounds have healed and you are back home.
6. It is a tremendous relief to know that you have finally recovered from the old illness and put our doubts at rest.
7. Our boss also was extremely happy to know that you are being discharged from the hospital.
8. It is a matter of great relief that you have, at last, recovered from your illness.

Then congratulate for recovery from illness:

9. Accept my heartiest congratulations on your recovery from the severe illness.
10. My wife/ family joins me in congratulating you on your recovery.
11. I understand your illness had made everybody panicky. Now that you are better, everybody can take a sigh of relief.
12. Congratulations on your being back to a new life.
13. We heartily congratulate you on your recovery.
14. Hearty congratulations on being cured of such a dangerous ailment.
15. Please accept our heartiest congratulations on your daughter's recovery from such a dreaded disease.
16. I congratulate you on surviving from such a massive heart attack.

Express good wishes for a complete convalescence:

17. I am sure you will be up and about within a few days.
18. I don't think your bones should give you any more trouble now.
19. We are looking forward to your joining us in the office.
20. I am sure, now you will be able to accompany your husband on the foreign trip, next month.
21. I don't think your health will be affected anymore like this.
22. Finally, you will be able to accompany your children to Simla, this summer
23. Hope you will start going to office soon.

A word of advice for regaining the health would convey your sincere feelings to the person:

24. Why don't you join us here for a few days? It being a hill station, the climate is very good here.
25. Still you should take care not to exert yourself too much.
26. Please take care of your diet as per the doctor's advice.
27. Please be sure to take some good tonic in consultation with your doctor.
28. Take full rest for some more days/ according to the doctor's advice.
29. Don't let him/ her play around too much for a few days.
30. Thank God! Your parent's worries are over now.
31. I am sending you a few novels and comics to give you a company during your rest time.
32. Thank God that you are back to good health now.

Conclude with a few words of 'Good Wishes':

33. I will drop in one of these days. Best Wishes.
34. Accept my best wishes for a speedy recovery.
35. I hope this is your last trip to the hospital.
36. As soon as I get some time, I will come to Delhi to see you.
37. The moment I get some time, I will be with you in Delhi. Take care.
38. I hope to meet you soon.
39. Wishing you all the best.

Sample Letter

Dear ....,

I am delighted that the plasters on your thighs have been finally removed and you have been discharged from the hospital.[2] I understand your illness had made everybody panicky. Now that you are better, everybody can take a sigh of relief.[11] I am sure you will be up and about within a few days.[17] Still you should take care not to exert yourself too much. I will drop in one of these days to see you.[36]

With love and regards,

Sincerely Yours,

Congratulations on Success in Elections

Winning an election gives greater mileage in one's social and political life. It is won on the basis of public support. On such an occasion, a letter of felicitation helps build up a pleasant understanding. Any one can send a letter of congratulations and start building a rapport with the elected personality.

Begin with expressing your happiness on getting the news :

1. It's really exciting to know that you have won the Lok Sabha / Rajya Sabha seat.
2. How delighted I am / we are to learn that you have become a Metropolitan Councillor.
3. Your victory with a large majority in the university elections has filled me with great joy.
4. I am extremely happy to know that you have won the election for Council Membership.
5. Your amazing victory in a local Assembly election has filled me with excitement.
6. We are happy to hear that you have won the election with a substantial margin.
7. It is great to know that..........

Thereafter, express your greetings :

8. Accept my heartiest congratulations on your magnificent / glorious success.
9. You must be feeling quite elated on this victory. Kindly accept my greetings.
10. I know how keen you were to get elected. Kindly accept my greetings.
11. My wife joins me in congratulating you on your brilliant success.
12. Congratulations on your great victory/ victory once again/ unprecedented success.

Now, wish for the person's bright future:

13. I am sure you will, now, be looking forward to a deserving seat in the Cabinet.
14. I know this is only the first step on the ladder of your success.
15. Now you will be able to put things on the right track a great deal with your extra-ordinary qualities of leadership and administration.
16. I am sure you will, now, be able to solve the problems of the masses and sincerely look after their welfare.
17. You will, now, be able to put many things on the right track.
18. I know you were the right candidate to get elected, and that happened.
19. You will, now, be able to set certain things right with your qualities of leadership and administration.
20. We are sure you will make a difference in the current political scenario.

Make enquiries about concerned person's future plans. This would show your personal interest and closeness to him:

21. Do you intend to contest for the leader's post in the party?
22. Are you going to support the new constitutional amendment which your party plans to bring in the opening session.

23. I am sure you won't forget the electorate which has sent you to Assembly/ Parliament.

24. I am sure that you will, at any cost, stand up to the faith the electorate has reposed in you.

25. Now you should find out ways and means to fulfil the promises made in the election manifesto of your party.

26. With your gift of powerful oratory you can bring home to members the reality on many burning issues of the day.

27. You can now well persuade the Government to allocate more funds to your area, so that new projects are chalked out for its fast development/ for the overall development of your area.

28. With the gift of the gab you are blessed with, I am sure you will open the eyes of many others to the real problems of the people.

Make a reference to some outstanding achievements:

29. I, of course, remember the valuable services you rendered during the flood last year.

30. Your dedication has made your victory in the elections more realistic.

31. Your success with a thumping majority is indicative of your popularity and mass support.

32. Your success has brought to the fore a student leader excelling in all fields including studies.

33. It is indeed a remarkable achievement to get Loka Sabha seat for the third time.

34. I knew you were the right candidate to get elected and that happened.

35. I am sure you will stand up to the faith the people have reposed in you.

Close your letter by wishing once more for his brilliant future success:

36. Wishing you all success in your political career

37. Wishing you to have a constructive role in the politics of our country.

38. I hope you are able to shine more because of your brilliance.

39. Best of luck in your political career.

Sample Letter

Dear ....,

It is really exciting to know that you have won a Lok Sabha seat.[1] Accept my heartiest congratulations on your magnificent success in the elections.[8] I know this is only the first step on the ladder of your success.[14] Your dedication has made your victory more realistic.[30] Wishing you all success in your political career.[36]

With regards,

Yours sincerely,

Sample Letters for other Occasions :

(Elevation to an Important Post)

My dear........,

It is a matter of great delight that you have been elevated to the post of the Chairman of Electricity Board, a position which you rightly deserve. Accept my heartiest congratulations on your achievement/ on your remarkable recognition. I am sure, with your administrative capabilities, the power distribution system in the city will definitely improve. I hope you make a popular Chairman.

Wishing you all success in meeting new challenges.

Sincerely,

(To some Author on His Work)

My dear........,

I am delighted to learn that you have been nominated for Gyanpith Award for your famous novel 'Dard'. My wife joins me in congratulating you on this great recognition and achievement. I feel proud of being associated with a great writer like you. Hope you win more and more awards and gain recognition in the years to come.

Sincerely,

(On getting some Academic Degree)

My dear........,

How excited I am to know that the Delhi University has conferred upon you a Doctor of Philosophy degree. Please accept my congratulations on this great achievement. In fact, I never had any doubt about your getting the degree.

Hope you keep on winning more and more fame in this field. Congratulations on this great achievement.

Best Wishes,

Sincerely,

(To an Artist/ Actor/ Scientist on Winning an Acclamation)

Dear........,

It is really exciting to learn that you have been selected for the President's award for the best acting in 1999-2000! Please accept my heartiest congratulations on this happy occasion. In your case this award, in fact, was long overdue. Anyway, better late than never. Your parents must be feeling extremely proud of you.

Wishing you all success and fame in the years to come,

Sincerely,

Letter of Thanks

It becomes socially desirable to send a letter of thanks on certain occasions. It speaks of your gratitude for a favour shown by the other person. It is a sign of good breeding and culture, a polite gesture which aims at lasting social ties. Such letters normally have only a few appropriate occasions.

Receipt of any of the following would call for a letter of thanks:

1. Wedding gifts.
2. Gift·for baby
3. Birthday greetings
4. Festival greetings
5. Condolences and sympathies
6. Staying as a guest
7. Financial help
8. Favour
9. Receiving information.

Thanks for Congratulations on Marriage

Start with conveying our thanks on receiving a letter of congratulations :

1. I was extremely happy / delightful to receive your letter of congratulations/ greetings on my marriage.
2. Thanks for your letter/ telegram of congratulations on my marriage. I knew it was coming.
3. Thank you for your nice words congratulating me on my marriage.
4. Thank you for your letter of congratulations, but I missed you on my marriage.
5. We are not only glad but also thankful for your good wishes on the occasion of our marriage.
6. It was very nice of you to send us your congratulations/ best wishes on....
7. It was really thoughtful of you to have sent a beautiful gift on.....

Gladly accept the good wishes for happy future :

8. Both my wife and I deeply appreciate your nice gesture on this occasion.
9. I deeply appreciate your gesture.
10. I am sure your good wishes will bring us all the happiness/ luck and prosperity in life.
11. Your blessings will certainly help them in making their married life happier.
12. With your blessings and wishes, we look forward to many prosperous and peaceful years together.
13. I know you have always treated him like your own son.
14. Your blessings and wishes will go a long way in making our life happy and prosperous.
15. Your blessings will go a long way in making our life meaningful .
16. We believe that your blessings and best wishes matter a lot in our life being happier.
17. It was nice of you to say good words about...........
18. We are honoured by your good words and gesture which speak also of your goodness.

Convey thanks for getting appreciation for your spouse:

19. It was really nice of you to speak so well of my wife. I am surely lucky to have her./ She is indeed a wonderful girl.
20. It was extremely kind of you to speak so high of Deepak. I am, of course, very lucky to have him.
21. Your high opinion about my wife/ husband speaks for the kindness of your heart.

Again express your thanks in conclusion:

22. I am proud that you hold such a high opinion of.............. We both are extremely flattered and thankful to you.
23. We intend to pass Jammu on our honey-moon trip to Srinagar. We will drop in at your place for a day or two.
24. Thank you once again for your good wishes.
25. We both are eagerly looking forward to your visit here.

26. Rita could hardly get to know you on the day of marriage. Please do drop in one of these days.

27. I hope to meet you all soon.

28. Look forward to meeting you sooner.

29. Also, thanks for your invitation. We will be coming over soon

30. Thanks for your thoughts.

Sample Letter

My dear........,

Thanks for your letter/ telegram of congratulations on my marriage. I knew it was coming.[2] Both my wife and I deeply appreciate your nice gesture on this occasion.[8] I am sure your good wishes will bring us all the happiness.[10] Rita could hardly get to know you on the day of marriage. Please do drop in one of these days.[26]

With best wishes,

Sincerely,

Thanks for Wedding Presents

Start your letter by giving thanks:

1. Thank you very much for your wonderful gift.
2. Thanks a lot for your well chosen present on my marriage.
3. How exciting it was to receive your beautiful wedding gift!
4. It was very nice of you to have arranged a wedding gift from hundreds of miles.
5. Thanks for your unique present on my wedding. As I opened I knew it would be from you only.
6. My husband joins me in thanking you for such a lovely gift on our wedding.
7. Thanks for the lovely gift sent on the eve of our marriage.
8. It was really thoughtful of you to send us a beautiful gift on……..

Writing about the gift itself and its importance to you makes the reader happy. Select your phrases according to the gift received:

9. The gift you sent was lovely and a utility item, and we really liked it.
10. Thank you for sending such a lovely gift.
11. We very much liked the wonderful piece of gift which is of great use and value to us.
12. The gift you sent was a really well-chosen item and we liked it.
13. We liked it very much and have kept it at a prominent place in my office.
14. The dressing table you have presented us is really useful.
15. Why don't you drop in to see how cute your alarm clock looks on our dressing-room wall.
16. The decoration mirror you sent was exactly what we needed for our dressing room.
17. Everybody at home has taken a fancy to the crockery-set you presented.
18. The attractive painting you sent us looks exquisite on our drawing-room wall.

Again express thanks:

19. Thanks/ Thank you once again for the lovely present.
20. Once again we thank you very much.
21. We convey our thanks once again.
22. Many many thanks, again/ Thanks a lot for your wonderful gift.
23. Please drop in soon and see how well your painting looks in our drawing-room.
24. We look forward to seeing you next month.
25. I hope you will be able to visit us soon and see how well the sari presented by you looks on me.
26. We wish to have you with us very soon.
27. We are sure you won't turn down our invitation to visit us this time.

28. Thanks for your nice gesture.
29. Thank you for everything.
30. Thanks a lot.

Sample Letter

My dear...........,

Thanks a lot for your well chosen present on the day of my marriage.[2] The decoration mirror you sent was exactly what we needed for our dressing room.[15] We really liked it. Looking forward to seeing you next month.[24]

With regards,

Sincerely,

Thanks for Birthday Gifts

A letter of thanks is written by parents on getting a gift on their child's birthday. This is almost similar to a letter of thanks sent on receiving a wedding gift.

Start the letter with thanks:

1. It has been really nice of you to send/ to have sent a precious gift on my son's birthday.
2. Thanks a lot for the beautiful birthday present.
3. Raju is delighted to have the toy train which you presented on his birthday. He sends his thanks.
4. It was extremely thoughtful of you to have presented me with a leather bag on my birthday.
5. My wife joins me in thanking you for the lovely gift you presented to Rita on her birthday.
6. Thank you for the lovely gift you presented to my daughter on her birthday.
7. It was really thoughtful of you to send such a beautiful gift to my son/ daughter on his/her birthday.

Describing the utility and loveliness of the gift in the letter would be appropriate:

8. The pullover you presented her looks just exquisite on her.
9. In fact, I was about to buy a good leather bag. Now, of course, there is no need of buying.
10. Music doll is perhaps the most liked play-mate of my son, and you have chosen the same!
11. Barbie is her beloved doll and now she sleeps only with it.
12. He has taken such a fancy for it that most of the time he is busy with it.
13. The little baby simply adores the cute little doll. If she could write she would have told you that you were the best auntie in the world.
14. You have definitely made a perfect choice of the toys as they are not only playthings but also good mental exercise for our child.

Repeat your thanks again as done on the occasion of getting a wedding gift:

15. Thank you once again for the lovely present.
16. I wish I could find words to express my thanks!
17. Many many thanks again.
18. He/She conveys his/her thanks to you.
19. A lot of thanks for the lovely gift.
20. Thanks for the nice gesture.
21. Thanks once again/ Thanks for your thought.
22. Thanks a lot for your thought.
23. Thank you very much and hope to meet you soon.

Talking of the baby will add to the charm:

24. Please do drop in one of these days to spend some time with us.
25. Please do call on us when you are in Delhi.
26. We hope you will come and see the baby soon.
27. I am sure he will be quite grown up when you come to India next year
28. Thank you very much and hope to meet you soon.
29. And our naughty junior is waiting to see you.

Sample Letter

My dear........,

Raju is delighted to have the toy train which you presented on his birthday.[3] He has taken such a fancy for it that most of the time he is busy with it.[12] Thank you for the lovely gift.[19] Please do drop in one of these days and spend some time with us.[24]

With best wishes,

                                                   Yours sincerely,

---

Thanks for Festival/ New Year Greetings

Printed cards on special occasions like Diwali, New Year day, Christmas etc. are sent to friends and acquaintances. One should acknowledge their receipt in the form of a short letter. Such a letter usually as three parts (i) pleasure on getting greeting (ii) thanks for it and (iii) reciprocating the greeting.

Express your happiness on getting the greetings:

1. It has been a great pleasure to receive your greetings on Diwali.
2. It was nice to receive your Greetings and Best Wishes.
3. How delighted we were to receive your New Year Card!
4. Your Greetings will definitely lead us to a happy and prosperous New Year.
5. It was nice of you to wish us on the auspicious day of ....!
6. I am delighted to receive your greetings on the occasion of Holi/ Dussehra/ Diwali.
7. It has been extremely nice of you to send greetings on the eve of Independence Day/ Republic Day/ Martyrs. Day.
8. I appreciate and feel happy to get your greetings on Guru Nanak's Birthday.
9. Thank you for your Diwali Greetings and Best Wishes which I heartily reciprocate.
10. It was nice to receive your Greetings and Best Wishes.

Express thanks for the greetings:

11. I am grateful to you for your good wishes.
12. I reciprocate your sentiments and wish you all the best in the New Year.
13. We thank you for your greetings for the New Year and wish you too the same.
14. Thank you so much/ Thanks a lot for your good wishes on the eve of..........
15. I know you cannot ever forget me on such occasions. Thanks.
16. My wife joins me in thanking you for your good wishes.

Return the sentiments:

17. I too wish you a very happy and prosperous New Year.
18. Please accept my greetings also on this happy occasion.
19. May the festival mark the beginning of a great year ahead.
20. I send you my sincere greetings of the season.
21. I reciprocate your sentiments and wish you too..........
22. We heartily reciprocate your sentiments.
23. My wife/ family joins me in wishing you a happy New Year/ Diwali.
24. And here also wishing you a happy and prosperous New Year.
25. May God give you and family the best of everything in life.
26. I too wish you happy returns of this auspicious day.
27. I return your sentiments and wish you too all the best in the New Year.

Sample Letter

My dear……..,

It has been a great pleasure to receive your greetings on Diwali.[1] Thanks a lot for your good wishes.[14] I too wish you happy returns of this auspicious day.[26]

With regards,

Yours sincerely,

Thanks for Condolence

It is a letter written on a sad occasion like the death of someone. Thus, it should be short and straightforward. It is often written by a member of the aggrieved family. At times even gratitude is conveyed for some help received or offered.

Begin the letter in this style:

1. Your letter has been very comforting at this tragic juncture of my life.
2. Thanks/ Thank you for your kind note of sympathy and your offer of help.
3. My mother deeply appreciates your sympathies at this tragic hour of her life.
4. Your words have been a source of comfort at this hour of my life.
5. Your words have helped me regain my lost energy and will.
6. It is difficult to express in words how much relief your letter has given me in my grief.
7. Since my sister is not in a position to reply to your note of sympathy, I am expressing our gratitude for your comforting words.
8. In this hour of trial your letter of sympathy has given me tremendous courage and strength.
9. Although separated by thousands of miles your letter of sympathy has brought me nearer to you and consoled me a great deal.
10. Thank you for your words of comfort which have helped me face this difficult time.

Express gratitude for the affection shown:

11. I am trying to cope up with the reality.
12. With friends like you, I am sure, the burden of sorrow will be less painful.
13. Your touching letter has timely expressed your deep love for us.
14. No one knows better than you what Meena meant to me.
15. How can I express my gratitude to you for standing by me at this hour of trial.
16. I was feeling very helpless, but your letter of sympathy has indeed helped me a lot to sustain myself.
17. Your words of comfort have given me a new life.

Express gratitude on receiving help or offer of help :

18. In fact, during Mohan's illness also you had been a great help.
19. I am deeply moved by your offer of help. I will definitely approach you whenever the need arises.
20. It was very kind of you to make such an offer of assistance and I appreciate it more than I can express.
21. I really don't know what I would have done but for your assistance on this critical occasion.
22. Your words were, of course, consoling and I really appreciate it.
23. You have indeed been a great help in my hour of distress.

24. My sister, of course, needs assistance at this crucial juncture of her life, and I am sure you will be a great help.
25. It was really kind of you to have made this offer of help. I will soon get in touch with you.
26. I am indebted to you for your help and support.
27. Had it been without you, I don't know what could have happened to me.
28. If it is not a great trouble, please drop in one of these days. Your company will be a great comfort.
29. Had it not been for you, I would have been a totally shattered man today.
30. Your invaluable help has been a tremendous prop to me at this hour of crisis.
31. I am back to work and hope to sit with you for some time.

Close the letter in this style:
32. Of course, only time can heal this deep wound.
33. You have been really very kind to us.
34. Thanks for your sympathy.
35. Please excuse me for such a short letter of thanks.
36. My mother/sister feels indebted to you for your kind concern.
37. I am really grateful for your generosityt.
38. Be in touch.
39. I am back to work and hope to meet you soon.
40. Be in touch and thank you for the offer of help.
41. Thanks for everything.
42. Leaving everything to God as we all are only characters in his drama.

Sample Letter

My dear........,

Thank you for your note of sympathy and your offer of help.[2] With friends like you I am sure the burden of sorrows will be less painful.[12] You have, indeed, been a great help at this hour of my distress.[23] Please excuse me for such a short letter of thanks.[35]

With good wishes,

Sincerely,

Dear........,

Thank you for your words of comfort which have helped me face this difficult time.[10] I am trying to cope up with the reality.[11] Be in touch and thank you for the offer of help.[40]

Regards,

Sincerely,

Thanks for Hospitality During Stay as a Guest

> Courtesy demands that you acknowledge the hospitality extended to you by a friend, acquaintance or a relative. A cordial way of doing is by sending a letter of thanks after you have returned from the stay.

At the start mention about the pleasure of being together :

1. This summer vacation/ week/ week-end spent with you was a real treat/ was worth remembering.
2. It was extremely nice of you to have invited me for a stay at your place.
3. It is difficult to adjust to Delhi's weather now, after spending a delightful week at your place.
4. What a nice time I had in your company!
5. The time spent with you just seems to have flown away.
6. How I wish this vacation spent at your wonderful place had gone on and on.
7. My whole family is absolutely thrilled by the stay at your place.
8. The memory of the good time spent with you shall remain fresh for ever.
9. I had always wished to visit Calcutta/ Bombay/ Madras. Thanks to you, I got a chance to see it and had a nice time at your place.
10. I had always liked to spend a few days in a hill-station and thanks to you, now that dream is fulfilled.
11. My children remember you affectionately and the good time they had with Vikas and Dolly at your place.
12. I remember every bit of the fun we had during our stay.
13. I will not forget the courtesy extended to us by you and your hospitable wife.
14. The break I had because of you from this busy and hectic life, has done wonders in me.

Discuss the memories of the hospitality you have cherished :

15. Everything at your place was just about perfect.
16. Everything, including weather, scenery and your company was just wonderful.
17. How can I ever forget those long treks with you in the hills.
18. The relaxation I enjoyed at your place has totally recharged me.
19. I am sure there couldn't be a better way of enjoying a holiday.
20. It was really a happy time with you though a little hectic.
21. Helping you build up that shed at the rear was a real fun.
22. The credit of our happiness of being with you as your guest goes to your better half too.
23. The trip to the old palace has become a permanent part of my memory now.
24. Had it not been for you, we could never see Paris.
25. Oh, bathing in that river was a real fun and I just can't forget it.
26. I am missing those long rides in the woods and mist.

27. Our special regards to your aunt who was such a dear and excellent cook.

28. Our kids have started pestering us to make another programme to visit you during next vacation.

29. I still miss the company of your cousin, Manish, and the spicy jokes I had with him.

30. The photographs have come out nicely and I will send a few copies to you.

31. I consider myself very fortunate in having such a hospitable friend as you.

32. Please take care of the lichi tree which we planted. I hope it will be quite big when I visit you next time.

33. There is certainly no other house where I go with so much pleasure and leave with so much pain.

34. I tried a recipe which you gave and the dishes came out wonderfully.

35. My children remember with great delight the fairy tales your grand-mother told them.

36. I am extremely grateful to all of you for treating me as one of the family.

37. I am looking forward to more shooting sprees which we had while staying with you.

Close the letter thus :

38. I hope I too will get opportunity to entertain you soon.

39. Why don't you please come here with your family in the coming autumn.

40. I do hope my stay with you didn't cause inconvenience to your family.

41. Next Sunday, we are hosting a dinner party. Why don't you also join us?

42. I would like to enjoy your company once again, but this time at my place.

43. Don't forget to spend next Sunday with me here at my residence.

44. We await to have you amongst us.

45. Thanks for everything and be in touch.

Sample Letter

My dear........,

This summer vacation spent with you was a real treat.[1] The time spent with you just seems to have flown away.[5] How can I ever forget those long treks with you in the hills.[17] My children remember with great delight the fairy tales your grand-mother told them.[35] I would like to enjoy your company once again, but this time at my place.[42]

With love and regards,

                                        Yours sincerely,

Thanks for Financial Help Received from a Friend

Start your letter with a mention about receiving the help :

1. In today's mail I got your cheque for Rs.5000/-. I really do not know how to thank you for this timely help.
2. I did not know you would be so quick in sending the money that I asked for.
3. How grateful I am to you for this timely assistance!
4. At this hour of financial crisis, I knew that I could turn towards you only.
5. You don't know what a relief I have got by your timely assistance.
6. It was really kind of you to have come to my help at a time when I had none else to tall back upon.
7. The money you sent to me came as a great boon to me.
8. I knew that it would be you only who could send an M.O. so timely.
9. With your timely financial help you've not only done me a favour but also given me the much needed moral support. .
10. How relieved I felt when I got the M.O. you sent to me.
11. The money you sent to me came as a great relief.
12. Your timely help has relieved me of a lot of tension and I don't know how to express my thanks to you.

Now write about the utility of the aid received:

13. You understand that my father is not in a position to send money and the hostel dues had to be cleared.
14. This money will help me pay off some pressing debts, giving me great/ tremendous mental relief.
15. I got the much needed support from you. Your loan will help me make some urgent investments in my business and consolidate it.
16. With this money, I will be in a position to ensure good medical treatment to my wife/ son/ daughter/ father.
17. Being on a job which requires a lot of travel, I badly needed a scooter. And yet, did not want to ask my father for it. I am greatly thankful to you as you solved my problem by providing me the money for a scooter.
18. This amount will help me pay for my son's college education which otherwise would not have been possible.
19. You did the role of a friend indeed.
20. With this money now I can buy some important equipment for my workshop which I badly needed.
21. In fact, needed this money to buy a gift for Ashok's wedding. As I am virtually broke these days, I couldn't buy on my own.
22. With this cash in hand I now needn't worry about the completion of my house/ project.
23. I knew you would be there to help me at a time like this.

24. Now, I am able to clear the monthly instalments due to the authority which were pending for long.
25. Now the future of my kids' schooling is ensured for which I needed this money.

Do not forget to mention about repaying the loan

26. I will be returning this amount soon, most probably within two weeks.
27. I will return you this amount within the next six months, in two instalments.
28. Next month, I am expecting the payment of the goods I supplied last week. I will repay your loan as soon as I get that.
29. I am sure of returning this money in a month's time.
30. I will try to repay the loan at the earliest, but within a period of one year.
31. As I mentioned to you in my earlier letter, we will adjust this amount against the printing work I am going to do for you, next week.
32. I promise the complete repayment of the amount as early as possible and positively in a month's time.
33. My LIC policy matures next month and the moment I get the cash, I will return your money.
34. As you know I am quite tight nowadays. At the moment, I can't give any specific date for returning the loan. But I will repay as soon as I can.
35. As I told you, I should get my arrears next month and I will pay back this loan on getting the same.
36. I will honour the faith you have in me and will return the money in 2 weeks.

Once again express thanks:

37. I am really indebted to you for this kindness.
38. If not for you, I don't know what would have happened to me.
39. I wish to thank you again for the help which I can never forget.
40. Thank you for your timely help.
41. Of course, I will repay the money, but I won't be able to repay your kindness.
42. Once again I thank you for being so considerate and helpful.
43. Thanks again for saving me at this hour of crisis.
44. Please accept my thanks again for your very timely help.

Sample Letter

My dear........,

In today's mail I got your cheque of Rs.5000/-. I really do not know how to thank you for this timely help.[1] At this hour of financial crisis, I knew that I could turn towards you only.[4] You understand that my father is not in a position to send money and the hostel dues had to be cleared anyhow.[13] I will return you this amount within the next six months in two instalments.[27] Please accept my thanks again for your very timely help.[44]

With regards,

Sincerely,

Thanks for a Favour Received

At the very outset, express your gratitude for the favour received :

1. This is just a line of thanks for the certificate you have sent to help my son in his forthcoming interview.
2. Thanks a lot/ This is to thank you for the hospitality extended to my daughter at your place in Calcutta.
3. It was very nice of you to have received my wife at the Delhi Airport.
4. I learn that you spent a lot of time showing my family the important places in Bombay. I am really grateful to you for the courtesy.
5. It was very kind of you to have extended all your help to my son during his stay in Bombay.
6. It has been very nice of you to have spoken to my General Manager for my promotion which has been long overdue.
7. Had it not been for you, it would be almost impossible/ extremely difficult for my son to get admission to such a renowned school.
8. This is to thank you heartily for your help in procuring an import-export licence for my firm.
9. It has been very nice of you to get me a cute puppy.
10. Thanks a lot for campaigning so well for my election as the President of the University Students' Union.
11. I don't know how to thank you for managing my estate so well during my absence.
12. Your letter of recommendation did make an impact on the realization of my claims.
13. Had you not advised me timely, I would have continued in the wrong way.
14. Your guarantee has enabled me to secure a big contract.
15. I am sure I could not have got this job without your help.
16. It is only because of your help that I have been able to get my case settled.
17. Without your advice I could not have my appeal pursued so effectively.

Expectations to return the favour/ good deed

18. I hope I will soon find an opportunity to return/reciprocate your kindness.
19. I don't know how to return your kindness which has overwhelmed me.
20. My wife is very keen to have you with us for at least a few days.
21. Hope to get an opportunity soon to show my appreciation for your kind gesture.
22. Please do not hesitate to let me know if I can be of any help to you.
23. I have asked my son to get a Video System for you when he returns from the U.S.A. next month.
24. Please let me know if I can help you get the right contacts in the bureaucracy.
25. Please let me know if I can be of any similar help to you.

Once again convey thanks:

26. Thank you once again for your kindness.
27. I again express my appreciation for all the trouble you have taken for me.
28. My wife/ daughter sends you her best wishes.
29. It is of course difficult to return your kindness.
30. My son too sends his thanks to you for your prompt help.
31. Please accept my thanks again for all the help you have extended to me.

Sample Letter

My dear........,

This is just a line of thanks for the certificate you have sent to help my son in his forthcoming interview.[1] I hope I will soon find an opportunity to return your kindness.[18] My son too sends his thanks to you for your prompt help.[30]

With regards,

Yours sincerely,

Thanks for Birthday Greetings

A reply to such greetings is usually short. It consists of two parts; pleasure on getting the Greetings and Thanks for it.

Convey pleasure on getting Greetings:

1. I was extremely happy to get a greeting card from you on my birthday.
2. It was a real pleasure to receive your charming note of birthday greetings this morning.
3. I knew you would not forget my birthday even in England.
4. I am overjoyed to learn that you still remember my birthday even after so many years.
5. Pappu was thrilled to receive a card of birthday greetings from you.
6. It was nice of you to send Greetings and Best Wishes on my Birthday.
7. A communication from you after so long, in the form of a birthday card, is indeed a pleasure.

Then express your thanks :

8. Thanks a lot for your good wishes.
9. Thank you very much for your Greetings.
10. It has been extremely nice of you. Thanks.
11. I am deeply touched by your kind remembrance.
12. Thanks for it. But when are you dropping in here?
13. Thank you and I appreciate your remembrance.
14. Thanks for greetings and blessings which I need not only now, but also for all such occasions to come.
15. I am sure your nice words will keep me going.
16. It is your good wishes that keep me going

Sample Letter

My dear.........,

I was extremely happy to get a greeting card from you on my birthday.[1] Thanks for it. But when are you dropping in here?[12]

With love,

Sincerely,

Thanks for Information Received

> Very often information is needed from a certain source. It could be an individual or a certain authority. After one has received the desired information, one should thank the sender.

In the beginning acknowledge the information and convey thanks :

1. This is to thank you for the information you sent in response to our letter.
2. I have received the form you sent in reply to my enquiry and thank you for the same.
3. This is to thank/ Thanks a lot for sending the press clippings on Indo-American relations in reply to my letter.
4. The circular you have sent in response to my letter is very informative. Thanks for it.
5. The literature you have sent is very relevant to my research. Thanks a lot for your help.
6. I thank you for your prompt and informative reply to my enquiry.
7. This is to thank you for sending the rate list for your books.

Write about the utility of the information received :

8. On the basis of your information I can now write to the concerned authorities.
9. The form you have sent to me will help me lay my claim before the concerned authorities.
10. Thanks for the information. I will, now, be able to contact the concerned officer and expedite the matter.
11. The proforma is certainly useful and meets my requirements fully.
12. Now I can write my article without any problem.

Once again, express your gratitude:

13. Thank you again for your help.
14. It's been extremely nice of you. Thanks.
15. I do not know what I would have done without your cooperation. Thanks.
16. Please accept my thanks once again for your prompt and informative response.
17. I feel highly obliged and thank you for your kind cooperation.

Sample Letter

My dear........,
This is to thank you for sending the press clippings on Indo-American relations in reply to my letter.[3] Now I can write the article without any problem.[12] I feel highly obliged and thank you for your kind cooperation.[17]

Regards,

Sincerely,

Letters of Invitation

There are moments of happiness and joy in everyone's life. And one wants to share them with others. Thus, on special occasions invitations are extended to friends, acquaintances and relatives. Very often printed cards are used for this purpose. But, if the number of invitees is small, just letters are sent. Here are a few sample sentences which can form letters of this type.

However, acknowledgement of the letter of invitation should be sent, expressing if one is going to attend the function or not. Such a gesture is a mark of courtesy and good manners on the sender's part.

If a person can't attend the ceremony or function, he can send a letter of regret in response to the invitation. Such a letter should be a little longer than that of invitation. The reason for not joining the function also should be expressed. Care has been taken to include all possible occasions while preparing these drafts.

The occasions on which such letters are sent :

1. Engagement/ Marriage party
2. Child's birthday party
3. Religious, social or cultural functions
4. Inauguration of new establishment
5. Spending holidays/ vacation together
6. Inauguration of a new house/ House warming party.
7. Dinner, Lunch, at Home, Tea Party, Garden Party etc.
8. Ceremonies – Christening of child, Tonsures, Tilak etc.
9. Picnic, Cinema, Boating
10. Social gathering/ Get-together/ Meetings.

Engagement/ Wedding Invitation

In the beginning write about the date and the place of ceremony :

1. I wish to inform you that I am getting engaged on June 20, 2000.

2. Engagement of my son/ brother/ daughter will be solemnized on September 1, 2000.

3. This is to inform you that my son's/ brother's daughter's sister's engagement has been fixed for May 2, 2000.

4. This is to inform you that April 20 has been fixed as the date of my marriage.

5. I am pleased to inform you that the date and place of my wedding ceremony have been finally fixed. It is on February 8, 2001 at my residence.

6. The barat will start from our residence in the evening at 6.00 p.m.

7. The marriage ceremony of your daughter will be solemnised on January 15, 2001 at 10.00 a.m. at Agarwal Dharamshala, Model Town.

8. I would like to inform you that........

9. You will be happy to know that........

Now extend Personal Invitation:

10. Of course the printed invitations have been sent, but I must write personally to a close friend like you to join us on the occasion.

11. It will be a great pleasure to have you among the guests.

12. Why don't you come a little early and help me with some work here.

13. I needn't tell you that without you the wedding celebration would lack the charm.

14. Of course, you are one in the reception party to receive the barat.

15. You are also invited to attend the reception ceremony which is on the next day of the marriage.

16. I am keen to have you among us on ....

17. You know well that the functions will lack the charm if you are not there.

18. I heartily invite you..........

19. It is also your duty to make the functions gay and lively.

Once again insist on the person's joining:

20. You know that I won't take a 'no' from you.

21. I am counting a lot on your coming. So don't disappoint me.

22. My mother is very eager to have you as my best man.

23. Let me remind that you have to be there. I am not going to accept a negative answer.

24. Hope to meet you on the day of the wedding.

25. Please come two days before the marriage as I have to talk to you about certain important matters.

26. I shall expect you to be at my place two days before.

Sample Letter

My dear........,

This is to inform you that April 20 has been fixed as the date of my marriage.[4] Of course, the printed invitations have been sent, but I must write personally to a close friend like you to join us on this occasion.[10] Please come two days before the marriage as I have to talk to you about certain important matters.[25] You know that I won't take a 'no' from you.[20]

Love,

Yours sincerely,

Acceptance of Invitation

> It is not a very long letter. The details are left for the meeting (?). Thus, try to be as brief as possible.

Start your letter by acknowledgement :

1. Received in today's mail the invitation of your brother's marriage.
2. Thank you for your invitation to attend the wedding of your son/ daughter/ brother/ sister to be solemnized on ....
3. It was nice of you to invite me to attend......
4. Ramesh just now conveyed to me your invitation to the dance party.
5. I have received your note regarding a dinner party at your place.
6. Thanks a lot for the invitation to your birthday party.
7. My wife joins me in thanking you for your invitation to the dinner party.
8. We are thankful to you for the kind invitation to your daughter's marriage.
9. My children are quite thrilled by your invitation to Ranjana's birthday party.

Convey acceptance with a note of gladness :

10. Of course, I will come to the function.
11. How can I miss the engagement/ wedding of such a dear friend?
12. In fact, all of us have been eagerly waiting for this great day.
13. The question of not joining does not arise.
14. My daughter, Divya, has already bought a new set of dress for the occasion.
15. Thanks a lot for your kind invitation.
16. You don't know how thrilled everybody is on receiving the invitation.
17. It will be my pleasure to be present on this occasion.

In the end express your pleasure on getting a chance for a personal get-together.

18. More when we meet.
19. Looking forward to meeting/ seeing you.
20. I am sure it is going to be very exciting.
21. Just wait till I meet you. I am bursting with news about our common friends.
22. I hope to enjoy your company soon.
23. Please be present at the station at 9.00 a.m.
24. Please confirm whether you will wait for us at the station or not.
25. Looking forward to this day with full of happiness.

Sample Letter

Dear........,
I have received your note regarding dinner party at your place.[5] Of course, I will come to the function.[10] More when we meet.[18]
Regards,

                                                    Sincerely,

---

Invitations on Different Functions and Ceremonies

> Functions and ceremonies are often organised by individuals or groups. To invite guests, letters are sent. Informal invitations can be even hand-written. The following sample sentences can be properly arranged to get a letter of this type.

Give an account of the occasion, its reason, time, date, and place etc.

1. We are pleased to inform you that on account of my son's recovery from a long illness, we have arranged for a Satya Narain Puja on May 5, 2000 at our residence.

2. It is a great pleasure to inform you that on the auspicious occasion of Janmashtami, we are holding a Gita Path at our residence, on August 12, 2000.

3. We have pleasure to inform you that the Mundan Ceremoney of my son will take place on May 7, 2000 at my residence.

4. This is to inform you that the cultural society of our college is holding a show of Shakespeare's 'Hamlet' on July 2, 2000 at Kamani Hall.

5. It is our pleasure to have you with us at the cocktail party we are hosting on November 21, 2000 at our residence.

6. We are having a get-together at our place on December 8, 2000 to mark the commission of our son into the Indian Army.

7. I am pleased to invite you to join me for a small get-together I am hosting to mark the publication of my first novel/ book.

8. On the occasion of my receiving 'Padmashree' I am hosting a party on July 8, 2000 at my residence.

9. To mark the Golden Jubilee of my wedding anniversary, I am hosting a get-together at my residence on January 10, 2001.

10. This is to inform you that the Christening/ Tonsure/ Yagyopavit/ Tilak ceremony of my brother/ son will take place on January 8, 2000 at Nirankari Colony, Delhi.

11. I have the privilege to inform you that a concert by Amjad Ali Khan/ Variety Show is to take place at 6.30 p.m. on March 10, 2001 at Salwan Public School.

Extend invitation to come on the auspicious occasion :

12. You are cordially requested to join us on the occasion.

13. We will be delighted to have you amongst us on this auspicious day.

14. Your gracious presence on this auspicious occasion is sincerely solicited.

15. This is just a line to request you to join us on this occasion.

16. How I wish you could just fly down for this occasion.

17. Please come with your family to attend the function.

18. Please don't forget to bring your wife and children along.

19. I am eagerly looking forward to meeting you on this occasion.

20. Please request your parents also to join us on this happy occasion.

21. Keeping in view your hectic schedule in Delhi, we won't detain you for long.

22. Of course, you have recently recovered from your illness, but I am sure, sparing a few hours won't make much difference to you.

23. I trust you can arrange your tour in such a way that you are here on this auspicious occasion.

24. I realize this is a short notice, but hope you will manage all the same.

25. Though you will be busy with your job on that day, I insist on you to spare a few minutes for us.

26. Please drop in a little early to help me with preparations.

Close the letter in the following style :

27. Please drop a line in reply and I hope it is positive.

28. Don't disappoint me on this crucial occasion.

29. Please do come. You know I will be quite lost without you.

30. My children are eagerly waiting to see their dear Saroj Auntie.

31. Needless to say, without you it will be a very dull affair for me.

32. I have taken your presence in this function for granted.

Sample Letter

Dear........,

We are pleased to inform you that the Mundan ceremony of my son will take place on May 7, 2000 at my residence.[3] We will be delighted to have you amongst us on this auspicious day.[13] Please drop a line in reply and I hope it is positive.[27] Needless to say, without you it will be a very dull affair for me.[31]

With regards,

Yours sincerely,

Invitation to Child's Birthday Party

Start the letter with the Happy News

1. I am happy to say that my son/ daughter will be completing four years next Monday.
2. We have pleasure to inform you that next Sunday is the fifth birthday of my son, Rohit.
3. It is a matter of great pleasure for us to inform you that we are celebrating the first birthday or our son, Chandan.
4. I am sure you remember our Ashok's birthday which falls on 15th of this month.
5. My daughter completes two years next Friday and we are celebrating her birthday with friends like you.
6. We have great pleasure in informing you that our son will be completing three years day after tomorrow.
7. With great pleasure, we wish to inform you that we will be celebrating the first birthday of our son, Ajay, on the coming Thursday.

Extend invitation to grace the occasion:

8. On this happy occasion, may I invite you to join a small get-together at my place.
9. We are having a small get-together on this happy occasion.
10. My wife joins me in cordially inviting you to grace this occasion.
11. You are cordially invited to attend the get-together on this happy occasion.
12. We eagerly look forward to your joining us on this occasion.
13. Please don't forget to bring your family along.
14. The party will be held at 6.00 p.m. on the coming Thursday at my residence.
15. I wish you could join us on this happy occasion.
16. Ashok is really keen to have you amongst us on this happy occasion.
17. The party will be held at 7.00 p.m.

Express hopes of acceptance of invitation :

18. I hope you will come by all means.
19. May we hope that you will spare a little time for the party/ ceremony.
20. You know I won't take a 'no' from you.
21. Although you are sitting thousands of miles away, we can often feel your presence amongst us.
22. I am sure you have completely recovered from your throat trouble now. So, please do come.
23. I remember how strongly you were insisting on our hosting a party on this occasion. So, don't pull out an excuse now.
24. I think you will be back from your Patna trip by that time. So, please do come.
25. Rakesh is very keen to see his 'Ramesh Uncle'. So, don't disappoint him.

26. I am sure Bhabhiji must have come back from the maternity home. So, please do come with her.

27. If you are badly tied up with your business, at least send your wife and children.

28. We are sure to enjoy your company on this occasion.

29. I am sure that you will come.

30. Please don't forget.

At the close of the letter, again give thanks:

31. We will feel highly obliged by your graceful presence.

32. It will be a privilege for me to find you amidst our guests on this occasion.

33. It will be a great pleasure to have you with us on this occasion.

34. Although you can't make it, I know your wishes are always there with him.

Sample Letter

My dear........,

We are pleased to inform you that next Sunday happens to be the fifth birthday of my son, Rohit.[9] We are having a small get-together on this happy occasion.[2] My wife joins me in cordially inviting you to grace the occasion.[10] I hope you will come by all means.[18] Please don't forget.[30]

With best wishes,

Yours sincerely,

Invitation on Inauguration of Business

Announce the happy occasion first :

1. It is a great pleasure to inform you that I am opening a medical store on the first of next month. Mr. .... has kindly consented to be the Chief Guest at the inaugural ceremony.

2. It gives me great pleasure to inform you that I am opening a clinic next Monday and Mr. .... will grace the occasion with his presence.

3. You will be happy to know that I am launching a Tourist magazine. The inaugural issue will be released by Mr. ...., the Minister for Tourism.

4. You will be pleased to know that I have got the distributorship of Atlas Cycles, and I am opening an office with a small inaugural ceremony at Darya Ganj on the 15th of next month.

5. I am pleased to inform you that I am setting up an Engineering Consultancy firm and opening a small office for this purpose.

6. I am glad to inform you that I have been appointed the Wholesale Dealer of Fine Cloth Mills, Bombay and will be opening a depot of the mill next month. The opening ceremony will be performed by Mr............., Chairman, Delhi Chamber of Commerce.

7. We are pleased to inform you that we are opening a branch of our bank in your colony.

8. It gives me great pleasure to inform you that we are opening a restaurant in your colony/ market.

Request for personal presence on the occasion :

9. May I request you to grace this happy occasion by your presence.

10. It would be a great pleasure for all of us if you could join us in the opening ceremony.

11. Please grace this occasion by attending the opening ceremony along with your wife.

12. Needless to say, without you the ceremony won't have any charm.

13. Your presence and blessings on this auspicious occasion would make me feel fortunate enough.

14. Please try to make it a little early to help me with the arrangements.

15. We keenly look forward to your presence and need your blessings and good wishes.

16. Please grace the occasion by your benign presence.

17. We seek your blessings on this occasion and, hence, kindly make it convenient to attend.

Give details of time and place of the festivity

18. We will have it (the ceremony) at 9.00 a.m. on November 8, at the new office at No.6, Nehru Nagar.

19. The address of the shop/ store is No.6 Khan Market and the inauguration will take place at 6.00 p.m. on March 9, 2001.

20. We have decided to start evening working hours from 5.00 p.m. to 7.00 p.m. for the convenience of our customers.

21. The shop/ depot will be inaugurated at 9.00 a.m. on Vijaya Dashmi day at Industry House, Ground Floor, Textile Street, by the Commissioner for Commerce, Mr. ....,

22. Our restaurant will be open from 10.00 a.m. to 10.00 p.m.

23. Our new shop will be inaugurated by Mr. ...., President, Traders Association at 219, Main Market on the 24th November at 11.00 a.m.

Close the letter in the following way:

24. I hope it will be possible for you to accept this invitation.

25. I am sure it won't be a problem for you to make it.

26. I consider your presence a must, so please do not disappoint me.

27. You know I feel quite lost without you.

28. We hope you will grace the occasion by your presence and extend your patronage in future also.

29. Of course, this invitation includes all your family members and I hope to meet all of you on the occasion.

30. Please drop a line to confirm your arrival.

31. We hope to continue and maintain this relationship forever.

32. I look forward to your delightful songs on this occasion.

33. Your jolly mood would certainly captivate the guests on this occasion.

34. With a person like you around the whole party will get enlivened.

35. We are sure our décor will appeal to you.

36. Looking forward to your delightful company.

Sample Letter

My dear......./ Dear Mr........,

It is a great pleasure for me to inform you that I am opening a medical store on the 1st of next month. Mr. .... has kindly consented to be the Chief Guest at the inaugural ceremony.[1] May I request you to grace this happy occasion by your presence.[9] The address of the shop/ store is No.6 Khan Market and the inauguration will take place at 6.00 p.m. on March 9, 2001.[19]

Best regards,

Yours sincerely,

Invitation to Spend Holidays/ vacation Together

At the outset, express happiness on getting a vacation:

1. At last, the summer vacations have started and we can relax now.
2. I am absolutely thrilled at the thought of Puja Holidays starting next Monday.
3. How exciting it is to learn that you have finally been granted leave.......!
4. To think of Diwali, just at hand, makes me quite happy.
5. The thought Diwali makes me quite thrilled.
6. The very thought of winter vacation starting from the first of next month makes me jump with joy.
7. I am happy to inform you that we will spend next Sunday evening together.
8. Thank God, finally you have taken out some time from your busy schedule.

Now, enquire about the reader's programme:

9. What are your plans for the vacation? Do you plan to go somewhere during the vacation?
10. How do you propose to spend your Puja holidays?
11. I hope you haven't fixed anything for this Diwali/ winter/ summer vacation.
12. Please let me know your programme for the winter vacations so that I can arrange accordingly.

Thereafter, extend your invitation to spend the holidays with you:

13. I gladly invite you to spend your holidays with us.
14. It will be our pleasure to have you with us during these holidays.
15. Please make it this time which has been postponed a lot.
16. Why don't you spend this vacation with us?
17. I remember you had promised to spend this vacation with us, so don't back out now.
18. My wife and Babloo have been pestering me to ask you to spend your vacations with us.
19. I invite you to accompany us to Simla this vacation.
20. I know your Babu and Buntie are quite keen to see Simla. So why don't all of you spend your vacations here with us.
21. It will be very exciting if you could spend this vacation with us.

Mention the activities on being together :

22. You know we have a number of tourist spots in the vicinity and we could go on trips over here.
23. As we have a lot of greenery all around, it remains pleasantly cool even during summers.
24. Even if we don't go very far from the town, we could have enough time to spend together in entertaining ourselves.
25. We could go for swimming and boating and even surf-bathing during these days.
26. This place is full of lichis (Strawberries) and plums during this season. You can look forward to enjoy them here.

27. We have a busy cultural season in the winter here and I know you love theatre and music.

28. If you want to get away from the crowd and din of Delhi, you wouldn't find a better place than our village.

29. We look-forward to have nice long treks in the hills with you.

30. My parents also are quite keen to have you with us.

31. I admit that the weather now is not very good here, but I am sure we will make delightful company. And that makes all the difference!

32. Please do not worry about the accommodation, as we have a bigger house now.

33. I have already got the guest-room ready for you.

Then insist on coming to you and confirm the date and time of arrival:

34. Please reply soon and let me know about the date and time of your arrival.

35. Please don't disappoint us. We are all keenly looking forward to see you.

36. Please don't hesitate at all – just pack up your suitcase and come down.

37. On getting your travel intimation, we will arrange to receive you at the railway station/ airport.

38. You know that I won't take a 'no' from you.

39. You know you can't back out after the promise you made last month over here.

Sample Letter

My dear…….

At last, the summer vacations have started and we can relax now.[1] I hope you have not fixed up anything for this summer vacation.[11] I remember you had promised to spend it with us, so don't back out now.[17] My parents also are quite keen to have you with us.[30] Please don't hesitate at all – just pack up your suitcase and come down.[36]

With good wishes,

Sincerely,

Invitation to House Warming

Start by announcing the completion of house building:

1. I wish to inform you that my house which was under construction, has now been completed.

2. I am pleased to inform you that the finishing touches have been given to our new bungalow.

3. How happy I am to inform you that we have been allotted a DDA (Delhi Development Authority) Flat under the Rohini Scheme!

4. The construction work of the apartment is now over. Only white-washing is left which will take hardly two or three days.

5. I am quite excited to inform you that finally we have been allotted a house under the Haryana Housing Scheme.

6. We are pleased to inform you that we have purchased a new house in Friends Colony last month.

Thereafter, give details of time, date and place of shifting into the building:

7. We plan to shift into it on November 7, 2000. The address is 5, Bungalow Road.

8. Our family priest has fixed 8.00 a.m. as the Muhurat time.

9. Since my son is coming down from Bombay next Saturday, we plan to shift into it on Sunday itself, when we have a Muhurat at 8.00 a.m.

10. My newly wedded son has decided to move into it with his wife. Muhurat takes place on April 8, 2001.

11. According to our Purohit, December 7, 2000 is the most auspicious date to shift into the new building, and the time fixed is 8.00 a.m. The address is 17, Rajpath, New Delhi.

Mention some programme/ activities of the occasion:

12. We have planned to have a 'hawan' on this day in the morning. There will also be recitation of Vedic hymns.

13. Satya Narain Katha will be narrated and fast will be observed on this day in the new flat before we start living in it.

14. We have decided to have a get-together on this occasion.

15. A 'kirtan' function is being arranged to recite kirtan for two hours on this day.

Request for participation on this occasion:

16. Please do come and grace this occasion.

17. I hope you will come and grace the function.

18. Needless to say that the functions won't be complete if you don't grace it.

19. We are quite keen to have you among the first entrants into our new house.

20. As you are quite fond of bhajans, I hope you won't miss it.

21. My wife joins me in soliciting your esteemed presence on this occasion.

22. Please bring Raju and Rohit also. They were really keen to see our new house.

23. Swami Videh has kindly consented to mark the occasion with his discourse.

24. Our thanks in advance for your benign presence on this occasion.

Sample Letter

Dear ....,

I am pleased to inform you that the finishing touches have been given to our new bungalow.[2] We plan to shift into it on November 7, 2000. The address is 5, Bungalow Road.[7] Our family priest has fixed 8.00 a.m. as the Muhurat time.[8] We have planned to have a 'hawan' on this day in the morning. There will also be recitation of Vedic hymns.[12] Please do come and grace this occasion.[16] We are quite keen to have you among the first entrants into our new house.[19]

With regards,

Yours truly,

Invitation on Social Gathering/ Meetings

Start by giving time and date of meeting:

1. It has been decided to hold a meeting of Rotary Club at 6.00 p.m. on October 2, 2000 in the Community Hall.

2. Please be informed that a meeting of the Tenants' Association will be held on .... the 5th November, 2000 in the Public Library, 58 Ashok Vihar at 1.00 p.m.

3. This is to intimate you that the annual meeting of Youngmen's Sports' Club is to take place on November 4, 2000 at 4.00 p.m. in Quarter No.1138, LIG Flats, Phase-III, Kalyanpuri.

4. This is to inform you that the General Body meeting of Delhi University Teachers Association will take place on November 9, 2000 at 5.00 p.m. in Kirori Mal College auditorium.

5. I have the honour to inform you that a meeting of the Central Government Employees' Association will be held at at 3.00 p.m. on 3rd October, 2000 in Room No.21, Shastri Bhawan, Janpath, New Delhi.

6. This is to inform you that a meeting of the Drama Association of our college will take place at 3.00 p.m. today in Hall No.16 of the College.

Give some details of the meeting:

7. The agenda for the meeting includes the following items:
   (a) A review of our sportsmen's performance in the inter-state tournaments in the previous year.
   (b) Budget for the current year.
   (c) Discussion on providing new kits to our sportsmen.
   (d) Suggestions to evolve new methods to improve their performance.

8. Enclosed is a list of items to be discussed in the meeting.

9. We are also sending an agenda for the meeting separately. Kindly go through it and have your views/ comments ready.

10. We hope to bring about substantial improvements over our earlier performances. For this purpose, we would like to have the suggestions from our members.

11. This meeting has been called hurriedly to discuss the steps taken recently by the Central Government regarding the pension of the employees.

12. The main objective of the meeting is to discuss regularisation of the temporary staff. Other items can also be discussed with the permission of the chair.

Now extend the invitation:

13. You are invited to attend the meeting and participate in the proceedings.

14. Please make it convenient to attend the meeting in time.

15. Don't miss this opportunity to attend the meeting. I am inviting you for some specific reasons.

16. Please try to get along as many members as possible, since it's a show of strength for us.

Stress on attending the meeting:

17. You know that with greater number of members around, we will be assured of good support.
18. I am sure you must have recovered from your illness by now. So do come.
19. Since jobs of many of our colleagues depend on this crucial meeting, don't take it lightly.
20. We must make it a point to convince the President of the financial irregularities being committed by the Treasurer and the Secretary.
21. Please come armed with ideas to floor the opposition.

Convey our thanks in anticipation:

22. We will be extremely thankful for your valuable presence which seems indispensable.
23. Your presence will lend a lot of weight to our case.
24. I express my thanks and await your participation in the meeting.
25. You will oblige us by your esteemed presence in the meeting.
26. I am eagerly looking forward to your speech which I am sure will be quite impressive.

Sample Letter

Dear Sir,/ Dear Mr........,

This is to inform you that the General Body Meeting of the Delhi University Teachers' Association will take place at 5.00 p.m. on 8th October, 2000 in Kirori Mal College auditorium.[4] Enclosed is a list of items to be discussed in the meeting.[8] The main objective of the meeting is to discuss regularization of the temporary staff. Other items can also be discussed with the permission of the chair.[12] Don't miss this opportunity to attend the meeting. I am inviting you for some specific reasons.[15] I express my thanks and await your participation in the meeting.[24]

With regards,

                                                    Yours sincerely,

---

Invitation to Dinner or Dance Party

Begin with the information about the time and place :

1. We are having a dinner/ dance party at 8.00 p.m. on next .... i.e., November 7, 2000 at the Ashoka Hotel.

2. It is my pleasure to inform you that a dinner/ party is being arranged at 7.00 p.m. on December 8, 2000 at Janpath Hotel.

3. You will be glad to know that we are having a dinner/ dance party at 7.00 p.m. on November 2, 2000 at our place.

4. You will be pleased to know that we have arranged for a dinner/ dance party at 8.00 p.m. on January 1, 2001 at Mohan's place.

5. You will be happy to know that a dinner/ dance party is being held at 9.00 p.m. on 1st January, 2001 at my residence at 11/138, Shakti Nagar, New Delhi.

Some details of the programme:

6. Our programme shall include soft drinks, light entertainment and then dinner.

7. We have invited all of our friends.

8. After the dinner, we will have a programme by Runa Laila who has been especially invited to the function.

9. We will have both vegetarian and non-vegetarian dishes.

10. Don't be late because cultural items will start immediately after the dinner.

11. You had been pestering me for such a party for a long time. I hope you will not have any complaint now.

12. It is/ is not exclusively a dance party. So do/ don't bring a partner along.

13. I am sure you will like the pop group, Rolling Stones, who have been especially invited for this function.

Extend invitation:

14. I/ We cordially invite you and your wife to this party.

15. Please try to make it in time, although you don't believe in punctuality!

16. I hope being a bachelor, you will not miss this golden opportunity of the winter season.

17. Being the organiser of the party, I extend this invitation to your family to join us in the party.

18. Do bring along Rita also. I know she is very fond of dancing.

19. I am sure the party will be cheerful by your delightful company.

20. I know I can count on you. Please be in time.

21. Please block your diary. I know how easily you forget things.

22. Please bring along Raju and Munni also. They are going to be delighted by the music.

23. Hope to meet you all together.

Sample Letter

Dear........,

We are having a dinner/ dance party at 8.00 p.m. on next .... i.e., November 7, 2000 at the Ashoka Hotel.[1] Our programme shall include soft drinks, light entertainment and then dinner. [6] Please bring along Raju and Munni also. They are going to be delighted by the music.[22] Hope to meet you all together.[23]

Warm personal regards,

Sincerely,

Invitations on other Occasions : Sample Sentences

Express your joy according to the occasion :

1. I am overjoyed to learn that you have been finally blessed with a son after a long wait.
2. It is a great pleasure to learn that your daughter has got first division in her M.A. examination.
3. It is very comforting/ I am very happy to learn that your son has finally recovered from his serious illness.
4. I am delighted with your invitation to 'Yajna' at your place.
5. I am glad to learn that you are going to start a new business of chemicals at Khari Baoli.
6. I am overjoyed at your invitation to spend my summer vacation with you at Simla this year.
7. It will be a pleasure for me to enjoy your company in the new house.
8. I feel much honoured to have got the invitation to participate in the Republic Day Celebrations.
9. I eagerly look forward to the get together you have arranged to mark this happy occasion.
10. It has been very kind of you to invite me on this occasion.

In the end express your blessings :

1. All my blessings are with your new born child.
2. My good wishes are always with you in your new trade.
3. May you prosper well in your new business.
4. I sincerely hope that he develops into a fine young man.
5. I will be there to attend the ceremony to mark this occasion.
6. I hope this new house gives you a comfortable stay.
7. It has been nice of you to have arranged the meeting with such promptness.
8. Wishing a grand success to your dinner/ dance party.
9. May your son have a long and healthy life, after Tonsure/ Yagyopavit ceremony.
10. You know my blessings are always there.
11. May your child have good health and long life.

Declination of Invitation

A letter of acceptance of invitation is brief in expectation of the personal meeting. But that of regret is a little longer since it includes the reasons for regretting.

Start your letter with thanks for the invitation:

1. Thank you for your invitation to the wedding of .... to be solemnized at Gurgaon on ....(date).
2. Thanks a lot for your invitation to the dinner/ dance party.
3. Thanks for remembering and inviting me for the Mundan/ Tonsure ceremony of your son.
4. Thank you for your kind invitation.
5. It has been really nice of you to invite me on your daughter's marriage.
6. Many thanks for remembering me on this happy occasion.
7. My wife joins me in thanking you for the invitation to your brother's marriage.
8. It was an honour to receive your invitation.
9. It was a great surprise to hear from you after so long and that too in the form of an invitation to your sister's marriage.
10. It has been extremely nice of you to invite me and my wife to the party.

Subsequently, express regrets for declining the invitation:

11. I would have been delighted to be with you, but......
12. I wish I could participate in the functions and see you all personally, but......
13. In fact I had been looking forward to this for quite some time, but........
14. Everyone at home is so excited about this, but........
15. I would have liked to participate, but.....
16. My wife was really keen to see the bride, but......
17. You don't know how bad I am feeling for my inability to attend it.
18. I regret to say that I am in no position to accept your invitation because.....
19. Bunti was really keen to see his Asha Aunty's wedding, but.....
20. It would have been our pleasure to participate in the functions, but.......
21. You know I would have loved to attend the party, but....

Complete the above sentences by adding the ones given below:

22. ....unfortunately I am down with fever.
23. As I have not recovered completely from my recent illness, doctor has advised complete rest for a week.
24. ....our son is ill for the last few days, and there is nobody to look after him in our absence.
25. .....my wife's parents are coming down from Kashmir, and we would not like to leave them unattended.

26. ....I have to go to Calcutta on an important official business.

27. ....I cannot leave the town for the next few days due to some pressing personal problems.

28. .....I have already accepted and consented to a similar invitation from another friend for the same day.

29. .....I am badly tied up with my business engagements for the next week.

30. .....I will not be able to make it as I will be in the US next week.

31. .....I will be out of India on this day and hence won't be able to make it.

32. ....due to prior engagements, I do not think I will be able to attend the functions.

33. ......regret that I will not be able to make it due to pressing official commitments.

34. .....you know it is the closing for banks and I just cannot leave my work.

35. .....it is difficult for me/ us to make it.

Convey your greetings on the happy occasion:

36. All the same my best wishes are always with you.

37. I convey my best wishes on this happy occasion.

38. At the same time, let me heartily congratulate you on this happy event in your life.

39. My family joins me in wishing you the Best of Luck.

40. We wish you a very long and happy married life.

41. Best of Luck in life.

Sample Letter

Dear........,

Thanks a lot for your invitation to the dinner party.[2] I would have been delighted to be with you, but, our son is ill for the last few days and there is nobody to look after him in our absence.[11] So, it is difficult for us to make it.[35]

I convey my best wishes on this happy occasion.

Best of luck,

Sincerely,

(Another sample not taken from the above)

Dear........,

It was nice of you to invite me to the wedding of Reshma with Rahul on 2nd October, 2000. I wish I could attend the function and meet all of you personally, but, regret that I will be out of India on that day.

Please convey our best wishes to the newly weds for a long and happy married life.

Congratulations to you.

Sincerely,

Letters of Condolence

A letter of condolence is written to the closest surviving relative of the deceased. It could be his/her father/mother, brother/sister, son/ daughter, wife, or husband. The letter should be prompt, and preferably brief.

Such a letter should appear genuine and not a mere formality. One can also talk about some of the outstanding qualities of the deceased. Element of praise is desirable.

If one is capable of assisting the bereaved family financially or otherwise, one should not forget to mention it in the letter. Such an offer shows one's genuine concern for the family even if it is not accepted.

At times such letters are written to express condolences in business circle. The writer might not have even known the deceased and would be writing on behalf of an organization. In such cases, a touch of formality cannot be avoided. But one should be careful not to write in a light vein.

The outlines of a condolence letter should be:

i. Expression of grief on getting the sad news

ii. Paying tributes to the departed soul.

iii. Willingness/ offer to help on the sad occasion.

iv. Repeating the condolence.

Condolence on Death in Business Circle

Express grief on getting the news:

1. It was with deep regret that we learnt about the sad demise of Shri Manohar Lal, your esteemed Managing Partner.
2. Your father's sudden death has shocked all of us.
3. It was shocking to learn about the untimely death of your young partner, Shri Ram Prasad.
4. I have been extremely distressed to learn from today's newspaper about the sudden demise of your Managing Diréctor.
5. I am shocked to hear about the sudden demise of Shri.....
6. I understand what a serious loss it is to you and your business, caused by the passing away of......
7. I learnt with great sorrow about the untimely demise of your partner, Mr. Kishore Jain.
8. It was shocking to learn about the sudden/ untimely/ premature death of your partner/ colleague/ Managing Director.
9. We were shocked to hear about the passing away of your partner.
10. The news about the sad demise of your partner Mr........was really shocking.

Discuss the good qualities of the deceased:

11. He was a remarkable person and will always be remembered by all friends and acquaintances.
12. The tremendous progress your firm has made under his astute guidance is a tribute to the departed soul.
13. That he built up such a big enterprise from scratch speaks of the great talents and business acumen he had.
14. He was not only a leading industrialist but a thorough gentleman also.
15. I have had the honour of meeting him personally. And I have always cherished the memory of that meeting.
16. Although I did not have an occasion to make a personal acquintance with him, I have heard that he was very much esteemed.
17. It is indeed very difficult to fill the gap, created by his sudden death.
18. He was the father of your organisation and the fountain-head of all progressive ideas.
19. I am sure your employees too will be quite distressed at his demise.
20. Whoever came into contact with him was impressed by his sagacity and business acumen.
21. I sincerely hope that the relations we had with him be maintained even after his departure.
22. He was a source of strength and inspiration to many other entrepreneurs.
23. Some of his pioneering work will go a long way in benefiting the future generations.
24. His remarkable achievements, in such a short span of time, indeed speak of his creditable performance.
25. As the whole industry knows, he was not only a great industrialist, but also a philanthropist and his contributions to your organization are memorable.

26. Worth mentioning is the fact that he was a rare and great personality not only in business but also in social circle.

27. The gap left behind by the deceased is difficult to be filled.

28. He was such an unmatchable personality that it would be difficult for your organisation to fill the gap.

Repeat your sympathies:

29. Please accept my sincerest sympathies on this sad occasion.

30. My colleagues join me in sending their deepest condolences on this occasion.

31. May his soul rest in peace and guide in the years to come.

32. We hope that the tree he has planted flourishes and bears many more fruits in the years to come.

33. Please convey my heart-felt condolences to his family.

34. May God give his family the strength to bear this sudden shock.

35. We share your sorrow and pray for peace for the departed soul.

36. Since words cannot really express our feelings, at this time, we send our heart-felt condolences.

37. We express our heart-felt condolences on this sad occasion. May the departed soul rest in peace and be a driving force to all of you.

Sample Letter

My dear........,

It was with deep regret that we learnt about the sad demise of Shri Manohar Lal, your esteemed Managing Partner[1]. I have had the honour of meeting him personally and I have always cherished the memory of that meeting[15]. Some of his pioneering work will go a long way in benefiting the future generations[23]. My colleagues join me in sending their deepest condolences on this occasion.[30]

With prayers for the departed soul,

Sincerely,

Condolence on a Death in Family

> It is neither necessary nor proper to mention specifically the deceased person in your letter, because the sad event is still fresh in the mind of the reader. You should not attract his/her attention to the tragedy.

At the outset express grief on getting the news:

1. We are shocked to learn about the sorrow that has come upon you so untimely.
2. I don't know how to express my grief at this tragedy in your family.
3. The sad news completely stunned me/ us.
4. I cannot tell you how grief-stricken I am to learn about your brother's sudden demise.
5. I can well imagine your condition on this sudden tragedy.
6. I have just heard the sad news and don't know how to console you.
7. Today Ashok brought the news of your brother's death and it left us speechless.
8. It was a great shock to hear about your father's tragic death.
9. I could hardly believe the news about your mother's death when I picked up the paper today.
10. The heart-breaking news came as a stunning blow.
11. What is more shocking is the fact that it was nothing but an accident.
12. The other day only I met him and he appeared so cheerful and healthy.
13. The other day when we met him who knew he would be with us only for a few days.
14. I know what dreams you had for him.
15. Although your revered father was of ripe age, I could never think that his end was so near.
16. I simply can't imagine the grief of your dear mother.
17. He/she was always kind to me. Whenever I went to your place, he/she treated me like his/ her own son/ daughter.
18. With such a good academic career/ job, he was on to a bright start. But who knew?
19. I still remember very vividly the long meetings I have had with her.
20. She was the darling of everybody who knew her.
21. All his friends are quite stunned by this sad news.
22. I know how deeply attached you were to Rajan and what a wonderful brother he had been to you.
23. Your sister was an adorable girl.
24. It was a real shock to hear about the tragedy that has occurred in your life.
25. We were/ I am shocked to learn about the untimely passing away of your.......
26. The sad news came as a sudden shock to all of us here.
27. We were spell-bound to learn about the sad news.
28. It left us deeply pained to learn about the tragedy that occurred in your life.

Extend all possible help (only in case of family/friend – not in business circle)

29. I hope I can be of some help to you in this hour of distress.
30. Please don't hesitate to tell me if I can do anything for you.
31. Why don't you come here for some time. The change might help you.
32. My mother sincerely wants you to come here to stay with us.
33. I will very soon drop in at your place.
34. May I offer you some financial help that you might need on this occasion.
35. We have to bow/ are helpless before the fate.
36. I/ we pray to God to give you enough strength to face/ withstand this irreparable loss.
37. Let God give you enough inner strength to stand this loss.
38. Please be courageous enough for the sake of others in your family, though your sorrow is inconsolable.
39. If I/ we can be of any type of help to you please do not hesitate to tell us.

Repeat your sympathies at the close of letter:

40. May the departed soul rest in peace.
41. You must put up a courageous front for the sake of your children.
42. My deepest sympathy in your bereavement.
43. Please don't give in to this sorrow. All of us have to suffer such shocks at one time or the other.
44. Time alone will heal your wounds.
45. The void that the sad demise of your dear husband/ wife has created in your life can never be filled.
46. Heart-felt condolences.
47. Please accept our heart-felt condolences.
48. Condolences.

Sample Letter

My dear........,

We are shocked to learn about the sorrow that has come upon you so untimely.[1] What is more shocking is the fact that it was nothing but an accident. Time alone will heal your wounds.[44] Our heart-felt condolences.[46]

With regards,

Sincerely,

Condolence on the Death of a War Personnel

> There are brief and skillfully conceived letters. Be sincere and avoid philosophizing on death.

Express your grief on knowing the news:

1. I am deeply grieved to learn about your husband's death on the front.
2. I am terribly shocked to learn about your brother's death in the Kargil operation.
3. It was with great distress that I learnt about the aircrash during test flight and your son's death who was aboard.
4. I am very much grief-stricken to hear the sad news of your eldest brother's death, while parachute landing into the enemy's territory.
5. It's heart-rending to know about your pilot son's death in the enemy lines.

Write about the good qualities of the deceased:

6. There is no doubt that he was a brave and fine young man.
7. There is no doubt that by his death, the country has lost a brave son.
8. I still remember vividly his handsome young face.
9. Everyone at our place is deeply shocked at your tragic loss.
10. I have never come across such a man having so sincere sentiments for his country.
11. Ofcourse, it is for the country that he has laid down his life.
12. He has set an example for the growing generation of our country.

Express your sympathy at the close of the letter:

13. May his soul rest in peace.
14. History will remember him for his deed of patriotism,
15. He proved himself a worthy son of his motherland.
16. His martyrdom is a great tribute to the martial tradition of your family.
17. May God give you strength to bear the burden of grief.
18. Be proud to be the father of such a great son.
19. His name will be written in golden letters of gallantry.

Sample Letter

Dear........,

I am deeply grieved to learn about your husband's death on the front.[1] There is no doubt that by his death the country has lost a brave son.[7] May his soul rest in peace.[13]

Regards,

Sincerely,

Letters of Sympathy

The tragic events/ sad occasions on which letters of sympathy are written may be classified as under:

i. Financial loss

ii. Failute in examinations

iii. Accident

iv. Illness

The emotional stress in a letter of sympathy is toned down as against the letter of condolence because the loss of property has less significance than the loss of life. Still, the reader must be able to get genuine sympathy from the letter.

The outlines of a letter of sympathy are as under:

i. Regrets on getting the tragic/ sad news

ii. Happiness over saving the precious life and sustaining lesser loss

iii. Innocence of the reader over the event

iv. Enquiries about recovery/ revival

v. Offer of help

vi. Repetition of sympathies and good wishes.

Sympathy on Loss/ Damage

Start your letter with regrets on getting the news:

1. I am extremely sorry to learn that a part of your house was destroyed in a fire yesterday.
2. It was very distressing to learn about the theft in your house last Monday and the loss of valuables.
3. It was very upsetting to learn about the loss you have suffered in the business deal last month.
4. How sad it was to know from your letter that recently some miscreants damaged your car while attempting to steal it.
5. I am extremely sorry to learn about the theft of your suitcase in the train.
6. I am quite upset to learn about the damage occurred to your house because of the recent earthquake/ floods/ blast in your city.
7. I was quite disturbed to learn about your loss of BHEL contract over a small technical point.
8. It is quite sad to learn about the loss of your prized lottery ticket.
9. I am sorry to know about the loss of your lovely dog, Rover.

Express your relief on lesser loss:

10. At the same time I am relieved to learn that all of you are physically safe.
11. However, it is a matter of relief that the damage was of a minor nature.
12. It was, however, quite fortunate that nobody was in the house.
13. It was, however, fortunate that your jewellery was in a locker at the bank.
14. I am relieved, however, to see that the loss is not such that your flourishig firm cannot bear.
15. It is quite a relief to learn that police has got some clues about the theft.

Convey your belief in the reader's innocence:

16. Don't get tensed over this matter. After all it was not your fault.
17. I think with a little care you could have avoided the loss.
18. I suggest that you get your household goods insured now.
19. One could not, possibly, have foreseen such a recession in business.
20. I am sure it was none of your fault.
21. Please don't take it to heart. One should learn to take these things in the stride.
22. You must, of course, have done your best to minimise the loss.

Mention anything else of importance:

23. I am confident that your business skills will help you make up for this loss very soon.
24. I hope you have contacted the insurance people immediately.
25. I hope the health authorities in your city have taken precautions against the possible epidemic, which the floods are likely to bring.

26. The Government will certainly do something to help you and others affected by this natural calamity.
27. As your son is an engineer, the repairs of the house can be done speedily at a moderate cost.
28. Have you reported the loss to the police?

Extend your offer of help:

29. Don't worry. You have many good friends and I will be happy to be of any help to you.
30. I am sure your loss will be shared by others too.
31. May I offer you financial assistance to help you tide over the difficulties?
32. I would be happy to help you in any way on this occasion.
33. We have two dogs of excellent breed. You can take one of them.
34. You are most welcome to come and stay with us while your house is under repairs.
35. I have contacted my brother who is the IG of your city, and he has promised full cooperation.

Repeat your sympathies:

36. You have all my sympathies on this unfortunate event.
37. I feel extremely concerned about your loss.
38. Please convey my deepest sympathies on the sad event to everybody at your home.
39. My wife joins me in sending her sympathies on this sad occasion.
40. Best Wishes for a quick recovery.

Sample Letter

My dear........,

It was very distressing to learn about the theft in your house last Monday and the loss of valuables.[2] At the same time I am relieved to learn that all of you are physically safe.[10] I suggest that you get your household goods insured now.[18] Have you reported the loss to the police?[28] You have all my sympathies on this unfortunate event.[36]

With good wishes,

Sincerely,

Sympathy on Accident

Basically the contents of this letter are the same as those written on the occasion of loss or damage.

Express your grief on getting the news:

1. I am extremely sorry to learn from your father that you met with an accident yesterday.
2. It is quite distressing to learn from your brother that you had a fall and have broken a leg.
3. It is quite upsetting to learn that you had a scooter accident yesterday.
4. It was quite sad to learn that yesterday your wife suffered burns while cooking.
5. I was quite disturbed to know that you slipped down the staircase and injured yourself.
6. I am quite distressed to learn that your brother got an electric shock yesterday.

Convey your relief/ happiness over lesser injuries or surviving the accident:

7. At the same time, it is a relief to learn that the injury is of a minor nature.
8. It is, however, quite a relief to learn that the burns are not very serious.
9. But, it is a great relief to learn that although it was a major accident, you had a narrow escape.

Express your belief in reader's innocence:

10. I am sure there was nothing wrong on your part.
11. I am sure you were not at fault as the truck hit you at the back.
12. You should be a little more careful about the children.
13. Tell her not to wear nylon saris while cooking.
14. Tell her to be more cautious while cooking on the gas oven.
15. Nowadays, accidents occur even when we are not at fault.

Now, make enquiries about the victim's proper care being taken:

16. I am sure you are being looked after well in the hospital.
17. I hope she will be discharged from the hospital soon.
18. I hope the injury will heal soon.
19. Even if the injury seems small, I must urge you not to neglect it.
20. Luckily, your son is a doctor and I am sure he will look after you well.
21. When will his plaster be removed?

Anything else which may be relevant:

22. I am sure the operation will be successful.
23. I will drop in at the hospital one of these days.
24. Although the other driver must have been at fault, please be more careful while driving, in future.

25. Now, you must not exert yourself for atleast one or two weeks.
26. When you are fit enough to travel, please drop in here.

Repeat your good wishes for fast recovery:

27. As the injury is not serious. I am sure you will be up and about soon.
28. Don't worry. It will be over soon like a bad dream.
29. Hoping to see you hale and hearty very soon.
30. I hope he will be healthy soon and back to his school and games.
31. There are some good Ayurveidc tonics for speedy recovery of which I am enclosing a list.
32. Trials test a man in adversity to bring out his best.
33. Don't take it to heart. All these are in the game.
34. I wish you a speedy recovery.

Sample Letter

My dear........

I am extremely sorry to learn from your father that you met with an accident yesterday.[1] At the same time it is a relief to learn that the injury is of a minor nature.[7] I am sure there was nothing wrong on your part.[10] As the injury is not serious, I am sure you will be up and about soon.[27] I wish you a speedy recovery.[34]

Good luck,

Sincerely,

Sympathy on Illness

The contents of this letter are similar to those written in the event of a loss or an accident.

Start the letter with a show of your concern:

1. I am quite disturbed to learn from your brother that you have been hospitalised for quite a few days.
2. Its quite upsetting to learn that you have jaundice.
3. I am quite distressed to learn that your wife has developed post operation complications.
4. It is quite disturbing to learn that your new born baby has developed some problem.
5. It was quite disturbing to learn today that you have been down with typhoid for the last many days.
6. I was quite worried to know that you had to be hospitalised because of your liver problem.
7. It's quite shocking to learn that your brother has got tuberculosis.
8. Your chronic diabetes is indeed a source of worry to me.

Make enquiries about the treatment:

9. I am sure you are getting the right treatment from an experienced doctor.
10. Don't feel allergic towards Allopathic treatment, if you feel better than before.
11. Why don't you get yourself examined in the All India Institute of Medical Sciences.
12. I wish, the specialist you are consulting now, makes the right diagnosis.
13. Has your surgeon advised an operation?
14. Don't worry; it is a minor problem and perfectly curable.
15. You need not worry. T.B. is perfectly curable now.

Ask if you can be a source of help:

16. My wife can take care of your children while you are away in the hospital.
17. Can I be of any help as long as you are in the hospital?
18. I am enclosing a recommendation letter of Dr. Gokhale. I am sure it will help you a great deal to get good treatment.
19. I have asked my daughter to take food for your children regularly till you are in the hospital.

Repeat your good wishes:

20. We all are waiting eagerly for you to get well.
21. Get well quickly/ fast.
22. I am sure you will be back from the hospital soon.
23. We all miss you badly and are eagerly waiting for you to return from the hospital.
24. Vikas is planning to host a party when you return from the hospital.
25. Everybody in our family is praying for the speedy recovery of the child.
26. I don't think it will take more than a week to get discharged from the hospital.

Sample Letter

My dear........

I am quite disturbed to learn from your brother that you have been hospitalised for quite a few days.[1] Has your surgeon advised an operation?[13] My wife can take care of your children while you are away in the hospital.[16] I am sure, you will be back from the hospital soon.[22]

With good wishes,

                                                      Sincerely,

Sympathy on Failure in the Examinations

Express your sympathy on getting the news:

1. I am quite disappointed to learn that you have not been successful in your B.A./ M.A./ Higher Secondary/ I.A.S. examinations.

2. It is quite disappointing to learn about your brother's sister's/ daughter's/ son's failure in the B.A. exams.

3. I am sorry to learn about your failure in departmental examination.

4. It is indeed upsetting to learn about your Pappu's failure to get into the N.D.A.

5. I am quite distressed to learn about your daughter's failure to get through her music training diploma, this year.

6. It has pained me to learn that you have failed to secure a scholarship for the U.S.A.

Convey your reassurances:

7. However, I quite understand your circumstances. It is not easy to handle a full time job and studies together.

8. I understand how badly you were tied up with your family problems.

9. I am quite sure that you would have passed, if you had enough time to prepare for it.

10. It was mainly your illness that let you down.

11. With your sister's marriage taking place around that time, you hardly had any time to study.

Close the letter by wishing for future success:

12. I have no doubt that you will succeed next time.

13. Once you have recovered from this illness, you will easily get through/ secure it. (scholarship).

14. For a boy of your talents, this degree is certainly not out of reach.

15. You should not lose heart. It is very difficult for most people to make it in the first attempt.

16. With enough time for preparation, I am confident you will clear this examination next time.

17. With no disturbance around, clearing this exam won't be a problem for you.

Sample Letter

My dear........,

I am quite disappointed to learn that you have not been successful in your B.A. examinations.[1] I am quite sure that you would have passed if you had enough time to prepare for it.[9] I have no doubt, you will succeed next time.[12]

With best wishes,

Sincerely,

Letters on Educational Matters

There are occasions when teachers and children's parents have to correspond with one another. More often than not such correspondence relates to the absence of the child from school. However, there can be other matters too, concerning some other educational problems.

Some of these are:

i. Getting a certificate.

ii. Complaint on lack of facilities in school or other inconveniences.

iii. Inquiries about child's progress in his/ her studies and the teacher's reply.

Letter to School for Certificate

Start your letter by giving reasons for asking for the certificate:

1. This is to inform you that I have been transferred to Hyderabad and will be leaving Delhi on the tenth of this month to take charge of my new post.

2. You will be pleased to learn that my son Rajiv who has passed his higher secondary from your school this year, plans to apply to an American university/ Education Ministry for a scholarship for higher studies.

3. It will be of interest to you to learn that my son, Chandra Kiran, who has completed/ finished his education this year at your school, plans to apply for a job with the Government of India/ Escorts Ltd.

4. You will be happy to know that my daughter, Rani Rao, who is a student of Class X in your school wishes to participate in the Science Talent Competition next month.

Request for Certificate itself:

5. Hence, I would request you to issue a school leaving certificate to my son, Amit Kumar, a student of VII D of your school so that he can be admitted to a school there.

6. Therefore, you are requested to give him a character certificate to be enclosed with such an application.

7. This is to request you to give a provisional certificate of passing the said examination to be produced at the time of interview.

8. I learn that a merit certificate from her school is necessary for entry to this competition. Therefore, I shall be grateful if you issue the certificate.

9. He has been asked to get a character certificate and mark sheet from the school when he appears for the interview. Therefore, please issue the same.

Inform if the certificate is required by a fixed date:

10. Kindly arrange to issue this certificate by the end of this week.

11. For your information, this certificate has to be submitted before the first of next month.

12. As I have to leave Delhi in the first week of next month, kindly instruct your office to make testimonials available to us by this month end.

13. Since the interview is scheduled for next Monday, he requires it before that.

14. I request you to let me have the certificate immediately as there is only one week left for the final interview.

15. I will feel obliged if you release the certificate before the 15th of this month.

Express thanks:

16. Thank you for the trouble.

17. Please excuse me for putting you to trouble.

18. Thanking you.

19. I will feel obliged for this favour.

20. I will be grateful for your timely gesture.

Sample Letter

Respected Sir/ Madam,

This is to inform you that I have been transferred to Hyderabad and will be leaving Delhi on the tenth of this month to take charge of my new post.[1] Hence, I request you to issue a school leaving certificate to my son Amit Kumar, a student of VII D of your school, so that he can be admitted to a school there.[5] Kindly arrange to issue this certificate by the end of this week.[10]

Thank you for the trouble.[16]

Sincerely,

Letter of Complaint to the Head Master

> If there is lack of educational or other facilities in the school, a letter of complaint can be written to the Headmaster of the school.

Start the letter in this way:

1. I am deeply pained to learn from my son about the attitude of some of your teachers towards the students.
2. As the father of one of your students, I consider it my moral duty to bring to your notice the sad state of affairs in some classes of your school.
3. May I take this opportunity to express my concern on the teaching standard in my son's class.
4. I am writing this letter mainly to bring to your kind notice the unsatisfactory sanitary conditions/ catering arrangements that I noticed during my recent visit to your school.
5. This is to bring to your kind notice the misbehaviour of the school bus driver/ conductor with students.
6. This is to suggest you a few measures you could take to improve the general conditions in your school.
7. I am quite disturbed to learn about the unhealthy conditions around your school.
8. It is quite surprising that your school, although well established, is totally lacking in sports' facilities.

Then mention some complaints (educational):

9. I have been informed by my son that during the course of one month the Physics teacher has been changed thrice, and as a result, the studies have suffered badly.
10. My daughter tells me that her Sanskrit teacher has been on leave for more than a month now and no substitute has been arranged.
11. I can see from my daughter's homework that her Mathematics teacher expects the students to know things that he/she does not teach in the class.
12. I have noticed that my son gets much more homework than a child of his age can handle.

After that, mention other complaints:

13. For the last few days the school bus has been arriving half an hour late and, as a result, my son always misses his first period in the class.
14. I noticed that the school canteen totally lacked hygiene, with flies hovering over the eatables.
15. According to my son, the toilet in the school is badly maintained and he fears that this might lead to the spread of diseases.
16. The desks are not dusted properly and, as a result, the students' clothes get spoiled.
17. The water tank which provides drinking water to the students is not regularly cleaned and hence there is always a danger of spreading infection.
18. I am quite pained to learn that young children are beaten mercilessly by some teachers for minor offences.
19. It is quite disturbing to learn that some students bully other children.

Close the letter by expressing hopes for early corrective measures:

20. I hope I have managed to bring home to you the basic problem and you will take prompt action to solve it.
21. It is clear that you will have to employ better staff and offer them better terms if you don't want your students to suffer.
22. Strict supervision of your canteen/ sanitary staff is necessary and I expect you would arrange for it.
23. May I request you to see that the students are not unnecessarily burdened.
24. I hope you will consider my suggestions in good spirit and my complaint will be heeded to.
25. May I request you to reprimand the bus driver.
26. May I request you to kindly instruct your teachers not to beat the children very harshly.

Sample Letter

Respected Sir/ Madam,

May I take this opportunity to express my concern on the teaching standards in my son's class?[3] I have been informed by my son that during the course of one month the Physics teacher has been changed thrice and, as a result, the studies have suffered badly.[9] It is clear that you will have to employ better staff and offer them better terms if you don't want your students to suffer.[21]

With regards,

Yours faithfully,

Letter from Teacher to Parents Regarding Students' Progress

> This letter can be written by the teacher on his/her own or he/she can do so in reply to the parent's/ guardian's letter.

Begin the letter in this way:

1. Thank you for your letter enquiring about your son, Atul's progress in the school.
2. Thank you for your enquiry about your son's progress in the class.
3. I have received your note asking for information regarding your son's progress in school.
4. I am pleased to learn that you have been showing a keen interest in your sister's progress at school.

The following sentences are suitable in reply:

5. I am writing this note as I feel you are interested in knowing how your daughter is doing at school.
6. I think it is my duty to inform you about your son's performance in the class.
7. I am sure you would like to know how your son is faring in his studies.
8. May I take this opportunity to inform you of your son's progress in his studies.
9. I am informing through this letter about your son's progress in sports and other extra-curricular activities.

Now, apprise of the student's progress in studies:

10. I am sorry to inform you that of late he has been careless in his work.
11. I regret to inform you that in the class he is more busy talking than listening.
12. He is certainly an intelligent boy, but remains inattentive in the class.
13. Mira is certainly/ definitely trying to make up in Mathematics, but I feel she will take some mere time to catch up with the rest of the class.
14. I am happy to say that Leela has now improved a lot and is doing well.
15. But for a slight weakness in English, Prakash has now come up to the average standard of the class and continues to make good progress.
16. Govind is a bright boy and if you arrange for a private tuition in English for just a month, he will be able to make up the deficiency.
17. Anita, of course, finds Geometry a little tough, but I am paying individual attention to her and hope she will catch up with the rest of the class.

Some other matters relating to the student can also be mentioned:

18. If Prakash maintains his touch, he will soon be selected for cricket team of Delhi State.
19. Although he is an intelligent boy he is a little quarrelsome.
20. I am happy to note that Deepak shows leadership qualities in all school activities.
21. I have noticed that Neelu has a flair for painting and she should be encouraged in that.

Suggest ways for improvement of the student:

22. I am sure, with a private tuition in English, Gopal will be able to do well on the whole in the annual examination.
23. May I suggest that your daughter needs special coaching in Mathematics to prepare herself for the final examination.
24. He does not need anything but a little supervision in his home-work.
25. Just a little more care on his part will improve the quality of his work considerably.
26. With her talents she might emerge as a good painter in future.

Give suggestions for improvements in student's conduct/ behaviour:

27. Perhaps a few words of parental advice from you would be enough.
28. It has to be explained to him that his quarrelsome nature creates problems for everybody.
29. I am happy to say that Renu is a very well-behaved girl.
30. With a little more supervision he will manage to do quite well.

The letter can be closed in this way:

31. I hope this information is of some use to you.
32. If you need any more information about your son's progress in school, you are most welcome to call on me.
33. Sometimes young boys take time to settle down. So I do not think you should worry too much about Kewal.
34. However, there is no need to worry. I am sure he will improve soon.
35. I am sure you will appreciate this information.

Sample Letter

Dear Mr........,

Thank you for your letter enquiring about your son, Atul's progress in the school.[1] He is certainly an intelligent boy, but remains inattentive in the class.[12] Just a little more care on his part will improve the quality of his work considerably.[25] I hope this information is of some use to you.[31]

With regards,

Yours sincerely,

Letter from Parent to Teacher Regarding
Student's progress

Start your letter by giving reasons for doing so:

1. As I had been away on an official tour for more than a month, I could not supervise my son's studies.

2. As a result of pressing business engagements for quite a few weeks, of late, I could not attend to my daughter's studies.

3. On account of my illness, I have not personally attended to my son's studies for quite a few days.

4. This being the end of the financial year, I was tied up with the office work and thus, could not pay much attention to my sister's studies.

5. The annual examinations are approaching nearer and I felt it necessary to know about the performance of my daughter in the class.

6. As I was away to Europe for three months on a sales promotion campaign for my company, I could not pay attention to my daughter's studies.

Now, enquire about your son's/ daughter's progress in studies:

7. May I ask you to let me know in detail about his/her progress in the class.

8. I would, therefore, request you to let me know if his progress is satisfactory.

9. So, please let me know how he is doing.

10. Could you let me know about his/her progress?

11. His last monthly report indicated that he was a little weak in English. So I would like to know if he has improved this time or not.

12. His performance in the last quarterly exam. was unsatisfactory. Do you advise me to arrange for a private tuition?

13. Please let me know how he can improve to catch up with the rest of the class.

14. Please inform what lessons he/she has missed during his/her absence.

15. Please write to me at the earliest about the progress she has made during this period – and also about the subjects she is weak at.

Write about the usefulness of the information to be received:

16. This would help me considerably to supervise his studies in a better way.

17. Your letter will help me decide whether he needs private coaching in any subject or not.

18. If you suggest, my sister who is a university teacher could coach him.

19. Information about his performance in the class will enable me to make some tutorial arrangements, if needed.

20. Your suggestions will help me considerably in my attempt to improve her/ his performance.

21. With your suggestions I shall feel better equipped to help her in her examinations.

22. Your information will enable me to monitor his/her improvement.

Close the letter by giving thanks:

23. I will feel obliged if you help me in this regard
24. Please excuse me for the trouble.
25. Thanking you.
26. Your advice will go a long way in improving/ helping her/ his career.
27. I shall feel highly obliged for your invaluable help in this regard.

Sample Letter

Respected Sir,

As I had been away on an official tour for more than a month, I could not supervise my son's studies.[1] So, please let me know how he is doing.[9] Your letter would help me decide whether he needs private coaching in any subject or not.[17] Please excuse me for the trouble.[24]

Thanking you,

Yours sincerely,

Letter to the Headmaster/Principal on Student's Absence

Give details about the child and his absence:

1. This is to request you to grant my son, Atul, a student of VIII B of your school, leave for a week, i.e., from July 3 to July 9.

2. My son, Rakesh Arora, is unable to attend the class for two days, i.e., 14th and 15th of this month.

3. My daughter, Priti Kumari, student of class VIII B will remain absent from her class for three days, i.e., from 1st to 3rd of this month due to a marriage in the family.

4. This is to intimate you that my niece, Rashmi, a student of class VI B won't be able to attend her class tomorrow.

Give reasons for absence from school:

5. The boy is running high temperature and the doctor has advised him complete rest.

6. Her sister has had a baby and there is nobody at home to look after her for two days.

7. He is accompanying us for the marriage of one of his cousins in Kanpur.

8. He is going to visit his grandmother who is seriously ill.

9. His mother has been admitted to the hospital for an operation today.

10. We have a function today on the occasion of his younger brother's first birthday.

Request for granting leave:

11. Kindly grant him/ her leave for this period.

12. She/he may be granted leave for these days/ this period.

13. We will try to make up for whatever loss in studies she/he suffers.

14. Kindly sanction leave for the said period.

Express your thanks:

15. Thanking you.

16. I will feel obliged for your kind help.

Sample Letter

Sir,

This is to request you to grant my son, Atul, a student of VIII B of your school, leave for a week, i.e., from July 3 to July 9.[1] The boy is running high temperature and the doctor has advised him complete rest.[5] Kindly grant him leave for this period.[11]

Thanking you,

Yours sincerely,

Letters on Office Matters

Writing an application for sick or casual leave is a normal official practice by an employee. However, there are many other subjects on which he might write a letter to his superior. Some of these are:

  i. Increment or promotion.

 ii. Resignation.

iii. Request for a transfer

 iv. Request for a reference

  v. Complaint on some inconvenience in the office.

Out of the above letters, the application for sickness or letter of resignation can be brief. The current trend in most of the offices is that there will be printed forms like Printed Leave Application Form, in which details can be filled, but, still the learners should know how to write a leave application. Other letters mentioned above can be detailed, listing the reasons for writing such a letter.

Letter of Increment/ Promotion

Start the letter by giving your tenure and performance in the job:

1. I have been employed with your company for the last three years and during this period, I have discharged my duties to the best of my abilities.

2. Ever since I joined this company, I have put in my best efforts and all my colleagues appreciate my work.

3. As you are aware, I have been working as an Accounts Assistant in this office for the last five years and have also officiated as an Accountant whenever the latter was on leave.

4. I am sure you are aware of the fact that I will complete five years in this office by the end of this month.

5. This is to inform you that I have completed five years of service with the organisation.

Now give reasons for the necessity of writing the letter:

6. However, I think my performance has gone unnoticed because I have not got any increment so far.

7. Although I have been entrusted with some additional work, my salary has not been revised for almost three years.

8. I hope I deserve a promotion to the next rank which is long overdue.

9. However, despite the general appreciation of my work, I have not got any promotion/ I have been superseded by Mr. Pillai who had been my junior.

10. I learn that Mr. Das is leaving by the end of the year and his post is likely to fall vacant.

11. I think I should have got a better increment than what I got this time.

12. I learn that the Accountant under whom I have been working, is being transferred to the Head Office on promotion.

13. I understand that a new branch of our company is being opened in Kanpur for which you require experienced staff.

14. I feel that an increase in my salary is long overdue.

15. After such a long period of sincere service I feel I deserve a promotion.

Thereafter come to the point by giving suggestions :

16. You are well acquainted with the fact that of late the inflation has been very high.

17. Therefore, may I request you to consider my case for an increment/ a promotion?

18. You know about the increasing cost of living in Delhi and now I struggle to make both ends meet.

19. I, therefore, enclose an application for that post and hope that considering my past record, you will take a favourable view of it.

20. I, therefore, apply for the post of Manager of the new branch and hope that my competence and experience will assure you of my ability to serve the company to the entire satisfaction of the management.

Close the letter with an expectation of a favourable consideration.

21. I hope you will consider my case favourably.

22. I earnestly hope that this request will be given due consideration.

23. As you are aware of my family circumstances, I hope you will take a favourable view.

24. I feel confident that the management will be generous in recognizing and rewarding my merit.

25. I am looking forward to a favourable response from you.

26. All my colleagues also feel the same way.

27. I assure you that I will do my best to justify your confidence in me.

Sample Letter

Dear Sir,

I have been employed with your company for the last three years and during this period, I have discharged my duties to the best of my abilities.[1] However, despite the general appreciation of my work, I have not got any promotion.[9] I learn that Mr. Das is leaving by the end of the year and his post is likely to fall vacant.[10] Therefore, may I request you to consider my case for a promotion?[17] I assure you that I will do my best to justify your confidence in me.[27]

Thanking you,

Yours faithfully,

Resignation

In the beginning give reasons for resignation:

1. I feel happy to inform you that I have been appointed the Manager of Delhi Branch of Bharat Tubes and have been asked to take charge in a month's time.

2. I am deeply concerned to learn that you have turned down my request for increment/promotion despite the fact that I have always been very serious with my work.

3. Since my husband has been transferred to Bombay, I am sorry to state that I can't continue in my present job here.

4. You are, perhaps, aware of the fact that I am expecting within a few months. I feel I can't continue with my job as the baby will require constant attention for the first few years.

5. I am sorry to say that my salary is too meagre as compared to the duties I perform in the office.

6. I am happy to inform you that I have been offered an Executive's post with an advertising company.

Thereafter, submit resignation for acceptance:

7. I, therefore, tender my resignation from my present post.

8. My resignation may, therefore, be accepted with effect from the first of next month.

9. Therefore, I am hereby giving one month's notice prior to my resignation.

10. As I am required to join there immediately, I pray that you waive the clause of three month's notice and relieve me immediately, considering my long service with you.

11. It is requested that my accounts be settled as soon as possible.

12. It was a pleasure to work with you and I very much regret to have to leave.

13. The leave that is due to me may kindly be encashed.

14. The leaves lying to my credit may be adjusted against my notice period.

15. I will always remember with gratitude the encouragement I have always received from you and shall definitely miss you.

16. I am indebted to you for all the knowledge and experience I have gathered during my stay with you.

Sample Letter

Dear Sir,

I feel happy to inform you that I have been appointed the Manager of Delhi Branch of Bharat Tubes and have been asked to take charge in a month's time.[1] I, therefore, tender my resignation from my present post.[7] It is requested that my accounts be settled as soon as possible.[11] I am indebted to you for all the knowledge and experience I have gathered during my stay with you.[16]

With regards,

Sincerely,

Request for Transfer

At the outset give reasons for seeking transfer:

1. I regret to inform you that for the last one month because of internal bickering among the staff members I have been feeling quite uncomfortable here in the Bombay branch.

2. You may have observed that the prolonged illness of my aged father has made it necessary for me to make frequent trips to Delhi.

3. This is to inform you that my husband has recently been transferred to Bombay and, therefore, it would no more be possible for me to continue here.

4. I am sorry to say that because of the humid climate here in Bombay/ Calcutta, I have not been keeping good health ever since I joined this branch.

5. I am afraid, I don't find the atmosphere in this branch very congenial.

6. Since housing problem is very acute in Calcutta and I cannot afford to pay very high rent, I find it difficult to work here.

7. This new branch being very small, I find myself unable to exercise my capabilities fully.

Then make a request for transfer:

8. May I, therefore, request you to transfer me back to the Head Office?

9. So, I would request you to transfer me to our branch office in Bombay/ Calcutta/ Delhi, so that I could live with my husband.

10. It would be very kind of you if you could kindly transfer me to Delhi so that I can properly look after my ailing father.

11. I may, therefore, be permitted to regain my health and serve the organization better by being transferred to a place where the climate is healthy.

12. I am sure that my transfer to the main branch will help me expose my potential better and thus help the organization too.

13. We have branches at many small places also where I could easily get a decent accommodation at reasonable rent.

14. I would request you to kindly accede to my request and do the needful.

15. I hope, considering my past performance, you will take a favourable view of this request.

Sample Letter

Dear Sir,

You may have observed that the prolonged illness of my aged father has made it necessary for me to make frequent trips to Delhi.[2] It would be very kind of you if you could transfer me to Delhi so that I can properly look after my ailing father.[10] I would request you to kindly accede to my request and do the needful.[14]

Thanking you,

Sincerely,

Request to Employer for Reference

Start by giving reasons for your request:

1. I had applied for the post of an Accountant in a Bombay based organization. Now they require a letter from my previous employer.

2. I have been called for an interview for a position in Air India's Junior Management Cadre. As I have to submit a letter of reference at the time of interview. I would request you to issue the same to me.

3. I would like to apply for the post of an Asstt. Manager in General Mills which was recently advertised. I need to enclose a certificate of experience alongwith this application and, hence, would request you to issue the same to me.

Now describe your activities :

4. I hope you would appreciate my requirement and do the needful.

5. I think you have always been satisfied with my work, and hope you will say all you can in my favour.

6. This is a promising offer and can ensure me a bright future within the limits of my qualifications and experience.

7. I hope my work for this firm has been satisfactory and you will always encourage me to seek better prospects.

8. This is a permanent post and there are many chances for my career advancement.

Close the letter hopefully :

9. Of course, I will always feel indebted to this Organization which has taught me a lot.

10. I hope I will always receive encouragement from you to make progress in life.

11. Although I am applying for a new post, I would request you not to take it as my dissatisfaction with your organization.

12. Even if I don't get this job, I will, of course, keep on working with you. But it is my earnest request to you not to have any apprehension about my sincerity towards work.

13. I hope you will appreciate the fact that all of us always try for better prospects in life. You understand how badly I need a transfer. And this job will get me that.

```
                    Sample Letter
Dear  Sir,
I  had  applied  for  the  post  of  an  accountant  in  a  Mumbai  based
organization.  Now  they  require  a  letter  from  my  previous  employer.[1]
I  hope  you  would  appreciate  my  requirement  and  do  the  needful.[4]
With  regards,

                                        Yours  faithfully,
```

Leave Application

First of all give reasons for the application for leave :

*(I regret to inform you that.........)

1. due to a sudden attack of influenza/malaria I have been confined to bed with fever and am unable to attend the office.
2. due to the sudden demise of my father, in Bombay, I have to leave immediately to perform/attend to his last rites.
3. of late I have been having shooting pain in my back/head, and hence, I need a few days' rest.
4. my son has suddenly taken ill and he has to be admitted to the hospital.
5. I have to perform Shradha ceremony of my late mother.
6. I have to go out of town for two days to attend my brother's wedding.
7. This is to inform you that my B.A/M.A. examinations begin from next month and so I require two weeks' leave in the beginning of the month.

After that make a request for sanctioning leave :

8. It will be very kind of you if you grant me casual leave for today only.
9. It is, therefore, to request you to grant me leave for two days, i.e., today and tomorrow.
10. So, please grant/sanction me leave for a week from today.
11. Whatever pending work there is, I will finish them soon after I join duty.
12. Please grant me leave for these two days and oblige.
13. Enclosed is a medical certificate for your kind perusal.
14. The leave may kindly be granted. The medical certificate will be submitted later on.
15. In my absence Krishnan has agreed to handle some of the urgent matters I deal with.

Sample Letter

Sir,

I regret to inform you that due to a sudden attack of influenza I have been confined to bed with fever and am unable to attend the office.[1] It is, therefore, to request you to grant me leave for two days i.e., today and tomorrow.[9]

Thanking you,

Yours faithfully,

*This part of the sentence will only be used with letters concerning illness or death.

Letter for Office Complaints

One often has occasions to complain about certain matters regarding one's office. It could be concerning lack of amenities or some other inconveniences. Such a letter is in two parts, first describing the cause of complaint and the second offering a solution.

Start the letter by giving the nature of your complaint :

1. I regret to say that because of over-crowding in our room, free movement has become extremely difficult.

2. This is to inform you that the lighting in our room is inadequate/insufficient. Thus, it becomes very difficult to work, especially in winter evenings.

3. I regret to inform you that our room is exposed to the sun and in summer it becomes too hot to work there .

4. I have to inform you very reluctantly that the gentleman on the table next to mine used objectionable language which should not have been used in the presence of a lady.

5. I regret to inform you that the new clerk we have appointed is rude and discourteous.

Suggest some corrective measures, if possible

6. I hope you will look into this matter and take corrective measures soon.

7. I am sure a slight reprimand from you will correct his ways.

8. May I, therefore, request you to provide us with more electric bulbs.

9. We, therefore, request you to get the water cooler repaired immediately.

10. I hope you will take care to get a few curtains for the windows to prevent the glare of the summer sun.

11. I am sure you will look into our grievances and take proper remedial action.

12. Please oblige us by taking necessary measures.

Sample Letter

Dear Sir,

This is to inform you that the lighting in our room is insufficient. Thus, it becomes difficult to work, especially in winter evenings.[2] Please oblige us by taking necessary measures.[12]

With regards,

Yours faithfully,

Letters between Landlord and Tenant

The tension between the landlord and the tenant is of comparatively recent origin. This is more acute in big cities. Earlier when there was not much pressure of houses, this problem was non-existent.

Now, sometimes the landlord is the harassed party and sometimes the tenant. At times, the tenant comes to occupy the house and virtually becomes the landlord. On the other hand, sometimes the greedy landlord wants to charge exorbitant rent. All these things result in quarrels and litigation.

For all the above reasons, some correspondence between a tenant and the landlord has become rather necessary. The general circumstances which may require such correspondence are as under:-

1. Repairs, renovations, white washing and upkeep of the tenanted portion/premises.

2. Increase in the rent.

3. Non-issuance of the rent-receipt, etc.

Since this correspondence is fraught with apprehensions of quarrels leading to litigation, the language used in the letter should not be self condemning. It should be well drafted so that it can stand in good stead at the required time in the shape of a documentary evidence.

Letter to a Tenant for Increasing Rent

Describe your reasons for increasing the rent :

1. I feel constrained to inform you that for the recent repairs done in the house, including the portion you are occupying, I had to incur considerable expenditure.
2. I am constrained to inform you that because of a steep rise in the cost of building material, the recent additions to the house have put a great financial strain on my resources.
3. Please take note that the municipal authorities have recently announced a very big increase in the house tax.
4. As you are aware my husband has passed away recently and I don't have any other source of income, I have to ask you, though reluctantly, to increase the rent.
5. As I am a retired person now, my only source of income is the rent of this house, which seems to be insufficient.

It can also start saying :

I am compelled to write to you...../ I am forced to inform you that because of..../ I am to tell you that..... etc.

Now propose the increase in rent :

6. Under the circumstances, I have been left with no other alternative but to increase the house rent by Rs.1000 /- per month w.e.f. the 1st of next month.
7. I have, therefore, to raise your monthly rent by Rs.500 /- per month from next month.
8. As a result, an increase in the house rent by Rs.500 /- per month from August 1, has become inevitable.
9. I, therefore, request you to consider an appropriate increase in the house rent.
10. So, please increase the monthly rent by an amount which suits your pocket.

Close the letter, expecting cooperation from the tenant :

11. I hope you will understand and appreciate my point of view.
12. I hope you will understand my position and won't take it as an exploitation.
13. I hope you will not find this increase unreasonable under the circumstances and will accept it in the right spirit.
14. I am sure you won't find it burdensome as you have recently got a pay hike.

Sample Letter

Dear Sir,

I am constrained to inform you that because of steep rise in the cost of building material, the recent additions to the house have put a great financial strain on my resources.[2] Under the circumstances I have been left with no other alternatives but to increase the house rent by Rs.1000/- per month w.e.f. the 1st of next month.[6] I hope you will understand my position and won't take it as an exploitation.[12]

With best wishes,

Yours faithfully,

Tenant's Refusal to Increase Rent

First, acknowledge the landlord's letter:

1. This refers to your letter concerning an increase in rent for the house I am occupying.
2. I have received your letter asking for an increased rent for my accommodation from next month.
3. I am amazed to receive your letter demanding more rent for your house rented to me.
4. I have received your letter demanding higher rent for your house rented to me.

Now, give reasons for declining the proposed increase in rent:

5. However, I don't see any justification for this increase and can't comply with your demand.
6. The poor condition of the house does not warrant any increase in rent and hence I cannot agree to your proposal.
7. It was only last month that you increased my rent by Rs.500/- per month and hence I cannot agree to another increase so soon.
8. I think you should not try to realise the amount that you spent on repairs by increasing the rent as you already collect high rent.
9. I regret to say that, however justifiable the increase in rent may appear to you, my present financial means don't permit me to spend any more on rent.
10. I feel that your demand is unreasonable as I am already paying more rent than your other tenants.

Stress on good relations:

11. I hope you will look at this proposal from my point of view and not press your demand.
12. I hope you will understand my position and withdraw this demand for the time being.
13. However, I will definitely try to agree to your demand, provided you get the house properly repaired as you often promise.
14. I expect you to please bear with me for the time being.

Sample Letter

Dear Sir,

This refers to your letter concerning an increase in rent for the house I am occupying.[1] I feel that your demand is unreasonable as I am already paying more rent than your other tenantes.[10] I hope you will look at this proposal from my point of view and not press your demand.[11]

With good wishes,

Sincerely,

Tenant's Regret at Late Payment of Rent

In the beginning give reasons for delay in paying the rent and regret the same :

1. I am sorry that I could not pay last month's rent in time as I was out of station for two weeks.
2. This is to apologise for not paying this month's rent in time as I had to meet certain other urgent expenses.
3. I very much regret my inability to pay this month's rent in time due to some unforeseen financial difficulties.
4. I am sorry that on account of bank holidays I could not pay last month's rent in time.
5. I am extremely sorry for not being able to pay the house rent in time.
6. I can understand your position at not getting my rent in time.

Now, inform about paying the rent :

7. However, enclosed herewith is a cheque towards the payment of rent.
8. I hope you understand my position and do not mind the delay.
9. At the moment I cannot promise any certain date. But I will pay as soon as I get money from my father in Calcuta.
10. As I had to spend very heavily on my son's illness I would be greateful if you could accept two month's rent together next month.
11. I have already arranged to pay it to you immediately.
12. I will pay as soon I get some payments from some of my clients.

Close the letter with due apologies:

13. Hoping to be excused.
14. Kindly excuse me for the inconvenience caused to you.
15. I again regret the inconvenience caused to you.
16. I request you to bear with me for the time being.
17. The inconvenience caused is regretted.

```
                    Sample Letter
Dear Sir,
This is to apologise for not paying this month's rent in time as
I had to meet certain other urgent expenses.²  I can understand
your position at not getting my rent in time.⁶ However, enclosed
herewith is a cheque towards the payment of rent.⁷ I again regret
the inconvenience caused to you.¹⁵

With good wishes/regards,

                                          Yours Sincerely,
```

Letter to an Estate Agent

Start the letter by informing about the requirement of a residential apartment:

1. I have been recently transferred to here from Bombay and thus I am looking out for a suitable accommodation.
2. I have recently come to Delhi, and my brother, Naresh Vij asked me to contact you if I needed an accommodation.
3. The colony in which I am living at present is getting over-crowded and I want to shift to a quiet place.

Describe the house of your liking/choice :

4. I want a small flat of two rooms in a posh colony.
5. I want a two bed room house/flat, preferably with a store.
6. I want a single bed room flat with a spacious kitchen at a place where there is no scarcity of water.
7. The accommodation I require is three bed rooms, a spacious drawing-dining room, a kitchen and a store. Enough water and modern sanitary arrangements are important.
8. My requirement is a barsati, with kitchen and toilet, in a good colony.

Express your opinion regarding the rent payable :

9. My estimate for the rent is between Rs.6000/- and Rs.8000/-
10. Rent is not a problem if the accommodation is good.
11. I am prepared to pay a rent upto Rs.12000/-.for a really suitable place in a decent colony.
12. I cannot pay more than Rs.6000/- for a spacious barsati.
13. For an accommodation of my requirements I propose to pay around Rs.8000/- as rent.

At the end, request him to search for a house :

14. I shall feel obliged if you arrange for such an accommodation.
15. Since I am staying in a guest house, I would require it as soon as possible.
16. I would request you to suggest a flat of this description and in this range of rent.
17. So, kindly let me know if you can arrange for such an accommodation.
18. I would not mind paying whatever reasonable commission you ask for if I get accommodation of this kind.

Sample Letter

Dear Mr........

I have been recently transferred to here from Bombay and I am looking out for a suitable accommodation.[2] I want a two bed room flat preferably with a store.[5] Rent is not a problem if the accommodation is good.[10] So, kindly let me know if you can arrange for such an accommodation.[17]

With best wishes,

Yours faithfully,

Request to Landlord for Repairs

Start your letter by giving reasons for repairs :

1. I must bring to your notice that the railing of the staircase has got broken at a few places and thus it has become quite hazardous

2. This is to inform you that on account of last night's heavy rain a lot of plaster from our sitting room's ceiling has come off.

3. I feel it must be brought to your notice that the wood used in our flat has become quite old and, as a result, it has developed cracks.

4. Now that the monsoon has set in, water is seeping into the floor of my rooms and I fear that it might affect the health of my family.

5. I have repeatedly reminded you that the basin in our bathroom has become very old. It has developed cracks and cannot be used any longer.

6. I regret to inform you that despite my repeated requests you have not repaired our flat.

7. The wiring in our flats has become old and it has become quite dangerous.

Stress on the landlord for early repairs :

8. So please, get it repaired quickly.

9. Therefore, kindly arrange for early repairs.

10. Please get it done before the winter sets in.

11. If you want I can contribute a share of the expenses.

12. I you like, I can get it repaired and debit the expenditure towards the rent.

13. Please get it repaired before it becomes and a serious hazard.

14. As I have small children at home, the open wires are quite dangerous.

15. Please see to it that repairs are done soon, as the festive season is approaching fast.

Close the letter with your thanks :

16. I will be thankful for your cooperation.

17. I hope I am not putting you to too much inconvenience.

18. Thanking you in anticipation.

19. Thank you for doing the needful

Sample Letter

Dear Sir,

This is to inform you that on account of last night's heavy rain a lot of plaster from our sitting room's ceiling has come off.[2] So, please get it repaired quickly.[8] I hope I am not putting you to too much inconvenience.[17]

Regards/Thanking you,

Yours sincerely,

Letters of Complaint

Complaints can be of two types; personal and social. If you have bought an article from the market and it turns out to be defective, a complaint concerning it would be personal. However, if a complaint is lodged with the municipal authorities concerning the general sanitary conditions, it would be social.

Whatever be the nature of the complaint, the purpose is to seek a remedy. For this purpose the letter should be very clear

A letter of complaint can be split up into 4 parts:-

1. In the beginning , give the specific complaint
2. In the middle, suggest remedies
3. In the third part, make a request for carrying out the remedial measures
4. At the end, express thanks/gratitude.

Complaint about Insanitary Conditions

Describe the insanitary/unhygienic conditions :

1. I regret to inform you that a dead buffalo has been lying in our street for the last two days and nobody has cleared it.

2. I regret to inform you that the unhealthy conditions prevailing in our locality for the past few days are now posing serious health hazards.

3. This is to invite your urgent attention to the heaps of dirt and garbage that have been accumulating in our colony.

4. I take this opportunity to inform you that the municipal garbage dump is right in front of our house.

5. This is to complain about a car workshop in our street which does its works on footpaths and has made the place slippery and dirty with oil and grease.

6. This is to bring to your notice the fact that sewage system has stopped working in our locality. It has become a breeding place for mosquitoes and is posing a hazard to the health of the people of the locality.

7. I would like to bring to your notice that most of the roads in our locality remain unswept for days together resulting in an unbearable stench.

8. I am sorry to inform you that now a days, particularly on account of the rains many lanes in our locality are full of stagnant water.

9. For the last two weeks, the sweepers of our area have been absent. As a result, heaps of garbage are lying along the roadside.

10. I have observed that the public toilets in our locality are not properly cleaned. As a result, the poor people of the locality use open public places for toilet purposes.

11. A sewerage pipe appears to have burst in our street two days back and dirty water has been spreading all around causing obnoxious smell. No sanitary inspector has visited the spot so far.

12. On account of the general construction being done by the municipal authorities, there are heaps of sand and bricks lying on the pavements. As a result, they have become impossible to walk on.

13. The heavy rain last week had created deep puddles in all lanes of our locality, but till date nothing has been done to repair the lanes.

14. The stagnant water is a breeding place for mosquitoes and malaria is spreading rapidly in our colony.

Discuss how the problem can be tackled :

15. I hope you will take prompt action and help in making the surroundings healthy.

16. May I request you to see to it that the gutter is immediately repaired to prevent the spread of any disease.

17. Kindly remove this repair shop/worksop from the area which is creating health problems for the residents of this locality.

18. Please instruct your sanitary staff to control the mosquito menace in our locality before the disease takes the shape of an epidemic.

19. Kindly arrange to remove the garbage dump from such a congested locality.

20. Please arrange to get the drains of our locality cleaned before the monsoon breaks.

21. Please ensure that the public toilets and urinals are regularly cleaned.

At the end express thanks in anticipation :

22. Thanking you in anticipation.

23. I will be gratefull for an early action.

24. I will be obliged if you take a prompt action in this regard.

Sample Letter

Dear Sir,

This is to invite your urgent attention to the heaps of dirt and garbage that have been accumulating in our colony.[3] For the last two weeks, the sweepers of our area have been absent. As a result, heaps of garbage are lying along the road side.[9] I hope you will take prompt action and help in making the surroundings healthy.[15]

Thanking you,

Yours faithfully,

Complaint against Pavement Encroachment

Bring the complaint to attention/notice :

1. I consider it my duty, as a citizen, to bring to your notice the blatant misuse of the footpaths in our locality by various kinds of repair shops.
2. This is to complain to you against the encroachment of the footpath by a tea-shop owner in front of my house.
3. This is to complain to you that the cattle from a nearby private dairy, have been spoiling the pavement opposite to my house, everyday.
4. This is to inform you that the footpaths of our streets have become camping places for the beggars.
5. I wish to lodge a complaint that a second-hand scooter dealer, opposite my house often blocks the pavement by parking scooters in a row there.
6. This is to complain against Mr.Sharma who is constructing a house down our lane for quite a few months. On account of this construction, the pavements are always full of sand, heaps and bricks.
7. This is to inform you that in the last few days a hutment has sprung up on the pavements in our neighbourhood.

Suggest some remedial measures:

8. I suggest that you visit our area for a first hand appraisal of the situation.
9. Kindly prevent these shops from encroaching public places, using the existing law.
10. It is requested that one week's notice to vacate the place may be served on repair-shop holders, under the existing law.
11. The check-force meant to remove such unauthorised occupation may be asked to be more alert and vigilant.
12. You may kindly depute some junior officers to make an on-the-spot enquiry and empower them to take prompt action against law breakers/squatters.

Request for action/redressing :

13. I hope you will take immediate action in the interest of better living conditions for the citizens of this locality.
14. I feel that your promptness in this regard can make the things normal and win the goodwill of the public.
15. I am sure you will take necessary steps to keep the pavement clean and open.
16. I have full faith in your officials sincerity and competence and hope that necessary action will be taken by them at the earliest.
17. I am sure my letter will set in motion your official machinery and get the beggars removed from here.

Express your thanks :

18. Thanking you.
19. Thanks in anticipation.

20. I will be thankful for an early action.

21. I will feel much obliged for your earliest action.

Sample Letter

Dear Sir,

This is to complain to you against the encroachment of the footpath by a tea-shop owner in front of my house.[2] It is requested to issue instructions for removal of all unauthorised occupation in public places. The check-force meant to remove such unauthorised occupation may be asked to be more alert and vigilant.[11] I will be thankful for an early action.[20]

Thanks,.

                                        Yours faithfully,

Complaint for Over-billing of Power/Phone

Start your letter expressing surprise and regrets for over-billing

1. I am quite surprised to receive such a heavy bill for domestic power consumed during the last two months.

2. I am quite disturbed to see an inflated telephone bill for calls made in the quarter, January to March 1999.

3. I regret to say that you have overcharged me for domestic electricity in the bill for January 1999.

4. I must point out to you that the telephone bill I have received from you for calls made in the last two months is much more than my expectation.

5. I feel there is definitely some mistake in billing such a big amount towards electricity consumed in my house during the last two months.

6. I am astonished to see an inflated bill for telephone calls made during the last quarter.

7. I am surprised to receive the electricity bill of Rs.5500/- for the quarter ending July 31, 1999.

Discuss the main objections :

8. It was just not possible for me to have used so much of power during this period as I was out of station with my family for more than a month and the house was locked.

9. If you compare it with our bill of last quarter, you will clearly see the gross mistake your department has made. While in the last bill meter reading was 48923, the reading in this bill starts from 47282.

10. The number of calls you have charged work out, on an average, to 20 calls a day, and it is impossible for us to make so many calls every day, as we do not even have STD connection.

11. Our phone is used only by a few family members and that also not for business purposes. It is therefore, not possible for us to have made such a large number of calls as you have shown in the bill.

12. If you compare our bill for winter when power consumption is at its peak, you will see that it is just not possible for us to have used so much electricity in the summer months for which you have billed so heavily.

13. The power-meter in our house appears to be faulty. It moves rather fast and that is why it indicates such a large consumption.

14. Our power consumption has always been low and we have never received a bill for more than Rs.200/-. If necessary, you may check it from the earlier records.

Urge for rectification of the bill :

15. Please rectify the bill so that I may make the payment.

16. You are, therefore, requested to have the meter checked and send me the amended bill for payment.

17. You may kindly send me a provisional bill, till this dispute is settled.

18. Therefore, please revise this inflated bill and send me a fresh bill for prompt payment.

19. I, therefore, request you to check if our phone is being misused.

20. Please arrange to make necessary amendments and oblige.

21. I am making the payment now under protest. But, please arrange to make the necessary corrections and adjust the excess amount charged in future bills.

Sample Letter

Dear Sir,

I am quite surprised to receive such a heavy bill for domestic power consumed by me during the last two months.[2] It was just not possible for me to have used so much of power during this period as I was out of station with my family for more than a month and the house was locked.[8] Please arrange to make necessary amendments and oblige.[20]

With thanks,

Yours truly,

Complaint against Postman's Carelessness

Describe the complaint :

1. This is to point out that for the last two weeks I have not been getting my mail.
2. This is to complain against the carelessness of the new postman who has recently been transferred to our colony.
3. This is to bring to your kind notice that instead of coming up, the postman has been giving our letters to people downstairs.
4. I regret to inform you that for the last one week or so, my mail is being given to small children in our building, for being delivered to me.
5. I take this opportunity to inform you that the new postman has been very careless and has often delivered my letters at wrong addresses, in the colony.
6. This is to inform you that the mail is not being delivered to our block in time for the past few days.
7. It has come to our notice that for the past few days, our mail is being tampered with.
8. This is to bring to your notice that for the last two months I have not been getting my issues of 'Reader's Digest' which I used to get regularly.

Then urge for proper attention to the complaint :

9. It is, therefore, requested that this postman should be warned against such lapses in his duties.
10. I hope you will ensure that this postman takes his duties more seriously in future.
11. If this postman continues with such practice, he should be replaced.
12. Please take prompt action in this regard as I have already written two such letters to you.
13. Please arrange to get our mail delivered in time.
14. We request you to ensure safe delivery of our mail.

Close the letter with your thanks :

15. I will feel highly obliged if an early action is taken in this regard
16. I express my thanks in anticipation of your prompt action.
17. I will be obliged for your taking necessary action.
18. Your prompt intervention will save the residents from a lot of tension.

Sample Letter

Dear Sir,

This is to complain against the carelessness of the new postman who has recently been transferred to our colony.[2] It has come to our notice that for the past few days, our mail is being tampered with.[7] We request you to ensure safe delivery of our mail.[14] I will feel highly obliged if an early action is taken in this regard.[15]

With thanks,

Yours faithfully,

Complaint for Faulty Repairs

Bring the complaint to proper notice :

1. I regret to inform you that, despite your recent repairs my television set's reception is very poor.

2. This is to inform you that even after your repairs, our two-in-one/ washing machine/ inverter is not functioning well.

3. This is to complain against your mechanic who has done a careless job on our music system.

4. The water-supply pipe which we got repaired through you continues to leak as before.

Request to do necessary repairs again :

5. It is, therefore, requested that you check up the set properly and remove the fault.

6. Please reprimand your mechanic and send another man to correct the fault.

7. Therefore, please come again and set it right.

8. As water rates have increased recently, please rectify this fault, at the earliest.

Discuss payments :

9. As the guarantee period for the repairs is not yet over, we hope there will be no further charges.

10. As the first repairs were not carried out properly, there would be no question of my making a second payment for the same repair job.

11. As it is mechanic's fault, I do not think I will have to pay anything extra now.

12. I think I do not have to pay for the repairs as the set is still under guarantee.

Sample Letter

Dear Sir,

I regret to inform you that despite your recent repairs my television set's reception is very poor.[1] It is, therefore, requested that you check up the set properly and remove the fault.[5] I think I do not have to pay for the repairs as the set is still under guarantee.[12]

With thanks,

Yours faithfully,

Complaint about Defective Goods

Bring to notice the defective goods/articles:

1. This is to complain against the electric iron/mixer/ cooler I bought from your shop, last month.
2. This is to inform you that the refrigerator I brought from your agent here about six months back does not cool to the required degree.
3. I regret to inform that the TV set I bought last month from your dealer here, does not have good picture quality.

Give details of defect noticed :

4. The iron does not heat up to its maximum temperature.
5. The iron at times gives shock.
6. I feel that its thermostat/compressor is not functioning properly.
7. The mixer refuses to run and I feel there is something wrong with its motor.
8. The fault seems to be major as we have already tried all adjustments of the controls.
9. The lid of the cooker is defective and the steam leaks out.

Ask for replacement or repair of the article :

10. I am sending the said item by rail parcel. I will be obliged if you could rectify the defect and send it back at the earliest.
11. I would be grateful if you could replace the faulty part and return the cooker/it as early as possible.
12. I will feel highly obliged if you get our set/refrigerator replaced.
13. I would be grateful if you could rectify the defect at the earliest.

Mention about the documents enclosed :

14. Enclosed herewith is a photocopy of the guarantee card.
15. All particulars of the set and its purchase are enclosed herewith.

Sample Letter

Dear Sir,

This is to inform you that the refrigerator I bought from your agent here about six months back does not cool to the required degree.[2] I feel that its thermostat is not functioning properly.[6] I would be grateful if you could rectify the defect at the earliest.[13]

Thanking you,

Yours faithfully,

Complaint to Railway about Lost Luggage

Reporting the missing article/luggage :

1. This is to report the loss of a trunk that I had booked form New Delhi to Bombay Central in the brake van of Rajdhani Deluxe/Air Conditioned Express that left New Delhi station on June 8, 1999 at 9 a.m./p.m.

2. This is to report the disappearance of a bicycle booked by me from Delhi to Bombay in the luggage van of the Froniter Mail which left New Delhi station on September 9, 1999 at 8.00 p.m.

3. This is to inform you that I have lost a basket of fruit I had booked in the luggage van of Rajdhani Express leaving Delhi for Bombay on November 15, 1999. I had also travelled by the same train.

4. The luggage I had booked in the Delhi-Howrah Express on the 15th of this month could not be traced at the destination.

Details of the lost article/luggage ;

5. I myself saw it being labelled and put in the brake van which was booked vide receipt No.R/54321. But at Bombay Central it was missing.

6. I have the booking receipt of my Atlas bicycle.

7. The said fruit basket, for which I have the booking receipt No.R/368325 contained 3 dozen apples of the 'Delicious red' variety. My name and Bombay address had been boldly written on its white cloth cover.

8. The said luggage booked under RR no.43913 was insured and clearly marked for delivery at the destination, Howrah.

Stressing an early tracing of the missing article :

9. I shall be highly obliged to you, if you could take a prompt action in this regard, as the trunk contains some important documents/valuables/medicines.

10. Kindly try to trace the bicycle fast as it was meant for a birthday present for my nephew.

11. May I request you to trace the basket and restore it to me before the apples are over-ripe or become rotten.

12. I request you to get my luggage traced or get the insurance claim settled.

Sample Letter

Dear Sir,

This is to report the loss of a trunk that I had booked from New Delhi to Bombay Central in the brake van of Rajdhani Express that left New Delhi station on June 8, 1999 at 9.00 p.m.[1] I myself saw it being labelled and put in the brake van which was booked vide receipt No.R/54321. But at Bombay Central it was missing.[5] I shall be highly obliged to you if you could take a prompt action in this regard, as the trunk contains some important documents.[9]

With thanks,

Yours faithfully,

Complaint to a Neighbour

Start your letter by expressing reluctance for having to do so:

1. Although I feel most reluctant, I think it is necessary to draw your attention to the mischievous habits of your little son, Pappu.

2. May I draw your attention to the nuisance caused by your dog.

3. I hope you will not mind my making a small suggestion that could help us maintain a cordial relation.

4. Had I not felt deeply offended I would not have written this note to you.

Give the nature of your complaint :

5. Whenever any of our family members passes by your house, it (your big Alsatian) barks quite fiercely. My younger son is particularly afraid of it.

6. It/your dog seems to be in the habit of barking at every passer-by and has become a nuisance.

7. He/your son often fights with my son for no reason.

8. Your radio keeps on blaring till late at night and invariably disturbs our sleep.

9. Your car is always parked in front of our house in such a way that the front passage to our place is obstructed/blocked.

Urge to mend the ways :

10. So, may I request you to keep a check on it.

11. So, can you please politely ask him to be friendly with him.

12. I do not mind your listening to the radio but may I request you to keep the volume low at night.

13. I can understand that you have to park your car wherever you get space. But, may we request you not to block our entrance.

Sample Letters

Dear Sir,

May I draw your attention to the nuisance caused by your dog.[2] Whenever any of our family members passes by your house, it barks quite fiercely. My younger son is particularly afraid of it.[5] So, may I request you to keep a check on it.[10]

With best wishes,

Yours faithfully,

Letters of Apology

We often commit mistakes. And a good culture calls for admitting those mistakes. This can be done with the help of a letter of apology. Even if one has not committed a mistake, a clarification should be made if the other person has taken an offence over something. A letter of apology should be prompt and sincere in tone as otherwise it will be self-defeating.

The outlines of a letter of apology are as under :-

1. Reason for writing a letter of apology;
2. Apology itself;
3. Justified pleadings in self defence;
4. Making amends;
5. Assurance for avoiding repetition of lapse/omission;
6. Repeating the apology.

Apology for Damage Done by Child/Pet

Give reasons for the apology :

1. I have been told by my wife that one of your window panes has been broken by my son while playing cricket.
2. I learn from my son that this morning our dog entered your garden and trampled over the rose plants spoiling many flowers.
3. I learn from my daughter that today morning our cat ate up one of your chicken.
4. I have come to know that my son has abused your daughter.

Beg forgiveness/tender your apologies :

5. I apologise on his behalf and promise to ensure that it is not repeated.
6. This is indeed regrettable and I apologise sincerely for the damage caused.
7. I am really sorry for what has happened and have asked my son not to unleash it.
8. I am extremely sorry for his behaviour and have scolded him severely.
9. I express my regret for the misbehaviour of my son towards your daughter.

Give cogent pleadings, if possible :

10. I am sure you will appreciate the fact that in our crowded locality children have to play wherever there is a little space. Still I have asked them to be careful in future.
11. Unfortunately we do not have a playground in our locality and children have to play in streets and courtyards.
12. Our cat is usually well behaved and I cannot imagine what got into her this morning.
13. Moti is by and large a sensible dog, but, then such an act is not inexplicable.
14. I know that my son is getting a bit impertinent these days, and I will take care of it.

Make amends :

15. Anyway, I would feel relieved/happy if you get a new window pane and charge me for that.
16. Even so I would like to make amends by paying for a new window pane.
17. Unfortunately there is no remedy for the flowers spoilt, but I sincerely hope that you may kindly accept a few of my rose plants as compensation, if you don't mind.
18. Moti has been properly punished and I am sure it will not bother your cat again.
19. I have severely scolded my son and warned him against repeating such acts.

Give assurance of non-recurrence/non-repetition :

20. I have reprimanded the children and assure you that they will be more careful in future while playing with each other.
21. I have asked my children to keep an eye on Moti/our cat and see to it that it does not cause you any inconvenience or damage in future.
22. His elder sister has been asked to keep a strict watch over him in future.

Repeat apologise

23. I solicit your forgiveness.
24. Apologies again.
25. I am sorry for what has happened.
26. My sincere apologies.
27. Once again I express my regret for the mishap.

Sample Letter

Dear Sir,

I have been told by my wife that one of your window panes has been broken by my son while playing cricket.[1] This is indeed regrettable and I apologise sincerely for the damage caused.[6] Unfortunately we do not have a playground in our locality and children have to play in the streets and courtyards.[11] Anyway, I would feel relieved if you get a new window pane and charge me for that.[15] I solicit your forgiveness.[23]

With best wishes,

Yours sincerely,

Apology for Not Keeping an Appointment

Start with apologies :

1. I am extremely sorry for being so forgetful and not keeping our appointment last evening.
2. I am sorry for my carelessness in not keeping our appointment, yesterday.
3. I am really ashamed to admit that the appointment of yesterday completely slipped out of my mind.
4. I very much regret my forgetfulness to keep the appointment last evening.
5. I am sorry for not being able to keep my appointment with you despite your reminder in the morning.

Then give justifications, if any :

6. There is, of course, no justification for this carelessness on my part.
7. I really do not know how I forgot it. Please forgive me.
8. In fact, I have been so deeply disturbed by my son's/daughter's illness for the last few days that I have become forgetful.
9. Of course, I had not forgotten the appointment, but at the last moment something unavoidable turned up at the office.
10. All along the day I had the appointment in mind but towards the evening I got so busy that it just slipped off my mind.

Close the letter with hopes of renewing the appointment :

11. Do you think we could have it on next Sunday?
12. Let's make it next Wednesday. Do we ?
13. So, will you mind having our meeting sometime next week, of course, at your convenience?
14. Kindly let me know when you are free now?
15. I am taking leave from next Monday. I can see you any time during this week wherever you find it convenient.
16. Please excuse me this time and let me know of the next appointment

---

Sample Letter

Dear Sir,

I am extremely sorry for being so forgetful and not keeping our appointment last evening.[1] There is, of course, no justification for this carelessness on my part.[6] Please excuse me this time and let me know of the next appointment.[16]

With regards,

Yours sincerely,

Letters between Couples

The letters between couples -unmarried or married- smack of intimacy. It is difficult to prescribe any limits or suggest any definite format for them.

However, there is a difference between the letters exchanged between married couple and unmarried couple. In the letters of married people there is a talk of domestic and family matters. But, the unmarried couples basically talk of mutual love and affection.

Letters between Husband and Wife

Start the letter with a love talk :

1. I am excited to receive your sweet letter today.
2. Your loving letter this morning has come like a ray of sunshine in darkness.
3. Your sweet letter is again a reassurance of the love between us.
4. I have read your letter at least five times and still I feel like reading it again and again.
5. Your charming letter has reminded me of how lucky I am to have a husband like you.
6. Your letter today has flooded me with happiness.
7. .I find it difficult to express how happy I am to receive such a loving letter from you.
8. Your loving letters are my only friends in the loneliness of the hospital.
9. I was feeling quite depressed for the last few days and your loving letter cheered me up.

Then come to the point :

10. You have written that you will be back by next Monday. I am extremely thrilled by the news.
11. Everything is fine here, except that I miss you.
12. Don't work too hard or keep late hours.
13. Has our little Meenu recovered from her cough?
14. Please take Babuji for his monthly check-up.
15. When are little Deepu's examinations going to start? Please help him out in his studies.
16. I have felt bad being unable to attend Kumar's wedding. You must have gone. What present did you take? How does his bride look? Of course, she cannot be as lovely as our Asha.
17. What is the news about your mother's illness?
18. Please bring a nice nylon frock for Sarita.
19. If you want me to bring anything special from Bangalore, do write to me. Of course, I have bought one Mysore silk sari for you.
20. If you need anything just let me know. I will have it sent from here.

Again repeat love coaxings :

21. Please do not delay writing, I am getting impatient.
22. I wish I were there with you now!
23. I am excited at the news of your arrival next week.
24. Once again I must tell you how deeply I love you.
25. Write back soon and tell me again that you love me.
26. I am now doing my work at a very fast pace as I want to join you as soon as possible.
27. I am counting the days and hope you will come back next week.

Close the letter with some compliments

28. You are the sweetest of my dreams.
29. Your memory keeps me radiant.

30. I am desperately waiting for your arrival.

31. I always find your face shining like full-moon.

32. You are the greatest thing that has happened in my life.

Sample Letter

Dearest….

I am delighted to receive your sweet letter today.[1] Your charming letter has again reminded me of how lucky I am to have a husband like you.[5] What is the news about your mother's illness?[17] Please do not delay writing. I am getting impatient.[21] Once again I must tell you how deeply I love you.[24]

With love,

                                        Yours lovingly/Yours ever,

---

Letters between Fiance and Fiancee

Begin the letter with eloquence of intense love :

1. Whenever I begin to write to you I try to tell you how deeply I love you but somehow cannot express even a part of it in the letter.

2. Whenever I sit to write to you I get stuck for word-for no word is capable of expressing the intensity of my love for you.

3. Received your sweet/loving letter this morning. It means that now I have to wait for five long days before I get another from my darling/dearest/love.

4. Has any one told you that your letters are the most wonderful things in my life-next only to you.

5. How on earth can you write such sweet letters full of emotions.

6. You don't know how I wait for your letters.

7. I hardly cherish anything so dearly as your letters.

Thereafter, meaningful talk takes place :

8. Have you applied for leave for the wedding? Please come soon darling, I can't live without you.

9. Have you started looking out for a flat? You don't know what beautiful plans I have to decorate the house.

10. Mummy has already started preparation for the marriage. I am sure you will love the gorgeous saris she has bought for me.

11. I have already fixed up a small two bedroom flat with the property dealer. It is only when you, the lady of the house, arrive that it will become a sweet home.

12. The engagement ring you gave me is just exquisite. My friends have been teasing me about it. And of course, I do not mind all that.

13. There are still two long months to pass before we are married. So you must promise to write to me every week without fail — why not every day?

14. Although there is only one month left for our marriage, it seems longer than eternity to me.

15. Thank God! Finally the marriage date has been fixed. I was so desperately waiting for that.

16. I swear, you are the greatest thing that has happened to me.

17. Your sweet memory haunts me every time and your smiling face, whenever I recollect, fills me with joy.

18. I have great plans for our future life together. I will tell you when we meet next time.

19. I always keep adorning your handsome personality, in my heart.

20. I am sure, like me, you too find this separation unbearable.

21. You don't know how eagerly I am waiting for our beautiful life together in future.

Close the letter with tender talk :

22. It is impossible to bear the agony of this separation.

23. It is time to get back to the grindstone, so good bye, sweetheart. Write back immediately-and tell me you love me so much.

24. Goodbye now, darling and don't ever stop loving me.

25. I must stop here now. But let me tell you again that I cannot live without you.

26. In the end, I send you all the love of my heart, my beloved Prakash.

27. Write back soon. Time becomes still when there is no letter from you, darl;ing.

28. You know how deeply I love you and do not know what I would be or do without you.

29. You know, I will always remain yours and only yours.

30. No man has ever loved a woman more than I love you.

Sample Letter

My sweetheart/My darling Renu,

Received your sweet letter this morning. It means that now I have to wait for five long days before I get another from my love.[3] The engagement ring you gave me is just exquisite. My friends have been teasing me about it. And, of course, I do not mind all that.[12] There are still two long months to pass before we are married. So you must promise to write to me every week without fail-why not every day?[13] You know how deeply I love you and do not know what I would be or do without you.[28]

With love,

Lovingly yours,

Letters between Lover and Beloved

Express intense love :

1. You know how your beautiful eyes have pierced me deep in heart.
2. You are my greatest joy ever.
3. Words fail to express my deep and intense love.
4. I see your reflection in every beautiful object of nature.
5. My soul aches for you in loneliness. I cannot live without you now.
6. I do not know what I would do without you.

Revive the past incident:

7. I can't forget the day, when I had first seen and fallen in love with you.
8. Your charming nature and personality has totally blinded me.
9. I know we are made for each other.
10. Now, it has become impossible to live without you. You are always uppermost in my mind.
11. I feel that despite our parents reservations about love, we must tell them everything plainly and be ready to face the consequences boldly.
12. If you permit and agree, I can send my mother to your house for a matrimonial talk.
13. I feel we must not take any delay in our marriage now.
14. We should be prepared to face any opposition to glorify our true love.
15. I think, not caring for consequences, we must get ready to face the world boldly.

Sample Letter

My sweet........,

You know how your beautiful eyes have pierced me deep in heart![1]
I cannot live without you now.[10] I feel that despite our parents'
reservations about our love, we must tell them everything plainly
and be ready to face the consequences boldly.[11]

With only love,

Always lost in you/Always yours,

Replies to Matrimonial Advertisements

Now a days, especially in big cities, matrimonial alliances are brought about with the help of newspaper advertisements. Some of the prominent national dailies are full of such advertisements in their Sunday editions/supplements.

These advertisements are carefully perused. A lot of marriages have been solemnised with the help of these columns. Letters of response to these advertisements can be outlined as under:

1. Reference to advertisement.
2. Detailed particulars of bride/bridegroom.
3. Family background.
4. Financial position of the father/candidate.
5. Request for a photograph.
6. Awaiting the reply.

Replies to Matrimonial Advertisements

(Replies by Boy's and Girl's Parents to Matrimonial Advertisements).

First give reference to advertisement :

1. In response to your matrimonial advertisement in the Hindustan Times dated April 30, 1999, I furnish here the particulars of my daughter.
2. In response to your advertisement for a suitable bride for your son, I would like you to consider my daughter, whose details are as follows:
3. This is in reference to your matrimonial advertisement in The Times of India dated November 8, 1999.
4. I have seen your recent advertisement for a suitable bridegroom for your daughter and would like to furnish the following particulars about myself/my son.

Then give particulars of the boy/girl such as :

5. Name, age, health, education, appearance, vocation and earnings.
6. Brothers, sisters and their descriptions.
7. Parents and their descriptions.
8. Sub-caste.

End the letter in this way :

9. In case you are interested, please send more details about the boy/girl and one of his/her recent photographs.
10. If you require any more information, I would be happy to furnish it.
11. If you are interested, kindly send me details about the boy/girl and also a copy of his/her horoscope along with one of his/her latest photographs.
12. In return it would be a pleasure to receive more information about the boy/girl and also his/her photograph.
13. Since we want the marriage at the earliest, please be prompt in reply.

Sample Letter

Dear Sir,

In response to your advertisement in The Hindustan Times dated April 30, 1999, I furnish here the particulars of my daughter.[1] She is 23 years, very healthy and good looking. A commerce graduate from Delhi University, she is presently employed as an Accountants Assistant with a nationalised bank at a basic salary of Rs.8000/- per month. She has two brothers and one sister. The brothers are well settled and married in respectable families. One is a Business Executive with a local firm and the other is a Captain in the Indian Army. Her sister is a student of class VII in an English medium school. I am a retired Company Executive and we live in our own house in South Extension, New Delhi. We are Kayastha by caste. A recent photograph of the girl is enclosed. If you are interested, kindly send me the details about the boy and also a copy of his horoscope along with one of his latest photographs.[11]

With regards,   Yours sincerely,

Family Letters

In our country the family ties are stronger than in the West. As a result there is a heavy exchange of correspondence between family members. Such letters may relate to a variety of subjects concerning personal problems or general topics. Thus, it is difficult to suggest a definite format for such letters.

But, whatever be the theme of the letter, a family is informal and affectionate in tone and content. There cannot be any limit on its size or shape. Ordinarily, family letters are longer than others. These letters must be simple, clear and so natural as if we are talking over a cup of tea.

These letters can be split up in two types :

1. *Letters from father/mother to son/daughter*
   1. living abroad
   2. serving at some other place
   3. living in a hostel at some other place
   4. irregular in correspondence
   5. seeking financial help and
   6. married at another place
2. *Letters from son/daughter to father/mother in similar situations as above.*

Letters from Father/Mother to Son/Daughter or from Son/Daughter to Father/Mother

In these letters the 'beginning' and 'end' remain alike. Some suitable sentences are being given below to illustrate the point. Appropriate sentences can be selected out of these to suit your requirement. Later, some other model sentences have been given according to some possible situations/occasions. These can be selected as per the situation that arises.

Start your letter with acknowledgement and your happiness over it. It should be followed by giving the home news:

1. We were delighted to receive your letter by today's morning mail.
2. Your mother was delighted to receive a letter from you after such a long time.
3. All of us here were/are deeply concerned about your health.
4. Your letter has now filled us with joy and removed all our doubts about your health and well being.
5. Thank God, you are coming home on your annual leave.
6. Your letter in the morning filled me with great joy.
7. Your letter has disturbed everybody here and filled with apprehensions about your health.
8. I was very happy to receive your letter a couple of days back.
9. Although I am delighted to hear from you after such a long time, I am getting a little disturbed over your relations with your wife.
10. I received your letter yesterday and was delighted to go through its contents.
11. I was filled with joy when I got your letter today.
12. In fact, we had been waiting for your letter for a long time and all of us were thrilled when we got it yesterday.
13. Pappu was particularly keen to hear about you. And now, having received your letter he is jumping with joy.
14. The postman delivered your letter just today.

Give information about family members :

15. Your mother has now completely recovered from her recent attack of malaria. So, there is no need to worry about her.
16. I am glad to tell you that your father has recovered from his recent attack of cold and flu. So, there is no need to worry now.
17. We could not write to you earlier, because Raju was ill last week and he gave us some anxious moments. He is much better now, and so you don't have to worry.
18. I am very happy to inform that last Friday, Renu gave birth to a son and both mother and child are in good health now.
19. Sanjay and Sunita have finished with their annual exams, and hope to do well.
20. Sonu is much better now and will start moving around, in the house at least, in a couple of days.

21. You will be quite delighted to know that your Didi has written from New York about their trip to India next month.

22. We are all fine by the Grace of God. Your brothers and sisters also wish you a very happy stay there.

23. Your Anita aunt from Kanpur is here for a week. And the kids are having a super time.

24. I had not been well for a few days because of the change of weather. But now I am fine.

25. Sujata remained bed-ridden for a complete fortnight due to chicken-pox, but now she is normal and regaining health.

26. Pramod has got a visa for Tanzania and he is leaving shortly, most probably, by the end of this month.

27. Don't forget to write to us every week. If that is not possible, every fortnight, definitely.

28. Don't miss to write letters regularly about your health and how you are getting along generally.

29. All of us get deeply worried if your letter is delayed.

30. Raju is keen to see Hyderabad. So, he might come to stay with you in the coming autumn vacation.

31. Ritu has got admission to Medical College. And I am sure you will really be happy since you were very keen to see her become a doctor.

32. Don't add to our anxieties by any more delay in writing a letter.

33. If you are generally very busy with your studies, there is no need to write a detailed letter. You can just drop us a line on a post-card about your well-being.

34. We have got the books you had asked for. We will send those through Vikas who is leaving for Bombay next week.

35. Let us have your reply by the return post. May God bless you.

36. Remember us to your parents-in-laws.

37. Tell Ramesh that we congratulate him most heartily on his promotion.

38. Take care of the baby.

39. Keep writing regularly so that your mother does not worry.

40. Give our due regards to your in-laws and ask Ramesh to write to us.

41. We are expecting both of you to visit us during the Dussehra festival.

42. Your mother lives by your letters only. So, don't be careless in that.

43. Your mother keeps worrying about you. So don't be irregular in writing letters.

Letters on Various Situations

> Different occasions call for different types of letters. The sentences given here can be used to form the middle of such letters. Opening and closing sentences of such letters have already been given.

Letter to a son living in some other town :

Middle of the letter may give some information about the family :

1. Your mother is going on a pilgrimage for a month from 1st October. Your uncle Harish will accompany her.

2. The final house examinations of the school are starting from next Monday. So, all your brothers and sisters are busy with their studies.

3. If Pramod does well, we will ask him to take the I.I.T. entrance examination. Last year he could not do well.

4. We are going to buy a T.V. with the money you have sent. Sonu and Monu are quite thrilled.

5. There are a number of proposals for your marriage. When you come here during Diwali holidays, you can make a choice for yourself.

6. Try to be more conscientious about your work.

7. We are really happy about the recent promotion you have got.

8. Keep good company and be away from vices.

9. Be careful/discreet in spending money. You must try to curb your extravagant habits.

10. We have reposed full trust in you for the fulfilment of our aspirations. So never disappoint us by doing anything unbecoming of you or your family.

Asking for financial help :

11. As you know, Sheela's marriage is approaching fast and we have to buy a lot of things. So, please send us the maximum money at the earliest.

12. As you are aware, I have spent a lot of money on your mother's illness and it has now become difficult for me to carry on with the salary I get. Your mother has suggested that you should contribute to the family expenditure by sending Rs.3000 per month for at least one year.

13. Subhash has passed his Higher Secondary Examination creditably and now he is planning to join college. But that is possible only if you send Rs.1000/- every month for his higher education.

14. Now that I have retired from the service, I find it difficult to manage the household expenses on my own. So, your mother expects you to share the responsibility and send me money regularly.

15. Keeping the present circumstances in view, it has become necessary for me to ask you for some financial help.

16. Although I feel quite ashamed to ask for money, at the moment I cannot help it.

Expressing hopes of getting money :

17. We are sure you will be able to arrange this sum/amount at the earliest.

18. Your mother feels that it won't be difficult for you to send such a small amount since you get a handsome salary now you have been recently promoted.

19. As we receive money form you, we will start the wedding preparations.

20. We have to pay the doctor's bill by the end of this month. So please send the money before that.

21. We hope you will start sending money from this month itself.

Letter to a son studying in some other town :

Discuss his studies and food arrangements, in the middle of the letter

22. You have written that your exams are drawing nearer. So you must be studying hard but at the same time, take care of your health also.

23. Your mother is quite apprehensive about hostel food. So, please write soon to her about it.

24. Are you sharing the room with somebody? What sort of a boy is he?

25. Do you find the hostel atmosphere congenial?

26. As desired by you I have sent a DD for Rs.3000/- today, but I suggest that you try to save as much as you can.

27. I don't mind sending you more money, but would like to know why you need it?

28. Your mother says, if the hostel food is not good, you make arrangements outside.

29. Don't you have a playground nearby? I hope you play regularly.

30. I hope you are studying regularly for your exams. Let me know if you require anything from here.

Write some other family matters :

31. All are very keen/eager to have you here for the Diwali vacation.

32. Your mother misses you very much and is eagerly waiting for you to join us during winter vacation.

33. There are all kinds of boys in a hostel. So you should guard yourself against falling into bad company.

34. Is your room near the school/college or at a distance? If you need a two-wheeler, I can send you mine. I will manage somehow.

35. Please try not to put any extra burden on your uncle with whom you are staying. You should, of course, move out when you get the hostel accommodation.

36. If you cannot manage hostel accommodation, rent out a single room in any colony near your college.

Letter to a married daughter living in another city :

Some special enquiries can be made and concern expressed while writing to a married daughter :

37. We are expecting you and Suresh here on Diwali. So, do not disappoint us.

38. Please try to adjust in your new family. I feel they are very nice and affectionate people.

39. We are really lucky to have got a son-in-law like Dinesh. Take good care of him.

40. Your mother is quite concerned about Sonu's teething troubles.. But these are usual things and you should not get anxious about it.

41. Now that Anu's exams are over, why don't you send her here for the vacation? Your mother has not seen her for a long time, and she has particularly told me to ask you.

42. This morning we received a letter from your father-in-law and were extremely happy to learn that Anu has now got a little brother.

43. We are happy to know that Anil has got a promotion and he has now become the Deputy General Manager. You are indeed lucky to have got such a fine husband.

44. I was delighted to learn from your letter that your younger brother-in-law has passed the Higher Secondary examination in 1st division. Please convey to him my heartiest congratulations.

45. We are very much disturbed to learn that your mother-in-law is seriously ill. You must not spare any efforts in taking care of her.

46. We are glad to receive the invitation to your younger sister-in-law's wedding. We have sent her all good wishes and a small present which we hope she will appreciate.

47. I was delighted to learn that Sanjay has got a special increment. Your husband is indeed a very competent young man.

48. It is good to learn that you have taken up a job. But, you must not neglect your duties as a wife and mother.

49. We are delighted to learn that you and Ramesh have been blessed with a son.

50. We are quite happy to learn that your in-laws have become quite fond of you.

Letter to a son/daughter living abroad :

Some special topics to write about :

51. We are delighted to inform you that Manju's marriage has been fixed for March 9, this year. But we wonder if you will be able to make it.

52. You have written that you can send air tickets to us to visit England, but I doubt if your mother would be able to stand such a long journey at this stage.

53. It is nice to hear that Meenu can speak English very fluently now. But don't let her forget Hindi.

54. You have been away for more than three years. Now, your mother very much wants you to visit us at least for a few months.

55. It was very nice to know that you have now bought a new house near London. We both wish you all the best.

56. I hope you have by now overcome the initial difficulties in speaking English/by now you have got used to the English weather.

57. Your suggestion that we should come and stay with you in England is of course nice. But we wonder if the climate there would suit us at this old age.

58. It is nice to know that you have learnt continental cooking too. We surely would like to have a taste of it.

59. Now that you have completed the assignment there, what do you plan to do next?

60. We are glad/happy to know that you don't intend to settle there permanently.

Letter to a son in defence services :

The middle part of the letter can discuss things of defence/military interest :

61. Please write to us about your daily routine there. Your mother fears that it is very strenuous.

62. Do you have to work under extreme temperatures? Are you able to bear all this?

63. I presume, sometimes you have to stay at high altitudes and that too during nights. How do you manage all these?

64. Have you finished with your commando course? Please write to us about its thrilling moments.

65. Aren't you scared of death during war? Write to us how you react to the situation?

Write something in appreciation :

66. I am proud of you, my son. You are serving the nation bravely.

67. I am proud of the fact that you maintain the glorious martial tradition of our family.

68. Service to the nation is the greatest of all. The other day I met Colonel Sharma and he was speaking very highly of you.

69. My son, even if you have to sacrifice your life for the nation, you should not hesitate.

70. I hope you will glorify the name of your Motherland by your bravery and courage.

Letter from a son/daughter to father/mother :

The middle part of the letter from a son studying in a different town. Give some highlights of hostel life in case you are a resident in a hostel.

71. I am glad/pleased/happy to tell you that I have got a good room here in the hostel and my partner is also a very nice boy. We have already become good friends.

72. The hostel food is quite good. So please tell mother not to worry about it.

73. The only drawback I find in the hostel is that it is about two miles away from the college. So I think I will have to buy a bicycle.

74. There are a few boys in the hostel who troubled me initially in the name of ragging. But, now they have become friends.

75. As we have to pay the hostel fee in advance, please send me Rs.2000/- by DD.

76. We have a large playground just opposite/across the hostel and we play hockey every evening.

77. A new wing is being added to our hostel and I hope to get a single room for myself in a couple of weeks.

78. My seniors here are very helpful and I have got a lot of books and notes from them.

79. Living in the hostel also gives me good company and entertainment during free hours.

Write some more things about the progress in studies etc :

80. My exams are drawing nearer. So please don't worry if I am a little late in writing letters.

81. Sometimes I do feel lonely, but gradually I hope to get used to the hostel life. So, please do not worry/so, there is no need to worry.

82. The laddus which mother sent, were extremely delicious. All my friends liked them.

83. I have already bought most of the books. The rest I can borrow from the library which is very near our hostel.

84. There are a few good singers in the hostel. We often have musical sessions during our free time.

Discuss matters relating to boarding and lodging in case you are not a hosteller :

85. This room which I have got is quite good and the landlord is very accommodating.

86. I am still taking my meals in the hostel because it is quite a problem to prepare them in my own room.

87. Staying with uncle is good fun. Mohan and I have become good friends.

88. Now I have taken another room which has more space and other facilities.

89. I have been very regular with my studies and hope to do well in the annual exams.

The middle part of a letter from the son studying abroad. The reason for delay in writing can be mentioned, if so desired :

90. I have been thinking of writing to you ever since I arrived here. But it has taken me some time to settle down.

91. As I am still not used to the ways of living here, I could not find time to write to you earlier.

92. Despite my best efforts to find time to write you back/to reply to your letter, I could not do so because of my busy working schedule.

93. I know you must have been waiting for my letter for many days. But I was busy writing my term paper which I have submitted today. And so, now I have got down to writing this letter.

Give some reference about life and people of the foreign country :

94. Things are quite different from our country, but the people in general are very friendly.

95. Life is very fast here. People don't waste even a single minute.

96. The educational system here is quite different from the one in India, but I very much like the system of informal group discussions which they have here.

97. The course is quite tough and we have to work very hard, but our professors are very helpful and mix with us quite freely.

98. During the Christmas vacation we will be going on a tour of the Continent. It is working out quite cheap.

99. London is full of Indians. So, I don't feel lonely at all. Please don't worry about me on that account.

100. It has taken me some time for me to adjust myself to the food here, but now I have begun to like it.

101. The climate here is very pleasant and healthy and I already find improvement in my health.

102. It was both a pleasure and surprise to find that Indian food is readily available here.

Now I regularly have it.

Make enquiries about things at home :

103. How is mother getting along? In winter her asthma usually revives.

104. I am eagerly waiting for the results of Anju and Raju.

105. How do you meet the expenses of the house because we are already in debt on account of my studies abroad.

106. If you have a passport, you can come here for a short while. It is an exciting place and the change will be good for you.

107. Where are you getting transferred now? I hope you get Bombay.

Close the letter as usual :

The middle part of the letter from a married daughter living elsewhere. Give some information about the in-laws :

108. I have adjusted with the new family very well. Everybody is extremely nice to me.

109. My younger sister-in-law, Ritu is very sweet and has taken quite a fancy for me.

110. I have got two brothers-in-law. They always crack funny jokes to make me laugh.

111. My mother-in-law is a little difficult person. But I hope soon I will win her over.

112. The general atmosphere in the family is quite cordial and congenial.

Give assurance of acquitting yourself creditably at your in-laws :

113. I remember well what mother had told me. I am not going to give them any occasion to complain.

114. In the beginning, I passed many embarrassing moments, when I could neither speak nor express my feelings. But now I have adjusted myself well.

Close the letter as usual :

Letter to a son who is irregular in correspondence

Start the letter by expressing your anxiety at not receiving the letter :

115. Your mother has been anxiously waiting for your letter for more than two weeks.

116. Your long silence for many days has got all of us quite worried.

117. What is wrong with you? Why have you not written to us for so long?

118. As it is, your mother is a heart patient. Don't increase her agitation by being so careless in correspondence.

119. It has been more than two weeks since I wrote to you last, but you have not replied so far.

120. We understand that you are very busy with your project. But, one can always take out a little time to write a letter to home.

Make enquiries for not receiving the letter :

121. Please let us know immediately about your health and the reason for this long silence.

122. Is it because you are not well?

123. We know you have a lot of work in the office but please take out some time to drop letters regularly.

124. It is quite possible that there is nothing serious for this delay in writing to us but we will like to be assured of this.

Stress the need for regular correspondence :

125. Your letters are a great solace/comfort to us in our old age. So make it a point to write regularly.

126. Your letters are a great comfort to your mother. So be regular at least for her sake.

127. You know, how your sister worries about you. So don't give her such anxious moments.

128. Remember that we are always worried about your welfare. So please keep us informed.

Explain some possible results of not writing the letter:

129. Your mother is already under medical care. If there is any more delay on your part, her situation might deteriorate.

130. If you do not reply to this letter immediately I might have to come down to see what is wrong.

131. If you delay any further in writing a letter, I will have to send Gopal to you to see what is wrong?

132. In case I still do not hear from you I will have to write to your hostel warden.

Close the letter in the following manner :

133. We hope that you are in good health by God's grace.

134. Please do not add to our anxieties by any more delay in writing a letter.

135. If you are very busy with your studies, you can just drop a line on a post card instead of writing a detailed letter.

136. Reply to this letter immediately. May God bless you.

137. Let us have your reply by return post.

138. If your are not finding time to write, you can just book telephone call from your office.

Letters between Brothers/Sisters

> The relationship between a brother and a sister is everlasting. Even after their marriages the bonds remain quite firm. As a result letters are often exchanged between them. So, these form an important section of family letters. The beginning and close of these letters are akin to other such family letters. In the last sentences, the elder gives blessings to the younger whereas the younger seeks advice and good wishes from the elder. These letters are mainly exchanged between those living in different cities.

Letter from a younger brother to his elder one or vice-versa :

Here is the middle part of the letter from a younger brother to his elder one or vice-versa. The beginning of the letter has already been explained in the earlier part.

Give some information about the members of the family :

1. Your bhabhi has been blessed with a son. They have come back home and are quite well.
2. Raju has taken his Higher Secondary Examination this year. I am sure he will come in the merit list. He has been doing very well in studies.
3. Father is very keen to see you. Please take out some time from your busy schedule and come down here for a few days.
4. Please come here for a few days. I want to discuss with you certain important matters relating to Sheela's marriage.
5. I think it is high time we asked our uncle to vacate our house.

Some advice or instruction can be given :

6. You should be very regular and particular about your studies. We have pinned many hopes on you.
7. You should be very careful about the company you keep. This is a very slippery age.
8. You must make it a point to keep the boss satisfied. It will pay you in the long run.
9. Good health is a blessing. So have good meals and some regular exercise.
10. It takes all sorts to make the world. So you must learn the art of adjustment.
11. Now, I understand my responsibility as an employee. I always do my work according to my superiors' directions.
12. I have been very regular in my studies.
13. My training at National Defence Academy is very rigorous. But, I feel it is necessary for the profession I have chosen.
14. I am very careful with my expenses now. I have cut down on all unnecessary things like shave lotion etc.
15. We have finished with our course and now we have got the preparatory leave. Our examinations begin from next Monday.
16. Our college has arranged a tour to the South during the coming winter vacation. So I won't be able to come home this time. Kindly send me Rs.1000/- for this programme.

17. I have passed my second term examination with distinction in Physics and Chemistry. I hope to do well in the final examinations also.

18. Our company is managed by professionals and my superiors are quire happy with my work.

19. Please don't think about arranging a match for me until I am settled in a good job.

Letter from a younger brother to his elder sister or younger sister to her elder brother(middle portion of the letter)

Give news about things at home :

20. Since I remain idle the whole day I am thinking of taking up an embroidery course.

21. Soon we are going to fix up the marriage of my sister-in-law Rakhi, I will send you the details later.

22. We have recently shifted to our newly built house. It has enough facilities and we feel quite comfortable in it.

23. My father-in-law has recently been discharged from the hospital. He had been admitted after he complained of acute gastric trouble.

24. Our little Amit is now growing up. He smiles sweatly and has started lisping.

25. The Rakhi which I sent you last week must have reached you by now. Kindly tie it round your right wrist on Rakhsha Bandhan.

26. I have received the presents you sent to me in return to my Rakhi. We all have liked the clothes, bangles and other things.

27. We all remember you very much, especially on social and religious occasions. Father and mother haven't yet got used to your absence.

28. Alongwith this letter I am also sending a Rakhi. Kindly tie it round your wrist at the auspicious time.

29. Narendra has not only been doing well in his studies but also helping us out in the household work.

30. Since this is my final year at the college I have to work quite hard. I feel quite bad that I cannot help out mother in the kitchen.

31. I have been very careful with my office work. My immediate boss is very happy with me.

32. Being the eldest member of the family, you should take care of the old parents. You should also look after your younger sister's and borhter's studies.

33. Although I am quite happily settled after the marriage, I miss all of you.

34. I hope bhabhi treats our parents like her own and gives them all the affection and love.

35. I know you can pay it off soon. But if you can't, I could help you out.

36. After your marriage, we feel a vacuum here in the family. Mother and Rita miss you terribly.

37. It is nice to hear that you have adjusted well to your new house and are loved by all.

38. I will try to come and stay with you in this winter vacation.

39. Bunti and Raju must be quite grown up now. I am desperate to see them.

Letter from elder sister to her younger one or vice-versa (middle portion of the letter)

Start by giving domestic news :

40. After your marriage, I missed your company very badly. You were doing everything for me and now I have to do everything myself.

41. During my stay with you, Sony had got strongly attached to you. And, now he is finding it difficult to adjust here.

42. I am, of course, very happy with my marriage. God has fulfilled all my expectations and dreams. I have got a very kind and loving husband.

43. I am very fortunate to have got such loving in-laws. They treat me like their own daughter.

44. Why don't you come here and stay with us for sometime after your exams? Change will be good for you and I will have your company.

45. Ever since you left this house, I feel quite lonely. Every moment your loving face haunts me.

46. I have got a beautiful Kashmiri shawl for you. I will give you when we meet next month.

47. Mother had become so dependent on you that now at times, she feels helpless despite all my help in household affairs.

48. I intend to join Secretarial Course during my summer vacation. This might help me in hunting for a job later.

49. Didi, I am planning to take the medical entrance exam. You know, how keen I am to become a doctor.

50. You should try to see that Rani studies well. I am told by Mohan that she is a little careless about work.

51. I am eager to see my younger sister become a doctor. So please work hard to obtain a good position in your Higher Sec. Exams.

52. Since mother's health is deteriorating you should not let her do too much of work now.

53. Your health is quite weak and the studies at M.A. level are very strenuous. Why don't you go and see a doctor?

54. You have got a good engineering degree and a permanent job. Now you should not disagree to the idea of a marriage.

55. Mother has been pestering father and Ravi to find a match for me. Didi, will you please ask them to drop the idea for the time being so that I could complete my studies?

56. Here is a good news for you. I have been awarded Ph.D. degree on my thesis, which I had submitted six months back to Delhi University.

57. Although I take a nourishing and balanced diet, I am still very thin. Doctor tells me that there is nothing wrong with my system. Kindly advise me what should I do to improve my health.

58. Ever since you left the house, Mohan has become very careless about his studies. He was scared of you only. So, please write a strong letter asking him to study well.

59. We are eagerly awaiting your arrival. Bhaiya told me that you would be coming here on Raksha Bandhan. Pinky was on bed for a complete fortnight due to chicken pox, but now she has recovered and is regaining her health.

The letter can be closed by giving blessings and also by urging for regular correspondence:

60. Don't forget to write a letter every week, or at least once in a fortnight. May God bless you with all success in life.

61. I know you are generally very busy, but, still you can spare some time to write to your sister.

62. Rest, till we meet on Vikas's marriage next week.

63. Please don't add to our anxieties by delaying your letter. We always pray for your happy life.

64. We wish you all the best. Let us have a reply a return mail.

65. Tell Ramesh that we are delighted and heartily congratulate him on his promotions. May God bless him with many such events in life.

66. Take care of the baby. May God bring good fortunes in her life.

67. Give our regards to your in-laws and ask Ramesh to write to us. May God give you happiness and prosperity in life.

68. All of us are really keen to have you here for Diwali. So, why don't you come.

69. Mother keeps worrying about you. So keep writing to her. She wants you to take a decision about your marriage.

70. I wish you good health. In future I will be very particular in writing regularly.

71. Please convey my regards and respects to Mummy whom I miss here every moment. I pray to God for her long life.

72. I am very keen to meet your Rohit and Rita. I hope you will bring them along when you come here next month.

73. If you find writing letter monotonous you can make a trunk-call once in a while.

74. Hope to hear from you soon.

75. I hope this letter will find you in good health. In future I will be very particular in writing letters.

76. Please ask Jijaji to reply to my letter which I sent to him last week.

77. I will bring something for my loving younger brother and sister when I come home.

Sample Letter
(To a son serving in another city)

Dear........

Your letters have indeed been a treat to go through. Your mother is going on a pilgrimage for a month from 1st October. Your uncle Harish will accompany her. Under these circumstances, it has become necessary for me to ask you for some financial help. We hope you will start sending money from this month itself. Keep writing to us regularly so that your mother does not worry. My best wishes are always with you.

With love,

Affectionately yours,

Sample Letter
(To a son studying in some other city)

My dear........

The postman delivered your letter today. You have written that your exams are coming nearer. So you must be studying hard. Also, at the same time take care of your health. Your mother is missing you very much and desperately waiting for you to join us during winter vacation. We wish you all the best. Let us have a reply by return mail.

Take care,

Affectionately yours,

Sample Letter
(To a son staying in a hostel)

My dear........

Your mother was delighted to receive your letter after a long time. I am very happy to tell you that last Friday Renu gave birth to a son. Both mother and child are in good health. You have written that your exams are coming closer. So you must be studying hard. But take care of your health at the same time.

Your mother keeps worrying about you, so don't be irregular in sending letters.

Love and take care,

Yours affectionately,

Sample Letter
(To a married daughter living in another city)

Dear........

We got your long awaited letter only three days back. We are expecting you and Suresh here on Diwali, and don't disappoint us. Give our regards to your in-laws and also ask Suresh to write to us. May God bestow on you good fortunes in life.

With love,

Affectionately yours,

Sample Letter
(To a daughter living in another city)

Dear........

We got your letter only today after a long waiting. Don't be so irregular in writing letters. How is Ritu? Now that her exams are over why don't you send her here for the vacation?

Your mother has not seen her for a long time and has particularly told me to ask you. Give our regards to your in-laws and ask Ramesh to write to us.

With love,

Affectionately yours,

Sample Letter
(To a son/daughter residing abroad)

Dear.......

We were quite relieved on receiving your letter. You have written that you could send us air tickets to visit England but I doubt if your mother can stand such a long journey at this age. Reply to this letter immediately. May God bless you,

With love,

Affectionately yours,

Sample Letter
(To a son serving in the army)

Dear.......

We were quite worried as we got your letter after a long time. Write to us about your daily routine there. Your mother fears it is very strenuous. I presume you have to stay sometimes at high altitudes; that too during the nights. How do you manage all these? I am proud of you, my son, that you are serving the nation bravely. Don't forget to write a letter every week. If that is not possible, write once in a fortnight definitely. May God bless you with all success.

With love,

Yours affectionately,

Sample Letter
(To a son who is irregular in sending letters)

My dear.......

For the last three weeks your mother has been waiting for your letter, but, no news from you. Your silence for many days has got all of us quite worried. Please let us know immediately about your health and the reason for this long silence.

Remember that we always think of your welfare. Therefore, please keep writing to us.

Take care,
With blessings,

Yours affectionately,

Sample Letter
(From a son living in another city)

My dear Father/Mother,

I had been thinking of writing to you for quite a few days but could not do it because I was tied up with my studies. My exams are drawing nearer and, therefore, please don't worry if I am a little late in writing letters. I hope you are all fine and in good health. In future, I will be very particular in writing letters.

Respect to elders and love to Raju and Pappu,

Yours affectionately,

Sample Letter
(From a son/daughter studying in another city)

Dear............

Your letter reached me yesterday and I was delighted to go through it. The room I have got is quite good and the landlord is very accommodating. I am still taking my meals at the hostel because it is quite difficult to prepare food in my room. Despite my best efforts to find time to write you back I could not do so because of my busy working schedule. Please convey my love and regards to mother whom I always remember, I pray to God for her long life.

With love,

Affectionately yours,

Sample Letter
(From a son studying abroad)

My dear........

I got your letter only a couple of days back. Things are quite different from our country here, but the people in general are friendly. I have taken some time to adjust myself to the food here, but now I have begun to like it. I wish you all good health. I will be very particular about writing letters in future.

With regards,

Affectionately yours,

Sample Letter

Dear Father/Mother,

I received your letter yesterday and was delighted to go through its contents. I am quite fine here. Now a days I am busy preparing notes for my final exams. I am glad to tell you that I have a fine room here and my partner is a very considerate boy. We have already become good friends. My exams are now drawing nearer and, hence, please do not worry if I am a little late in writing letters. Has Didi come from London? It is a long time since I saw her. Let me know when she comes so that I can plan a trip to home around that time. I am in good health and wish you all the same.

With regards and love to all,

Affectionately yours,

Sample Letter
(From a married daughter living in another city)

Dear........

I was delighted to receive your long awaited letter yesterday. I have adjusted with this family very well. Everybody here is extremely nice to me. The younger sister-in-law, Ritu is very sweet and has taken quite a fancy for me. Convey my regards and respects to mother whom I always remember. I pray to God for her long life.

With regards,

Affectionately yours,

Sample Letter
(From younger sister to elder brother)

My dear.......

We were delighted to receive your letter yesterday. Narendra has done very well in his final exams. He has come 11th in the merit list. How are Rohit and Ashok? I hope they are doing well in studies. Mother keeps worrying about you; so don't be irregular in writing letter. She always wishes for your safe and prosperous life.

With regards,

Affectionately yours,

Sample Letter
(From elder sister to younger sister)

My dear.......

I was delighted to get your letter yesterday. Ever since I got married I have missed you terribly. I hear that Ravi is getting quite careless about his studies. See to it that he becomes serious about it. We wish you all the best. Let us have your reply by return mail. We are planning to come down to Delhi in the beginning of next month.

Take care,
With love,

Yours lovingly,

Sample Letter
(From elder brother to younger brother)

My dear.......

I was quite thrilled to receive your letter yesterday. Your bhabhi has been blessed with a son last Monday. They have returned from the hospital and are quite well. You should be very regular and particular about your studies. We have pinned many hopes on you. Don't forget to write letters regularly about yours and others' health. My best wishes are always with you.

With love,

Yours lovingly/affectionately,

Sample Letter
(From younger brother to elder brother)

My dear.......

I received your letter yesterday and was delighted to read it. Now I have begun to realise how one has to deal in the professional world. Every fortnight our office work is assessed and my superiors are quite pleased with me. Please, convey my regards and respects to Mummy who is always there in my mind. I pray to God for her longevity.

Affectionately yours,

Sample Letter
(From younger sister to elder sister)

My dear........

I received your letter yesterday and was delighted to go through it. Mother has becomes so dependent on you that now she feels somewhat helpless, despite my full cooperation in work at home. She is always persuading father and Ravi, for settling my marriage. Didi, will you please ask them to drop the idea for the time being, so that I can complete my M.A.? We are expecting both of you to come down here during the Dussehra festival. We wish you both a happy and harmonious life.

With regards,

Affectionately yours,

Request to a Friend for Loan or Favour

Begin your letter with hesitations :

1. I really don't know how to start this letter.
2. This is to ask you for a personal favour, and I hope I am not asking for too much.
3. Although there should not be any formalities between good friends, I am a little hesitant to write this letter to you.
4. I am writing this letter to you very reluctantly.
5. It is with a little hesitation that I am writing this letter to you.
6. Although I am well aware of your situation, I have to write this to you.
7. Although I do not wish to, I have to write to you about it.

Now, urge him for doing the needful :

8. It has now become an urgent necessity for me to ask you for a loan of Rs.20,000/- as I have to make an immediate payment and my money is all blocked.
9. To be frank with you, my rather reckless expenditure this year has landed me in debts of over a ten thousand rupees. And, I thought perhaps you could help me now.
10. I have recently incurred a lot of expenditure on my wife's treatment, and I can't turn to anyone else, at this hour of exigency.
11. As you know, my daughter Sheela is coming to Delhi for her college education, and I was thinking if she could stay with you till she got admission to a hostel.
12. My younger brother is passing through Bombay on his way to Madras. I would appreciate if you could see him at the station. His coach number is ....at seat No.............
13. Could you find time to take the packet accompanying this letter to my cousin, Anil at Bandra?
14. I would request you to speak to Mr. Krishnamurthy, our General Manager about my promotion.
15. Of course, I don't have to tell you that it would be a great favour from you.
16. I know I can always count on you for a help.
17. I will, of course, very much appreciate if you could help me out. But even if you can't, don't feel bad about it.
18. As we are good friends, please feel free to say, "no". if for any reason, you can't make the arrangements.
19. I know you will do your best, and that would be enough for me.
20. I know you/I hope you will help and oblige me.
21. I hope to hear from you.

Sample Letter

Dear........(name)

This is to ask you for a personal favour, and I hope I am not asking for too much.[2] As you know, my daughter Sheela is coming to Delhi for her college education and I was thinking if she could stay with you till she got admission to a hostel.[11] As we are good friends, please feel free to say "no", if for any reason you can't make the arrangements.[18]

I hope to hear from you.

Yours sincerely,

Letter regarding Serious Illness in the Family

Start the letter by giving the news of illness :

1. I am very sorry to inform you that since yesterday your grandmother has been seriously ill and admitted to the hospital.

2. You are already aware that grandfather has not been keeping well for a few months.

But since last night his situation has started getting worse.

3. Meenu had been running temperature for a few days. And now the doctor says that it is typhoid.

4. Your father is again suffering from bronchitis and this time it is so severe that he is confined to bed.

5. Your mother's disc prolapse has been again troubling her. Yesterday we had to take her to the Medical Institute for physical therapy.

6. Babuji had a mild heart attack. And he had to be admitted to Sir Ganga Ram Hospital.

7. Sheela got a second attack of pneumonia last week. She had become so weak that she was hospitalised.

Give information about medical treatment/medicare :

8. She/he is under constant medical attention.

9. We have got a room in the nursing home and engaged a nurse too.

10. The doctor has prescribed an injection course for her and comes to our place daily for the treatment.

11. She/he has had ECG and many other tests and we are awaiting the reports.

12. Yesterday I took her to an X-ray clinic and got a chest X-ray which I have sent to the hospital.

13. All the medicines prescribed by the doctor are given regularly and she/he seems to be responding to the treatment.

Give comforting and soothing assurances to the person concerned :

14. In view of his present critical stage I suggest that you come here for a few days.

15. If his/her situation does not improve we will have to take her/him to another hospital.

16. In case of any unfavourable development we will let you know immediately.

17. We are taking all possible care of him; so do not worry too much about him.

18. He/she is under expert medical treatment, but in view of his/her advanced age we should be prepared for the worst.

19. Doctors are doing their best and, now, let us pray to God so that she gets well soon.

20. Your Kamala aunty's son, Dr.Naresh Chadda, who is a famous cardiologist is taking a special care of him.

21. Please don't worry too much as the doctor has assured us of her complete recovery within a fortnight.

22. Please keep some cash ready as we may need it any time.

Close the letter by expressing hopes of recovery of the patient from his/her illness:

23. I pray to God for his/her early cure.
24. We hope this crisis passes by us without doing any serious damage.
25. At the same time all of us earnestly wish her/him early recovery.
26. We pray that she recovers fully before Ramesh uncle's wedding.
27. May God bless her/him with a long life.

Sample Letter

My dear........,

I am very sorry to inform you that since yesterday your grandmother is seriously ill and has been admitted to the hospital.[1] We have got a room in the nursing home and engaged a nurse too.[9] She is under expert medical treatment, but in view of her advanced age we should be prepared for the worst.[18] At the same time all of us earnestly wish her early recovery.

With good wishes,

Yours loving/affectionately,

Reply to a Relative Asking for Advice

Start the letter with acknowledgement and thanks for seeking advice :

1. It was a pleasure to hear from you after such a long time.
2. I was delighted to receive your letter this morning.
3. I received your letter this morning. Thanks for seeking my advice.
4. I have your letter seeking my advice on such a sensitive issue. I wonder if I am capable of it.
5. Thanks for trusting me to seek advice on such an important matter.
6. Received your letter and thanks for finding me capable of giving you advice.

Write some good pieces of advice :

7. You are a brilliant boy and you will be successful in any line. But since you are particularly good in Mathematics I suggest that you go in for engineering.
8. You have always been very good in Biology. So, I feel that you should opt for medical profession.
9. Personally, I like very much your idea of becoming a journalist but I am afraid it is not a very paying profession in our country.
10. In response to your inquiry about some special medical line I suggest that you do a course in physiotherapy. It is comparatively a popular profession and has a lot of prospects.
11. If your like the girl, you should go ahead and marry her. The fact that you belong to different communities should not weigh against it.
12. Yes, it is true that since you are only 26, you don't really have to hurry for marriage.
13. Regarding the delicate matter on which you have sought my opinion, I advise you to be frank with the girl and express your feelings for her.
14. Frankly, I am of the opinion that you should not think of marriage till you are properly settled in life and have sufficient income to support a family.
15. I suggest that you go in for the job offered to you instead of starting an independent business. It will be difficult for you to raise the resources needed for an enterprise of this kind.
16. Unless you take chances you cannot forge ahead. So, my advice is that you accept this attractive contract rather than go in for a badly paid job.
17. I feel you should wait for some more time, and if he still does not make the payment, you can go in for legal action.

While closing the letter, tell the person concerned that the ultimate decision would be his/hers :

18. However, I must say that the final decision in this matter lies entirely with you.
19. In the final analysis, however, you have to take your own decision.
20. This is what I feel. You can, of course, decide for yourself.
21. Finally, whether you take my advice or not, I wish you all the best.
22. I have consulted my lawyer and he also feels the same way.

Sample Letter

My dear........,

I was delighted to receive your letter this morning.[2] Thanks for trusting me to seek advice on such an important matter. I feel you should wait for some more time, and if he still does not make the payment, you can go in for legal action.[17] I have consulted my lawyer and he also feels the same way.[22] Finally, whether you take my advice or not, I wish you all the best.[21]

With good wishes,

Sincerely yours,

Letter to Family Regarding Proposed Visit by a Friend

Start the letter by giving the news of welfare and then inform the visit of your friend and his stay :

1. I am quite fine here and wish the same for everyone at home.
2. I have got adjusted to the life here quite well and there is no need to worry.
3. I am quite fine here by God's grace and hope the same for you too.
4. The hostel life is quite enjoyable here and I am having good time.
5. Life is worth living here amidst the company of good friends.
6. In fact, I am writing this letter with a special purpose. Anil is going on a tour to Bombay and I have asked him to stay at our place.
7. Actually my close friend Rajiv, is visiting Delhi on some business, and I have asked him to stay with you rather than in a hotel.
8. You will be happy to know that my friend, Gita/Mohan is passing through Delhi and I have asked her/him to stay with you for two days.
9. I am writing this letter because my friend, Gopal, has been called to Bombay for an interview, and I have suggested to him that he could stay at our place.

Now write to the family to make his stay comfortable :

10. I am sure his stay will not cause any inconvenience, as you can put him up in my room.
11. Please take care that he does not have any problem since he is new to the city.
12. After he is free from his business, Raju can take him around for sightseeing.
13. Ask Papa to please put our car at his disposal since he has to do quite a bit of running around.
14. Govind is rather shy, but I am sure he will feel comfortable at our place and also mix freely with others.

If the letter is to be carried personally by the friend, there would be a slight change in the style of the letter :

15. I am sending this letter with my friend Anil, who is coming to Bombay on a tour and whom I have asked to stay at our place.
16. The bearer of this letter, Mr. Anil Deshpande is one of my colleagues who has to appear for an interview for a job.
17. This is Mohan, about whom you have heard a lot from me. He was going to Delhi on a short visit and I insisted that he stayed at our place.
18. This is to introduce my friend, Gopal who has been called to Bombay for an interview. I have suggested to him that he could stay at our place.

Towards the close you can take up other personal matters :

19. I am sending a cardigan for Leena through him. I hope she likes it.
20. Ask mother to send me my favourite laddus through him when he returns.

21. If you want anything in particular from here let me know immediately so that I can send it through him.

22. When he returns please send the blue shirt which I forgot on my last visit.

23. Please send with him some latest photographs of the baby.

Similar letter, if written to a friend, would be closed with your gratitude/thanks to him :

24. I am putting you to some trouble, but I am sure you will find in Mohan a very pleasant company.

25. Thanks in anticipation for all necessary arrangements which you will make for his stay.

26. I know I can count on you for making Rajiv's visit to Delhi a pleasant experience.

27. I know I am bothering you, but I look upon this as an opportunity to introduce two of my good friends to each other.

28. If you find it taxing, you can ask Rita to help you out. Now even her exams have ended.

29. Love to Raju and Bunti and regards to elders.

On similar lines you can draft a letter to one of your friends on the occasion of a visit by some member of your family.

Sample Letter

My dear........,

I am quite fine here and wish the same for everyone at home.[1] In fact, I am writing this letter with a special purpose. Anil is going on a tour to Bombay and I have asked him to stay at our place.[6] I am sure his stay will not cause any inconvenience as you can put him up in my room.[10] I am sending a blanket for Papa and hope he likes it. Ask mother to send me my favourite **laddus** through him when he returns.[20]

Love to Raju and Bunti, and regards to elders.

Yours lovingly,

Inquiry about Hotel Accommodation

Start the letter by giving your introduction :

1. This is to inquire about the availability of accommodation in your hotel in November, this year.
2. I will be coming down to Bombay on a business tour for two weeks from May 15, and want a suite of rooms in your hotel for this period.
3. I have to come down to Delhi on a short transfer for about two months in the beginning of April and propose/plan to stay at your hotel.
4. Our Managing Director is scheduled to visit Bombay for five days from November 15 to 19, and he intends to stay at your hotel.
5. I have asked my son who is shortly visiting Delhi to stay in your hotel.

Subsequently mention about your requirements of accommodation :

6. I want a well furnished double room suite, bath attached.
7. I will need a bath attached single room.
8. A small but decently furnished and well-ventellated room would be quite enough for me.
9. I would prefer an accommodation on the ground floor.
10. If air-conditioned rooms are over booked, I can do with the other accommodation.
11. Please confirm reservation for one double bed/ single bed room with attached bath and air-conditioning.
12. Please confirm reservation of a single deluxe tower room.

While closing the letter, make enquiries about the incidence of rent payable:

13. Please let me know your tariff and availability on the dates I have mentioned.
14. Please let me have your rates for various types of accommodation and whether you can book a room for me in advance.
15. Enclosed is a cheque for Rs.3000/- as payment towards advance.
16. Please confirm

Sample Letter

Dear Mr........(name),

This is to enquire about the availability of accommodation in your hotel in November this year.[1] Our Managing Director is scheduled to visit Bombay for five days from November 15 to 19 and intends to stay at your hotel.[4] Please confirm reservation of a single deluxe tower room.[12] Please confirm.[16]

Thanking you,

Yours sincerely,

Letter to Insurance Company regarding Car Insurance

Begin your letter by giving information about the vehicle to be insured:

1. This is to request you to insure my new Honda City car which is being delivered to me on the 1st of next month.

2. I have bought a second hand Maruti Zen and would like to get its insurance cover changed from third party to comprehensive insurance.

Make enquiries about insurance premium:

3. Kindly let me know your terms and conditions for the comprehensive insurance policy.

4. Please send me the details and the requisite forms for this purpose.

5. Please let me know the additional insurance premium for my car.

6. Please let me know if the premium is the same as before.

Inform the insurance company if a damage is caused to the insured vehicle:

7. I am sorry to say that my car which is insured with you (vide policy number.........................) was damaged extensively in an accident this morning/ on ....

8. I am extremely sorry to inform you that my car which was insured with you (Policy No....................) was stolen from my office parking yesterday. I have lodged a complaint with the Tilak Nagar police station.

9. I am sorry to inform you that last evening some miscreants broke the wind-screen of my car while it was parked outside my house.

Claim for the damage caused:

10. Please, therefore, send your inspector immediately to M/s. Auto Service Station, where my car is kept for the assessment of damage and repairs.

11. Am I eligible for compensation from your company for this damage?

12. I would like to know whether your paying for the new wind-screen would mean that I lose the no-accident rebate which I have been getting for the last four years.

Sample Letter

Dear Sir,

This is to request you to insure my new Honda City car which is being delivered to me on the 1st of next month.[1] Please send me the details and the requisite forms for this purpose.[4]

Thanking you,

                              Yours faithfully,

Letter about Repair Job Estimate

Begin your letter giving details of fault:

1. This is to complain about the Fridge/ T.V./Washing Machine/ Stereo System which I bought from your shop last month.
2. The picture keeps on rolling despite adjustment.
3. There appears to be something wrong with its speed.
4. Perhaps, because of some loose connections, the T.V. does not light up immediately.
5. The cooler's water pipe leaks.
6. The cooler's blower is very noisy and expels a lot of water.
7. It appears that the fridge's thermostat has burnt out.
8. Although the sound is perfect, the picture is very hazy.
9. Thus, this is to request you to send a mechanic as early as possible to rectify the defect.
10. Will you please send your engineer to have a look at my TV?
11. Since we do not have any competent engineer in our town, please advise me what I should do.
12. My fridge seems to need repairs and I would be glad if you could come and tell me what it would cost to put it right?
13. If you want we can drop it at your workshop.
14. I would like to have an AMC with you for a routine check-up of all the electrical gadgets at our place.

Urge for early repairs:

15. As this is an article of daily use, please give prompt service.
16. Please do the needful at the earliest as children are very keen to see this Sunday's film.
17. As the marriage of my daughter is approaching nearer, please complete all the repairs early.
18. I will feel highly obliged if you finish with all the repairs within one week as I expect a few guests soon/ as I am leaving for Bombay soon for a month.

Vocabulary

A

abundant	plentiful
academic	scholarly, literary
accomplish	perform
accumulate	to heap up
acumen	sharpness and accuracy
acute	sharp
adequate	sufficient
adopt	to take idea
adore	to worship
aesthetic	appreciating the beauty
affluent	wealthy
ailment	illness
alacrity	readiness
alert	vigilant
alternative	choice between two things
amend	change for betterment
anticipation	expectation
apologise	regret
appropriate	proper
article	substance
assess	to estimate value
assets	property
astounding	surprising
astray	on wrong path
auspicious	favourable
availability	state of being available

B

belongings	movable possessions
bereavement	loss by death
bestow	to give
beyond	at, on or to the farther side
blatant	rough
bronchitis	inflammation of windpipe tubes

C

calamity	a disastrous event
captivate	to charm
ceaseless	continuous
celebrate	to rejoice on an occasion
celestial	of the sky / of heaven
cherish	to hold as dear
christening	giving a name
commence	to start
committing	entrusting
compensation	making up for
compliment	praise
comprehensive	having a wide scope
concert	musical entertainment
conferred	granted
confidence	full trust
congenial	agreeable
conscious	aware
constancy	permanency
constituency	area sending a representative
contended	satisfied
contents	listing of matter that a book contains
contest	to debate
contract	agreement
contribute	to give help, money etc.
convalescence	gain health after illness
cordial,	hearty
courtesy	polite behaviour
cosy	warm and comfortable
creditable	bringing credit
crucial	decisive

D

damp	humid
debit	an entry of a sum owing
dedicate	to devote
delicate	soft, not strong
delighted	pleased
dereliction	neglect of duty
destination	place, point aimed at
deterioration	becoming worse
deviate	turn away

diagnose	to determine the nature
diligent	hard working
disappointed	frustrated
discharge	to release
distinction	excellence
distinguished	prominent
distress	pain, difficulty
dividend	profit divided to share-holders
document	reliable paper
duration	time, period

E

eager	strongly desirous
earnest	sincere, serious
efficient	fit, capable
elate	to make highly spirited
election manifesto	public declaration of principles and policies by a ruler, political party
embarrass	cause mental discomfort
enhance	to increase
ensuing	coming near after
entail	to impose
enterprise	difficult undertaking
entertainment	amusement
entire	full
entrust	to trust
environment	surroundings
equipment	things needed for a purpose
establish	to fix firmly
esteem	to respect greatly
exaltation	elevation
exceedingly	very much
exclusive	with the exclusion of all others
exhilarate	to make joyous
expedite	to speed up
expel	to drive out
explore	to enquire thoroughly
extend	to enlarge
extent	range
extra-ordinary	exceptional

extremely	in the utmost degree
exuberate	to abound
exult	to rejoice exceedingly

F

fancied	imagined
favourably	in a favourable manner
felicitate	to congratulate
fervour	earnestness
festival	public celebration
fiance	a betrothed person
fiercely	cruelly
flatter	to praise insincerely
flourishing	prospering
fluent	smooth and ready in speech
forge	to fabricate
forgive	to pardon
forthcoming	about to happen
fountain-head	source
fragrance	sweet smell
frequent	occurring often
frighten	to fill with terror
furnish	to equip

G

gaiety	cheerfulness
garbage	rubbish
gay	full of fun
genuine	true
gesture	expressive movement
glorious	splendid
gorgeous	magnificent
gratitude	thankfulness
grief	deep sorrow
grievance	cause for complaint
gruff	rough

H

harmonious	in agreement
harsh	disagreeable
haunt	appear repeatedly
hover	remain in one place

I

impact	strong impression
impertinent	inapplicable, rude
impression	influence
incur	to bring on oneself
indistinct	not clear
inevitable	unavoidable
interrupted	discontinuous
invariable	unchangeable

J

jubilant	shouting with joy

K

keenly	in a keen manner

L

lavish	profuse, abundant, generous
lax	not strict
leisurely	without haste
liabilities	responsibilities
litter	scattered rubbish
livelihood	means of living
lofty	high
loneliness	isolation
lucrative	profitable

M

magnificent	splendid
marvellous	astonishing
materialise	to take material shape
maternity	related to child birth
matrimonial	connected with marriage
meagre	scanty
merit	worth
meritorious	praise-worthy
mirthful	jovial
misbehaviour	misconduct
miscreant	villain
mishap	unlucky accident
monotonous	unchanging
monsoon	rainy season

N

neglect	pay no attention
negligence	carelessness
neighbourhood	adjoining area

O

obnoxious	very disagreeable
obstruct	to block up
obvious	clear
opportunities	good chances
overwhelming	cover completely

P

pangs	sharp sudden feelings
particular	special
passionate	with strong feeling
pensive	thoughtful
performance	notable action
perquisites	casual profit
pilgrimage	journey to a sacred place
pledge	promise
possess	own
potentiality	latent capacity
praise-worthy	laudable
prefer	to select
privilege	special benefit
probation	period of trial
procure	to obtain with effort
project	scheme
prolong	extend
promptly	without delay
proportions	dimensions
prosaic	dull
puddle	small dirty pool of rain water
punctual	in time

Q

quarrel	a dispute
quarterly	every quarter of the year
query	a question

R

radiant	shining

rally	to assemble
rear	back part
rebate	discount
recent	not long before
rectify	to put right
regularly	properly
relax	cause to become less rigid
relevant	pertaining to purpose
relieve	to lessen pain or distress
reluctantly	unwillingly
remarkable	attracting attention
reminiscence	recollection
reprimand	rebuke officially
requirement	need
requisite	required
resource	means
response	reply
revive	to restore
reward	something given or received in return for service or merit
ripe age	mature age
rippling	flowing in small waves
rung	step of a ladder

S

sagacity	soundness of judgement
saviour	deliverer
scheduled	according to a programme
scold	to rebuke
secured	safe, guaranteed
sentiments	feelings
sewage	waste matter carried in sewers
shirk	to avoid
shower	fall of rain
solace	comfortable in grief
solemn	serious looking
speculate	guess, form opinion
spirits	courage
splendid	glorious
sprightly	lively
steep	rising or falling sharply

stunned	astounded
suitability	suitableness
surroundings	environment
sustain	to uphold

T

temper	state or condition of mind
terrible	frightful
testimonial	certificate
toilet	a room for dressing self cleaning
token	sign
tragic	mournful
trample	to tread
treks	paths
tremendous	astonishingly large
tribute	praise
twine	twisted threads

U

ultimate	last, basic
undergo	experience, pass through
undisputed	without dispute
upkeep	act or cost of support
upliftment	rise
urge	to press urgently

V

vacuum	empty space
valuable	of great value
venture	to take risk
vice	bad habit
vicinity	nearness, closeness
vigilant	watchful
virtual	being in fact
vital	pertaining to life
void	empty, vacant

W

warrant	to guarantee
wastage	loss by waste
well behaved	of good behaviour
well being	welfare
withdraw	to draw back
worsen	to get or make worse

SECTION - II

Job Applications

Job Applications

Here we give certain important points which must be borne in mind while applying for a job :

1. Remember that the immediate objective of your application is not to secure the job but to get a chance for an interview.
2. Highlight your qualities briefly.
3. Give complete particulars, as desired by the prospective employer, in a simple and straight forward manner.
4. Avoid using stereo typed sentences like 'hoping for the favour of an early, assuring of my best services!'....etc.
5. Type the application neatly and correctly.
6. The format should be like that of a business letter.
7. Do not send cyclostyled applications, or pre-printed application forms with details filled in.
8. Always send the original typed copy and not the duplicate copy.

Type I : Application which includes the details of Resume

Dear Sir,

In response to your advertisement in 'The Hindustan Times' dated September 8 1999, I wish to apply for the post of Private Secretary to the Managing Director.

I graduated from Delhi University in 1996 securing 76% marks in B.A. (Hons) English.

This was followed by a one year Secretarial Course at the well-known Reliance Secretarial Institute, New Delhi, from where I acquired proficiency in Business Correspondence, Shorthand, Typing, Operating Computer & Secretarial Practice.

At present I am employed with Bright Light Company, New Delhi, as an Office Assistant. The present job calls for handling of routine correspondence besides other Secretarial Work. My shorthand and typing speeds are 120 and 60 w.p.m. respectively.

Having lived in various parts of the country I can speak Hindi, Punjabi and Marathi fluently and have working knowledge of Gujarati and Bengali.

I am 25 years old, excellent in health; and had been a good player of hockey during my college days. My work with the present employer has been highly appreciated (testimonials are attached) but I feel that your job offers greater scope for career growth and use of my potentiality.

I take the job with a great sense of responsibility, enjoy the challenge of new situations, and expect to make a positive contribution to your organization.

Hope to get an interview call from you.

Thanking you,

Yours faithfully,

Encl : Testimonials

Type II : Application with Separate Resume

Dear Sir,

In response to your advertisement in 'The Hindustan Times' dated November 8, 1999, I wish to apply for the post of Private Secretary to the Managing Director.

At present I am employed with Bright Light Company, New Delhi, as an Office Assistant but feel that your job offers greater scope for career growth and use of my abilities.

I take the job with a great sense of responsibility, enjoy the challenge of new situations and expect to make a positive contribution to your organization.

Hope to get an early interview call.

Thanking you,

Yours faithfully,

Encl : Copies of testimonials

Bio-data

Name	:	
Date of Birth	:	April 15, 1976.
Present Address	:	
Permanent Address	:	
Academic and Professional Qualifications	:	B.A. (Hons) English from Delhi University in 1996 securing 76 % marks.
		Did a one year course of Secretarial Practice at Reliance Secretarial Institute, New Delhi. Acquired proficiency in :
		Business correspondence, Shorthand, Typing, Operating Computers, & Secretarial Practice. Shorthand/Typing speed : 120 / 60 w.p.m. respectively.
Working Experience	:	Have been working with Bright Light Company, New Delhi, as Office Assistant for 11/2 years. The job involves handling of routine correspondence, filing taking dictation and answering visitors' queries.
General Qualifications	:	Can speak Hindi, Punjabi and Marathi fluently and have working knowledge of Gujarati and Bengla.
Personal Details	:	Excellent health. Have been a good player of hockey during college days.
Present Emoluments	:	
Salary Expected	:	

The present trend is slightly different. Mostly the applicants send a bio-data to the prospective employer along-with a Covering Letter. This Covering Letter may be as small as that of two-three sentences, but in the style of a formal letter. A few examples of such letters are given below:

---

1)

Dear Sir,

With reference to your advertisement in the Times of India dated 22nd November, 2000, for the post of an Executive Secretary, I wish to offer my candidature.

I am enclosing a copy of my bio-data for your perusal and kind consideration.

I hope to hear from you about the date of interview.

Yours Sincerely,

---

2)

Dear Sir,

In response to your advertisement in the Employment News dated ...., for the position of an Accountant, I would like to apply for the same.

I am sending herewith a copy of my resume/ curriculum vitae for your consideration.

Could you let me have an interview with you at an early date.

Yours Sincerely,

---

3)

Dear Sir,

I have come to know through reliable sources that there exists a vacant post of Sales Engineer in your esteemed organization.

Please find enclosed a copy of my resume for your perusal and kind consideration.

Should you require any further information, the same will be provided to you at the time of interview.

Hope to hear from you,

Yours sincerely,

Let us study how to frame a good resume, in the latest style, which is the first interface of a candidate with the potential employer:

- ◆ The employer should get an idea by the first glance itself. Thus make it briefer and stick to the points only. Ideally a resume should be of one page or maximum two.
- ◆ Sell yourself using friendly language, addressing only the employer's need, without using large paragraphs and repetitions.
- ◆ Make the 'experience portion' clearer, mentioning how long, in what capacity, and what you have done for the previous organizations. It has to be specific, measurable, action oriented and realistic.
- ◆ Be candid and unambiguous so that the employers feel comfortable in hiring your services.

- Don't write much about your hobbies and interests, age, height, weight etc. unless it is relevant to the position.
- Make it neat, clean, in good stationery absolutely error-free.
- Avoid using the pronoun 'I' like "I have conducted...etc.". Use only "conducted ....".

The sample resume of a senior level Executive Secretary in the latest style:

K. RAMACHANDRAN PILLAI

17F, Pocket A-I
Mayur Vihar-III
Delhi-110096
Ph. Resi: 91-11-2615270
EMail: KR.Pillai@PSINetCS.com

Experience

15 years of service as Executive Secretary, Personal Secretary etc. providing support to Senior Management functionaries in large Indian Corporate Houses and Multi-Nationals. (Starting from the latest is as below):

- Currently (for last 3 years) attached to the Managing Director, PSINet Consulting Solutions, a $2 billion multi-national with HQs in US, as Executive Secretary. Besides routine Secretarial Tasks, work includes coordination, communication with sister companies and counter-parts spread across the globe, team-oriented assignments, drafting and editing of key materials, handling MD's personal work etc.
- 3 ½ years in Xerox as Secretary to GM-HRD and then CEO-Staff Affairs. Besides Secretarial work, "updated and edited the Company's Personnel Policy Manual; Designed and implemented events and programmes, Arranged residential and non-residential Training Programmes and other Management Development Programmes; handled preparation of Minutes and Training related materials, Maintained interaction and communication with Company's JV partners, excelled in drafting and editing key and critical business related correspondence.
- Six years in Godrej (an Indian Giant group) as a Steno Secretary, where besides Secretarial Work, had to handle customers all over the world.
- Three years in Camphor and Allied Products Ltd. as a Steno-Typist. Work included inter-Company/ Departmental coordination and general Office Work, liaison with Import, Export and Insurance people.

182

Qualifications	:	B.Com from the University of Kerala. Pre-Degree Course in the first division and First Rank in the district.
Tech. Qualifications	:	Kerala Govt. Technical Examination Diploma in Typewriting & Shorthand. Speed 60 w.p.m. and 100 w.p.m. respectively.
Software knowledge	:	MS-Word, Excel, Power Point, eMail and Internet and a little exposure to Adobe Page-Maker.
Training Exposure	:	Have undergone:

Have undergone:

- Five-day Course on TQM ; familiar with Quality Tools and Processes.
- A course on Train-the Trainer.
- Kaizen Principle in work-life
- Six months Banking Training in Canara Bank
- Well exposed to ISO tools and processes.

Merits & Recognition	:	Won prizes/ Certificates in English Elocution, Essay Writing, Debates, Many times winner of Long Term Productivity Awards etc.
Personal	:	Highly interactive, team-oriented & empathic, Good in communication, Principled, Religious, Honest, candid and hard-working

General job Application

Starting the letter :

1. In response to your advertisement in 'The Times of India' dated August 8, 1999, I wish to apply for the post of Office Superintendent in your institution.
2. I have learnt from reliable sources that the post of Labour Welfare Officer in your office has fallen vacant.
3. I am interested in the vacancy you have advertised in 'The Hindustan Times' dated July 8, 1999, for a Sub-editor and wish to offer my services for the same.
4. This is to inquire whether you have a vacancy of an Office Assistant in your office.
5. I understand from Mr. Sunil Kumar, one of your suppliers, that you wish to appoint a Sales Engineer.
6. As Mr. Arun Kishore will be leaving your office on 31st July, I wish to offer my service for the same post.
7. I wish to offer my services for the post of Sales Officer which, as I understand, falls vacant by the end of this month.
8. This is to apply for the post of Sales Manager in your office which you have advertised in 'The Times of India' dated 8th September, 1999.
9. With reference to your advertisement in 'The Statesman' dated 21st October, 1999, I wish to offer my services for the post of Steno-typist in your organization.
10. I have learnt from a reliable source that the post of an Accountant is lying vacant in your office. I wish to offer myself as a candidate for the same.
11. In response to an announcement made in the Employment News on 10th September, 1999, I wish to apply for the post of a Translator (Hindi to English).
12. Going through Employment News, I found that a situation of a lecturer in English is lying vacant in your college. I offer myself as a candidate for the same.
13. Please refer to your advertisement in 'The Times of India' dated 14th July, 1999, for the post of a Law Officer, I wish to offer my services for the same.
14. Having come to know through a monthly bulletin of your Deptt., that you need a travelling Salesman, I offer my services for the same post.
15. Through a circular issued from your office, I have come to know that the post of a Draftsman is lying vacant in your office. I offer my candidature through this application.

Middle portion of the letter is given separately in the forthcoming pages :

Closing the letter:

16. I look forward to hear from you.
17. I trust you will consider my application favourably and give me a chance to meet you.
18. I would appreciate an interview with you when I could give you more details about myself.
19. I can come for an interview, at any time convenient to you. I enclose a self-addressed and stamped envelope so that you could respond to me.
20. I look forward to the opportunity of a personal interview.
21. I shall be grateful to you for an interview call at your convenience.

Various Job Applications
(Middle portion of the application for all types of jobs)

There are two different types of applications — one containing the particulars in the application itself and the other with a bio-data separately made. Their samples have already been given. You can select anyone of those, according to your requirement.

Here we give particular samples of various types of approaches for different job applications.

Private Secretary

1. I completed my education in June this year and have been employed as an Office Assistant with Bhatia Electric company. Although I do not have long experience, I am hard-working and take the work with great sense of responsibility. I am confident that your Managing Director will find me a competent Private Secretary.

2. For more than two years, I have been working as P.A. to the Sales Manager, India Trading Corporation. I am confident that I would prove to be a competent Personal Secretary to your Managing Director.

3. Although I am working in the same capacity in India Marketing Agency, I am applying for this job as your company is well-established and can offer greater scope for career advancements.

4. I have good knowledge of word processing and can work on MS Office, besides handling eMails and surfing Internet.

Accountant/Accounts Assistant :

1. I am a Commerce Graduate from Bombay University and have good knowledge of Accountancy, Auditing, income-tax procedure and company Law.

2. I can also draw up Balance Sheets and Profit and Loss Accounts.

3. Apart from my work as Accountant you may find my knowledge of Secretarial work also useful.

4. Now I have enough experience to take independent charge of maintenance of Accounts, preparation of bills and writing of account books.

5. I am computer literate and friendly with the software Tally.

Cashier

1. I passed B.Com from Delhi University in 1975, securing 52% marks and specialised in Book-keeping and Accounting.

2. I am, therefore, quite well versed in book keeping and billing etc.

3. Having worked for three years as a Cashier in the Delhi Textile Emporium, I have the requisite experience for the job.

4. I am computer literate and friendly with the software Tally.

5. If your rules require a security deposit I am willing to do so to a reasonable extent.

Typist-cum-Clerk

1. I can type accurately at a speed of 60 w.p.m.

2. I am excellent in word processing on Computer and is familiar with MS Word, Excel and MS-Outlook

3. I am fairly acquainted with office work such as filing, indexing etc. and also possess elementary knowledge of book-keeping.

4. I have also been attending short-hand classes for the last six months.

5. I have the ability to work for long hours and can cope with work pressure easily.

6. I take the work with a great sense of responsibility.

Labour Welfare Officer

1. I have studied Labour Welfare at the Delhi School of Social Studies, and am a registered member of the Labour Welfare Officers' Association.

2. I speak Hindi, Punjabi, Bhojpuri and Bengali fluently, and this enables me to deal easily with labour hailing from different parts of the country.

3. I am well versed in labour and factory legislation and possess the requisite qualifications as provided under the Factories Act.

4. On account of my present job in the textile mill I have adequate experience in handling industrial labour.

5. I have done a short-term course in computer and know its basics.

Librarian

1. I completed my MLISC (Master of Library & Information Science from IGNOU in 1999 securing 60% marks.

2. I am fully conversant with the DEWEY decimal classification systems.

3. I can competently manage all aspects of Library routine, including classifying and cataloguing of books and periodicals.

4. I have worked in computerized environment and am familiar with the relevant software.

5. I am good at various search methods which include CD search and Internate surfing.

Driver

1. During my five years of driving career I have not had any accident.

2. I have never been challaned even for minor violations of the Traffic Rules.

3. I have fairly good knowledge of automobiles and can do minor repairs.

4. I am ready for a trial any time, at your convenience.

Nurse

1. I completed B.Sc. in Nursing from the Delhi University in 1996 and am a registered member of the Trained Nurses' Association of India.

2. I also hold the St.John's Ambulance Certificates of Proficiency in First Aid, Nursing and Hygiene.

3. My work has generally been appreciated by my superiors.

4. I can undertake both medical and surgical nursing and have long experience in handling children and the aged.

Personnel Officer

1. I hold an M.A. degree in Social Science from Bombay University and have also completed a correspondence course in Personnel Management from the London School of Correspondence Courses.
2. I have sound knowledge of modern principles and practices of personnel management, aptitude tests, work incentives, etc.
3. I am also acquainted with the methods of merit rating and performance audit.
4. I have five years' experience as Assistant Personnel Officer in a public sector undertaking.
5. A short-term course on Computer that I have undergone with NIIT, Delhi, has enabled me to improve my productivity during my career.

Stenographer

1. My Short-hand and Typing speeds are 140 and 70 w.p.m. respectively.
2. I have also completed a course on book-keeping and secretarial practice.
3. I am good at English and thus can handle correspondence independently.
4. If required, I can also work in the capacity of a Secretary.
5. I am good at MS Office Software like Word, Excel, Power Point and Access, besides handling eMail and Internet.

Store-keeper

1. I am fully conversant with the theory and practice of store-keeping.
2. Having worked as an Assistant Store-Keeper with Mehta Surgical Company for two years, I have fairly good knowledge of handling and recording stocks.
3. I am fully conversant with all aspects of store-keeping.
4. Since I have also worked on a computerised Store Management System, I could increase my productivity by 200%.
5. On account of my training and experience, I am in a position to discharge efficiently all duties that are assigned to me as an storekeeper.

Telephone Operator-Receptionist

1. I have good command over spoken English and can also converse fluently in Hindi.
2. I have a pleasing personality and a well modulated voice, and can handle all inquiries on the telephone.
3. I can handle the most modern EPABX and other Voice Storage systems.
4. I have completed a three months course of Telephone Operators and Receptionists from Reliance Commercial Training Institute, New Delhi.
5. I do maintain all my official contacts on computer and am well-versed on how to appropriately manipulate these data.

Private Tutor

1. I am a IInd class Commerce Graduate from the Delhi University and have been giving private tuitions for the last ten years.
2. As I have been an English teacher in Delhi Public School for five years, I am familiar with all school requirements.

3. I can coach your son in all subjects and guarantee his progress in the subjects he is weak in, at present.

4. We can, of course, discuss the terms and conditions when we meet.

Typist

1. After completing my SSLC in 1999 with 2nd division I attended the Delhi Typewriting Institute and have now acquired good speed and accuracy in typing.

2. Besides office routine I can do simple invoicing and tabulation work, etc.

3. I can also cut stencils well and can operate any standard duplicating machine.

4. I am very good at Computers and can work on Windows '95, especially all software on MS-Office.

Salesman

1. Besides being a Commerce Graduate, I have taken a diploma in Business Management and Control and other subjects related to retail sales.

2. For the last three years I have been working as a part-time Salesman for a well-known cosmetic company and my sales, on an average, have exceeded Rs.50,000/- a month.

3. I am in perfect health and prepared to travel anywhere in India.

4. I have a way with people and know the art of persuading prospective customers into placing orders.

Sub-Editor

1. I also have a diploma in Journalism from the Nagpur University.

2. Since June this year I have been working as an apprentice with 'The Hindustan Times' and as a result have become conversant with the process of producing a paper.

3. I am proficient in English and can process data in a computerised environment.

4. I am of good health and prepared to work even in night shifts.

Hotel Cook

1. I have got a diploma in catering from the College of Catering, Bombay University.

2. For two years I have worked as an Assistant to my father who was the Chief Cook at the famous Leela Vilas Hotel in Shimla for more than 15 years.

3. I can prepare Indian, Continental as well as Chinese dishes.

4. At times, I have prepared meals for more than 100 people at very short notices.

Manager

1. I completed M.B.A. from the College of Business Administration, Hyderabad in 1995, securing 87% marks and have done a one year course on Computers.

2. I have three years experience as Assistant Manager in Bharat Auto Industries, Yamuna Nagar.

3. I can handle matters regarding Accounts, Finance, General Administration and Board Meetings competently.

4. My work with the present employer has been highly appreciated, as I have managed to establish harmonious relation between the staff and the management.

Mechanic

1. I have got a diploma from the Polytechnic Institute, Delhi, specialising in the working of Internal Combusion Engines, Electric Motors and allied subjects.

2. As a trainee at the Polytechnic, I have had the opportunity to dismantle car engines and reassemble them.

3. As an apprentice with Yantra Industries since last year, I have efficiently handled engines of various types and makes.

4. Having worked for some time in a tool manufacturing industry, I have acquired the knowledge of various types of tools required for the repair and servicing of engines and machines.

Technician

1. I have completed a two year diploma in Mechanical Engineering from the Industrial Training Institute, Malviya Nagar, New Delhi.

2. As an apprentice with Pratima TV company, Ghaziabad, I have also acquired fairly good knowledge of electronics.

3. My present job has given me adequate experience in various technical jobs like welding, soldering, wiring, etc.

4. If required I can also deal with customers.

Teacher

1. I completed M.A. History in 1995, from the Bombay University securing 76% marks. In 1996 I got B.Ed (Bachelor of Education) from the same University securing 78% marks.

2. I have been teaching English and Geography to IX and X classes for the last two years, in a Municipal School in Poona.

3. For more than five years I have been giving private tuitions to high school students.

4. I have an impressive personality and have the knack of handling students well.

Space Seller

1. After completing B.Com. in 1978 I have been working as Space Seller on behalf of "Blend" a monthly magazine published from Nagpur, with a circulation of 25,000 copies.

2. The monthly average of advertisement business which I procured for the magazine has always been at least six times of my remuneration.

3. I have been an active campaigner of advertisements for "Perception" a Calcutta monthly, with a circulation of more than 18000 copies and have established good contacts in the advertising circle in Bombay.

Air Hostess

1. Having wide-ranging interests Is have sound basic general knowledge.

2. I am fluent in English as well as Hindi and interested in hospitality industry.

3. As desired by you in the advertisement, I have a pleasing personality and am modest in approach.

4. I am unmarried and prepared to undergo any vocational, aptitude and physical tests that may be necessary to prove my suitability for the job.

Apprentice

1. I have been taking keen interest in everything mechanical ever since my childhood.
2. Of late, I have also got exposed to computer applications and am good at CAD.
3. Basically, being interested in mechanical work I have a small workshop at home in which I tinker about. I have also forged certain hand-tools.
4. The stipend you offer during my apprenticeship is acceptable to me.
5. I am of good health and take pride in working with my hands.

Canteen Manager

1. I have taken a Diploma in Hotel Management and Catering from the Catering College, Bombay.
2. I can efficiently supervise a large kitchen equipped with all modern cooking appliances.
3. I have also studied dietetics and nutrition thoroughly and can prepare meals for a big group.
4. For two years I have worked as an Assistant to the Canteen Manager of Messrs. Globe Industries, Faridabad.

Draftsman

1. My work with the present employer has been highly appreciated and I was also sent to West Germany for an advanced course in this line.
2. During my three years of service with Delhi Engineering Company, I have gained valuable experience in structural and mechanical drawings.
3. I am extremely good at all the related software and have worked in a computerised environment.
4. I have also done some architectural sketching and tracing.
5. My plans and blue-prints in the present job have been frequently praised for their accuracy as well as in the overall perspective.

Headmistress of School

1. I am M.A. M.Ed. from the Bombay University and have specialised in modern methods of education.
2. I have 15 years of experience as a senior teacher and two years experience as an Assistant Headmistress in reputed High Schools in Delhi including St. Francis Public School.
3. I am fully conversant with the administrative functions of a large educational institution.
4. I have a knack \for handling children, and along with maintaining discipline, I can win their confidence and love.

Hotel Manger

1. I have five years experience as Assistant Manager in the well-known Badshah Hotel of Bombay.
2. I am conversant with all aspects of hotel management, from daily menus to security and from public relations to arranging conventions.
3. I can fluently speak English, Hindi, Punjabi and Gujarati and also have working knowledge of French.

4. I have the experience of having worked in a computerised environment.

5. I have sufficient experience in handling foreign guests.

Lawyer for Industrial Concern

1. I have five years experience as Legal Adviser to M/S Delhi Steel Industries.

2. I have passed the L.L.M. examination and have sound knowledge and experience of Industrial Legislation, Factory Act, Labour Law etc.

3. On a number of occasions I have represented my Company in legal disputes in the High Court and the Supreme Court.

4. For more than three years I have worked as an Assistant to the reputed legal expert of Bombay on Industrial Legislation, Mr. F.M. Kanoonwala.

5. I generate most of my documents and affidavits on a computer without depending on a typist.

Publicity Officer

1. I have a diploma in Journalism from Nagpur University and have also done a correspondence course in Publicity, Public Relations and Advertising from the London School of Journalism.

2. I have a good knowledge of computer and all related software an am expert in design and lay-out.

3. As an Assistant Publicity Officer for Rose Cosmetics Ltd., Nagpur. I have conducted several successful advertising campaigns, trade fair, road-shows etc.

4. I am well versed in printing and production techniques and also conversant with all publicity media like Press, Radio and T.V. etc.

Press Reporter

1. I have a Diploma in Journalism from the Punjab University.

2. I am excellent in handling English language besides being good in Hindi and Punjabi.

3. I am a computer literate and can generate reports on computer.

4. I was closely involved in the publishing of the students' news paper brought out by the University Department of Journalism.

Sales Manager

1. As an Assistant Sales Manager I have been able to achieve creditable sales results and exceed the targets.

2. I have a sound knowledge of maintaining accounts and modern business methods specially in sales management.

3. I am known in my field for effectively handling tough sales related problems.

4. I have a good knowledge of modern methods of publicity, public relations and advertising which are prerequisites to sales.

5. I know how to generate spread-sheets and sales statistics on a computer.

Travelling Salesman

1. I have five years' experience in door-to-door sales canvassing of various consumer products.

2. I am prepared to travel to any part of the country and find pleasure in meeting people.

3. I am in excellent health which, I believe, is essential for a travelling salesman.

4. I know the art of dealing with the people and can speak English, Hindi, punjabi, Bengali and Gujarati fluently.

Agent

1. As the sole representative of Gala Cosmetics Ltd., for entire Maharashtra I have built up personal contacts with all major cosmetic dealers in the state.

2. Although I am new to this line I am confident of performing well in the business on account of my old contacts in the city.

3. I am confident that my connections in the trade circle will result in a large turnover for your firm in this region.

4. We could negotiate the agency terms at an early date and I would accept any reasonable offer.

Accounts Assistant

1. I have passed B.Com degree examination from the Punjab University with 90% marks in Advanced Accounts.

2. I have been an apprentice with Dena Bank, Karol Bagh, New Delhi, for more than 6 months.

3. I can easily maintain the books of accounts of any type of business.

4. I have a good handwriting and can speedily enter data into a computer. I am also familiar with the software 'Tally'.

Lecturer

1. Apart from having a good academic record I have also published papers in literary journals like Humanities Review, etc.

2. I am a writer and one of my books was chosen for an award by the Maharashtra Literary Conference.

3. I am a good orator and have often compered many cultural programmes during college days.

4. I am fond of teaching and I make it interesting for the students.

5. Despite the fact that I have done M.A. in Hindi, I have also good command over the English language.

Copy-writer in Advertising Agency

1. I have done a correspondence course in Advertising from the London School of Correspondence Courses.

2. I have made a special study of the 'copies' of leading Indian advertisers, and my paper on this subject has been appreciated by the London School of Advertising.

3. I have a flair for writing and can produce forceful and punch packed 'copy' on any product.

4. I can also visualise advertisements and have working knowledge of lay-outs.

5. My basic knowledge of computers has made my work more productive and speedy.

Engineer

1. I completed my B.E.(Electrical) from I.I.T. Kanpur, in 1994 securing grade A (90% marks).

2. I have worked as an apprentice engineer for 4 years with Hindustan Electric company, Calcutta, and am very familiar with computerised environment.

3. I have more than 2 years of experience in working at power generation plants.

4. I have also been designing and making small electrical gadgets for everyday domestic use.

Advertisement Manager

1. Over the years I have managed to establish close personal contacts with all major advertising agencies in Delhi.

2. I also have personal contacts with many major advertisers in Calcutta.

3. I have more than 5 years of experience in coordinating the activities of Creative Departments and the Studio. I am very good at presentation software like Adobe, Coreldraw, Photoshop etc.

4. I also have sound knowledge of block-making, offset printing and various other production techniques.

Shop Assistant

1. I have passed the Higher Secondary Examination.

2. I can speak Hindi and English fluently.

3. I have a pleasing personality.

4. I like any job involving public dealing and can be successful at the counter of any commercial establishment.

Proof-reader

1. I have a sound knowledge of English and am very good at spellings.

2. I know all the signs of proof-reading and can read proofs without omissions.

3. I have read proofs at home for the New Book Publishing Company, on assignment basis.

4. I am quite used to working on a computer and very familiar with most of the types/fonts, designing magazine lay-outs and book pages etc.

Business Letters
(Daily Contacts Series)

SECTION - III

Business Letters

Business Letters
(Main Characteristics)

"Good correspondence is the soul of successful business. Without correspondence there can be no trade. Modern business is the greatest romance of the age. It spins out money which can buy law and life".

A business letter needs a careful drafting because a well-written letter can go a long way in producing desirable results. It may clinch a sale, sort out a complaint or fetch a customer. It is a very straight forward document, but, at the same time, friendly and conversational in tone. It is also a substitute for a personal talk or conversation a on telephone.

Let your letter be a credit to yourself and your firm. Such a letter cannot be written by just anybody. It is an expert's job. If the letter has mistakes and faulty constructions it can do serious damage to business dealings.

However, there is nothing very complicated about these letters. In every company large amount of business and considerable sales are done through mail. Thus, every letter has its bearing on the balance sheet. Every outgoing letter is a spokesman of the company's policy. It is silent but not dumb. It helps to increase the reputation of the firm. It opens markets and outlets for goods and services. It is a way to make profit.

Since the business has become extremely complicated now a days, the ability to write good business letters is an asset. The correspondence between the head office, branches, production units and sale depots makes the functioning of a company smooth. Thus, a letter has both internal and external uses and importance.

Considering the fact that a letter gets only a few minutes of the reader's attention, the message must be clear, correct and concise. The letter should be well organised as to perform multiple functions of conveying a message, building good will and creating a favourable response. It is difficult to avoid negative ideas but what matters most is how they are put. A skilful correspondent handles the negative attitude with a tactful positive approach. Almost all negative ideas can be put in a positive way e.g.,

Negative	Positive
1. We cannot despatch the consignment until you inform where it is to be delivered.	We shall despatch the consignment as soon as you let us know where it is to be delivered.
2. We shall be careful to avoid delay in future.	We shall take care to ensure prompt delivery in future.
3. Unless the old dues are cleared, further goods cannot be despatched.	You are risking your own goodwill by delaying our payment.

Everyone has a style of his own. But, however good it might be, there can be scope for further improvement. A good style is an asset to a writer. And it can be perfected with practice and training. For an effective letter the correspondent must have a clear knowledge of the product, the services or the subject he is dealing with. And he must put all this with a flow of good and impressive language.

For an organisation or a commercial set-up, correspondence has a vital bearing on its relations with customers. Invaraibly, the prime need for giving a clear-cut and simple message is that there is no difficulty in understanding the message conveyed.

Simple and natural language is the key to good business correspondence. The letter should be friendly in tone and content. In your telephonic conversation you would not say, "It is regretted that the goods cannot be delivered today". Rather say, "I am sorry, we cannot deliver the goods today". Thus, the letter should be framed keeping in view what the situation demands, and as emplicity as one spends with the other.

Some tips for good letter writing :

For writing effective business letters, we are giving some useful tips below :-

1. While writing a business letter keep in mind whom you are writing to. Give all the information he needs clearly so that there is no guessing on his part.
2. Catch the attitude of the incoming letter and reply accordingly.
3. Use conversational language in the letter, wherever required.
4. Be clear, courteous and precise. Avoid ambiguity.
5. Be as polite and polished as possible.
6. Avoid using high sounding words. If the letter demands, the reply should be elaborate and detailed one.
7. Discard stereotyped language.
8. Use effective phraseology.
9. Avoiding monotony and dryness, introduce variety in the letter.
10. A long letter should be divided into paragraphs.
11. The opening should be particularly catchy, as it has lasting impact on the reader.
12. Revise the letter before closing it.
13. Avoid repetitions.

The tips explained in detail:

Keep you letter's reader in mind :

This can be best done by keeping the reader's point of view in mind. Anticipate his feelings, requirements and give sure and subtle replies. Visualise the letter's impact on yourself. If it is impressive and effective, the job is done.

Catch the attitude :

The reply should be in tune with the letter received. Think out the objective clearly and then reply accordingly. Skill, tact and practice are necessary for tackling different queries and approaches.

Use natural and conversational language :

The letter's tone should be friendly and natural. It should be simply written to convey a message for impressing the reader :

Avoid	Write
1. I have pleasure in informing you	I am pleased to tell you (or to say)
2. Please be good enough to advise us	Please let us know

Write clear and definite language , avoiding ambiguity :

Think before you write. Express yourself in clear and simple language. Avoid using stereotyped language. It should not cause reader's guessing, but being definite. It should also be unambiguous.

Be courteous and considerate :

'Courteous' does not mean that unnecessary adjectives are used. E.g.,'Your esteemed order', etc. Your approach should be on the positive side without meaning any discourtesy.

Avoid business jargon :

Avoid the use of words and phrases which the reader fails to understand easily. Jargons are the words that are specific to a subject and should not be used in general letters. The letter should be short, simple and to the point. Lengthy letters bore the reader.

	Avoid	Write
1.	We express our regret at being unable to fulfil your order on this occasion with customary promptness	We are sorry we cannot meet your present order immediately.
2.	Under active consideration	Being considered
3.	With reference to	About
4.	in connection with	For
5.	it should be noted that	Please note

Discard stereotyped language :

Modern business letters do not use old terminology that make the letters stereo-typed.

	Avoid	Write
1.	Adverting to your letter	Referring to your letter
2.	We beg to acknowledge	We have received
3.	Your esteemed favour to hand	Received your letter
4.	The favour of your early reply will oblige.	An early reply is expected
5.	Under separate cover	Separately
6.	Your goodself	You
7.	Kindly take into consideration	Please consider
8.	Assuring you of our best attention at all times.	We will pay full attention We assure you of the best of our attention.

Use effective phraseology :

The letter should be simple and easily understandable. Use of familiar and easy words is desired.

	Avoid	Write
1.	Communication	Letter
2.	Will you be good enough	Will you please
3.	In the near future	Soon, shortly
4.	It gives much pleasure	I am pleased; I am happy

5.	We will execute your order expeditiously	We will process your order promptly
6.	We beg to acknowledge receipt of your favour	Thanks for your enquiry/order

Introduce variety:

Avoid monotony and repetition. Use active voice on the whole but for variety use passive voice at places.

Avoid	Write
(i) Please let me know at once if you are unable to deliver the goods or not.	If you are unable to deliver the goods, please inform me/us immediately.
(ii) We have noted with surprise the contents of your letter.	It was with surprise that we noted the contents of your letter.
(iii) We despatched the goods on 15th	The goods were despatched on the 15th.
(iv) You did not sign the order form	The order form was not signed.

Opening and closing of effective letter :

A. Opening

Although 'Thank you for your letter', This refers to your letter' etc., are normally used one can introduce variety with expressions like 'I was glad to receive your letter', 'When I received your letter of.........' etc.

B. Closing :

Avoid	Write
1. We shall deal promptly with any orders you place with us.	Your orders will be dealt with promptly.
2. Thanking you in anticipation.	Thanking you/Thank you.
3. Hoping to hear from you soon.	I hope to hear soon from you
4. Trusting this meets with your approval.	I trust you will approve of this.

Revising the letter :

Peruse your letter before signing and revise if necessary before mailing it. Also put the following questions to yourself:

(i) Is the letter impressive?

(ii) Is the letter well drafted?

(iii) Are spellings and punctuation correct?

(iv) Is the message clear and simple?

(v) Does the letter fulfil the reader's needs?

(vi) How would you, yourself, react to such a letter?

If all the above questions have a positive reply, your letter is ready to be mailed.

Construction of Commercial Correspondence

The letter is like an organic being, having a head, body and tail. Business letters, unlike personal letters, have certain formalities to observe. Effective correspondence is the mainstay of any business. Successes and failures in business depend also on effective communication.

Since a good deal of money is involved in business dealings, the correspondence has to be handled with a lot of tact. Everything has to be calculated and complete. Even the stationery used should be of good quality. A shabby letter can spoil company's image. Be brief and natural, courteous and conversational.

It is discourteous to start a letter with the expression of regret or remorse. Express pleasure in hearing from the other party. After this, go on to the business aspects of the letter, enlisting in different paragraphs the items you want to bring to the reader's notice.

As in case of personal letters, the main parts of a letter, apart from the text of the message, are: the heading, date, inside address, salutation, close and signature. However, certain variations can be there in different cases. The letter must first make a visual impressions as the first impression counts.

The appearance of a letter largely depends on the quality of paper and print, neatness of the fold, the style of lay-out etc. In every good Company neat and efficient clerical attention is paid to the make-up of the letter.

Essential parts of a letter with special emphasis to business letters:

1. Letterhead,
2. Date,
3. Inside address,
4. Salutation,
5. Body of the letter,
6. Complimentary closure,
7. Signature and designation,
8. Enclosure reference,
9. P.S. (Post script)

1. Letterhead:

The letterhead is the printed heading giving the name and address of the company. Generally it occupies about six and a half centimeters of space from top. Use types of moderate size and with a modern face. Simplicity of design is an essential requirement. The letterhead should have only necessary information and that too in a brief form. But, it must have :

(i) Name of the company

(ii) Complete address

(iii) Nature of business

(iv) Telephone number, telegraphic address and eMail address, if any,

(v) Address of Registered Office and branch office, if any.

(vi) Logo of the company, if any

2. Date:

The date should appear on the right hand margin two spaces below the upper margin. The year is written in full as 1999. The date can be written in any of the following ways:-

(i). On the right hand margin e.g.,

2nd August, 1999.

or

August 16, 1999.

On the left-hand side top:

2nd August, 1999.

or

August 16, 1999.

3. Inside Address

The inside address includes the name and address of the addressee. This is exactly the same address as given on the envelope.

Fully-indented style:

To

    M/s. Universal Book Stall,

    Post Box No.540,

    New Delhi-12.

Blocked style :

    M/s Universal Book Stall,

    Post Box No.540,

    New Delhi-110 012.

A business letter must have the address of the addressee inside too, because, when the copies of such letters are filed, their identification is necessary.

4. Salutation/Attention line:

The salutation is a complimentary term used to begin a letter. A letter addressed to an organisation or a firm begins as under: -

    Sir/Madam

    Dear Sir

    Dear Sirs

    Gentlemen*

    Dear Mr....(Name)**

Originality, of course, pays in business correspondence and equally so in business contacts. If one is writing to somebody familiar it is preferable to begin the salutation by name e.g.,

    Dear Mr. Sharma,

---

*It's use is usually an American practice

**This is more prevalent now a days

5. Body of the letter:

A reference line will help the addressee to understand the subject matter of the letter and refer it to the relevant file. This reference line can go below the salutation.

The body of the letter conveys the main message to the person or the firm. If the letter deals with different subjects they should be put in different paragraphs, in the order of importance.

6. Complimentary Close:

The complimentary close should be consistent with the salutation and the content of the letter. It should express regard and respect for the addressee. A good correspondent uses appropriate words. The pairs of salutations and the complimentary closures often used are given below :-

Salutation	Complimentary close
Dear Sir(s)/ Dear Madam	Yours truly/ Yours faithfully
Dear Mr.	Yours faithfully***
	Yours sincerely

7. Signatures:

There are different styles of putting the signatures after the complimentary close. Some times the letter is signed by some junior official on behalf of a senior. In that case, "for" is prefixed before the signature. In case of women 'Miss' or 'Mrs' is put in the parenthesis. Now a days, however 'Ms', is also being used for women which does not tell anything about their marital status. The name and designation of the signatory are typed leaving space for signature.

8. Enclosure reference:

Usually the letter is accompanied by some enclosures. It may be a bill, a proforma invoice, a copy of previous reference, a self-addressed envelope, a leaflet etc. In such a case it is necessary to mention the number of enclosures so that the despatcher can check the same at a glance. It also helps the addressee to identify the enclosures expected.

9. P.S. (Postscript)

In case of some important omission, it can be mentioned at the bottom of the letter P.S. It should not generally exceed three lines. Sometimes its aim is to get pointed attention of the reader. As it stands at last, it leaves a lasting impression on the leader.

P.S. 1. Don't forget that the sale closes on 9th of this month.

2. How is your new venture in Bombay coming up?

3. I read your latest article in The Hindustan Times and found it quite interesting and enlightening

10. The address on the envelope:

This is invariably the same as the Inside Address. Mr. and Esq., should never be used together. If you have to write Esq., after the name, do not use Mr. Noadays. However, Esqr., is scarcely used. It is preferable to use Dr. before the name instead of writing M.D. or Ph.D. after the name. Medical professionals, nowadays, write their names by prefixing "Dr." and suffixing their professional degree.

***This is the most widely used complimentary close

The address on the envelope should be typed or neatly written leaving a space of about 4 c.m. on the top. This space can be used for franking the postage mark or affixing the postage stamps.

The address should be broken into 3 or 4 lines:

i). The name and designation of the chief executive e.g., Proprietor, Partner, Manager, Managing Director etc., of the firm/office should be followed by the name of the business organization.

ii) Locality, Street, Road etc.,

iii) Name of the town/city preferably in bold letters.

iv) Name of the state and pin code e.g.,

>The Sales Manager,
>M/s. Leader engineering works,
>46, Darya Ganj,
>New Delhi -11 00 02.

>Mr. James T Sobers,
>Divisional Manager,
>125, Esplanade Road, (W.B.).

Different parts of the address like designation, name of the street etc., should preferably be used in separate lines.

Streamline your letter

Some General Guidelines :

1. Gone are the days when the business letters were written in hand. These days business letters are generally typewritten or computer generated. Handwritten letters can be illegible and thus hamper business dealings. Moreover, they create a bad impression on the receiver.

2. The typist should be efficient. Care should be taken to type letters and correctly. Erasers should be avoided. If a letter has too many corrections it should be re-typed. If done on a computer, it can easily be edited. The stationery should be handled with clean hands and it should be ensured that poor quality paper is not used for letters.

3. The typewriter should be kept clean and should have a good ribbon.

A good typist is one who sees to it that: -

i) the type is clean;

ii) the touch is even;

iii) the eraser's impressions are unnoticeable;

iv) there is absence of 'strike overs';

v) there are no ink/pencil corrections;

vi) alignment of capital letters with small letters is correct;

vii) spacing of the typed area on paper is correct;

viii) spacing between words and lines is correct;

ix) In case of Electric or Electronic Typewriter, most of the above are automatically taken care of. A word processor or a Computer has innumerable options and facilities to edit, and manipulate a letter or document. In the latest software like MS Office, most of these are menu driven in the system itself.

Forms of indentions

A letter may be typed or indented in three different ways.

1. Block or Straight Edge Form:

This is the most common one practised throughout the world. The introductory address, salutation, body paragraphs and complimentary close, begin at the left-hand margin. Single spacing is used with double spacing between paragraphs not indented.

2. Indented Form:

The inside address and subsequently each paragraphs are indented to the same distance from the margin. Single or double spacing may be used between the lines.

3. Semi-block or Combination Form:

This form is also quite popular. The inside address is in block form and not indented-while the body of the letter is arranged in indented paragraphs.

Block Form
Letter-head

May 12, 1999 / 12th May, 1999
M/s. Jugal Kishore & Sons,
Main Avenue,
Santa Cruz,
Bombay-55.

Gentlemen,

This letter is in full block form. Every line including the date and the complimentary close, is at the left hand margin. Since there is no indention, this form takes the shortest time to type. It is useful where correspondence is large. It is the latest in styles of lay-out and is now universally popular.

Yours faithfully,

Manager

Indented Form

Letter-head

November 18, 1999

M/s. Mehta & Company,
Green Avenue,
Calcutta.

Dear Sirs,

This is the indented form which is now out of date. The inside address is indented and each paragraph begins five spaces away form the margin.

Although the appearance is good, time is wasted because of indentions.

Yours faithfully,

....

Semi-Block Form

10 September, 1999

M/s. Sehgal & Sons,
M/s. Industrial Town,
Jullundur City.

Dear Sirs,

This is the semi-block form and is quite common in correspondence. Here, the date, complimentary close and signature are written on the right-hand side. It is a modification over the modern Block Form.

Yours truly,

Supervisor

Summary of a good business letter:

A good business letter is one which can:

1. Sell goods,
2. Revive old clients/customers,
3. Secure new customers and business,
4. Convince customers,
5. Stimulate dealers,
6. Create goodwill,
7. Collect bad debts,
8. Adjust complaints,
9. Open up new outlets,
10. Influence the balance sheet.

Other points to be remembered:

- Investment in correspondence for business pays in the long run.
- A good letter, like a seasoned diplomat, fetches goodwill and business.
- In correspondence, promptness is a must. It avoids delays in business activities.
- Try to understand all implications of assurances/commitments given in your letter.
- Business calls for action at the right time. Learn to cash it at the proper moment.
- Every letter should be well-written, well-typed, well-set. The stationery used should be the best that the company can afford.
- The language of the letter can do wonders. Be selective in the choice of words and phrases. A good style and expression can make the letter a treat for its reader.

Different Types of Business Letters

A modern business man has to deal with different kinds of letters in his routine activities. It is not easy to classify the business letters or to give a detailed list of all such letters. Different situations require different approaches. Different kinds of letters which are usually written are as under :-

Letters of enquiry and replies

Circular letters

Letters containing offers or quotations

Letters ordering goods

Letters acknowledging orders

Follow-up letters

Letters acknowledging goods received and making payments

Letters regarding claims, complaints and adjustments °

Insurance letters

Letters regarding forwarding of goods

Export and import trade correspondence

Correspondence with government offices

Banking correspondence

For every kind of letter, different styles and terminology are used. Care should be taken to understand different forms of letters, their requirements and their implications.

Letters of enquiry

Today, in business world there are numerous enquiries to be made as more and more goods and services are offered for sale, backed up by massive publicity. Interested parties wish to find out more about the product than the advertisement tells them. The letter of enquiry asks about specific details about the product. A hotel manager as a user may ask for information about a washing machine while a dealer may be interested to know about the trade terms for retailing the same. Such a letter may include the following points: -

1. Request for information with reference to the advertisement;

2. The purpose for which information is sought.

Circular letter

Some times information regarding change of address, opening of a branch office or getting a new telephone connection etc., is brought to customer's/client's notice through a circular letter. Such a circular letter is either cyclostyled or printed.

Letters containing offers or quotations

An offer is in the form of a circular and is meant for the general public including the regular customers. Here the intention may be to clear the old stock or to expand the market. However, a quotation is a specific offer for sale, in response to an enquiry. The language of such a letter should be persuasive in order to win over the customer.

Letters ordering goods

While placing an order for goods, mention the articles required by you. Such a letter must contain full directions on forwarding , full name and address of the sender etc. Lack of information causes unnecessary delay at both ends.

Letter acknowledging order:

All orders should be promptly acknowledged, especially if the order requires some time for its execution. The buyer feels satisfied on getting the acknowledgement. However, the probable date of despatch should also be indicated.

Follow-up letters:

Follow-up letters are important as they show a continuing interest in the client. The language of the letter must be persuasive to win over the customers. The aim should be to coax the wavering customer into buying the product.

Letters acknowledging goods received and making payments :

The acknowledgement of goods soon after they are received is an effective business practice. In case there is a delivery note from the sender, it should be signed and returned. The mode of payment may be through a cheque or a bill of exchange. Bill of exchange is used both for internal and foreign trade.

Letters regarding claims, complaints and adjustments:

Sometimes the goods are damaged in transit because of careless handling by rail or road transport. This results in complaints. Such a complaint should be firm and polite in tone. A feeling of adjustment and understanding should be exhibited.

Insurance letters:

Often the exported goods are insured to avoid future complications. The fire and marine assurance are necessary as it saves the businessmen from future losses and risks.

Letters regarding forwarding of goods:

The goods within the country are moved through private carriers and the railways. Usually there is no correspondence while despatching or receiving goods except filling up a few forms. Complaints or claims, however, may crop up on account of delays, losses or damage of goods.

Export and import correspondence:

This correspondence calls for not only skilful handling but alertness of mind, technique and complete knowledge on the part of the correspondent. The business is usually done through Forwarding Agents/Commission Agents. The Forwarding Agent is responsible for receiving the goods and their safe shipment. Since foreign correspondence is expensive unnecessary correspondence should be avoided. Email has brought a lot of relief in case of foreign correspondence in terms of cost, accuracy, speed etc. The exported goods should be insured against risks.

Correspondence with government offices:

Every company has to correspond with a number of Government departments. At times there are proformas to deal with them but correspondence is also necessary on a number of occasions. Some of the government departments with which an ordinary citizen may have regular dealings include those of Income Tax, Sales Tax and Posts and Telegraphs, CCI & E, DGS & D etc.

Banking correspondence;

The bank accepts deposits and maintains different types of accounts with its clients. The services of the bank are many and of varied types but usually done through printed forms and proformas like cheque, bills, hundis, bills of exchange etc., But some times correspondence becomes necessary. Take care to be polite and learn the routine bank terminology for effective correspondence.

Business Inquiries
Dealer's First Inquiry from Manufacturer about his Product

Introductory :

1. We have come across the advertisements about your domestic appliances in various magazines and newspapers.
2. Of late we have been watching with interest for your advertisement on television about the readymade garments for children and cotton shirts.
3. We have come across your advertisement in the "Industrial Journal" and understand that you are one of the major manufacturers of machine tools/office furniture/handlooms.
4. Thank you for the literature you have sent to us about your hardware products.
5. I have been informed about your high quality products by my friend, Mr.Gulab Sharma, who is one of your customers.

Ask for detailed information about the product :

6. Could you provide us with more details about their range, size, quality, prices etc. and send us samples through your representative?
7. Please send us samples and more information about their prices, quality, range etc.
8. Are the parts used in your machines indigenous or imported?
9. Our requirements are of 15 m.m. bolts. Do you manufacture this size? Can you supply us this size?
10. As we plan to place a huge order, please let us know what is the maximum quantity you can supply us by the end of January.
11. We attach much value to the sample. It is a must before placing the orders.
12. We understand that you manufacture silk saris and would supply us 100 pieces within 15 days.
13. How long will you take to deliver the goods as per our order? We would like to have the supply within 15 days.
14. What is the mode of transport to send the goods at the earliest. We want to place an early order and get the supplies within a week.
15. Time factor is very important. It is ascertained before we place orders for the supply of goods. We stick to it strictly.

Give information about yourself :

16. We are one of the largest dealers in quality bolts in this area and wish to expand our range of stocks.
17. We are the only big dealer of electrical gadgets in Bilaspur, and we would like to stock the latest items of this type.
18. We deal in all types of hand-tools and wish to be up to date about new products.
19. We are one of the biggest furniture suppliers to the government agencies in our area.
20. We have direct approach to the industries and they always look eagerly to us for supply. The brochure enclosed tells all about our organisation.

21. We have only last year acquired the dealership of Escorts Tractors, and we want to stock the ancillaries.

Ask about trade terms:

22. Kindly let us know your terms of trade and the best discount on large orders.
23. On what terms can you supply us the goods?
24. State in your reply your terms of payment as well as trade discount.
25. Please let us know at the earliest about the extra charges for the transportation of goods.
26. Mention clearly the discount on the goods and terms of payments.
27. Can you please arrange to insure the goods before despatch?

Any other enquiry:

28. Will you be able to manufacture the items if we specify the size, shape, weight, colour and range?
29. Do you have any dealer in our district?
30. Will you kindly send us information on various manufactures of your line? It will help us in future for a comparative study.

Mention your own specialities, if any:

31. We are eagerly waiting for an early response from you.
32. Payments are through our bankers, Bank of India, as mentioned in the letter.
33. Our practice is to make payments within a week after the arrival of goods.
34. We have been dealing in hand-tools for the last 10 years.
35. We have regard for the business relationship once created. We hope we will have a lasting association.

Mention other conditions, if so desired:

36. Prices quoted should be f.o.b or f.o.r.
37. We shall require delivery of the material at our plant in Faridabad.
38. Payment of goods received is made through our bankers.

Close of the letter:

39. If the goods are to our satisfaction we hope we will have a permanent business relationship.
40. As the matter is urgent we would appreciate an early reply, preferably within a week.
41. As our expansion plans are afoot we require the information at the earliest.

Enquiry about Advertised Goods

Referring to the advertisement :

1. We have seen the advertisement of your ball-point pen on the Door Darshan.
2. We have come across your advertisement of cooking-ranges in newspapers and magazines.
3. We have been recently introduced to your cosmetics through an advertisement film.
4. We are interested in the latest hair-tonic you have developed and have been advertising about.
5. We have seen your advertisement in The Times of India and shall feel obliged if you could send us particulars of the television you have advertised.
6. We shall feel obliged if you could furnish us with more details about your cooking range recently advertised in Femina.

Asking for more information :

7. The advertisement, however, does not give sufficient information.
8. Although the advertisement gives the price, other details like size, shape, quality and discount are missing.
9. The advertisement, however, is too brief to give much information about the product.
10. Ten seconds advertisement on TV cannot give sufficient information about the product.
11. A newspaper advertisement, however, gives only a rough idea of the colour and shape of the product.
12. We would, therefore, appreciate more details.
13. Since we are eager to give it a try, please let us know from where and how we can buy it.
14. So please let us have any printed literature that you might have on the product.
15. We would, therefore, request you to send us your catalogue, price list and printed publicity material on the product.
16. As I am leaving India soon and keen on your product, please let me know about the details at the earliest.
17. As we want to buy it in bulk we would appreciate more information.

Closing the letter:

18. Samples would be particularly welcome.
19. Can you please also arrange a demonstration of the product in our factory or at some other place convenient to both of us?
20. We would appreciate a call from your representative.
21. We would, in fact, appreciate a personal meeting with your Marketing Manager.
22. We hope this is the beginning of a lasting business relationship.
23. We usually make huge purchases. So we would like to get the relevant information about the products before hand.
24. Thus, please, send us complete information about your products.

25. We deal in steel furniture. And we hope this is the beginning of a lasting business relationship between us.
26. We are sure you will find dealing with us a pleasure.

Request for Catalogues, Price-Lists and Samples

1. I saw one of your executive-tables in a friend's office and found it quite impressive/elegant.
2. I have a large domestic appliance retail business and am interested in the electric-ovens you have been advertising on Door Darshan.
3. A friend of mine has recently bought electric shavers from you for his retail shop. I have liked them very much.
4. Your firm has been recommended to us by M/s. Kala Mandal Centre who happen to be our regular customers.
5. The other day I came across a demonstration of your C.D. player in our market and found it quite attractive and handy.
6. We shall feel obliged if you could send us samples and price list of your new range of shirting material by post, courier or through your salesman.
7. We are interested in buying fancy table-cloths being manufactured by you.
8. We have seen your advertisement on the Star TV and would be obliged to receive your catalogue for the new ball recently introduced by you.
9. We have a good demand for neckties at our end. And we would appreciate if you could send us your price-list at the earliest.
10. Your advertisement for the sewing machine interests us. Please send us complete details of the product at your earliest.
11. I am particularly interested in furniture suitable for a small office.
12. As we have an advertising agency we are particularly interested in art material like painting brushes, poster and pastel colours, etc.
13. I need a similar machine, but smaller in size, for small-scale printing.
14. With our large sales net work we hope to give you a substantial annual business.
15. Ours being basically an export house, we could introduce your products in foreign markets too.
16. So, could you please send us a copy of the catalogue and price-list of your new VCPs and leaflets to be given to our prospective customers.
17. Please, therefore send me a copy of your detailed catalogue.
18. So, please send me a copy of your catalogue and any other information that may help me make the best choice.
19. Please let us know what discount do you normally give on bulk purchases.
20. As we are planning soon an expansion of our business we would like to have this information at the earliest.
21. We would appreciate an early reply with up-to-date information.
22. When replying, please specify your delivery schedule.

23. Please let us know if you are in a position to supply the goods from stock as they are needed urgently.
24. We shall appreciate if you could offer extra discount on bulk purchases.

Request for Quotations

Give your introduction first:
1. We have recently started manufacturing transistor radio sets and will be in need of bulk supplies of dry batteries.
2. We are large-scale fabricators of children's garments and now propose to diversify into men's wear.
3. We will be shortly opening a crockery shop at main Chandni Chowk and wish to stock wide range of china and glassware.
4. We are the wholesale dealers in all types of cotton fabrics.
5. We undertake contract for door-to-door sales of consumer products.

Now make further enquiries from seller :
6. We have seen the samples of your battery-cell through your representative who called on us on the 4th of this month.
7. As you manufacture a wide range of men's shirtings we hope you will be able to meet our requirements.
8. As you are a major quality manufacture of glass ware and crockery in the region we would like to receive stocks from you.
9. Your range will add to our variety.
10. The new soap developed by you could be a saleable item in our list of products. It appears to be a profitable proposition.

Tell about your requirements:
11. If the quality is good and price reasonable we might place orders for 5000 or more cells with you.
12. However, at present, we propose to place a trial order with you.
13. We could, to start with, stock goods worth Rs.50,000.
14. We deal exclusively with wholesale dealers and, hence, we shall need huge supply of the products.
15. We are government suppliers/exporters and, therefore, shall need a high quality material.

Request for Quotations:
16. Could you send us at the earliest quotations for 10,000 dry batteries to be delivered over a period of one year.
17. We, therefore, look forward to your quotations for one thousand bone china tea-set along with the terms and time of delivery.
18. So, please send us your quotations for the following items of crockery.

19. It is, therefore, requested that you send us your quotations for bulk supply of this raw material along with your terms and conditions.

20. Please let us have your best and confirmed offers, valid for two months, along with your delivery schedule.

Brief instructions:

21. Please quote for the supply of 500 toddler baby frocks in assorted sizes and also delivery time and other details.

22. At present please send us quotations for 1000 meters of fine cotton shirting material. If its demand increase at our end, we shall place a bigger order.

23. Thus, please send quotations for the supply of 1000 pairs of nylon socks and kindly reply immediately.

24. Please let us have samples and lowest quotations for 2000 meters of curtain material.

25. We rely not only on quotations but also on samples. Therefore, please send both immediately.

26. We are keen to see the samples. So, kindly send one tea set so that we can evaluate the product and place orders accordingly.

27. Are you in a position to manufacture certain dress material of our own specifications? If so, we can first send the specifications and thereafter have the quotations for the same.

Close:

28. A prompt reply would be appreciated.

29. We hope your quotation is favourable enough to start a continuing business relationship between us.

30. The tenders will be opened on 21st December at 3.00 p.m. in the office of the Chief Administrator.

31. The emphasis will be more on quality rather than price.

32. If you can give us a really competitive quotation, we would like to place a large order.

33. If your price compares favourably with those of other suppliers we shall place an order with you.

Enquiry about Raw Material Supply

Introduction

1. We are large scale distributors of kitchenware and now propose to manufacture a variety of crockery and other modern kitchenware.

2. We are leading steel utensil makers of north India and import steel sheets from West Germany.

3. We are leading manufactures of synthetic cloth of different varieties and require large quantities of nylon and terene yarn for the purpose.

4. We have recently started manufacture of small rubber items like rubber bands, erasers and chappals. Thus, we require natural rubber in bulk supplies.

5. At present we are manufacturing men's wear. As such we require fabrics of diverse qualities and designs on regular basis.

Inquiry about supplies:

6. Please let us know at the earliest if you could supply us extruded raw plastic to meet our requirements?

7. As we plan to go in for import substitution shortly, can you meet our heavy demand of steel sheets of the following specifications?

8. Will you be able to supply us yarn as per our requirements.

9. Please let us know up to what extent can you meet our requirements? The details are given below.

10. Kindly send samples of your production range with details about supply capacity.

Close:

11. On getting your positive response we shall give you our requirements and other particulars.

12. If you can meet our requirements, please let us know at the earliest your terms and conditions regarding prices, trade-discount, delivery schedule etc.

13. We hope your terms and conditions are reasonable and we have a lasting business relationship.

4. Before despatching the consignment please inform us how you are sending it.

General Inquiries

Beginning:

1. Please let us know the terms on which you can supply us 100 boxes of full size nylon socks.

2. We have come to know that you are a reputed dealer in electrical goods. Would you supply 100 tube-lights immediately?

3. We are told that you are leading manufacturers of stainless-steel utensils and wish to know whether you can supply us 100 thalis from ready stock at the factory price.

4. This is to inquire if you can supply us zinc appliances in bulk. The list of the products required by us is enclosed.

5. This is to request you to supply us with photographic material. The list of items required is enclosed.

Closing:

6. We look forward to hearing from you within the next few days.

7. As the matter is urgent, we shall appreciate an early reply.

8. If the material matches our specifications we might place regular orders for large quantities.

9. We are depending on you for standard material and, therefore, be prompt to our enquiries.

10. As the demand is increasing at our end, we would like to get the supply at the earliest.

11. We are keen to hear from you soon. Our enquires may turn into big orders, if the terms are found satisfactory.

12. We will appreciate an early reply.

Sample Letters
(Dealer's First Enquiry)

Dear Sir,

Thank you for the literature you have sent about your hardware products.[4] Please send us samples and more information about their prices, quality, range etc.[7] We are one of the largest dealers in quality bolts in this area and wish to expand our range of stocks.[16] Kindly also let us know your terms of trade and the best discount on large orders.[22] Will you be able to manufacture items if we specify the size, shape, weight, colour and range.[28] Prices quoted should be f.o.r.[36] As the matter is urgent we would appreciate an early reply preferably within a week.[40]

Thanking you,

Yours faithfully,

(Enquiry about advertised goods)

Dear Sir,

We have seen the advertisement of your ball-point pen on Door Darshan.[1] The advertisement however, does not give sufficient information.[7] We would, therefore, appreciate more details.[12] Samples would be particularly welcome.[18]

Thanking you,

Yours faithfully,

(Request for catalogue, price-list and samples)

Dear Sir,

I saw one of your executive tables in a friend's office and found it impressive and elegant.[1] I am particulary interested in furniture suitable for a small office.[11] Please, therefore, send me a copy of your detailed catalogue.[17] We would appreciate an early reply with up-to-date information.[21] Please let us know if you are in a position to supply the goods from stock as they are needed urgently.[23]

Thanking you,

Yours faithfully,

(General Enquiries)

Dear Sir,

Please let us know the terms on which you can supply 100 boxes of full-size nylon socks.[1] We look forward to hearing from you within the next few days.[6] Our inquiries may turn into big orders, if the terms are found satisfactory.[11]

Thanking you,

Yours faithfully,

Business Replies

It, of course, costs considerable effort and money to get a prospective buyer prompted to enquire about one's product. Thus, a reply to his query has to be cleverly drafted.

It is just like a customer being attracted by a window display. It is then the job of the salesman to sell something to him. Similarly, the responsibility of one replying to the prospective customer is heavy. His deft handling may result in getting the enquiry turned into an order. Remember the prospective buyer wants to know how he can benefit from the deal. Thus, for the enquirer's convenience one can always attach a list of goods. They can be ticked by the customer for the placing of order.

At times the order cannot be immediately met because of lack of fresh stocks. In such cases, the order should be acknowledged and the customer should be assured of prompt delivery as soon as possible.

Reply to Dealer's First Inquiry from Manufacturer about his Product

Convey pleasure on receiving the inquiry :

1. Thank you for your letter dated May 23, 1999 inquiring about our domestic appliance range.

2. We are pleased to see your interest in the corduroy we have recently introduced in the market.

3. We are pleased to learn from your letter dated October 30, 1999 that you are interested in our plastic crockery.

4. We are highly obliged by the interest shown by a big dealer like you in our product.

5. We are happy to receive your letter regarding the information you want about our electronic appliances.

6. We are thankful to you for sending your representative to inquire about our ready-made garments.

7. We are privileged to have your letter inquiring about bulk purchase of our cosmetic items.

8. Since our goods are of high quality our wholesale rates are a little higher than the market rates.

9. We believe in quality and honest bargains, so we can assure you of our best service and fair-deal.

10. Although we give f.o.r. up to the destination, we charge for packing and local transportation.

11. The goods are guaranteed for six months and thus can be exchanged during this period if they have any manufacturing defect.

12. We send the goods by road transport as we believe in prompt service.

13. As desired by you we can insure the goods at your expenses

14. All money transactions will be made through our authorised bank, Punjab National Bank.

Express hope of mutual goodwill :

15. We shall be pleased to furnish any other information you may need.

16. We hope you will be able to place an order with us soon.

17. We shall deal promptly with any order you send us.

18. We are sure we shall have a long lasting business relationship.

19. Although at the moment we have many orders in hand we will try to execute yours at the earliest.

20. We have enough stocks to comply with your orders immediately.

21. We have the items in stock which you enquired of and can deliver as soon as we receive your orders.

22. We are confident that you will be satisfied with the quality of our goods and will associate only with us for your future requirements.

23. We assure you of our fullest co-operation and service in future too.

Reply to Enquiry about Advertised Goods

Express pleasure on customer's having marked the advertisement :

1. We are happy to learn that you have noticed our advertisement in last week's Indian Express and The Times of India.

2. We are delighted to learn that you have taken a special interest in our commercial programme on Door Darshan.

3. We are pleased to hear from you that you have seen our advertisement on Delhi Doordarshan and are interested in the hair-tonic manufacture.

4. It's been a pleasure to know that you have seen our short film on our latest tooth-paste.

5. We are pleased to know that our advertisements about Mopeds on radio and television have been impressing our customers and we are getting healthy response from them.

6. We are quite satisfied with the positive response to our advertisements.

7. We feel that our advertisements have served the purpose and are happy to find that you interested in our goods.

Give more details:

8. As the advertisement does not carry all the details, we enclose a printed folder enlisting our new line of products and their prices.

9. We hope that the literature being sent herewith would give you all the information you required about the product, its range and price.

10. We plan to diversify soon into ladies garments too.

11. We are sending you a detailed folder about our goods with further reference to our advertisements.

Give information about the goods :

12. We hope the enclosed list is sufficient to satisfy your interest and curiosity as it contains detailed information about the advertised goods.

13. One thing we can assure you is that our products are of high quality and will be up to your satisfaction.

14. The catalogue will indicate the variety of sizes and colours of this popular product.

15. We are sure that in addition to the advertised items there are many other products illustrated with details in the folder which might interest you.

16. In fact, we are a Company set up with German collaboration. Thus, you can rely on our quality.

17. Our goods are always the same as advertised. We are sure to satisfy you through our dealings.

Close the letter with a hope of getting the order :

18. We hope that the rates appeal to you and prompt you to place an early order with us.

19. If you place an order with us you can expect a delivery within a week.

20. We can arrange for a demonstration of our sewing machine at your convenience.

21. We are sure that the high quality of our products and our attractive trade terms will encourage you to stock these fast-selling items.

22. If you still want more information before placing an order, our representative would be happy to call on you at your convenience.

23. If you place a bulk order, we give discount. The discount terms are enclosed.

Reply to Request for Catalogues, Price-List and Samples

Express pleasure on receiving the letter:

1. We are pleased to receive your letter of April 8, 1999 in response to our advertisement for mixers.

2. Thank you for your telephonic inquiry of last Tuesday regarding various transistors of our make.

3. As requested in your letter dated 10th September 1999, we enclose a catalogue in respect of our different products.

4. This is in response of your inquiry dated 4th January 1999.

5. We are obliged for your inquiry of 3rd July regarding the prices of different items.

Fulfil the request :

6. As requested by you, we enclose a copy of our detailed catalogue.

7. Please find enclosed the catalogue of our domestic appliances.

8. I take pleasure in enclosing a catalogue and current price list of our mixers as per you inquiry.

9. We are enclosing a few photographs and arranging to send you some of our samples through our sales representative to give you an idea of our range of products.

10. Our sales men are going to conduct a door-to-door campaigning in your area next week. They will give you samples. A price-list, however, is enclosed.

11. We are sure you will find our enclosed price list very reasonable.

12. The catalogue lists costs of different range of items. These are the latest prices.

13. This is our latest catalogue with revised prices.

14. We have pleasure in enclosing a copy of our illustrated catalogue/latest price list asked for in your letter of 23rd May.

15. We are pleased to receive your inquiry of 13th December and enclose our catalogue with the endorsing letter.

16. On account of Diwali, we offer 15% reduction in items purchased. We suggest that you do not let this golden opportunity pass and place an order immediately.

17. We will arrange to send the samples of our shirting material soon. And if any of your representatives comes to our new market showroom he can collect them from there.

18. Samples of our shirting range, which you have asked for in your letter of 15th March, are being sent to you today through our representative.

Give detail of the catalogue:

19. We feel, you may be particularly interested in our No.3 mixer, In fact, this is our latest and the most economical model.

20. Our terms and conditions are printed on the back-cover of the catalogue.

21. The catalogue has been devised keeping in view of all the relevant information the buyer might require.

22. You will find particulars of the electric kettle and its illustration on page 10 of the catalogue.

Give details of the product:

23. Without any increase in fuel consumption it gives out 15% more heat than the earlier models.

24. We feel the item illustrated on page 4 of the catalogue is ideal for your present requirement.

25. All our current models are shock-proof, efficient in operation and more economical in fuel consumption.

26. As evident from the illustrated catalogue, all our new models come in elegant cases.

27. In case you want a smaller size, there are many suitable ones listed on page 12 of the catalogue.

Close the letter with the hope of getting the order :

28. We look forward to a trial order which will convince you of our product quality.

29. In case you want a demonstration before placing an order, we shall be happy to welcome you to our show-room at any time in the afternoon.

30. You will, of course, be able to explore the variety of items only when you call on us.

31. We sincerely hope that our price-list enables you to place orders and establish trade relations with us.

32. We hope the samples reach you safely and you place an order with us soon.

33. We hope to hear from you very soon and expect your orders.

34. We hope you will place an order in bulk and avail of our discount scheme.

35. We hope you will take advantage of our offer and place an early order.

36. On account of Diwali we are allowing special benefits to customers who place orders before the end of the current month.

Reply to Request for Quotations

Beginning:

1. Thank you for your inquiry of August 3, regarding quotation for 100 'Executive' model office tables.

2. This is with reference to your inquiry of November 5, 1999. As per your request, we will be glad to supply you nylon socks at the rate of Rs.15/- per pair.

3. In response to your letter of last Monday we are happy to send you the following quotation for the goods you have indicated.

4. The prices of the items required by you are as given below.

5. We submit herewith for approval our rates for all the items required by you.

Closure:

6. We hope you will find our rates reasonable and place an order with us.
7. Please let us know by return of post if we may book your order at the prices quoted.
8. As our stocks of these goods are limited we strongly recommend you to take advantage of this opportunity.
9. As the prices quoted are exceptionally low and are likely to rise soon, in view of the imminent hike in the raw material price, we would advise you to place your order without delay.
10. Our rates might be a little higher than those of many other manufacturers but our quality is incomparable.

Reply to Enquiry about Raw Material Supply

Beginning:

1. We are pleased to learn that you are a large-scale distributor of plastic crockery and plan to expand your business.
2. Thank you for the inquiry of April 2, 1999, for the purchase of steel sheets in bulk.
3. We are pleased to learn that you require nylon and terene yarn for the manufacture of synthetic cloth.

Closure:

4. We will, of-course, be glad to supply you extruded raw plastic as per your requirement.
5. We have enough stock of steel sheets and can deliver whenever you require them.
6. We are a big stockist of nylon and terene yarn and can supply the required quantity within a week of the request.

Reply to General Inquiries

Beginning:

1. We are pleased to receive your inquiry of January 3, 1999 about the multi-purpose electric iron marketed by us.
2. We are glad to learn from your representative that you are interested in our preserved food items.
3. We are pleased to learn that you are interested in a large variety of paper that we manufacture and wish to know more about your requirement.
4. It is a pleasure to know that you are interested in stocking our entire range of electronic instruments.
5. Thank you for the interest you have shown in our fabrics.

Close;

6. We will, of course, be happy to furnish any further information you may require.
7. We are looking forward to your order.

8. We have a reputation for being prompt and efficiency is our watchword.

9. Any order you may like to place with us can be met immediately from the ready stock.

10. We have the items in stock and can deliver them as soon as we receive your order.

11. We are confident that you will be satisfied with the quality of our goods.

12. We hope to have a long lasting relationship with you.

13. We assure you of our fullest co-operation in business.

Letter Rejecting Quotation

First thank the seller for sending quotation :

1. Thank you for sending your quotation for the proposed purchase of 1000 yards of handloom cloth by us.

2. You were good enough to quote on 19th August for 100 electric heaters we proposed to buy from you.

3. I appreciate the trouble you have taken in this regard.

4. In response to our inquiry dated 8th June, you were good enough to quote for 200 plastic buckets and send us a sample.

5. I am thankful to you for promptly quoting for 200 pairs of suede jackets I had proposed to purchase from you.

Express regret giving reasons:

6. Their quality is, of course, good but the prices are rather on the higher side. We have been purchasing the same kind of jackets at a much lower price.

7. Although the goods suit our requirements, their prices are much higher than we had expected.

8. The quality and prices of the fabric suit our requirements but your quotation reached us rather late. In the mean time we had placed an order with some other manufacturer.

9. Although your prices are quite competitive, the sample does not meet our specifications.

Close on a positive note:

10. We have asked for more quotations from other manufacturers. We shall take a final decision after taking their products' quality and prices into consideration.

11. However, next time we shall again invite quotations from you and hope that you will be prompt.

12. If you are able to supply us better quality material on the same price, we can renew our offer.

13. I shall now seek quotations from other dealers, but may find it necessary to refer to you again if their prices are not an improvement over yours.

Sample Letters
(Reply to First Inquiry)

Dear Sir,

Thank you for your letter dated May 23, 1999, inquiring about our domestic appliance range.[1] Since our goods are of high quality, our wholesale rates are a little higher than the market rates.[8] We are confident that you will be satisfied with the quality of our goods and will associate only with us for your future requirements.[22]

With thanks,

Yours faithfully,

(Reply to Inquiry about Advertised Goods)

Dear Sir,

We are happy to learn that you have noticed our advertisement in last week's Indian Express and The Times of India.[1] As the advertisement does not carry all the details, we enclose a printed folder enlisting our new line of products and their prices.[8] Our goods are always the same, as advertised. We are sure to satisfy you through our dealings.[17] We can arrange for a demonstration of our sewing machine at your convenience.[20]

Thanking you,

Yours faithfully,

(Reply to Request for Catalogue)

Dear Sir,

Thank you for your telephonic inquiry of last Tuesday regarding various transistors of our make.[2] As requested by you we enclose a copy of our detailed catalogue.[6] Our terms and conditions are printed on the back-cover of the catalogue.[20] As evident from the illustrated catalogue all our new models come in elegant cases.[26] We hope you will take advantage of our offer and place an early order.[35]

Thanking you,

Yours faithfully,

(Reply to Requests for Quotations)

Dear Sir,

Thank for your inquiry of August 3, regarding quotation for 100 'Executive' model office tables.[1] We hope you will find our rates reasonable and place an order with us.[6]

Thanking you,

Yours faithfully,

Business letters Promoting Goodwill

Apart from winning customers, business letters promote goodwill too. These are letters which are written when apparently there is no dire need for doing so. Writing such letters is part of official routine. However, care should be taken to keep in mind what are the customers' requirements, because customer deserves the best.

Goodwill letters should be courteous and cordial. A slight personal touch can work wonders. These letters should be precise and need not be too long.

Those engaged in sales promotion realize the real worth of correspondence building up goodwill. The best way to achieve customer's goodwill is to offer him the best services and look into his genuine complaints. Very often customer' letters of complaints are overlooked. It must be noted that goodwill letters promote mutual understanding and are of considerable help, in times of fierce competition. One has to have a constructive approach towards business. Such letters come in handy when important customers plan an expansion of their existing premises or seek a foreign collaboration. Sincere wishes and friendly approach can win many customers. For instance, an offer of credit in the event of a fire in customer's warehouse can win his life-long loyalty. These letters should be written by responsible officers of the company.

Manufacturer's Goodwill Letter

First of all, express pleasure over customer's inquiries :

1. Thank you for your inquiry dated May 10, 1999.
2. We are pleased to receive your letter dated August 8, 1999, inquiring about our hardware products.
3. We are pleased to have your letter of 3rd July 1999, seeking information about a variety of our plastic products.
4. We feel obliged to have received your letter of inquiry dated July 22, 1999.
5. We are glad to have received your note inquiring about the nature of polish used on our stoves.
6. We are pleased to know about your interest in our goods through your enquiry dated July 23, 1999.

Now come to the point:

7. As per your request we enclose our catalogue and price-list.
8. Accordingly, we are enclosing pamphlets of our various products.
9. This is our latest catalogue and we have tried to make it as attractive and exhaustive as possible.
10. This is our latest price-list and we hope it will convince you how competitive our prices are.
11. Through our representative, we are shortly sending a sample of our latest soap prepared by our manufacturing division.
12. The prices and particulars about various items mentioned in the enclosed catalogue and pamphlets will certainly answer your inquiries.

Now suggest some business aspects promoting goodwill :

13. You are most welcome to visit our factory whenever you are in Bombay.
14. We hope you would pay a visit to our factory so that we could show you our high-quality raw materials and excellent workmanship.
15. If you do not find it inconvenient, please join us for a seminar on the "Changing Patterns of Automotive Industry" hosted by the company at Ashoka Hotel on April 8, 1999 at 10 a.m.
16. We sincerely feel that the information you might collect on a visit to our factory would prove interesting as well as useful for your placing orders in future.
17. If you visit the current Trade-Fair at New Delhi please do not forget to call at our stall.

Close the letter offering your extra services :

18. If there is anything more we could do for you, please do not hesitate to write to us.
19. Please let us know how we can extend our services to you.
20. Please do not hesitate to say what else you would like to have from us.
21. Please let us know if we can be of any service to you, otherwise.
22. We are soon going to celebrate the silver jubilee of the company's inception. We will be soon requesting you to join us on the happy occasion.

Letter Explaining Late Reply

Begin with a slight touch of regret for delay :

1. I am extremely sorry for the delay in sending the catalogue and price-list requested by you in your letter dated October 8, 1999.

2. I am extremely sorry for the delay in replying to your letter of August 8, 1999.

3. I regret that because of the company's annual auditing I was tied up and could not reply to you earlier.

4. I express my regret for not giving a prompt response to your request of April 8, 1999 for a demonstration of our photocopier.

5. It is, of course, a lapse on our part that we could not respond promptly to your inquiry of May 9.

6. We are really sorry for the delay in replying to inquiries as per your letter of 15th July.

7. I am sorry, I could not reply to you earlier because I was out of station for more than two weeks.

Give reasons for delay:

8. Our new catalogue and price-list are expected within a fortnight and as soon as we receive the copies we will despatch you one.

9. The delay has occurred as I was on tour during the last week and could not attend to your request.

10. We have unexpectedly run out of samples, and as soon as they are replenished we will despatch you the ones you have asked for.

11. Our Technical Representative, who gives the demonstration, has reported sick last week, and so we could not arrange an early demonstration to you.

12. On account of some labour problem the work was disrupted and hence I cold not attend to your request earlier.

13. There was a strike notice from the labourers on some of their demands and thus we got delayed in replying to your inquiry.

Apologise again while closing the letter:

14. I hope you will bear with us for this short period of delay.

15. We hope you do not mind this delay on our part which will not recur.

16. I regret the inconvenience this delay has caused you.

17. A settlement between the management and the workers is in sight and I think by the beginning of next week we shall be in a position to send you the samples.

18. I honestly hold the responsibility for this delay, but request you to take it in good spirits.

19. This is the first occasion that we are at fault. So we hope you will not mind it.

20. It is, of course, a lapse on our part but we assure you that in future we will take care to meet on queries promptly.

Letter of Regret

Begin with conveying your pleasure :

1. Thank you for submitting your manuscript of "Business Letter Writing" to me.
2. Thank you indeed for the sample of your new cheese you have sent us.
3. I am grateful to you for the sample 'copy' you have prepared for the advertisement we plan to release soon.
4. You were certainly prompt in despatching your catalogue and price-list in response to our inquiry.
5. We appreciate your promptness in sending your representative for demonstration of washing machine.
6. Thanks for the sample of new detergent powder which you sent to us last week.

Express genuine regrets/inability:

7. I am, of course, impressed with the care with which you have written the book and I would have certainly accepted it for publication had we not released a book on a similar subject only last month.
8. Yours is definitely a fine product but unfortunately does not meet our requirements.
9. The advertisement 'copy' is definitely a sincere and a very good effort, but this is not the type of advertising we have in mind.
10. Your catalogue and price-list are, of course, informative but rather on the higher side and not suitable for the market in which we operate.
11. The demonstration performed by your representative was quite satisfactory, but we have postponed the project for the time being. I am sorry for our present inability.
12. Thank you for the promptness in attending to our inquiries but in view of certain unforeseen expenditure, I am sorry, at present we are unable to place the order.

Close the letter with a touch of regret :

13. I am, therefore, most regretfully returning your manuscript.
14. I am sorry for this negative reply.
15. I am sorry I am not in a position to utilise your services at the moment, but, I will definitely get in touch with you some time next month.
16. I am really sorry, we are not yet equipped to sell your fine product.
17. I hope our inability to place orders for your goods at present, will not disturb our good business relations.
18. I am sure we will continue to have business deals in future, despite this temporary gap.
19. We have filed your catalogue and hope to place orders at some appropriate time in future.

Letter of Regret for Oversight

Refer to the oversight:

1. It has come to our notice that the consignment sent to you on the 5th of the month has fifteen garments less than mentioned in our despatch letter.

2. We regret to inform you that the curtain material sent to you on the 8th of this month is of inferior quality to what you had ordered for.

3. This is to inform you of a mistake in the despatch of ten bone china tea-sets on the 10th of this month.

4. We regret to inform you that the 20 electric kettles despatched to you on 5th June are of the "medium" size while you had ordered for "large" size.

Express regret or concern:

5. We are, of course, extremely sorry for this oversight.

6. In fact, because of the oversight of the despatcher the lables of address on the boxes got changed.

7. In fact, our sales department followed the instructions given in your earlier letter and, by mistake, your second letter was overlooked.

8. The mistake is, of course, entirely ours and we deeply regret for it.

Now, talk of amends:

9. However, we have instructed our sales department to prepare a fresh consignment and despatch to you at the earliest. I hope you will receive it by the end of next month.

10. Please arrange to return the earlier goods at our expenses. The replacements are being despatched tomorrow.

11. We assure you that in future we shall not give you any cause to complain.

Sample Letters
(Manufacturer's Goodwill Letter)

Dear Sir,

We are pleased to have your letter of 3rd July, 1999, seeking information about a variety of our plastic products.[3] As per your request we enclose our catalogue and price-list.[7] You are most welcome to visit our factory, whenever you are in Bombay.[13] If there is anything more we could do for you, please do not hesitate to write to us.[18]

Thanking you,

Yours faithfully,

(Letter explaining late reply)

Dear Sir,

I am extremely sorry for the delay in sending the catalogue and price-list requested by you in your letter dated October 8, 1999. Our new catalogue and price-list are expected within a fortnight and as soon as we receive the copies we will despatch you one.[8] I hope you will bear with us for this short period of delay.[14]

Thanking you,

Yours sincerely,

(Letter of regret)

Dear Sir,

Thank you for submitting your manuscript on 'Business Letter Writing' to me.[1] I am, of course, impressed with the care with which you have written the book and I would have certainly accepted it for publication had we not released a book on similar subject only last month.[7] I am, therefore, most regretfully returning your manuscript.[13]

With regards,

Yours faithfully,

(Letter of regret for oversight)

Dear Sir,

It has come to our notice that the consignment sent to you on the 5th of the months has fifteen garments less than mentioned in our despatch letter.[1] We are, of course, extremely sorry for this oversight.[5] We assure you that in future we shall not give you any cause to complain.[11]

Thanking you,

Yours faithfully,

Business Letters of Thanks

Business relations often call for letters of thanks and appreciation. Such letters enlarge areas of influence and are profitable in the long run. The content has to weigh more in spirit than in letter. The art of writing a truly concise letter is a difficult one. One has to infuse the letter with a touch of goodwill, cordiality and friendship. This can be done in the opening paragraphs. Here are a few examples.

Opening paragraphs :

1. We received with thanks your order No....... dated.......
2. We acknowledge with thanks the receipt of your order No................
3. This is to thank you for your inquiry/order No...........
4. Thank you for your Order No........ dated..............
5. It gives great pleasure to receive your order..........

Some occasions for letters of thanks:

1. Getting an order from a new customer,
2. Getting large orders from old customers.
3. Getting prompt payments/remittances.
4. Getting useful promotional suggestions.

Getting an order from a new customer:

1. When you get an order from a new customer, send a personal letter of appreciation immediately. Such a letter should be written by a senior official. This will fetch a lasting goodwill.
2. Mention a definite date for executing the order.
3. Close the letter with a note of appreciation/goodwill and express your pleasure in serving your customer.

Getting large orders from old customers :

The old trade relations and customers are as important as the new ones. Due attention and recognition should be paid to letters and execution of orders. Here also the same methods can be followed as above besides the following.

1. Stimulate your customer's interest in your products by including some sales talk and selling points of the goods ordered by him.
2. Suggest the profits he can make from the sale of goods ordered by him.
3. Expectations of fresh orders should be given at the close of letter.

Getting prompt payments remittance:

Getting prompt payments are as important as getting orders. This keeps the business flow smooth. Therefore, it is necessary to express appreciation/gratitude over prompt realization of money.

Getting useful promotional suggestions:

These are the wholesale dealers or retailers who come in direct touch with the customers. And customers are the best judges of the products' quality. Their reactions go a long way in improving products' quality. Letters of suggestions, thus, should be acknowledged with appreciation.

Letter of Thanks for the First Order

Begin your letter with thanks:

1. Thank you for your order dated August 8, 1999. We shall be despatching 100 woollen blankets that you had ordered on next Monday i.e. 23rd August, 1999.

2. We acknowledge with thanks your order dated 13th November. We despatched the crockery yesterday and enclose herewith our invoice No.4321.

3. We are pleased to inform you that the glassware you had ordered on March 15, 1999, have been sent to you today by the passenger train reaching Delhi on 25th March.

4. Thank you for your order dated July 8, 1999, for 200 Oxford pocket dictionaries. The book will be despatched by the beginning of next week.

5. I hope you will receive your goods on next Monday definitely. We have despatched them through Kangaru Transport yesterday. I feel obliged in having executed this first order from you.

6. We feel proud to serve you for the first time and hope to establish good relations in future.

7. I am obliged for the opportunity you have given us, to have business transactions with you for the first time.

While closing the letter expect your customer to be satisfied:

8. We feel sure you will find the crockery up to the mark in every respect and perfectly suited to your needs.

9. We trust that the goods will reach you safely and in time and that you will be satisfied with the quality.

10. We hope to have further orders from you, in future too.

11. We look forward to serve you, in future too.

12. We hope you will be quite pleased with the goods and we can have pleasant and lasting business connections with you.

13. Please acknowledge the receipt.

14. May we hope that this order is a promising beginning of a pleasant and fruitful business relationship between us in the long run.

15. We hope this order will go a long way in creating an era of healthy business relations with you.

Letter of Thanks for Large Orders

Begin the letter with your appreciation/gratitude:

1. We appreciate the unusually large order for 'Weekend' shoes and thank you for your continued confidence in us.

2. This is just a personal note of thanks for the large order of dry battery cells you have placed with us. We appreciate your confidence in us.

3. Thank you for your large order dated 8th October for 'Deluxe' office tables. We are extremely pleased at your confidence is us.

4. We are thankful to you for such a substantial order of transistor sets and the trust you have maintained in us.

5. Our sales team is jubilant over the large order of 9th July for bed sheets that you have placed with us. We assure you of our prompt compliance of the same.

6. Your placing this large order for vegetable oil with us shows your good confidence resposed in us.

Discuss prospects of good business relations :

7. We have always valued our esteemed relationship built over years. And we will do our best to maintain it.

8. Our relationship with your firm has always been a matter of great asset for us, and we will do everything to strengthen it.

9. We have always regarded you as our esteemed customer. And we hope our relationship, built over years of mutual confidence, will grow further.

10. We assure you of our fullest co-operation in maintaining the past business relations between us.

11. We can assure you that despite your confidence in us there would not be any complacency on our part.

12. We have, in fact, always counted on you for big supplies.

While closing the letter convey your gratitude again:

13. Believe me, it has always been a great pleasure to deal with you.

14. Very soon we are planning a diversification of our business into hosiery industry and will despatch you samples as soon as they are ready.

15. Thank you again for this fine expression of your continued trust in us.

16. In the end, we extend our thanks for relying upon our prompt service and credit.

Thanks for Prompt Settlement of Accounts

Start the letter with thanks and a cheerful note :

1. This is to thank you for the prompt settlement of our accounts during the preceding year.

2. This is to express our sincere thanks for settling our bill promptly.

3. Thank you for the prompt settlement of our accounts during the preceding financial year.

4. We thank you for your promptness in settling all our outstanding bills despite the financial constraints your company is facing.

5. Ever since you have started our association, you have been very prompt in settling our accounts. We are indeed thankful to you.

Mention utility of promptness in payments:

6. It has eased our financial tightness as a number of bills were pending with us.

7. Your payment has been of great help to us at a time when we ourselves were facing heavy commitments connected with the expansion of our business.

8. The promptness in making the payments is indeed a proof of the high level of your business ethics.

9. Your prompt payment has come in handy as we had been planning to make some bulk purchases.

10. The promptness in settling the accounts is, of course, in keeping with your high reputation in this respect.

Expectations for cordial relations may be touched upon at the close of the letter :

11. We hope you will continue to give us the opportunity to serve you.

12. This promptness is a positive indication of our growing cordial relations.

13. It has always been a matter of great pleasure for us to be of some service to you.

14. This is our sincere hope that our business relationship will continue to grow in future, irrespective of the unintentional slips on our part.

15. I am sure we can count upon such good co-operation from you in future too.

16. It goes without saying that your co-operation will go a long way in establishing sound relationships with your suppliers.

Thanks for a Service Performed

Begin your letter with thanks:

1. Thank you for returning the draft of the catalogue, we propose to send to our customers, alongwith your detailed comments on it.

2. This is to sincerely thank you for your enlightening suggestions concerning the publicity folder we intend to publish soon.

3. This is a note of thanks for your valuable suggestions for improvement of our product's quality.

4. Thank you for contacting the transporter on our behalf.

5. Your tips for the boost of our sales will definitely help us modify and improve the quality of our product.

Discuss the services rendered:

6. We are indeed grateful to you for the trouble you have taken for us.

7. I realize how busy you are. And despite your pre-occupations you have taken out time for our job.

8. Your detailed examination of our proposal would indeed be useful to us.

9. I am sure your valuable suggestions will help us a lot in giving a thrust to our business activities.

10. The modifications you have suggested will certainly make our product more useful and popular.

Repeat your appreciation again at the close:

11. Thank you again for your very useful suggestions.

12. Please accept our thanks again for this kind service.

13. I hope we will be able to compensate for your valuable services in one form or another, in the near future.

14. We express our thanks for your valuable feedback.

15. Your ideas have indeed taken our publicity department by storm.

16. Perhaps, I will never be able to pay for the valuable services you have rendered us free of cost.

Sample Letters
(Letter of thanks for first order)

Dear Sir,

Thank you for your order dated August 8, 1999. We shall be despatching 100 woollen blankets that you had ordered on next Monday, i.e., 23rd August 1999. We trust the goods will reach you safely and in time and that you will be satisfied with the quality.[9] We hope this order will go a long way in creating an era of healthy business relations with you.[15]

With regards,

Yours sincerely,

(Letter of thanks for large order)

Dear Sir,

This is just a personal note of thanks for the large order of dry battery cells you have placed with us. We appreciate your confidence in us.[2] We have always valued our esteemed relationship built over years. And we will do our best to maintain it.[7] Thank you again for this fine expression of your continued trust in us.[15]

Yours faithfully,

(Thanks for prompt settlement of accounts)

Dear Sir,

Thank you for the prompt settlement of our accounts during the preceding financial year.[3] The promptness in making the payments is indeed a proof of the high level of your business ethics.[8] It has always been a matter of great pleasure for us to be of some service to you.[13]

Thanking you,

Yours faithfully,

(Thanks for a service performed)

Dear Sir,

Your tips for the boost of sales will definitely help us modify and improve the quality of our product.[5] We are indeed grateful to you for the trouble you have taken for us.[6] I hope we will be able to compensate for your valuable services in one form or another in the near future.[13]

With thanks,

Yours faithfully,

Sales Promotion Letters

Sales promotion calls for the basic knowledge of the product being marketed, the particular areas of its wide acceptance, effective distribution networks, smart and active representatives, flexible and competent management and good knowledge of the market conditions. No product can be successful just on the basis of publicity. Quality is a must. It is, therefore, imperative that the person handling sales correspondence is competent and keeps all these factors in mind. He must have a live wire understanding of all the involvements and implications of his approach in handling sensitive correspondence. A letter, of course, can make or mar the entire prospects of an upcoming business.

A good letter may cover the following points :

1. Stimulate interest.
2. Create the buying impulse.
3. Build confidence about the product.
4. Clinch the bargain.

Am effective sales letter should be easy to read and understand. The contents should be divided in short paragraphs. One should see to it that typing and stationery are clean. Certified and updated mailing lists for announcements and business circulars are essential for a progressive business house. The letter should be well-worded and posted in time.

A mistake in the letter can have an adverse effect on company's sales. A businessman is, of course, no writer or journalists, but he is certainly expected to be able to express himself well. The ability to choose the right words, and use them skillfully is essential for a good and effective correspondent. Punctuation, spellings, grammar, effective phrases and above all their meticulous use, make a world of difference in promoting sales.

Introducing a New Product

Begin with an introduction about the New Product:

1. May we take this opportunity to introduce to you our new can-opener/motor-cycle/filter which we have launched in the market.

2. This is to inform you of our new revolutionary concept in safety locks that we have recently marketed.

3. It is the result of painstaking research and exhaustive laboratory tests.

4. It is a major breakthrough that our engineers have achieved in automobile technology.

5. We are sure that the great utility and superb finish of the new product will convince you of its ready saleability.

6. Today, it is the best motor-cycle in the market in this price range.

Now build up confidence:

7. We have taken the liberty of sending you a sample of the product for your comments and reactions.

8. We have sent you a sample of this product and would welcome your putting it to test.

9. We will soon be despatching its sample and hope you will approve of its quality.

10. We have confidence that your inspection and testing of the product would prove to you the high quality of this product. And for this purpose you are welcome to our works anytime between 10.00 a.m. and 12.00 noon.

Discuss price range and business terms:

11. The enclosed folder is indicative of its competitive price.

12. We are giving 20% discount on orders of Rs.50,000 and above.

13. We can offer special terms even for your trial orders provided the orders reach us before the end of this month.

14. We can allow regular trade discount on a trial order if it is large enough.

Close the letter with an invitation for a trial order :

15. We hope that soon we will have a positive response from you.

16. So kindly send us a word by return mail.

17. When you call please ask for me.

18. As you wanted something of this kind we hope you will soon place an order with us.

19. We request you to place a trial order with us so that we can prove our efficiency.

Soliciting a Customer for a Product

Begin with asking customer's choice/selection:

1. Do you want pure and fresh butter at a moderate price?

2. Would you like to have a complete cooking machine that would save you time and energy by half?

3. Would you like to become popular with friends? /Do you have an inferiority complex? Are you suffering from a chronic disease?

4. Do you want to buy the latest exquisite variety of the best south Indian silk saris?

5. Are you on the look out for exquisite bone china crockery?

6. Do you want your dinner party to be a super success?

7. Do you plan to go on a vacation but would need better travel arrangements?

Mention your services/products:

8. The Pure Product Dairy will meet all your needs.
9. Then our 'Cook Master' is what you are looking for.
10. Become a know-all just by mastering our 'Treasure House of General Knowledge'.
11. Visit 'Silkalaya', our emporium, and see them all in a breath taking display.
12. Our exquisite, 50 piece dinner-set is the one for you.
13. All you have to do is to read our 'Fabulous Recipes'.
14. You can leave everything to us and just relax.

Give more details of available services:

15. Manufactured with the latest machinery, Delhi Dairy's butter has flavour and taste of its own.
16. Pure Product's butter is the proud owner of F.P.O mark of quality.
17. This unique domestic appliance is easy to handle and economical in power consumption.
18. At present it is in heavy demand and if you don't order for it fast our supplies might exhaust.
19. This fascinating digest brings you facts from all over the world to enrich your knowledge.
20. If you are looking for a treasure of knowledge in one place, this is the book for you.
21. All these saris are for you if you can make a choice.
22. Nowhere else will you find such exquisite saris at such reasonable prices.
23. The dinner-set will win all your guests' admiration and speak well of your taste.
24. In these exquisite pieces the art of the potter and the painter has come together in all its perfection.
25. The book is a real treat.
26. If you want to find international masterpieces of the culinary art at one place, this unique cookery book is what you are looking for.
27. We will treat you like a royal guest and plan minutest detail of your holiday meticulously.
28. Reservations, bookings, entertainment, tickets-we take care of everything.

Close your letter by insisting on definite business:

29. Lest you are late, please register with us by filling and posting us the enclosed form.
30. You are cordially invited to a demonstration of the machine at our factory, at your convenience.
31. We could let you have a copy on approval basis.
32. Just one visit is all you need to be fascinated.
33. You are most welcome to visit our shop any time and test our statement.
34. Book your copy before it is too late.
35. So, why don't you drop in at our office for a chat?

Soliciting a Customer for a Service

Begin your letter with a clear understanding of customer's requirements :

1. We have been informed by M/s Vishal Bharat Suppliers Ltd., that you are looking out for competent agents for clearing and forwarding of consignments.

2. It has been brought to our notice that you propose to publish a number of books next year, and that you are looking out for a good offset press.

3. I have been told by my friend, Mr. Suresh Jain, who is your Chartered Accountant that you are on the look-out for a representative with good contacts to handle your liaison work with the Government Departments in Delhi.

4. We understand from our client, Mr. Ramesh Gupta, that you require the services of a tax consultant for filing of your tax returns regularly.

5. I have been informed by one of your employees that you are looking out for a good part-time accountant.

Introduce your business standing and extend your services:

6. We have pleasure in placing our services at your disposal and providing you with the best facilities.

7. This is to inform you that our large printing establishment is capable of handling your publication programme.

8. You will be glad to know that I have been a liaison-officer with DCM for more than 10 years. And I am sure you can entrust me with your Delhi work.

9. I have been a practising tax-consultant now for more than 20 years, and it would be a pleasure for me to be of service to you.

10. I offer and guarantee you prompt and efficient service.

11. Our experience in this line has been of more than 20 years and we have been handling accounts of S.Kumars and Gopinath&Sons for the last 10 years.

12. Our staff is well-versed with the relevant procedures and all the work entrusted to us will be carried out with efficiency and promptness.

13. Enclosed are the details of our handling charges which are very competitive.

14. We have successfully handled similar work for other publishers too and it has been highly appreciated.

15. We also have modern computer typesetting facilities in our press.

16. Our rates for various types of printing jobs are enclosed herewith, which, you will find quite reasonable.

17. My contacts in this field have been profitably used by many leading business concerns.

18. For my professional experience and competence you can please refer to M/s. Machine Makers Pvt.Ltd., and M/s. Rang Nirman Pvt. Ltd., for whom I have done considerable work for this type.

19. I wish to inform you that several big and reputed concerns have appointed me their Tax Consultant.

20. I have 20 years experience to my credit as an accountant in various concerns.

While closing, express expectations of positive response:

21. We look forward to hearing from you.
22. I am sure you will be satisfied with our work.
23. I hope you will entrust this responsibility to me.
24. So, may I have the confidence that our association would prove mutually beneficial?
25. I would very much appreciate a trial of my services.

Manufacturer's Offer to Retailers

Begin with alluring offers:

1. Here is a fabulous offer. Research has now enabled us to offer you a large range of toilet soaps at highly reduced rates.
2. We are happy to announce that our increased production capacity has now enabled us to offer you our quality cosmetics at reduced rates for large orders.
3. Our researchers have recently developed a new high quality detergent powder which is much cheaper than the ones available in the market.
4. We have removed certain existing faults from our transistor-kits which were brought to our notice by our customers.
5. We are sure you will like our recently developed chemicals which are tested through a technical process developed by our scientists.

Give details of goods offered:

6. The details of price reduction are enclosed which comes to an average of fifteen percent.
7. As our prices are quoted c.i.f. Delhi you will agree that they are below those of all other manufacturers.
8. Moreover, we are offering 10% discount on purchase of Rs.25,000 and above.
9. You can easily find the increased rates of discount proportionate to the purchasing amount. We also give guarantee for one year for proper functioning of the appliance.
10. Although, of late, there has been a slight hike in our prices, our quality has also improved.

Other Relevant Topics:

11. The quality of our products, of course, remains unchanged.
12. You will see for yourself that the quality of our product has considerably improved.
13. Immediate despatch is guaranteed, as we have ample stocks.
14. In fact, these are the additional accessories which have some what pushed up its price.
15. You will find a slight rise in prices but it is due to the high cost of raw material.

Expectations of getting business:

16. We appreciate your confidence in us and look forward to serving you again.
17. We are sure that the new prices will encourage you to place still bigger orders with us.

18. We hope this new offer will put our relationship on a firmer footing.

19. We hope you will utilise this reduction to the maximum extent for the benefit of both of us.

20. We look forward to a big order from you as we feel our new product's quality speaks for itself.

Notifying Price Increase to Retailers

Announce the new prices and give reasons:

1. With effect from the 1st of next moth, the prices of all our products are being raised by 10%.

2. We regret to announce that on account of the hike in power rates, we are compelled to raise the prices of our plastic ware.

3. On account of the increase in overheads we have most reluctantly decided to raise the prices of our electric wires by 5% from the 15th of this month.

4. We are compelled to raise the prices of our items by 10% from the 1st of next month due to increased electricity charges.

5. Our new consignment will have an increase of 15%, due to the increased cost of raw materials.

6. We regret very much this increase which we have been compelled to resort to because of a directive from the All India Metal Product Manufacturers' Association.

7. We are extremely sorry for enhancing our products prices but a steep rise in the essential raw materials cost has forced us to take this unpleasant step.

8. We would certainly not have taken this step, had the Government not subjected our raw material to heavy duty in the new budget.

9. This increase has become unavoidable because of the rising cost of labour and raw material.

10. This hike is the direct impact of the heavy import duty recently imposed by the Government on our raw materials.

Assure good quality products:

11. However, please rest assured that there will be no change in the high quality of our products.

12. However, we are contending our case in the court of law and will bring down the prices once the Government gives us relief on it.

13. In the coming year, however, because of the expected better yield, the price of raw material might come down. Hence it could be a temporary increase.

14. You can, of course, rely without any doubt on our superior quality of goods, which has its own image in the market.

15. You can always return the goods if they are not up to your satisfaction.

Express hope of cordial business relations:

16. Our new price-list is under preparation and will be sent to you as soon as it is ready.

17. However, we are giving concessions to our old customers. And we will charge old rates for all orders received on or before 15th of next month.

18. We hope that our business relationship continues to be as cordial as before.

19. We assure you of the same prompt service as we have been rendering in the past.

20. We hope that this slight increase in prices will not make any difference to our good business relations.

General Sales Letter

Opening:

1. We are large scale manufacturers of leaf-springs and coil-springs and are taking the liberty of sending you a copy of our latest catalogue and price-list.

2. As you are our regular customer we have decided to make you a special offer.

3. We hope you will be interested in our latest plastic goods we have introduced in the market on the terms and conditions mentioned in the catalogue.

4. Having just made a special purchase of ready-made shirts on very favourable terms we are able to offer them to you at very attractive prices.

5. We have recently bought a large quantity of antique pieces at very attractive terms. And, we can offer them to you are very reasonable prices.

Closing:

6. We hope you will take full advantage of this exceptional offer.

7. We look forward to a large order from you.

8. We are offering you articles of the highest quality at a very reasonable price and hope you will take the opportunity to try it out.

9. We know that heavy demand of our books exists in the market. And so you will find an easy market for them.

10. We shall be pleased to send our representative to you on receipt of the enclosed enquiry form duly filled in.

11. We shall be pleased to welcome you to our show-room at any time to give you a demonstration.

Visits by Salesmen

Travelling salesmen are an asset to any company. They help to give a boost to the sales and popularize company's products. Very often they go out of station to explore markets. Thus, it is advisable that their visits are preceded by letters of introduction or details intimating about their visits.

Sometimes even senior officers of the company make business trips to further business interests. And in this context such letters acquire greater significance.

Sample Letters
(Introducing a new product)

Dear Sir,

This is to inform you about our new revolutionary concept in safety lock that we have recently marketed.[2] We have taken the liberty of sending you a sample of this product for your comments and reactions.[7] We can offer special terms even for trial order provided they reach us before the end of this month.[13] So kindly send us a word by return mail.[16]

Thanking you,

Yours faithfully,

(Soliciting a customer for a product)

Dear Sir,

Do you want to buy the latest exquisite variety of the best south Indian silk saris.[4] Come to'Silkalaya', our emporium and see them all in a breath-taking display.[11] All the saris are for you if you can make a choice.[21] Just one visit is all you need to be fascinated.[32]

Thanking you,

Yours faithfully,

(Soliciting a customer for a service)

Dear Sir,

I have been told by my friend, Mr. Suresh Jain, who is your Chartered Accountant that you are on the look out for a representative with good contacts to handle your liaison work with the Government Departments in Delhi.[3] You will be glad to know that I have been a liaison officer with the DCM for more than 10 years. And, I am sure you can entrust me with your Delhi work.[8] My contacts in this field have been profitably used by many leading business concerns.[17] So, may I express the confidence that our association would prove mutually beneficial.[24]

With thanks/regards,

Yours faithfully,

(Manufacturer's offer to retailers)

Dear Sir,

We are happy to announce that our increased production capacity has now enabled us to offer you our quality cosmetics at reduced rates for large orders.[2] Details of the price reduction are enclosed herewith which show an average reduction of fifteen percent.[6] Immediate despatch is guaranteed, as we have ample stocks.[13] We are sure that the new prices will encourage you to place still bigger orders with us.[17]

Thanking you,

Yours faithfully,

(Notifying price increase to retailers)

Dear Sir,

With effect from the 1st of next month the prices of all our products are being raised by 10%.[1] We are extremely sorry for enhancing our products prices but a steep rise in the essential raw materials cost has forced us to take this unpleasant step.[7] However, you can rest assured that there will be no change in the high quality of our products.[11] We hope that this slight increase in prices won't make any difference to our cordial relations.[20]

With thanks,

Yours faithfully,

(General Sales Letter)

Dear Sir,

We are large scale manufacturers of leaf springs and coil springs and are taking the liberty of sending you a copy of our latest catalogue and price-list.[1] We are offering you articles of the highest quality at a very reasonable price and hope you will take the opportunity to try it out.[8] Hoping to hear soon from you.

With thanks,

Yours sincerely,

(A follow-up letter)

Dear Sir,

In response to your enquiry dated July 9, 1999, we sent you our catalogue two months ago. We, however have not heard anything from you. Please note that our new mixer is a product of the latest technology. With the help of its accessories you can mix or grind a large number of food items. And in our bargain offer we are allowing 15% discount on large purchases. We hope you will avail of this opportunity. Assuring you of the best of our services.

With thanks,

Yours faithfully,

(Letter to save a lost customer)

Dear Sir,

It has been more than three months since we heard from you last. As our business has been fairly regular for the last two years. We have been wondering about this silence from your end. We hope this does not reflect your dissatisfaction with our quality or prices. However, we shall appreciate a frank reply in this regard and wish to know where we lack in satisfying our customers. As you know it has been our constant endeavour to better our service and quality. Moreover, our items have become much easier than before, on account of withdrawal of Government's duty on aluminium. Assuring you of best of our services.

With thanks,

Yours faithfully,

Orders for Goods

When an order for any goods is placed one must keep in mind various aspects of it, otherwise it can lead to delay and complications for both. Details of goods must be mentioned very clearly. There should be no confusion about the specifications, quantity, name of bankers and mode of transportation. The instructions are elaborated here.

1. Article, its quantity and quality :

If the product line is long it is advisable to mention numbers on the catalogue referring to your requirements. However, if there is no catalogue attached, one can clearly mention the specifications like size, colour, and quantity.

2. Packing :

For packing special instructions are a must. Different types of products come in different packings for convenience of transport. For instance, glassware and many chemicals call for a very thorough and specialised packing.

3. Delivery :

One must give very clear instructions about the delivery of goods. They can be sent through any convenient mode of transport like road, air or sea. The point of destination and date of delivery are again important points to be included. All these details are generally printed in a tabulated form to enable an easy and quick placing of order. Even the companies make suitable indenting forms or list of articles for easy placing of orders. It eliminates possibilities of omissions of important details.

General Letter for Placing Orders

1. We thank you for your letter dated 25th October, 1982 in response to our inquiry for the supply of 300 tea-cups and place the order for the following goods (list enclosed).

2. This is to confirm our telephonic conversation of this morning regarding the purchase of 15 portable Remington typewriters. We enclose an order for the same.

3. Thank you for sending your new price-list of 1st May. Hereby we place an order for the items listed below.

      200 White bedsheets   @ Rs.100 per item

      300 pillow covers   @ Rs.40 per item

4. As these items are urgently required by our customers we will appreciate if you send them immediately.

5. We agree to the prices you have quoted in your yesterday's letter and hereby request you to send the said goods immediately.

5. Please let us know if your offer of 15% reduction on these items still stands or not.

6. Please let us know if we can expect goods' delivery by 15th November.

7. Please send them by Kangaroo Transport which has an office in your city.

8. We hope to receive your advice of delivery by return post.

9. Please note that we would not be requiring the goods if delivered after 15th of next month as our customer leaves for abroad soon.

10. We shall be obliged for prompt delivery as the goods are needed urgently.

11. Since the crockery is a fragile item please see to it that packing is done properly.

12. A prompt execution of our order is solicited.

13. They can be sent through any goods train bound for Delhi.

Placing Order from Catalogue

First, indicate your requirements :

1. Please send me by V.P.P. the following machine tools as listed in your latest catalogue.

2. Thank you for your sending the catalogue. We have marked it for goods urgently required by us.

3. I have gone through your latest catalogue and request you to send the items listed against the following numbers.

4. The printed date of catalogue is June 1980. Please confirm if this is the latest one.

5. We need immediate delivery of the following items, as per your new catalogue.

6. We are sending our man tomorrow between 9-11 a.m. for a spot delivery of 200 electric shavers. He will carry the catalogue which is marked for the size and shape of the items.

Refer to delivery and payment :

7. Enclosed herewith is the cheque for Rs.50/- towards the total payment/advance mentioned in your letter.

8. I am enclosing herewith a crossed cheque of Rs.5000/- towards the part payment of goods.

9. Please acknowledge the receipt of this advance payment and despatch us the parcel.

10. Please let me know the mode of payment.

11. Our payments are exclusively through cheques or drafts. What is your preference?

12. We are very prompt in making the payments but only through banks. Our banker is Oriental Bank of Commerce.

13. We shall appreciate your giving prompt attention to this order.

14. We would like to make it clear that our payments are very prompt.

15. Please despatch the goods on receipt of this order.

16. Since we need the goods immediately, please do not delay.

17. We are making the payments in advance just to facilitate your sending the consignment at earliest. We know you have a tremendous regard for your old customers.

18. In case there is any hitch in the supply, please let us know immediately.

Placing Order for Advertised Goods

Make a mention of the advertisement :

1. I have seen your new tape recorder's advertisement in **The Hindustan Times** of August 4, and would like to place an order for one.

2. I have listened with keen interest to your advertisement of "Rapidex English Speaking Course" on radio. Please send me two copies by V.P.P.

3. I have come across your advertisement of 'Kitchen Master' and hereby place an order for one.

4. Advertisement of your detergent powder on the Delhi Television has convinced us about its good quality. Please supply the same as per our order.

5. I have been impressed by demonstration of your "Knit Master" in a television advertisement. I am placing order for one.

Give details of delivery :

6. Kindly send the books at the address given above.

7. Please despatch the article to the above address.

8. One of the two pieces is to be sent to my address given above and the other to the following name and address.

9. The address of the person, this is to be delivered, is as follows.

10. The moment you receive the advance payment of the item, please send it directly to the address given below.

11. Kindly execute this order immediately as I have to go out of station in the next week.

12. Please attend to this order urgently.

13. We can arrange for our truck to collect the goods from your Delhi office anytime it is convenient to you.

14. I would appreciate your promptness in sending the items mentioned in the order letter.

15. Please let me know in future too, about your new products.

Acknowledgement of an Order

Convey pleasure on getting the order :

1. We are pleased to have received your order No.123 for 20 immersion type water heaters.

2. We thank you for your order for 50 wall paintings (No.4B in our catalogue).

3. This is to acknowledge with thanks the receipts of your order for two dozen 'Constellation' neckties and matching hand kerchiefs.

Advice letter after executing the order :

4. It is, of course, your great favour to have given us a chance to serve you.

5. We thank you for this fresh order for our new items. We feel proud that you have appreciated our previous services.

6. As all the items were in stock, we have despatched them to you today by the passenger train.

7. Our workers are busy on your order and we hope the job will be completed well before the stipulated time.

8. The goods are being packed on a priority basis and will reach you within the next week.

Above details can be summed up as under :

9. The goods have already been despatch as per your orders. These have been sent by Mercury Transport and will reach you on Monday.

10. As per your request the goods are being flown to you by air.

11. We acknowledge with thanks your order of 5th May 1999, and enclose our invoice No. PL.840.

12. We are just awaiting a green signal from the shipping corporation. As soon as that comes we shall despatch the consignment.

13. Since your order was not large we have sent it through our representative Mr. Krishan Kumar and you will get the consignment by Tuesday.

14. We are pleased to inform you that goods against your order No.B-401 have been sent by goods train today.

15. Please note that the goods which you ordered on May 5, 1999 are now ready for despatch. We are awaiting your instructions.

16. We have instructed Messrs. Bharat Goods Movers to forward the under mentioned consignment to you by rail.

17. Since the staff of Air-India is on strike, we are planning to fly goods to you by some other airlines. We shall intimate soon the date of their arrival in your city.

18. The goods were sent to you this afternoon by express railway parcel.

19. To avoid the risk of breakage of glassware we have sent them by the road transport.

Close the letter with expectations of securing more orders :

20. We hope the goods will reach you in time and you will place more orders with us in future too.

21. We hope that the goods are to your satisfaction and will help us in establishing a lasting business relationship with you.

22. The goods are of very good quality and in view of our latest research we hope to give you better quality next time.

23. We trust the goods will reach you safely in good time and that you will be satisfied with them.

24. We have despatched them as per your instructions. But if in future you want them immediately, we could send them by air.

25. We hope you will be pleased with the goods and thus we can establish a strong and lasting business relationship with you.

26. We are pleased to inform you that the goods have been despatched today and hope for repeat orders.

Intimation of Goods Despatched

Advise despatch :

1. Please note that the 25 dozen sweaters you had ordered on 14th October, will be despatched to Bombay tomorrow by rail for shipment on S.S. Indian Trader which leaves for Colombo on 3rd December.

2. Enclosed herewith is our invoice for the 500 pieces of artificial wool blankets ordered on 6th February by you. The goods have been despatched to you by Kangaroo Transports yesterday.

3. The garments you had ordered for on 25th April have been despatched today by goods train to reach Bombay on 2nd of next month. Enclosed herewith are a copy of invoice and railway receipt.

4. In compliance with your order of 7th March, we have today sent the parcel of goods by passenger train and have forwarded the documents through your bankers, the Bank of India.

5. The crockery is being transported today by our trucks. And enclosed herewith is a copy of the bill.

6. We take pleasure in informing you that we have today sent the following goods as per your order by V.V.P.

Mention the documents enclosed or sent :

7. Enclosed herewith is our invoice and, we shall present shipping documents and our draft for acceptance through the Chartered Bank, as agreed.

8. We enclose herewith our invoice and draft for Rs.2,000 in your favour at 60 days'sight.

9. R/R No.508352 dated March 5, 1980 with a copy of your invoice No.158 has been sent to your Bombay office.

10. The R/R has been forwarded through Punjab National Bank, Karolbagh, New Delhi. It may be collected from its Head Office in Bombay.

11. The documents have been forwarded to you through your bankers and a copy of the invoice is enclosed herewith for your prior information.

12. Please honour the documents on presentation.

13. The remaining amount may please be paid on receipt of V.V.P.

14. Our bill No.541 for Rs.2198/- is sent herewith, in duplicate.

15. Please collect the R/R against payment.

16. As per our agreement we have surrendered the documents to Chartered Bank, Connaught Place, New Delhi, who have accepted our draft for Rs.2000/- at 60 days' sight.

Mention about the special features of consignment :

17. These sweaters have been manufactured from the finest lamb's wool especially for you. And we are sure you will find them worth the price.

18. Since the glassware are fragile items extreme care has been taken to pack them in straw and paper chippings.

19. The goods have been packed in four special cases lined inside with water proof cloth.

20. The machines are to your exact specifications and are securely packed in strong wooden boxes.

21. Each sewing machine has been tested again and again and carries five years' warranty.

22. Our technical representatives in Bombay will be pleased to advise you on any point of fitting or maintenance. They also hold an adequate stock of spare parts.

23. We are sure the goods will reach you intact.

24. If you find any manufacturing defect in any of the pieces you may kindly return them immediately.

25. We trust that the goods will reach you in excellent condition.

Closing the letter :

26. And we hope this is the beginning of a lasting business relationship between us.

27. We appreciate your trust in us and inclination to further business dealings.

28. We assure you that any further orders you may place with us will be attended to with similar care and attention.

Delay in Execution of Order

Begin by acknowledging the order and give reasons for delayed execution :

1. Thank you for your order for Mixers, dated November 8, 1981. We are sorry for the delay caused in the execution of the order on account of labour strike in the factory.

2. We are most thankful to you for your order for 500 pieces of item no.3 in our catalogue, but regret to say that there might be a slight delay in executing it because of its exceptionally heavy demand in the local market.

3. We are thankful to you for your order dated May 4, 19181 for 500 plastic buckets. But we regret to inform you that we might not be able to supply them by the end of the month as desired by you on account of power cuts.

4. We thank you for your order for 800 electric iron but regret that we cannot supply them immediately because of a recent fire which has extensively damaged our factory.

5. We are glad to receive your order of 2ⁿᵈ December, but very much regret that at present the make you have ordered is out of stock because of the exceptional demand for electric heaters in the prolonged cold weather.

6. Much to our regret, a strike of transport companies in Delhi is causing some delay in the despatch of a number of consignments, and the goods you ordered on 5ᵗʰ August are among those held up.

Requesting for more time for execution of order:

7. Soon, however, the work will resume in the factory as a settlement is being reached between the management and the workers. And we will be in a position to meet the demand.

8. We are, however, taking urgent steps to execute your order and shall be able to deliver the goods in not more than 15 days' time.

9. However, we hope to make the delivery in three weeks time and hope you will be bear with us till then.

Expecting the order to stand :

10. Please intimate if the delay is acceptable to you.

11. We do hope the slight delay will not be of too much inconvenience to you.

12. We would be grateful if you confirm your order as per the revised schedule.

13. We, of course, deeply regret this delay, but are helpless in this regard.

14. Meanwhile we apologize for the delay and trust it will not cause you much inconvenience.

15. As a new thermal plant is coming up in the district we hope the power supply will soon become regular thus enabling us to meet orders regularly without delay.

16. Meanwhile we deeply regret the delay and hope this will not affect our business relations.

Inability to Execute an Order

Begin with thankful acknowledgement :

1. Thank you for your order dated 8ᵗʰ May for 20 "Executive" leather chairs.

2. This is to express our thanks for your order dated 8ᵗʰ October, for 20 pieces of our "Tiptop" cooking tables.

3. We thank you for your order dated 9ᵗʰ September, for 500 "Toddler" baby frocks in assorted sizes and colours, with a request to deliver them by 14ᵗʰ of this month.

4. We are in due receipt of your order dated 2ⁿᵈ December, for 10 "Majestic" transistors/100 cutglass tumblers.

5. This is to confirm your order dated 8ᵗʰ November, for the delivery of 1000 embroidered ladies' handkerchiefs.

Regrets over inability :

6. We, however, have to express our inability in supplying the goods because of our earlier heavy commitments.

7. But we are sorry to admit that the tables/chairs requested by you are out of stocks.

8. However, we regret to inform you that we are unable to supply the requested goods as we have stopped manufacturing this make.

9. We regret to comply with your orders for being put in short supply of raw materials.

10. We are extremely sorry that we cannot supply the items as our production has suffered heavily on account of labour problems and we have many other earlier commitments.

Suggest alternatives :

11. But we could supply the same number of our 'Comfort' type junior executive revolving chairs, if you find them suitable.

12. However, plain glass tumblers of very high quality are available in case they meet your other requirements.

13. Perhaps Messrs Woodcraft, another leading office furniture makes, could fulfil your orders.

14. However, Messrs. Fancy Products might be in a position to meet your requirements.

15. However, we could probably meet your order after a few months.

Close the letter with the hope of repeat performances :

16. We sincerely hope you will give us another opportunity to be of some service to you.

17. However, we are sure the situation will improve soon and we will be in a position to meet more orders.

18. We hope this will not deter you from placing further orders with us in future.

19. However, despite this we look forward to a long and lasting relationship in future.

Offer of Goods on Approval

Begin with reference to earlier talks :

1. Confirming our telephonic conversation of this morning,

2. As per request by your Business Representative, Mr. Kamal Kishore, after discussions with our sales officer, Mr. Prem Gulati on the 3rd of this month,

3. As per instructions in your letter of 5th December.......

4. This follows the demonstration of our new electric toaster in front of your purchase officer.

5. After your talks with our representative and our samples test.......

Advice letter :

6. We are sending you, herewith on approval one toaster the retail price of which is Rs.225/- only.

7. .... we have despatched a parcel of 10 pairs of 'Nylotex' socks at the rate of Rs.9.50/- per pair.

8. .... we have despatched to you by goods train two lemon sets of our latest 'Royal Blue' variety.

9. We are shortly sending you 10 'Majestic' transistors through our representative.

10. We are despatching you five welding appliances.

Give reference of earlier talks/correspondence :

11. As agreed, we have arranged to leave the piece with you for a period of two weeks, and if by then you do not find a customer for it, it is understood that you may either return it to us at our expense or retain it at 30% discount on the retail price.

12. In case you retain the piece for more than a month we will require a settlement of accounts.

13. It is agreed that in case you are unable to sell these in one month from today you can send them back at our expenses.

14. Please note that the goods sent on approval can be accepted back only if received in good condition and within the stipulated time.

15. As per our agreement, if unsold, the goods will only be exchanged for other goods and not returned.

Request for Extension of Delivery Period

Express regrets over delayed delivery and give reasons :

1. This refers to your order No.314/52 dated 15th August, for supply of 500 sewing machines.

2. We very much regret to say that at present we are not in a position to execute your order, within a week, as per your stipulation.

3. We must reluctuantly request you to extend the delivery period of your order No.63/4 of April 1, for supply of 500 'Sharp' ball-point pens, by at least a month.

4. We shall feel obliged if you could favour us by extending the delivery period by only one week.

5. Kindly allow us to send your anticipated goods next week instead of this weekend.

6. In fact, recent transporters' strike has badly disrupted our deliveries and we are quite helpless in this regard.

7. Sudden strike by workers has affected our production badly. But, unfortunately a settlement between the management and the labour is in sight and we hope to supply the goods by next week.

8. The extension has become necessary because there is a temporary halt in our production due to the installation of new machinery. The extension has become necessary as there has been a temporary halt in production because of a fire in the factory recently.

At the closing, apologize again :

9. May we, therefore, request you to wait for at least two weeks more, by which time we will be in a position to supply the goods ?

10. We shall be grateful if you bear with us for this time.

11. We are, however, confident that we shall be able to effect the delivery by 15th of next month and hope that this schedule will meet with your approval.

12. We again apologize for this delay and hope that you will understand our position.

13. We hope you will realize that the delay is due to circumstances completely beyond our control and we shall very much appreciate if you allow us this additional time.

Substitute for Supplier's Order

Acknowledge order with a feeling of pleasure :

1. We are glad to learn from your letter dated 8th May that you wish to place order for 500 lace handkerchiefs/50 'Hi-Mod' T-shirts.

2. Thank you for your letter of 1th April, enclosing your order for 50 sky blue terene ready made shirts/'Blue Bird' T-shirts.

3. This is to thank you for your order for 50 'Playmouth' toy cars.

4. We are glad to receive your valuable orders for our plastic buckets.

Give reasons for offering alternate goods :

5. But, we are sorry to say that handkerchiefs ordered by you have been exhausted after we quoted for them. It will take around four weeks before we can get them ready.

6. We are sorry to say that on account of constantly changing fashions we have discontinued the manufacture of this dress material.

7. However, we can supply you the new dresses created by our designers, which have been highly appreciated by importers.

8. We have now new designs in readymade T-shirts which we can supply if you like them. Two samples are being sent to you.

9. You, of course, understand that in this fast changing world, we have to keep pace with it by bringing new designs and shapes.

10. As you required urgent execution of your order we have taken the liberty of substituting them with white cambric handkerchiefs of comparable quality.

11. If you do not have any objection we can supply you blue shade in the same material.

12. We, therefore, suggest that this product could be of greater interest to your clients and we can supply it in adequate quantities at short notice.

13. We can, of course, replace the toys cars by our new battery operated automatic 'flying car'. There is not much difference in the cost.

14. These new handkerchiefs have become very popular in our home markets.

15. The new transistors have been improved by our research and are much superior to the earlier ones.

16. These new toy cars are not only more attractive but are built to last longer.

17. At the rate of Rs.20/- a metre, this dress material is much cheaper than terene and is equally attractive in finish.

18. If you want the new longer lasting tools we can supply you these. The price is a little more than the earlier one but they are built to last.

Closing the letter:

19. Thus, we hope that this substitution is acceptable to you and will bring you more business.

20. We hope you can wait till then.

21. In case, however, you do not find it suitable you can return it at our expense.

22. However, if you are not satisfied with this substitute, we shall certainly take it back at our expense and replace it with your original requirement as and when it is available.

23. We are, of course, sorry for this change. And we hope you do not mind it.

24. We are, of course, looking forward to your appreciation of our new item.

Refusal to Reduce Price

Express regret and give reasons:

1. We have carefully considered your counter-proposal of 5th July, to our offer of children's woolen knitwear/glassware/decorative pieces but very much regret that we cannot accept it.

2. This refers to your request dated 8th July for reduction in our prices of stainless steel utensils.

3. Having given due thought to your proposal of 23rd April regarding a reduction in our prices for clutch-plates, we regret to say that it is not possible for us to accept it.

4. This is to express our inability to reduce our printing charges, in view, of high cost of labour and printing machines.

5. I am sorry to say that our prices are fixed. And therefore, we are unable to reduce them.

6. The steep rise in the cost of the raw materials has left us with no alternative but to slightly raise our rates.

7. The prices we have quoted in our letter of 3rd June, leave us with only minimum margin.

8. Our prices are in fact much lower than those of the same type of goods elsewhere in the market.

9. The cloth we use undergoes a special process that prevents shrinkage and increases durability.

10. In fact, we are unwilling to compromise on the question of quality. And as a result of that, our rates are slightly higher than the market rates.

11. As we have already agreed to a large discount, a further reduction is not possible.

12. As you know that these ivory pieces call for special workmanship it is not possible to cut down their prices.

Expectations of maintaining cordial relations:

13. If you are still interested in our original offer, please drop us a line.

14. We shall always be glad to hear from you and consider any proposals that might lead to business between us.

15. We hope this inability on our part to reduce prices does not affect our future business relationship.

16. We, however, look forward to your co-operation in future.

17. We hope you will understand our helplessness in this regard and give us an opportunity to serve you.

18. We will be always glad to serve you in future.

Cancelling an Order

Begin with giving reference of order placed:

1. Please refer to our letter dated 30th June, placing an order for 15 medium sized steel almirahs/steel sheets/picture-tubes.

2. Your Delhi representative, Mr. Arun Kumar, must have informed you about our desire to buy 10 dozen brass belt-buckles listed as "Deluxe" in your catalogue.

3. We had given you an order for supplying us 10 barrels of mustard oil at Rs.18/- per kg by the 30th of this month.

4. This refers to my telephonic conversation with your sales manager regarding purchase of 20 reams of lucky parchment.

5. Please refer to our order placed with your representative, Mr. Man Mohan, on the 1st of this month for the supply of 100 ink bottles of 800 milli litre.

Reasons for cancelling order:

6. Kindly treat the order as cancelled as the labour has gone on a lightning strike and at the moment we do not need the raw material.

7. I regret to inform you that the order now stands cancelled as per this letter.

8. We regret sending telegram to you cancelling the order as the delivery period has expired long ago.

9. We are compelled to cancel our order for 10 television picture-tubes as you are not in a position to meet our specifications.

10. The cancellation has become necessary because the delivery schedule suggested is not acceptable to us.

11. The necessity had arisen in view of the sheer oversight of our store-keeper who missed to register five dozen belt-buckles received by us last month.

12. It is because till now we have not received the goods nor any reply from you although the time of delivery has expired.

13. As we have got a much lower quotation from "Laxmi & Co.," for the same quality of almirahs we would like to cancel this order if they have not been despatched so far.

14. However, we have got stocks of an outgoing concern at much lower rates immediately and at the same time you have expressed inability to begin supplies till next month.

15. We have been compelled to take this decision in view of the latest market reports about fall in prices of this oil as a result of heavy import of a substitute.

Apologies and assurance for maintaining cordiality:

16. However, in three months time we are likely to require replenishment of our stock and then we shall endeavour to make good the loss.

17. We shall send you our instructions for other supplies in due course.

18. We again apologise for the inconvenience caused to you and assure you of further orders from us.

19. In case you have incurred any loss on this account, you may please debit it against our next bill.

20. Should you incur any loss on this account, we will arrange to reimburse the same as early as possible.
21. In order to compensate the loss sustained by you on this account we shall favour you shortly with an order for other items required by us.
22. Please, again accept our apologies.

Request for Forwarding Instructions:

Indicate about the position of order:

1. We are pleased to confirm that 25 portable "Deluxe" typewriters you had ordered on 18th April, are ready for despatch.
2. Please note that 2 tonnes of tea you had ordered on 2nd February, have been made ready for the final delivery.
3. We are happy to inform you that 200 yards of rayon you had ordered on 8th July have been ready for despatch.

Now request for instructions from buyer:

4. At the time of placing the order you had stressed upon the need of fast delivery and we are happy to inform that we have been able to improve on it by a few days.
5. Now, we are waiting for your shipping instructions to despatch the goods.
6. The arrangements have already been made for their despatch by passenger train. We are just awaiting your instructions.
7. Arrangements for shipment c.i.f. Hong Kong, have already been made with Modern Shipping Corporation.
8. We shall arrange for the shipping documents to be sent through Chartered Bank against our draft for acceptance, as agreed earlier.

Now closing hoping for a lasting business relationship:

9. We hope the goods reach you in perfect condition and in time.
10. As soon as we receive a word from you, we shall despatch the goods.
11. Thus, please inform us at the earliest regarding further action.
12. We appreciate this opportunity to serve you and look forward to more business with you.

Sample Letters
(General Letter for Placing Order)

Dear Sir,

We thank you for your letter dated 8th October, 1982, in response to our inquiry for the supply of 300 tea cups and place the order for the following goods (list enclosed)[1]. Please let us know if we can expect goods delivery by 15th November.[7] We shall be obliged for prompt delivery as the goods are needed urgently.[11]

Thanking you,

Yours faithfully,

(Placing order form catalogue)

Dear Sir,

Thank you for your sending the catalogue. We had marked it for goods urgently required by us.[2] We shall appreciate your giving prompt attention to this order.[13]

With thanks,

Yours faithfully,

(Placing order for advertised goods)

Dear Sir,

I have seen your new tape recorder's advertisement in 'The Hindustan Times' of August 4, and would like to place an order for one.[1] Please despatch the article to the above address.[7] Kindly executive this order immediately as I have to go out of station in the next week.[11]

Thanking you,

Yours faithfully,

(Acknowledgement of an order)

Dear Sir,

We are pleased to have received your order No.123 for 20 immersion type water heaters.[1] It is, of course, your great favour to have given us a chance to serve you.[4] As all the items were in stock, we have despatched them to you today by the passenger train.[6] We hope the goods will reach you in time and you will place more orders with us in future too.[20] The goods are of very good quality and in view of our latest research we hope to give you better quality next time.[22]

With thanks,

Yours faithfully,

(Intimation of goods despatched)

Dear Sir,

Please note that 25 dozen sweaters you had ordered on 14th October, will be despatched to Bombay tomorrow by rail for shipment on S.S. Indian Trader which leaves for Colombo on December 3rd.[1] Enclosed herewith is our invoice and we shall present shipping documents and our drafts for acceptance through the Chartered Bank, as agreed.[7] These sweaters have been manufactured from the finest lambs' wool especially for you. And we are sure you will find them worth the price.[17] And we hope this is the beginning of a lasting business relarionship between us.[26]

With thanks,

Yours faithfully,

(Delay in Execution of Order)

Dear Sir,

We are thankful to you for your order for 500 pieces of item No.3 in our catalogue, but regret to say that there might be a slight delay in executing it because of its exceptionally heavy demand in the local market.[2] We are, however, taking urgent steps to execute your order and shall be able to deliver the goods in not more than 15 days time. We hope that the slight delay will not be of too much inconvenience to you.[11] We would be grateful if you confirm your order as per the revised schedule.[12]

Thanking you,

Yours faithfully,

(Inability to execute an order)

Dear Sir,

Thank you for your order dated 8th May, for 20 "Executive" leather chairs.[1] We, however, have to express our inability in supplying the goods because of our earlier heavy commitments.[6] But we could supply the same number of our 'Comfort' type junior executive revolving chairs, if you find them suitable.[11] We hope this will not deter you from placing further orders with us in future.[18]

With regret,

Yours faithfully,

(Offer of goods on approval)

Dear Sir,

This follows the demonstration of our new electric toaster before your purchase officer, Mr. Gopal Srivastava.[4] We are sending you herewith on approval one toaster the retail price of which is Rs.225/- only.[6] As agreed, we have arranged to leave the piece with you for a period of two weeks, and if by then you do not find a customer for it, you may either return it to us at our expense or retain it at 30% discount on the retail price.[11]

Thanking you,

Yours faithfully,

(Request for extension of delivery period)

Dear Sir,

This refers to your order No.314/52 dated 15th August, for supply of 500 sewing machines.[1] We very much regret to say that at present we are not in a position to execute your order within a week, as per your stipulation.[2] In fact, recent transporters' strike has badly disrupted our deliveries and we are quite helpless in this regard.[6] May we, therefore, request you to wait for at least two weeks more, by which time we will be in a position to supply the goods.[9] We again apologize for this delay and hope that you will understand our position.[12]

With regret,

Yours faithfully,

(Substitute for suppliers' order)

Dear Sir,

We are glad to learn from your letter dated 8th May that you wish to place order for 500 lace handkerchiefs with us.[1] But, we are sorry to say that handkerchiefs ordered by you have been exhausted after we quoted for them. It will take around four weeks to get them ready.[5] As you required urgent execution of your order we have taken the liberty of substituting them with white cambric handkerchiefs of comparable quality.[10] These new handkerchiefs have become very popular in our home markets.[14] Thus, we hope that this substitution is acceptable to you and will bring you more business.[19]

Thanking you,

Yours faithfully,

(Refusal to reduce price)

Dear Sir,

This refers to your request dated 8th July for reduction in our prices of stainless utensils.[2] I am sorry to say that our prices are fixed and, therefore, we are unable to reduce them.[5] We, however, look forward to your co-operation in future.[16]

Thanking you,

Yours faithfully,

(Cancelling an order)

Dear Sir,

Please refer to our letter dated 30th June, placing an order for 15 medium sized steel Almirahs.[1] I regret to inform you that the order now stands cancelled as per this letter.[7] It is because till now we have not received the goods nor any reply from you although the time of delivery has expired.[12] We shall send you instructions for other supplies in due course.[17]

With regret,

Yours faithfully,

(Request for more information)

Dear Sir,

Thank you for your order of 22nd February for the supply of 20 pairs of "Weekend" shoes of size 8. The shoes are in our stock but before their despatch we would like to know about the colour you wish to have. They are available in three colours, namely beige, light brown and dark brown. As soon as we receive your instructions, we shall despatch the goods.

Thanking you,

Yours faithfully,

Letter of Complaints and Adjustments

Every business has problems to grapple with and difficulties to overcome. These problems may be complaints which come from different quarters. They can be about poor services, damaged goods, billing mistakes, undue delay in supply, discourteous treatment and so on.

As in business one cannot afford to lose temper, the complaints call for tactful handling. The letter should be well-worded and smack of good manners.

Thus while writing a letter of complaint or adjustment, the information about dates, order numbers, invoice numbers, description of goods and quantities must be specific. One must check up ones' reference properly. Unpleasant words like dishonest, careless, unfair, false etc., should be avoided. Confine your complaint to statement of facts and a polite enquiry as to what your supplier proposes to do about it.

Some occasions for writing complaints making claims are:

i. Delayed delivery of goods upsetting sales plans.
ii. Arrival of goods in damaged condition.
iii. Receiving goods other than those ordered.
iv. Difference in quantity/quality from that ordered.
v. Price charged higher than quoted.
vi. Unsatisfactory service.
vii. Goods delivered at the wrong place.
viii. Discourtesy shown by the staff of shop/office.
ix. Mistakes in a bill.
x. Breach of other terms and conditions.

Points to be remembered while complaining:

1. Promptness in making complaint.
2. Cause of complaint and your concern about it.
3. Details of order number, invoice number and other relevant details.
4. Asking for cause of delay and your further instructions about acceptance/cancellation.
5. Any inconvenience caused to you.
6. Your suggestions for adjustments, making up the loss or damage in transit etc.

Letter of complaint

M.M. Gupta,
45, D.N. Road,
Bombay-400 002
25th April, 2000

M/s. Modern Furniture Company,
6671, M.G. Road,
Calcutta.

Dear Sir,

Please refer to my letter dated 20th February, placing an order for a walnut table with six chairs. I am sorry that despite your promise to supply it within three weeks I have not received it.

In case the delivery is not made within two weeks, I will be compelled to cancel the order.

Please let me know at your earliest whether you will be able to deliver the furniture within the specified time.

Thanking you,

Yours faithfully,

M.M. Gupta

(Reply to complaint)
Modern Furniture Company
6671, M.G. Road
Calcutta.

28th April, 1999

Mr. M.M. Gupta.
45, D.N. Road,
Bombay-400 002.

Dear Mr. Gupta,

We received this morning your letter of April 25. I am sorry to learn that the dining table and chairs have not been delivered to you yet and regret the inconvenience caused to you.

The furniture was despatched by a truck of Rajput Transport on March 28 and should have been delivered latest by 8th April. I feel the delay is because of some transit problems.

We have checked with the transporters and have been assured that the furniture will reach you within a week. Please accept our apologies for the delay and our appreciation for bringing the matter to our notice.

Thanking you,

Yours faithfully,

(G.Malhotra)
 Manager

Complaint to Supplier about Non-delivery

Begin with reference to order number and its date etc:

1. I sent you an order for 50 copies of "Rapidex Professional Secretary's Course" on 5th June.
2. Please refer to our letter dated 3rd July, placing an order for two dozen Kashmiri silk saris.
3. Vide our letter No.B-14 dated 27th August, we had placed an order for 50 velvet cushion covers of standard size in four colours — blue, red, pink and orange.
4. This refers to our order No. C-18, dated 3rd September, 1999 for 100 battery eliminators.
5. We had sent you a letter requesting for supply of 25 'Super Tone' transistor sets on 11th August.
6. While placing the order we had stressed upon immediate delivery of books as the new sessions start on 25th June.
7. We had ordered for them as we planned to participate in a sari exhibition at Grand Hotel here.
8. As we were expecting to receive them in a week's time, we had made commitments to our retailers accordingly.
9. This order is for a friend settled abroad who is currently here and plans to leave the country within a week.
10. We believed that you would send the material within the stipulated time.

Give information about non-delivery of goods:

11. But, we are sorry to say that we received neither the books nor any intimation regarding the delay.
12. But, till today we have not received the goods.
13. So far we have not received any information from you regarding the supply of the material.
14. But, despite our reminders we have not received the supply.
15. We are sorry to inform you that we have not heard anything about the order we placed with you last week.
16. We are compelled to write that we have waited long enough for the ordered goods but failed to receive them so far.

Write about the inconvenience caused due to non-delivery:

17. As the session is about to start, the non-availability of books is going to cause great inconvenience.
18. As these items are urgently required, the delay will result in potential loss of business to us.
19. If the saris do not reach us within ten days, we will not be able to participate in the exhibition.
20. A lot of important work has been held up because of the non-delivery of this essential equipment.
21. As he is due to leave the country soon we request an immediate delivery of the goods.
22. However, we are prepared to wait till 15th January by which date we must receive the delivery of goods in full.

23. Please ensure a fast delivery to enable us to keep our commitments and maintain our image in the market.

24. As the goods have to be shipped we must receive them within a weeks' time. In case of non-delivery the order will stand cancelled.

25. This delay has caused us a lot of inconvenience, requiring many awkward explanations to our customers.

26. We would like to inform you that the goods are for export and the last date of shipment on the L/C is January 5, 1999.

Request for an early reply:

27. We shall be glad if you take an urgent step in this regard.

28. So, please let us know by return post by which date our order will be executed.

29. If we do not receive any intimation from you regarding delivery, we will consider it as cancelled.

30. Be kind to inform us immediately about the delivery of goods.

31. We shall be obliged to get a note from you on the supply position.

Complaint to Carrier about Non-delivery

Advice of non-delivery of goods:

1. We regret to inform you that the consignment of three packages of woollen blankets sent through you and addressed to M/S. Sunil Kumar & Co., Connaught Place has not yet been delivered.

2. This is to inform you that two packages of printed books from M/s Pustak Mahal were booked from Delhi by Frontier Mail bound for Bombay Central on March 5, 1999, vide R/R No.383349. But, despite a lapse of one week they have not reached the destination.

3. Our consignors, M/s. Yantra Machine Works, Bombay, had booked two boxes containing machinery parts at Patna by Tinsukhia Mail bound for Delhi. But, your parcel office at Delhi informs us that the goods have not yet been received.

4. We are sorry to say that the goods sent from Bombay to Delhi have not reached so far. The details are as under.

5. On March 5, 1999, we had booked goods with your Delhi Transport Office vide order No.B-18, but, they have not reached their destination yet.

Details of goods despatched:

6. The packages were delivered at your office on 2nd February for despatch by Passenger Train and should have been delivered at its destination by 5th February. The receipt No. is 2453.

7. The R/R against which the goods were booked bears No. DA/22456.

8. The parcels were duly booked at your booking office, New Delhi Railway Station, on November 15, as per R/R No. RB/22068 dated November 15, 1999.

9. Our sales representative, Mr. Sudhir Malhotra had booked the consignment with your Operation Incharge, Mr. Bal Kishore, on 8th April. The booking order No. is CA/8242.

10. Refer to your R/R No.972816 dated 2nd August 1999, regarding the material booked for Lucknow.

Request for tracing the goods:

11. Since we urgently need the goods, please try to trace them out.

12. Thus, please check up the whereabouts of the goods and inform us within a week.

13. As we require the goods within a week for distribution, please locate them immediately so that we can go ahead with our programme.

14. Kindly find out the reasons for non-delivery of the goods and inform us immediately.

15. Our important sales have been help up because of this non-delivery. Please take action in this regard immediately.

Complaint reg. Late Delivery

Inform about delayed delivery:

1. This is to bring to your notice the late delivery of ten 20kg boxes of Assam tea ordered on 3rd August.

2. Although you had promised the delivery of jeans by 5th of this month we received the supply only on 30th.

3. We had learnt from your representative that our order, placed with him, would be executed positively in the first week of this month, but we received the goods only today, at the end of the second week.

4. This refers to our order for 200 neckties, placed with you on 8th April. Please note that the supply has been received today after one month.

5. We had ordered for 10 dozen 'Sharp' ball-point pens on 8th May and requested for their supply within a week.

6. I regret to inform you that the goods reached us four weeks after the requested date of supply.

Write about similar delays in the past also:

7. Unfortunately, there have been similar delays in the past also.

8. I am sorry to point out that on various previous occasions also there have been such delays.

9. We have noticed that of late, such delays on your part have become more and more frequent.

Discuss the extent of loss due to delay:

10. This compels us to say that if such circumstances prevail, it will be difficult for us to have business dealings with you.

11. Under these circumstances it may not be possible for us to continue our business with you.

12. The goods have arrived after our customer has cancelled the order. As a result we have incurred substantial loss.

13. Please understand that the delay in delivery has been eroding our customers' faith in us.

14. Our own reliability in respect of deliveries of goods to our customers depends upon the punctuality of our suppliers like you.

At the close of the letter again lay stress on time-bound order:

15. We hope you will understand our position. Now onwards we will rely only on punctual supply of the orders.

16. We hope you will be more careful in future, stick to delivery schedules and give us no more cause for complaints.

17. We hope we would not get another occasion to complain, in future.

18. We shall be glad if you look into the matter at once and let us know the reasons for the delay.

19. Please note the order stands cancelled if the goods do not reach us by the end of next week.

20. We feel there must be some explanation for this delay and await your reply with interest.

Report on Damaged Goods

Begin by informing about the damage noticed:

1. We received a consignment of three packages of woollen blankets from you on 2nd March, as per our order. But, at least four blankets are in damaged condition.

2. We are sorry to inform you that of the parcel of nylon socks you sent on 15th of this month, at least 10 pairs were soiled and partially torn.

3. On 15th of this month we received 200 glass tumblers from you. But because of improper/ careless packing, at least 40 of them have got broken in transit.

4. This refers to your delivery of 50 cricket bats on 14th April. But, the handles of at least ten of them are coming off.

5. We are sorry to report that package No.15 containing glassware/Hydrogen peroxide despatched under our instructions of 15th March was received in a badly damaged condition.

6. And as the waterproof covering of the package was torn, six blankets got soiled. We will have to get them dry-cleaned before we can sell them.

7. As a result of careless packing some of the chemical solution has spilled in the package.

8. Although the package containing the goods appeared to be in perfect condition when unpacked, some of them were found broken. I am sure that this damage is the result of rough handling in transit.

Then ask for replacement or compensation:

9. Will you, please therefore, arrange to send replacement immediately and charge to our account?

10. As the sweaters were bought on 'ex-works' terms, we realise that the responsibility for damage is ours and we have taken up the matter of compensation with the railway authorities.

11. So please despatch the replacements soon at your cost and take up the matter with your transporters.

12. Please fix the responsibility for this damage and let us have immediate replacements.

13. We assume you will take up the matter with the transporter at your end.

267

14. Alongwith this letter we are sending you back the damaged socks.

15. Meanwhile, I have kept the damaged tumbler aside, in case you need them to support your claim with the railways for compensation.

16. We have also registered a complaint with the transporter and he has promised to settle the issue with you.

17. Upon learning the extent of damage we will write to you again.

18. Since this chemical solution calls for skilled packing, please be careful in its packing next time.

19. We will appreciate your sending us credit note for the value of the damaged items.

20. We feel we can share the value of damage amongst ourselves.

Complaint reg. Inferior Quality

Begin by informing about the inferior quality of goods supplied:

1. This refers to our order for 500 clutch plates/cardigans/hand-tools/electric heaters, dated 25th July.

2. We have received the delivery but are sadly disappointed with its quality.

3. We feel there has been some mistake in despatch on your part.

4. The clutch plats you have sent, are not of our specification.

5. We regret to inform you that your consignment of nylon threads of the 6th January, has not been satisfactory at all, in quality.

6. The goods appear to be sturdy but their finish is very poor.

7. When we came to examine the goods received against our order No.583 of June 3rd, we found that their finish was not at all as per our expectations.

8. Many customers have complained to us about the poor quality of fountain-pens supplied by you on 25th July.

Discuss inconvenience caused due to inferior quality of goods:

9. As a result, we are not in a position to offer these goods for sale.

10. It is not in accordance with our business standards to sell such inferior goods.

11. It is really unfortunate to have received such material in a trial order.

Mention further suggestions:

12. Consequently, we are left with no other alternative but to ask you to take the goods back and replace them with those of better quality.

13. If you cannot accept the goods back, you can send us the revised rates.

14. We are returning herewith the defective items and expect you to send us items of the quality we require.

15. If you get us the replacement we can extend the delivery period by two weeks.

16. In view of our long business relationship we hope you will be prepared to make some allowance for the inferior quality of goods.

17. We are sure, in view of our long business relationship, you will adopt an accommodating approach towards this and replace the goods/accept the goods back.

18. And we hope, in future we won't have any occasion to complain.

Complaint reg. Short Supply

How to begin:

1. We thank you for the prompt execution of our order No.L.314 dated 20th April. But while we had ordered for 20 immersion rod heaters, we have received only 10 in the package delivered to us.

2. On 20th of this month, we got the supply of 20 pairs of socks vide our order No.SVT/ADT/M-20, but we had ordered for 30 pairs.

3. Thank you for sending the shirting material we had ordered, but we have found on measurement that it is only 30 metres in length and not 35, as we required, vide our order No. M-14 of 23rd February.

4. I would like to point out that some articles, as per our order, are not found in the package delivered to us today.

5. Moreover, we have not received any intimation about the short supply.

Ask reasons for short supply:

6. Please let us know about the reason for such short supply.

7. Your transporter was unable to explain this short supply.

8. The consignment is not accompanied with an explanation from you.

9. And also please intimate when we might get the rest of the supply.

10. The cost of the missing articles will be deducted from the next payment.

Request for making up the deficiency:

11. We still need the rest of the goods. Please let us know how fast you can send them.

12. You are, therefore, requested to make good the shortage at the earliest.

13. As our customer is soon leaving for abroad, please deliver the rest of the goods at the earliest.

14. We will feel obliged if you can supply the missing articles at once or issue a credit note.

15. Thus, may we ask you to please find out the reasons for this short supply and compensate?

Complaint Against Incomplete Work/poor Services

Start the complaint giving a few facts:

1. On 8th July I received through your representative Mr, Ram Kumar, my Philips cassette recorder sent to you for repairs last month.

2. Last Monday, your Service Engineer, Mr. Gopal Sharma came to check up the faults in our Kelvinator refrigerator.

3. On 5th July I left my defective radio at your shop for repairs.

Now complain about unsatisfactory work:

4. Since he could not rectify the defect on account of lack of equipment he left with a promise to come the next day.

5. And when I played the recorder yesterday, I found that the old defect was still persisting. The recorder often produces a strange sound and the tape gets struck on its head.

6. At that time I had explained to your service engineer the defects in detail. Yesterday I received its delivery and surprisingly it has gone from bad to worse.

Refer to further complications, if any:

7. And since then the refrigerator has been lying like that and we are greatly inconvenienced.

8. Earlier its recorder had been running although at a low volume. But now the disc refuses to move.

Request for a prompt action in this regard:

9. I would request you to take an immediate action in this regard and send your engineer at the earliest.

10. Since the defect has not been rectified, mainly because of your negligence, please arrange to pick up from my place and do the needful.

11. I shall drop it at your shop at my convenience and request you to mend it by an early date.

Sample Letters
(Complaint to supplier about non-delivery)

Dear Sir,

I sent you an order for 50 copies of 'Rapidex Professional Secretary's Course on 5th June.[1] While placing the order, we had stressed upon immediate delivery of books as the new session starts on 25th June.[6] But, we are sorry to say that we neither received the books nor any intimation regarding the delay.[11] As the session is about to start, non-availability of books is going to cause great inconvenience.[17] So, please let us know by return post by which date our orders will be executed.[28]

Thanking you,

Yours faithfully,

(Complaint to carrier about non-delivery)

Dear Sir,

Our consignors M/s. Yantra Machine Works, Bombay, had booked two boxes containing machinery parts at Patna by Tinsukhia Mail bound for Delhi. But your office at Delhi informs us that the goods have not yet been received.[3] The R/R against which the goods were booked bears No.DA/22456. As we require the goods within a week for distribution, please locate them immediately so that we can go ahead with our programme.[13]

Thanking you,

Yours faithfully,

(Complaint reg. late delivery)

Dear Sir,

This is to bring to your notice the late delivery of ten 20 kg boxes of Assam tea ordered on 3rd August.[1] I am sorry to point out that on various previous occasions also there have been such delays.[8] This compels us to say that if such circumstances prevail, it will be difficult for us to have business dealings with you.[10] We hope you will understand our position. Now onwards we will rely only on punctual supply of the orders.[15]

With thanks,

Yours faithfully,

(Report of Damaged Goods)

Dear Sir,

We received a consignment of three packages of woollen blankets from you on 2nd March, as per our order. But, at least four blankets are in damaged condition.[1] And as the waterproof covering of the package was torn, six blankets got soiled. We will have to get them dry-cleaned before we can sell them.[6] Will you please, therefore, arrange to send replacements immediately for the damaged ones and charge to our account?[9]

With regret,

Yours faithfully,

(Complaint reg. Inferior quality)

Dear Sir,

This refers to our order for 500 cardigans dt. 25th July.[1] We have received the delivery but are sadly disappointed with its quality.[2] As a result, we are not in a position to offer these goods for sale.[9] Consequently we are left with no other alternative but to ask you to replace them with those of better quality.[12]

With regret,

Yours faithfully,

(Complaint reg. short supply)

Dear Sir,

We thank you for the prompt execution of our order No. L-314 dated 20th April. But while we had ordered for 20 immersion rod heaters, we have received only 10 in the package delivered to us.[1] Please let us know about the reason for such short supply.[6] We will feel obliged if you can supply the missing articles at once or issue a credit note.[14]

With thanks,

Yours faithfully,

Dear Sir,

On 8th July, I received through your representative, Mr. Ram Kumar, my Philips cassette recorder sent to you for repairs last month.[1] And when I played the recorder yesterday I found that the old defect was still persisting. The recorder often produces a strange sound and the tape gets struck on its head.[5] I shall drop it at your shop at my convenience and request you to mend it by an early date.[11]

Thanking you,

Yours faithfully,

Replies to Complaints : Adjustment Letters

Since nothing is perfect, complaints about one's products or services should not be taken with a frown. A large business is a complex network of various departments and people. There can always be a lapse somewhere which might lead to complaint by customers. At the same time a complaint from a customer cannot be ignored. If it happens, it might have repercussions on the business in the long run. One must keep one's customers satisfied. In some Western Countries, various companies invite criticism of their products. They even circulate printed forms for the customer to tick off the points regarding flaws in the goods. These help them to better their products quality. All professional businessmen are keen to introduce reforms in the business. This gives more credibility to their business. Thus, a prompt action on a complaint is a must.

Some Don'ts while handling complaints

Tact, sincerity and patience are required in handling letters of complaints:

1. Don't express surprise over customer's complaint. This undermines his assessment. However, to say that such an error did not occur earlier is to justify him.
2. Do not be too apologetic. He expects your sincere approach to his problem and will be satisfied if you show concern.
3. While making adjustment do not give the feeling that you are doing him a great favour.
4. Do not shift the blame to a junior member of the staff or make someone else a scapegoat of it.
5. Do not repeat the details of faults?
6. Do not try to sound unethical by saying 'our rules do not allow it', 'company's policy does not allow it' etc. The customer is above these internal definitions. He has the right to get satisfactory service.

Purpose/Function of a good adjustment letter

Whatever decision one might take in regard to complaints a definite set of rules has to be followed. A proper attitude and frame of mind are essential for handling delicate situations. One must try to realise the position of the customer. All adjustments must be made valuing customer's feelings. His shaken confidence in the company must be restored. This objective can only be achieved by a right attitude to the error pointed out. This means that the businessman must be able to (I) locate the source of error, (ii) control it and (iii) forgive it. Proper human relations with employees are conducive to better business relations.

Some Dos while handling complaints:

(i) Have an unbiased attitude to the error pointed out.

(ii) Remember, sometimes apart from the inconvenience, loss of money is also involved.

(iii) In such circumstances the tone is more important than the content.

(iv) Courteous attitude will get a favourable response.

(v) Sometimes the customer is only half correct and not fully justified. Still, be helpful, sympathetic and courteous.

Types of adjustment letters

Here a few important points have to be kept in mind, viz., responsibility for the fault, business relations with the customer and his earlier record of dealings. Such letters can be grouped as follows:-

(i) Letters of apology owning error and granting adjustments.

(ii) Letters explaining non-acceptance of complaint and refusing adjustment.

(iii) Letters offering a compromise.

(iv) Letters requesting the customer to wait while matters are under consideration.

(v) Letters of partial compromise according to the extent of error owned/admitted.

Reply to Complaint Re: Non-delivery

Acknowledge the letter informing of non-delivery of goods:

1. This refers to your letter concerning non-delivery of hand-tools booked vide your order No.AS/2448 of 5th May.

2. We regret to learn from your letter that the lipsticks ordered from us in the beginning of this month have not yet reached you.

3. We are surprised to learn from your representative, today that the shirts you had ordered on 23rd October, have not yet reached you.

4. It was quite surprising to know that the consignment of 20 tea sets despatched to you, as per your order No.SL/2881 of 10th November, has not reached you so far.

5. We are, of course, totally, in dark about their whereabouts.

Give proof of delivering goods in time:

6. We assure you that your order was executed on the same day it was received.

7. It is, of course, surprising because the next day itself, we had despatched the goods to our transporter.

8. We confirm that your consignment was delivered in time to the Parcel Booking Office at Bombay Central Railway Station for onward despatch by passenger train.

9. Our transporter inform us that the goods were delayed a little. And we feel that they must have reached you by now.

10. We feel very much concerned about the non-receipt of the goods by you. It was sent through registered post parcel. We have the postal receipt of the same.

Close the letter indicating future action:

11. Immediately on receipt of your letter we have taken up the matter with the railway authorities/ our transporters here.

12. We will immediately let you know about the developments this side.

13. We think it would be advisable that you also make inquiries at your end.

14. We are getting in touch with the transport company and will let you know about their reply.

15. We are complaining about the matter to the postal authorities and hope to advise you shortly.

Reply to Complaint Re : Late Delivery

Convey regrets in the beginning of your reply:

1. We have received your letter dated 8th January and regret the delay in despatching 20 reams of sunlit bond-paper you ordered on 30th December last year.

2. We have received your letter dated 2nd May regarding the supply of 20 easy-chairs and sincerely regret the delay in delivery of goods.

3. We are sorry to learn from your representative that you have not received the consignment of 20 dozen cotton-shirts we had despatched to you as per schedule.

4. Your letter dated 8th August, complaining about delay in delivery has come as a surprise. We had despatched the goods to you on the next day of receiving your order.

5. This has reference to your letter dated 2nd June complaining about the delivery of twenty 160 litre refrigerators on 29th May instead of 14th.

6. We are sorry to learn about the delay in delivery of the neckties that you ordered on 30th September.

Explain the cause of delay and its non-recurrence:

7. We admit that an unexpected rush of activities caused a slight delay in executing your order but we assure you that we are doing our utmost to expedit delivery.

8. We had already sent you a telegram informing of late despatch of your consignment which we hope you might have received by now.

9. In fact, a heavy demand of electric heaters this season somewhat delayed the delivery.

10. This delay has occurred because of the fact that our plant is not working full-time on account of regular power-cuts.

11. A recent labour strike had stalled the work for some time. Now the workers have resumed the duty and we can assure you that there will not be any delay in future.

12. We are the only manufacturers of these goods and our resources have been overtaxed.

13. Our transporters were heavily booked and so they could not deliver the goods in time.

14. It is our usual practice to send goods well in advance of delivery dates and the consignment of toys which you refer to was despatched on the 3rd of this month.

15. We are very much concerned that our efforts to give punctual delivery are disturbed by delays in transit.

Give adequate assurances for future dealings.

16. We are taking up the mater of delay with the transport company, in all seriousness.

17. In future, we are sure, we shall be able to supply the goods in time.

18. Till the recent rush we have never failed in delivering the goods within the scheduled time. We hope you will take a favourable view of the recent delay.

19. The power problems has eased off and our production has become normal. So, in future we shall be able to supply the goods in time.

20. We assure you that every effort will be made in future to guarantee the delivery in time.

21. We assure you that we are doing all we can to speed up delivery and apologise for the inconvenience caused to you.

22. Our transporter has assured us that in future they will make the deliveries in time.

Reply to Complaint Re : Damaged Goods

Begin by conveying your sincere apologies:

1. We are sorry to learn from your letter dated 3rd August that some of the glass tumblers were received by you in broken/ damaged condition.

2. This refers to your complaint dated 3rd August about the damaged parcel of socks.

3. Your complaint of 2nd October concerning the damaged cotton bed-sheets has caused us great concern.

4. We are sorry to learn that some of the tea-sets despatched to you on 8th April were found damaged.

5. We are surprised to learn that despite our tremendous care, knitwears have reached you in a soiled condition.

Give assurance of more alertness in future transactions:

6. To avoid inconvenience and annoyance to our customers , we have now employed a packaging specialist.

7. We have now started ordering for special packing cases to ensure safe delivery of goods.

8. We have to especially reinforce all future consignments by rail, and this, we hope, will prevent any damage in future.

9. We have decided to switch over to 'Modern Transport' for despatch of goods. This, we feel, will ensure a safe deliveries.

10. We are ready to meet half the cost of the damage occurred during transit.

Suggestions to rectify loss:

11. You need not return the broken tumblers. They can be destroyed. Replacements are following soon.

12. We realise the need to reduce your selling price for the damaged sweaters and are ready to allow a special allowance of 10% which you have suggested.

13. You can return the soiled blankets through our representative, Mr. Ashok Kumar, who will be visiting your area on 10th March. We shall replace them with new ones.

14. We take the responsibility of the damaged goods and shall adjust its cost in our next transaction.

15. Kindly send the estimate of the damaged goods. We shall deduct the amount in our next bill.

Reply to Complaint Re : Inferior Goods

Convey regrets at the beginning of your letter:

1. We regret to learn from your letter dated 29th May that you are not satisfied with the pens/books/bush-shirts supplied as per your order No.SL/7824.

2. This refers to your complaint of 29th May expressing dissatisfaction over the neckties quality supplied to you on 2nd May.

3. We are sorry for the inconvenience caused to you.

4. Your letter of 3rd April complaining about the quality of ball-point refills supplied as per your order No.265, has caused a great deal of concern in us.

5. We are very much disturbed at your complaint of 2nd May regarding the quality of the electric heaters supplied against your order of 28th March.

6. This is to express our concern over your complaint about the quality of shirting material supplied to you on the 3rd of this month.

Show gratitude on bringing the error to your notice:

7. We are, nevertheless, glad that you have brought the matter to our notice.

8. At the same time we are glad to receive your complaint.

9. Still, we thank you for promptly reporting this to us.

10. We really appreciate your frankness in the matter.

Give explanation, if possible:

11. We assure your satisfaction in future regarding the quality of the material.

12. We ourselves have tested the heaters and found them not up to the mark. Our technicians are advising ways to improve their quality.

13. We have inspected the goods from the same batch and agree that they do not tally with your specifications/feel that the goods were exactly as per your specifications.

14. In fact, there had been some mistake by our despatch department.

15. We admit that it has been a lapse on our part and we are taking steps to prevent such mistakes in future.

16. Since the goods you had ordered for were out of stocks, our sales department took the liberty of substituting them with those of a different quality

Indicate steps taken to rectify errors:

17. The defects in the goods have been traced to a fault in one of the machines, and it is being rectified now.

18. We are arranging to replace 50% (ie., 200pens) of your unsold stock.

19. We shall soon meet your order for terene bush-shirts in place of the cotton ones you received, and these are at present being fabricated.

20. As soon as fresh supply is ready we shall replace the goods.

21. We have arranged for immediate despatch of replacements.

Give suggestions for clearance of defective goods:

22. If it is not too much of inconvenience to sell the cloth already supplied, we can send you a credit note for the difference, as soon as we hear from you.

23. The defective books may kindly be returned at our expenses.

24. If you can keep the books for sale, we are ready to give 5% discount on them.

25. Please return the defective pens to us.

Express hopes of satisfying the complaint by your above action:

26. We trust the replacements we are sending now, will be upto your satisfaction.

27. We apologise sincerely for the trouble caused to you, and will take all possible steps to ensure that such a mistake does not recur.

28. We are ensuring stricter quality control tests and assure you that such a mistake will not take place again.

29. We admit our draw-back and promise you our best of services in future.

Indicate if complaints are not acceptable:

30. We have investigated your complaint and regret to say that we could not find any justification for it.

31. We have gone through your complaint but regret to say that we are unable to entertain it.

Explain reasons of non-acceptance and talk of future action:

32. As all our fountain pens are of the finest quality and subjected to a variety of quality control tests, we fail to understand your complaint.

33. All our products are thoroughly examined before passing into store.

34. Since we do not have any doubt about their quality, we are sorry to say that we cannot entertain your request.

35. Since our manufacturer refuses to take back the goods once sold, we express our helplessness in this regard.

36. Therefore, we shall have no option but to refuse to accept the goods, if returned.

Closure of a letter not accepting the complaint:

37. We hope you will take it as a fair and reasonable solution to the matter.

38. You will appreciate that no other course is open to us, under the circumstances.

39. We, of course, understand your point of view but are helpless in this regard.

Closure for the ordinary reply:

40. We hope this will now settle the matter to your complete satisfaction.

41. We trust you will have no further cause to complain.

42. We regret the trouble caused to you.

43. Please feel free to express your opinion in future too in case of any such problem.

Reply to Complaint on Mistake

Beginning:

1. Thank you for your letter of 14th June. It has given us the opportunity to set right the mistake regarding the address of your factory.

2. In fact, we have not received the circular you issued notifying the change of address.

3. We are grateful to you for pointing out the mistake regarding the despatch of an old paid bill.

4. The mistake you pointed out was indeed inadvertent but unfortunate.

5. We are obliged to you that you have given us a chance to mend our errors.

Closure:

6. We apologise for the trouble our mistake may have caused you.

7. We assure you that we shall be careful not to repeat such mistakes in future.

8. We deeply regret having given you a cause to complain and assure you that we shall do all we can to put matters right.

9. We are sorry that you have suffered our mistake. It will never happen again.

10. Kindly excuse for the undesirable happening. We assure you that it will not be repeated.

Reply to Complaint about Poor Services

Begin by acknowledging the letter:

1. We are in receipt of your letter dated 9th September and apologise for the carelessness of our service engineer.

2. We have received through your representative today your C.D. player which according to your complaint has not been properly repaired.

3. We regret to learn from your letter dated 8th October that the defect of the VCP you had sent to us has not been rectified.

4. We are sorry to learn from your letter dated 19th September that our service engineer has not yet paid you a visit.

Give explanation if possible:

5. In fact, our engineer who visited you on last Monday has reported sick since then.

6. We have made enquiries at our end and found that because of the absence of one of our supervisors the system was delivered without proper checking. The fault, of course, is ours.

7. As far as we are aware nothing leaves our workshop without a thorough check up. There is a possibility that during transit the recorder has got damaged.

Now assure of full co-operation:

8. However, we are instructing Mr. Krishan Kumar to visit you and rectify the defect in your refrigerator.

9. We are arranging for transfer of your system to our workshop and assure you that it will be mended to your satisfaction.

10. We apologise for the inconvenience caused and assure you that next time you will not have an occasion to complain.

11. We are arranging for an immediate repair of your system and hope that it will satisfy you.

12. We look forward to extend our services to you in future.

13. We hope you will ignore this lapse on our part and give us a chance to serve you in future too.

Sample Letters
(Reply to complaint re : non-delivery)

Dear Sir,

We are surprised to learn from your representative today that the shirts you had ordered on 23rd October, have not yet reached you.[3] We confirm that your consignment was delivered in time to the Parcel Booking Office at Bombay Central Railway Station for onward despatch by passenger train.[8] We think it would be advisable that you also make inquiries at your end.[13]

With thanks,

Yours faithfully,

(Reply to complaint of late delivery)

Dear Sir,

We have received your letter dated 8th January and regret the delay in despatching 20 reams of sunlit bond-paper you ordered on 30th December last year.[1] We admit that an unexpected rush of activities caused a slight delay in executing your order, but we assure you that we are doing our utmost to expedite delivery.[7] We assure you that every effort will be made in future to guarantee the delivery in time.[20]

Always at your service,

Yours faithfully,

(Reply to complaint regarding damaged goods)

Dear Sir,

We are sorry to learn from your letter dated 3rd August that some of the glass tumblers were received by you in broken/damaged condition.[1] We have now started ordering for special packing cases to ensure safe delivery of goods.[7] You need not return the broken tumblers. They can be destroyed. Replacements are following soon.[11]

Assuring you of fullest co-operation.

Yours faithfully,

(Reply to complaint regarding inferior goods)

Dear Sir,

We regret to learn from your letter dated 29th May that you are not satisfied with the pens supplied as per your order No.SL/7824.[1] We are, nevertheless, glad that you have brought the matter to our notice.[7] We have inspected the goods from the same batch and agree that they do not tally with your specifications. We are arranging to replace 50% (i.e.,200 pens) of your unsold stock.[18] Please return the defective pens to us.[25] We trust the replacements we are sending now will be up to your satisfaction.[26] We hope this will now settle the matter to your complete satisfaction.[40]

Assuring you of prompt attention,

Yours faithfully,

(Reply to complaint on mistake)

Dear Sir,

Thank you for your letter of 13th June. It has given us the opportunity to set right the mistake regarding the address of your factory.[1] In fact, we have not received the circular you issued notifying the change of address.[2] We apologise for the trouble our mistake may have caused you.[6]

Thanking you,

Yours faithfully,

(Reply to complaint about poor service)

Dear Sir,

We regret to learn from your letter dated 8th October that the defect of the VCP you had sent to us has not been rectified.[3] We have made enquiries at our end and found that because of the absence of one of our supervisors the system was delivered without proper checking. The fault, of course, is ours.[6] We are arranging for transfer of your system to our workshop and assure you that it will be mended to your satisfaction.[9] We hope you will ignore this lapse on our part and give us a chance to serve you in future too.[13]

Thanking you,

Yours faithfully,

Letters Regarding Transport of Goods

There are four modes of transportation available to us-road, rail, air and sea. In all big cities and towns there are agents to book goods for such transportation. Not just that, there are many independent agencies too who undertake the task of despatching goods. These agencies are fully conversant with legal formalities and transporting techniques. They even have printed material for replies and queries. However, at times, need arises for letters too.

Letter to Shipping Company Regarding Freight Rates

Begin the letter by giving goods' details and asking tariffs:

1. We shall soon have 20 cases of crockery ready for shipment to Kandy, Ceylon from Chennai. Each case weighs 70kg and measures 1 ¼ x 1 ¼ x 1m.

2. So, will you please send us details of present freight charges for despatch of these goods.

3. As we wish to send a consignment of leather garments in 10 wooden cases, each weighing 20kg from Bombay to Dubai, we would feel obliged if you could send us your freight rates.

4. Kindly inform us about the freight rates for packaged handicrafts from Madras to Port Louis, Mauritius. The consignment will consist of 4 wooden cases, each weighing 15kg and measuring 1 ½ x 1 x 1m.

5. We wish to inquire about the freight rates for shipment of packaged woollen garments from Bombay to London. These goods will be in 8 wooden cases, each weighing 10kg and measuring 1½ x 1 ½ x 1m.

Enquire about the actual shipment:

6. You may also inform us of the frequency of your sailing and the duration of the voyage.

7. Please also let us know about the sailing schedule and voyage's duration.

8. We understand that S.S. Ratnagiri is due to sail on 20th July but we would like an earlier sailing if possible.

9. As our customer has been pressing for the goods, please let us know when they can be shipped at the earliest.

10. Please inform us if we have to book the consignment in advance or not.

Inquiry of Freight Rates from Road Transport Company

Describe your goods:

1. We wish to send books in 25 wooden boxes measuring 50cm x 50cm x 25cm to Bombay early next month.

2. Will you please quote your freight charges to Bombay for 10 wooden cases containing glass tumblers. The size of the boxes is 50cm x 30cm x20cm.

3. We propose to despatch 10 cardboard cartons of ready-made garments measuring 1 x 1 x 0.25m to Bombay on the 1st of the month.

Make specific enquiries:

4. So please furnish the following information per return.

5. Therefore, please let us know about the following details at the earliest.
6. Can you arrange to collect the goods from our office at the above address?
7. Do we have to deliver the goods at your office or can you arrange to pick them up from here ?
8. How long will the goods take to reach Bombay ?
9. What would be the freight and other charges, if any ?
10. Are the insurance charges included in the freight or do we have to pay them separately ?
11. We shall feel obliged if you send us detailed information about the freight rates, time taken to cover the distance and the mode of lifting the goods.

Letter to Airlines Regarding Transport of Goods

Describe the goods first:
1. We are sending through our representative, Mr. Devendra Kumar, 100 cases of mangoes for despatch to London.
2. We wish to send by air 50 baskets of Mangoes to London.
3. Through the bearer of this letter we are sending 100 rose buds packed in cellophane bags for air freight to London.
4. We intend to send 100 cases of transistors to Port Louis (Mauritius) from Delhi.
5. We are a Handicraft Unit and plan to send by air handicrafts from Delhi to Paris.

Indicate the documents:
6. All papers, duly completed, are enclosed.
7. Enclosed please find all necessary documents, duly completed. Please let us know if any other documents are required or not.
8. We have completed all the papers which are enclosed.
9. All the formalities are over. The necessary documents are enclosed with the letter.

Mention about the invoice:
10. The freight bill for these cases may be sent to us in duplicate for payment.
11. Please let us know if you would require part payment in advance or full payment after the delivery.
12. You are requested to submit the freight bill for this cargo in duplicate for settlement.
13. To promote goodwill, we can make the payment in advance.

Letter to Forwarding Agent

Begin your letter with important points involved:
1. Our company has been operating a large network of parcel despatch service.
2. We receive and despatch large volume of parcel everyday.
3. Our business involves handling of large amount of parcel despatches.

Discuss your requirements:

4. We shall, appreciate if you·could send your representative to apprise us of your services and charges for the same.

5. So please let us know if you could handle this business as our Clearing Agent and intimate your charges for the same.

6. Could you act as our forwarding agents ? If so, please let us know about the details of your services.

Letter from Forwarding Agent Regarding Terms

Begin your letter with reference to the letter received/visit of the representative:

1. Thank you for your letter of 7th July.
2. This is to thank you for your letter dated July 7, 1999.
3. This has reference to the visit of your representative, Mr. Kumar to our office on 4th May.
4. This has reference to the meeting between your agent and our partner Mr. Rao.
5. We are glad to have had talks with your agent on Monday, the 10th July.

Indicate your trade terms:

6. We are pleased to state our terms as follows.
7. Please note our terms as given below.
8. We will collect all the goods from your factory for onward transportation by road or rail.
9. For transportation of goods from your godown to the transporters or railways, we will charge extra. The rates are given below:
10. A sum of Rs.50/- will be charged for our services for each inward and outward parcel, subject to a minimum of 200 parcels every month.
11. We deal in insured goods only.
12. All bills submitted by us should be paid within 30 days.
13. All our bills should be payable on the 1st of every month.
14. We shall keep on sending our revised rates from time to time.
15. The validity period of these terms will be subject to negotiation.

Close the letter hoping for favourable reply:

16. We hope you find our terms favourable and will have regular business deals with us.
17. We hope these terms will be acceptable to you.
18. Please confirm whether these terms are acceptable to you.
19. I am quite sure that you would accept these reasonable terms.
20. We look forward to a long and fruitful relationship with you.

Letter to Railway for Giving Open Delivery

Begin your letter giving reasons for taking open delivery:

1. Our representative Mr. Kulbhushan Kapoor, visited you on 18th August for taking delivery of two parcels of books against PWB No.226801 and found that they were badly damaged.

2. This is to report the damage to our packages containing glass tumblers. The damage was noticed by our representative, Mr, Shastri, when he went to your office on 18th April to take their delivery.

3. We regret to inform you that the parcel of woollen goods sent to us was found damaged and torn when our representative Mr. Manmohan, visited your office to take its delivery against PWB No.384983.

4. On 8th July, when our representative, Mr. Suresh Virmani, went to your office to take delivery of the parcel of garments addressed to us, he found it damaged and some of the pieces missing.

5. This is to inform you that the crockery packages despatched to us were very much damaged. Please refer to PWB No.14568 and note the extent of damage which is as under : (I) Handles of two tea pots broken, (ii) Three cups broken.

Now, request to take open delivery:

6. We, therefore, request you to give us open delivery of the parcels.

7. It is, therefore, requested that an open delivery of the said parcels be given to us.

8. So please give an open delivery of the damaged consignment. Our representative can call on you whenever you find it convenient.

Letter to Carrier to Release Goods from Customs

Mention details of documents:

1. Enclosed please find a letter from British Airways with invoice for 2 cases of ready-made garments despatched from London on 8th July, 1999.

2. Please find enclosed a letter from Singapore Airlines with invoice for a case of dress material despatched from the United States on August 2, 1999.

3. Please find enclosed a letter from Air India along with an invoice for 5 cases of dry fruits despatched from Kabul on September 9, 1999.

Advice for delivery of goods:

4. Please arrange to collect the same and deliver it to us at our office.

5. Kindly make arrangements to collect and deliver it at our office at the given address.

6. Please make arrangements to transport to us the luggage in the next two-three days.

7. Please receive these papers and arrange the delivery. Details are given in the letter.

8. Kindly acknowledge this letter sent through the bearer and manage to send the articles to our godown at the given address.

Sample Letters

(Letter to Shipping Company re. Freight rates)

Dear Sir,

We shall soon have 20 cases of crockery ready for shipment to Kandy, Ceylon, from Chennai. Each case weighs 70kg and measures 1 ¼ x 1 ¼ x 1m.[1] So, will you please send us details of present freight charges for despatch of these goods.[2] You may also inform us of the frequency of your sailings and the duration of the voyage.[6]

Thanking you,

Yours faithfully,

(Enquiry of Freight Rates from Road Transport Co.)

Dear Sir,

We propose to despatch 10 cardboard cartons of ready-made garments, measuring 1 x 1 x 0.25m to Bombay on the 1st of the next month.[3] We shall feel obliged if you send us detailed information about the freight rates, time taken to cover the distance and the mode of lifting the goods.[11]

With thanks,

Yours faithfully,

(Letter to Airlines re. Transport of Goods)

Dear Sir,

We are sending through our representative, Mr. Devendra Kumar, 100 cases of mangoes for despatch to London.[1] All papers duly completed, are enclosed.[6] The freight bill for these cases may be sent to us in duplicate for payment.[10]

Thanking you,

Yours faithfully,

(Letter to Forwarding Agent)

Dear Sir,

Our company has been operating a large network of parcel despatch service.[1] We shall appreciate if you could send your representative to apprise us of your services and charges for the same.[4]

Thanking you,

Yours faithfully,

(Letter from Forwarding Agent re. Terms)

Dear Sir,

Thank you for your letter of 7th July. We are pleased to state our terms as follows.[6] All our bills should be payable on the 1st of every month.[13] Please confirm whether these terms are acceptable to you.[18]

Thanking you,

Yours faithfully,

```
(Letter to Railway for giving Open Delivery)
Dear Sir,
Our representative Mr. Kulbhushan Kapoor had visited you on 18ᵗʰ August
for taking delivery of two parcels of books against PWB No.226801 and
found that they were badly damaged.¹ We, therefore, request you to give us
open delivery of the parcels.⁶

Thanking you,

Yours faithfully,
```

```
(Letter to Carrier to release Goods from Customs)
Dear Sir,
Please find enclosed a letter from Air India along with an invoice for 5
cases of dry fruits despatched from Kabul on September 9, 1999.³ Please
arrange to collect the same and deliver it to us at our office.⁴

Thanking you,

Yours faithfully,
```

Collection Letters

One of the primary issues of any commercial establishment is to keep the books of accounts in good order. This can only be done if firms' bills are paid in time, But, at times, the credit customers fail to make payments within the stipulated time. In that case one has to send reminders to customers. Such customers may be of three types.

1. Good Credit Customers:
The ones who pay up promptly and do not keep their suppliers waiting for money. These customer scarcely need any reminders.

2. Fair Credit Customers:
They fall behind in payments at times and await a few reminders before clearing dues. With them it becomes a kind of habit. However, after a few reminders they pay up.

3. Poor Credit Customers:
These are difficult to tackle. They make it a habit not to pay up until they are reminded repeatedly and they cannot delay any further. They require regular reminders until the money is realized.

After the bill, collection procedure starts with the monthly statements. Reminders are sent periodically to realise uncleared dues. Without them, of course, a company cannot run.

Usual/Formal Collection Letter

Formal Reminder:

1. Our records show that you have yet to clear your account No.L/123 dated 15ᵗʰ December, 2000.

2. May we remind you that the above account has not yet been cleared.

3. This is to remind you that we have not received payment of the above account already a month overdue.

4. According to the enclosed statements the outstanding amount due from you is Rs.5000/- only.

5. You have always been very prompt in settling your accounts; and we hope this bill also receives a similar response.

6. The outstanding sum, according to our books, amounts to Rs.5,000/- only.

Request for early response:

7. We hope that you will settle the account at the earliest.

8. An early settlement of the account will be appreciated.

9. We would request you to settle this account at the earliest.

10. We have always been very earnest in our dealings and hence we hope that our outstanding bill for Rs.2500/- will soon be cleared.

11. As we have received another order from your agent we would appreciate an early settlement of this account.

12. In view of our cordial business relations it is necessary to get our previous accounts settled.

First Collection Letter

Begin with a friendly approach and tone:

*In case the account No. is given at the top, do not write it again in the letter.

1. As you are usually quite prompt in settling the accounts, we wonder if there is any special reason for delay this time.

2. May we call your attention to our outstanding account for Rs.5250/- settlement of which is now overdue for more than a month.

3. We shall be glad if you pay attention to our statement of account dated 5th March 2000, which still remains unpaid.

4. We wish to draw your attention to our invoice No.PN/2041 for Rs.3,550/- which we have not yet received.

5. We have noted that your account, which was due for payment on the 15th of last month, is still outstanding.

6. We may remind you that you had promised for an immediate settlement of the account at the time of the delivery of goods.

7. While checking our accounts we have found that there is a balance of Rs.6220/- due from you for the purchases made in April 2000.

8. We regret to remind you that despite our letter of 8th November enclosing an invoice for Rs.8,500/- only, payable on 28 November, we have not received any communication from you.

9. While going through your account, we have noticed that a balance of Rs.1045/- is still outstanding against your name.

10. It seems you have inadvertently overlooked our invoices of February and March, or there is some other reason for the delay in payment.

11. We very much regret to inform you that we have not yet received the payment of our hundi which fell due on 12th September, 2000.

12. Our accounts department has been waiting for more than a week for the settlement of our account of December for Rs.25,000/-.

13. We regret to remind you that you have not yet paid the balance of Rs.7100.50 due on our statement dated December 3, 2000.

14. We hope you must have received the statement of account, dated 28th February, showing the balance of Rs.1500.00.

15. As our auditors have to balance the accounts by the end of this month, we request for a prompt settlement of our bill.

16. To expedite the matter, we are sending our representative with a copy of the invoice. Kindly make payments of our bill.

17. For ready reference we enclose a copy of the statement of March. These accounts are now overdue.

Request for early payment:

18. We shall be glad if you take an immediate action in this regard and settle our accounts.

19. We look forward to your remittance by return mail.

20. We hope to receive the amount overdue/cheque within the next few days.

21. We hope you will settle the account expeditiously.

22. As the financial year is coming to a close we request you make immediate payment of the bill.

23. Please let us know at the earliest when can we have the payment.

24. We will appreciate your making the payment at the earliest. If you cannot, please let us know the reasons.

25. We shall be pleased to receive your cheque in settlement of this account.

26. Kindly help us to bring your account up-to-date by paying the outstanding amount.

27. Please let us know the date when you retired the hundi so that we could write to your bankers for payment.

Second Collection Letter

Write a courteous but firm letter:

1. We regret to say that an amount of Rs.5195.50 is still outstanding against your name, and we have not received the payment despite a reminder dated 4th February.

2. On 17th January we sent you a letter reminding that on 3rd December we had sent you our statement for November 1999, showing an outstanding balance of Rs.2205.50 due for payment by 31st December.

3. Despite our reminder dated 24th May for an outstanding payment of Rs.2800/- we have not heard from you.

4. We regret to inform you that despite our request dated 3rd September for the settlement of the amount due on our invoice No.P.241 of 24th July, we have not heard anything from you.

5. This is to request you again for the payment of Rs.8851/- outstanding against your account. We had reminded you that your account, already more than a month overdue, had not

been settled.

6. We are at a loss to understand why we have had no reply to our letter dated 27th May requesting you to settle the amount outstanding on our March statement.

7. We regret to remind you again of our unpaid bill for Rs.8805.15, now nearly three months overdue.

8. We are sorry to draw your attention to your unpaid balance of Rs.6640/- which has not been paid despite the reminder sent through our representative last month.

Ask for reasons for delay and request for early payment:

9. No doubt there might be some special reason for this delay in payment. We shall welcome an explanation for the same and hope for the clearance within a week.

10. As this amount is overdue for more than two months, we must ask you either to send us your remittance within the next few days or at least offer an explanation for the delay.

11. We have not so far pressed you for a settlement because of your good past record.

12. For a regular customer like you, our terms of payment are 3% for one month. We hope you will not withhold payment any longer and thus compel us to revise these terms to your disadvantage.

13. You will understand that a prompt payment is in the best interests of a cordial relations.

14. We trust you will now attend to this matter without any further delay.

15. We are sorry to inform you that it is not possible for us to give you any further credit.

16. We regret to press for an immediate payment of the outstanding amount.

17. We hope you will give a positive response to our representative who is the bearer of this letter.

18. As the amount owing is considerably overdue, we shall be grateful to receive your cheque at your earliest.

19. Kindly send us the remittance immediately or explain any reason for further delay.

20. As we have to settle certain important bills, we must insist on the immediate clearance of our account.

Third Collection Letter

Mention earlier reference of letters:

1. We do not appear to have received any reply to our previous requests dated 4th and 17th August for payment of Rs.1,110.35 which has been outstanding against your name for more than four months.

2. We fail to understand why we have not received your reply to our two reminders dated 17th March and 4th April requesting you to pay Rs.2895.10/- due on our January 1999 statement.

3. We are surprised and disappointed not to have received any reply from you despite our two reminders dated 8th April and 5th May 1999 for payment of Rs.2,050/-.

4. We note with surprise and disappointment that we have not received any replies to our two previous reminders for payment of Rs.3000/- due on your account.

5. We have sent you two reminders earlier dated 2nd July and 24th July requesting you to pay us the amount of our invoice No.125/023.

6. We regret to inform you that we haven't had any reply to our previous requests for payment due on our statement of October.

7. Despite our two reminders of your delinquent account, we have not heard anything from you regarding the payment of Rs.5000/- due on our invoice No.DL/489.

8. Your balance of Rs.5750/- which dates back to November 1998 is still unpaid in spite of our two reminders.

Request for payment clearance by a specified date:

9. We regret to inform you that now we must press for immediate payment.

10. I hope you will understand our position and will not delay the payment any more.

11. As we would not like to harm your credit and reputation we propose to give you time till the end of this month to clear your account.

12. As our dealings over many years have been satisfactory we are giving you ten more days to settle this overdue account.

13. We still hope you will discharge this account without any further delay.

14. Unless we receive the payment in full settlement by the end of this month,......

15. Unless we receive the payment in full settlement by 23rd of this month.......

Indicate legal implications:

16. If you fail to stick to this date we will be left with no other choice but to resort to legal action.

17. I regret to inform you that this is the last reminder and if the payment does not come forth, we'll be left with no other option but to stop our business dealings with you and take recourse to law.

18. ....we shall have to consider seriously other further steps to recover the amount.

19. ....we shall instruct our lawyers to recover the amount due to us.

20. ....we shall have to take legal action.

21. ....we hope you will prevent the matter from going to court and thereby avoid inconvenience and heavy expenditure on both the sides.

22. ....we shall be compelled to hand-over this matter to our attorneys.

23. ....we hope you will not compel us to take the unpleasant step of handing over the matter to our solicitors.

24. ....we shall pass the matter on to our legal advisers for necessary action.

25. ....we shall be constrained to resort to legal action at your cost and risk.

Sample Letters
(Usual/Formal Collection Letter)

Dear Sirs,

Our records show that you have yet to clear your account No.L/123 dated 5th December, 2000.[1] We hope that you will settle the account at the earliest.[7]

Awaiting an early response,

Yours faithfully,

(First Collection Letter)

Dear Sirs,

As you are usually quite prompt in settling the accounts, we wonder if there is any special reason for delay this time.[1] As our auditors have to balance the accounts by the end of this month, we request for a prompt settlement of our bill.[15] We shall be glad if you take an immediate action in this regard and settle our accounts.[18]

Awaiting an early reply,

Yours faithfully,

(Second Collection Letter)

Dear Sirs,

We regret to remind you again of our unpaid bill of Rs.8805.15, now nearly three months overdue.[7] No doubt there might be some special reason for this delay in payment. We shall welcome an explanation for the same and hope for the clearance within a week.[9]

Yours faithfully,

(Third Collection Letter)

Dear Sirs,

We do not appear to have received any reply to our previous requests dated 4th and 17th August for payment of Rs.1110.35 which has been outstanding against your name for more than four months. As we would not like to harm your credit and reputation we propose to give you time till the end of this month to clear your account.[11] If you fail to stick to this date we will be left with no other choice but to resort to legal action.[16]

Yours faithfully,

Remittance Letters

The modern methods in accounting, new electronic devices and computers etc have up to a large extent, eliminated the need for letters of transmittal with payments. However, still in the local business transactions such letters are used. Moreover, in most of the cases today the business houses use printed letters.

Such a letter must specify the amount and nature of enclosure (cheque/draft/postal order/ etc.) and should give the date and number of the bill being paid. An expression of appreciation for service rendered is in good taste.

However, sometimes payments cannot be made because of certain errors in bills or statements of account or noncompliance with the terms settled earlier. On such occasions letters should be written promptly referring to delay in payment. These letters should be courteous in tone and tactfully written.

Acknowledgement of remittance:

A letter acknowledging receipt of the payment is not as necessary as the letter of transmittal. It can be sent as a matter of routine, token of appreciation or referring to further business orders.

Billing errors:

Claims of errors in billing should be carefully investigated and acknowledged as soon as possible. If the error is proved, admit it, apologise for it and offer adjustments. Send a corrected bill with a covering letter as soon as possible.

Stopping payment of cheque:

If it is necessary to ask a bank to stop payment of a cheque, it should be done promptly either by telephone/telegram or letter.

Letters Regarding Remittance for Goods Received

Give details of remittances:

1. Please find enclosed cheque No.568350 HB dated ...... for Rs. 2000/- drawn on the Punjab National Bank in full settlement of your invoice No.3942 dated 14th August 2000.

2. We are pleased to enclose the cheque No.SB 829421 dated ....for Rs.5000/- drawn on the Punjab National Bank, in full settlement of your invoice No.3428.

3. Enclosed is our cheque No.AB 408212 drawn on Grindlays Bank, Connaught Place for Rs.5250/- in full settlement of your invoice No.12 dated the 1st of this month.

4. We are finally settling all due accounts on our part and sending the amount of Rs.5682/- through cheque No.AB428641 drawn on the Syndicate Bank, Greater Kailash, New Delhi and regret any inconvenience caused to you.

5. With this cheque for Rs.3507/- you will find you have nothing due on us now.

Request for official receipts:

6. Kindly/please acknowledge the receipt.

7. You can send your acknowledgement in the normal course.

8. Receipt of the cheque/amount may be kindly acknowledged.

9. Please confirm the receipt of the cheque by return mail.

10. We hope to send a cheque for the balance (Rs.2320/- only) next month.

11. Kindly bear with us for the remainder amount till the next month.

12. We hope it is not too much of inconvenience to you if we send the balance amount (i.e., Rs.5800/-) next month.

13. The rest of the amount will be remitted to you positively next week.

14. The balance will be sent to you next month after we have gone through the details of the account.

Acknowledgement of Remittance

Convey thanks:

1. This is to thank you for your cheque for Rs.12000/- in full settlement of our invoice No.3942 dated 14th August 2000.

2. We are in receipt of your cheque for Rs.1850.75 in full settlement of our invoice No.521 dated May 7, 2000.

3. Thank you for your cheque for Rs.5750.50 sent in full settlement of our invoice No.150 of 15th March 2000.

4. We express our thanks on receiving the cheque for Rs.3540/- against bill No..... of.......

5. We are thankful to you for the immediate payment of Rs.5000/- through cheque against our recent supplies.

Also send the receipt:

6. Enclosed is the receipt for the cheque.

7. Please find enclosed our receipt for the same.

8. Our receipt for the amount is enclosed.

9. For your records, we are sending the receipt for the amount.

Express expectations for more flow of business:

10. We hope, now, you will place fresh orders with us.

11. May we now expect that you will favour us with further orders.

12. We hope that our promptness in dealing with you will encourage you to place fresh orders with us.

13. We are sure you will entrust us with more orders as our accounts are cleared.

Letters Disputing an Account

Give reasons for non-acceptance of bill:

1. We have received your statement for October, 2000 but are returning it herewith, as it is at variance with our account books.

2. Kindly find herewith your statement for July 2000, which we are returning, as it does not tally with our account books.

3. We regret we have to return herewith your statement for May, 2000 as it does not agree with our books.

Indicate details of errors in bill:

4. You have charged us for four dozen pens while we had purchased only three dozens.

5. Your statement shows that you have charged us for twenty pairs of kurta-pyjams while we had ordered and received only fifteen.

6. While you had agreed to give us 15% discount on the purchase initially, you have not done so.

Ask for an amended bill:

7. We shall be obliged if you could look into this matter and let us have the modified statement.

8. Kindly make necessary corrections in the statement and we will pay it immediately.

9. Please check up at your end and let us have the amended statement for payment.

10. If you feel there has been some misunderstanding and there is no mistake on your part, please clarify.

Sample Letters

(Letter regarding Remittance for Goods Received)

Dear Sirs,

Please find enclosed the cheque No.568350 HB dated ………. for Rs.5000/- drawn on the Punjab National Bank in full settlement of your invoice No.3942 dated 14th August 2000. You could send your acknowledgement in the normal course.[7]

Thanking you,

Yours faithfully,

(Acknowledgement of Remittance)

Dear Sirs,

This is to thank you for your cheque for Rs12000/- in full settlement of our invoice No.3942 dated 14th August 2000.[1] We hope, now, you will place fresh orders with us.[10]

Thanking you,

Yours faithfully,

(Letter Disputing an Account)

Dear Sirs,

Kindly find herewith your statement for July, 2000 which we are returning as it does not tally with our account books.[2] You have charged us for four dozen pens while we had purchased only three dozens.[4] We shall be obliged if you could look into this matter and let us have the modified statement.[7]

Thanking you,

Yours faithfully,

Business Circulars

Business circulars are meant for providing information about any change taking place in a particular commercial establishment. The general public can be informed through the media. But, the clients or customers have to be informed individually. Thus, the circular contains information which the customer would be glad to know. The inside address is given on each circular separately before it is mailed. Like other letters the circulars also should be effective and friendly in tone having a proper lay-out.

Circulars can be sent on several occasions-(I) expansion of a business (ii) introducing new product line (iii) opening a new branch (iv) shifting to other premises (v) repairs (vi) lockout or some other trouble (vii) clearance sales (viii) change of business terms or bankers etc.

Shrewd business circulars also carry a sales message with them. In fact, the big business thrives on flashing different types of circulars from time to time.

Example of a circular on the opening of a new branch

Dear customer,

We are glad to announce the opening of a new branch in Calcutta for the convenience of and service to our growing customers in the city and its upcountry towns. Our branch address is as under:-

> Pustak Mahal
> 405, Mahatma Gandhi Road,
> CALCUTTA-1 (W.B).

The new building that also accommodates other departmental stores is located in the heart of the new fashionable market which has come up on this prestigious road, Mr. Gupta, our salesman from Delhi will be incharge of this new branch. You are cordially invited to visit us on its inaugural ceremony on November 1, 2000.

We take this opportunity to express our thanks for your continued patronage over the last so many years and shall endeavour to provide our best service to you in future too.

Yours faithfully,

For M/s Pustak Mahal.

Circular Announcing Opening of New Business

Announce the new business:

1. We are pleased to announce the opening of a general store at the above address on the coming Diwali.

2. We take great pleasure in announcing the opening of a T.V repair shop in your colony's market (shop no.617) on the auspicious day of Janmashtami.

3. We are glad to inform you about the opening of a Refrigerator repair shop at No.5 Laxmi Road, Delhi on the New Year day.

4. This is to gladly announce that we are opening a book shop at 3145, Nai Sarak on the 14th August, 2000.

5. We take great pleasure in announcing the opening of Super Sari Emporium at 15, Ajmal Khan Road, Karol Bagh on the eve of ensuing Diwali festival.

Give introduction about yourself:

6. We have been in this line of business now for more than ten years and our product knowledge is extremely good.

7. My experience in this trade as a representative of M/s India Sales Corporation is of more than ten years. Therefore, it will help me a great deal to serve customers efficiently and meet their requirements promptly.

8. As technical supervisor for Fairview Television Company I have competently handled and repaired all kinds of T.V. sets.

9. We have been in this line for a long time. Wide and varied experience will help us to mobilise the business and satisfy the customers.

10. This has been our family business for three generations. Thus, we are well versed in cloth trade.

Make a mention about new premises:

11. The store's timing will be from 10 a.m. to 7 p.m.

12. The opening ceremony of the centre will take place in the morning at 10 o'clock on the above day.

13. We are offering 5 percent inauguration discount on all first day purchases.

14. Attractive gifts will be offered on all first day purchases of more than Rs.500/-.

Extend invitation:

15. We look forward to your patronage.

16. We hope you will grace the occasion with your presence on the opening day.

17. May I invite you to avail of the inauguration discount ?

18. You are cordially invited.

19. Kindly come and encourage us.

Circular Regarding New Branch

Announce the opening of a new branch:

1. We take great pleasure in announcing that on 1st January 2001, we are opening a new branch of ready-made garments at 15 Nehru Place, New Delhi.

2. We are pleased to inform you that as part of our expansion plans we have opened a new branch of our saree store in your colony.

3. Owing to the large increase in the volume of our trade in North Bombay we have decided to open a branch in Dadar.

4. We are pleased to inform you that our new store at No.7 South Extension Market, New Delhi will be officially inaugurated by the Minister of Tourism on Sunday the 9th April, 2000.

Give reasons for opening a new branch:

5. The new branch is just the expression of customers' growing faith in our products.
6. Although we have so far served you efficiently, you deserve still better services that await you.
7. Now with a branch in your locality we have virtually come to your door steps.

Give details about the new branch:

8. Mr. Sunil Kumar, our Manager for the last 20 years, will be, in charge of the new branch.
9. The new branch will be opened on 15th April, 2000. Therefore, from that date all orders and enquiries may be sent to Mr. Sunil Kumar at 18 Laxmi Road, Puna, instead of sending them to our Bombay office.
10. This branch is managed by some of the best salesmen of the line who will take pleasure in providing excellent service.
11. Mr. Prem Prakash who has been in charge of the wholesale division at our head office for the last 15 years will head the new branch.
12. Mr. K.L. Sharma will represent us in this new branch. His dealings with customers have always been highly appreciated.

Express hope for closer business patronage:

13. We take this opportunity to thank our customers and are sure that our services will further improve with this new arrangement.
14. We welcome a visit by you to our new branch.
15. We eagerly look forward to provide you with more extensive services.
16. At this new branch we hope to receive your orders as usual for prompt delivery.
17. Our association has been long lasting and we hope that it will continue likewise.
18. So in future please send your enquiries and orders to our Agra branch instead of sending them directly to our Head Office in New Delhi.

Circular Regarding Acquisition of a Firm

Inform about acquisition:

1. It is our pleasure to inform you that M/s Beauty Products Co., has been acquired by us from the 1st of this month.
2. We have recently purchased the sole interests in the silk sari business of M/s Mysore Sari Emporium, 15 Main Road, Shahdara.
3. We have pleasure in informing you that M/s Cosmetic Corner, Sunder Market, has been acquired by us from 1st May, 2000.
4. We take pleasure to intimate you that Modern General Stores, 14 Kamla Market, has been purchased by us. We shall start transactions from 2nd August, 2000.
5. It is our pleasure to inform you that we have taken possession of 'Fashion House', 28A, Shaktinagar, and from 15th August, 2000, we are starting a retail sale.

Give self introduction:

6. You will be pleased to know that we have been in this line for more than two decades.

7. Our long experience in this line and substantial investment place us in a position to offer better goods to the customers.

8. Being new in this line of business, we have hired highly professional and competent staff.

9. We are well known in the market in this trade and hope to fully satisfy the public.

10. We have been veterans in this field. Thus you can rely on us for quality products.

11. We shall not only continue to trade under the old name but also make every effort to adhere to our predecessor's policy of sound services on which the goodwill of the firm has been ·built.

12. The business will be transferred to a new department in our main store in Connaught Circus, New Delhi, with Mr. Sushil Kumar as the Manager.

13. Mr. Sushil Kumar was the General Manager of the old firm and his deep knowledge of the ready-made garments business, acquired during a lifetime spent in the trade, will continue to be at your disposal.

14. Mr. L. Kahyap who will be in charge of Fashion House is an expert designer and well versed in this trade.

15. We have completely renovated the premises and have spent a considerable amount on the décor.

16. In order to get acquainted with our prospective customers we are hosting a lunch at 2 p.m. on 8th August. You are cordially invited.

17. We propose to offer the old stock in a bargain sale next week on very attractive terms.

18. We have reduced prices by 10% on every item of old stock and, thus, we hope to get better acquainted with you.

Extend invitation for visit:

19. We hope you will be kind enough to extend your usual co-operation.

20. We can assure you of the best of our services. Please pay us a visit and see for yourself.

21. We are sure that even under the new management this firm will continue to receive your generous support.

22. We hope we shall build a·lasting relationship with you.

Notice of Change of Address

Inform about shifting of premises:

1. We take pleasure in informing you that we have shifted to larger premises at Nav Niwas colony from 1st August, 2000.

2. We have pleasure in informing you that the offices of Gorgeous Garment Company, Ajmeri Gate, Delhi, have been shifted to 5/6 WEA Ajmal Khan Road, Karol Bagh, New Delhi, w.e.f. July 19, 2000.

3. This is to inform you that we have shifted our offices to the new commercial complex at Kalyan Pur.

4. The new address of our firm is Nirmal Cheap Silk Store, 25 Ajmal Khan Road, Karol Bagh, New Delhi.

5. From 1st June 2000, we will be functioning from 15 Shri D.B. Gupta Road, Karol Bagh.

Give details of the new premises:

6. The need for larger premises on account of steady expansion has warranted this shift.

7. The place is centrally located and will facilitate prompt deliveries.

8. The new premises also provides scope for better methods of production that will increase output besides improving the quality of our products further.

9. The new site is in the heart of the city and within easy reach by rail and road.

10. At the new place transport has now become easier ensuring prompt deliveries.

Give assurance for better services:

11. We hope to serve you better with these improvements.

12. Although the new premises are on the outskirts of the city, we hope to meet deliveries promptly.

13. We are sure of serving you better from this place.

14. We can assure you of efficient services.

Announcement Regarding Clearance Sale

Make announcement of sales:

1. This is to advise you that we are holding a clearance sale from 15th March. We enclose a catalogue.

2. We take great pleasure in informing you that we are holding a clearance sale from February 14 to 19.

3. We are holding a clearance sale of our old stocks for a week commencing from Monday, February 14.

4. We are going to have a clearance sale for a week at very reduced prices from 1st Jan. to 6th Jan., 2000, at Janpath Hotel, New Delhi.

5. As the summer is coming we are holding a clearance sale, of our woollen clothes, starting from March 2, 2000.

Refer to attractions of sale:

6. All stocks will be cleared regardless of cost.

7. Attractive discount is being offered on all articles ranging from 10% to 40%.

8. Prices have been reduced in some cases by over 50% and in all departments exceptional opportunities are being offered to obtain high class goods at prices far below the cost.

9. The goods offered for sale are new and of high quality.

10. Stocks to be cleared are excellent, both in terms of variety and quality.

Extend invitation to sales:

11. As we expect heavy rush we suggest that you visit the shop in the morning hours when it is going to be more comfortable.
12. During the first few days of the sale you will find many bargains at very low prices.
13. We hope you will be able to pay us a visit during the sale and make your selections.
14. In case you are unable to visit we shall be happy to reserve for you any goods that you order from the catalogue, to be despatched on February 1.
15. Assuring you of the best and most efficient services.

Circular Regarding Retirement of a Partner

Start with main information:

1. We regret to inform you that our senior partner Mr. Rajaram Shastri has decided to retire from 31st March this year.
2. We regret to inform you that our senior partner Mr. Dharm Dutt Shastri has decided to retire from the firm.
3. We are sorry to announce the retirement of our valued partner, Mr. Man Mohan from this firm.
4. We are sorry to inform that our partner, Mr. K. Sharma, has opted to proceed on retirement from 3rd December, 2000.
5. This is to inform you that our partner, Mr. M.N. Gupta, has withdrawn his share from the company and thus he ceases to be our partner any longer.

Mention something about the outgoing partner:

6. He has sought this retirement on account of ill health.
7. Shri Das will, however, continue to act in an advisory capacity.
8. His absence, of course, will leave a gap which would be difficult to fill.
9. Mr. Verma has had to take this decision on account of old age and continuing ill-health.
10. Mr. Sharma has cut his share by 50% and appointed his son, Rajat Sharma, as partner in his place.
11. The withdrawal of capital by Mr. Shastri will be made good by the continuing partners. As a result the volume of firm's capital will remain unchanged.
12. The firm will continue to function under its present name of Shastri Kumar & Co., and there will be no change in its established policy.
13. The business will be conducted as it has been in the past.
14. In consequence of the withdrawal of capital by the retiring partner, we have applied for a loan from Industrial Finance Corporation and it has been sanctioned.
15. No further change will be made in the constitution of the firm, its name or its policy.

Express hope for cordial relations:

16. We hope that the new arrangements will not affect our long business relationship and you will continue to repose your faith in us.

17. We will ensure that the firm's present standard of service is maintained.
18. With the induction of young blood like his son, we hope to make our services more efficient.
19. We take this opportunity to thank you for your co-operation in the past and hope we can count on your continued support.
20. I take this opportunity to again remind you of our continuing cordial relationship and wish that it becomes better in the years to come.
21. We assure you of the same care and prompt attention to your orders as in the past.

Circular Regarding Admission of New Partner

Make announcement about new partner:

1. We take pleasure in announcing the induction of Mr. Bharat Bhushan as a partner in our firm.
2. We are pleased to inform you that Mr. Ram Prasad Gupta, our esteemed partner, has inducted his son, Mr. Ramesh Gupta, as the fifth partner of our firm.
3. We are pleased to inform you that we have now admitted Mr. Ramanath as a partner w.e.f. 8th July, 2000.
4. It is our pleasure to inform you that we have just taken Shri Raj Kishore, an experienced mechanical engineer, into partnership of the firm.
5. We are glad to inform you that with effect from July 1, 1999, Mr. Bhaskar Rao, our General Manager, will become a partner of this firm.

Tell the necessity for taking new partner:

6. This was, in fact, necessitated following the death of our friend and partner, Mr. Dhan Raj.
7. In fact, the substantial increase in the volume of business made it imperative for inclusion of another partner.
8. We were compelled to add a new partner because of our work-load and business expansion.
9. His inclusion has come in view of the proposed expansion of our business.
10. Entry of a new partner was necessary as one of our former partners had shifted his interests to some foreign concern.

Give introduction of the new partner:

11. Mr. Prakash has been our General Manager for the past ten years and is well acquainted with every aspect of the firm's business.
12. Although Mr. Gupta is young he is dynamic and has a lot of drive.
13. He has worked as Sales Manager with Telco for more than 10 years.
14. We are sure his experience will come in handy and further boost our business.
15. A specimen of Mr. Bharat Bhushan's signature is given below.
16. Our dealings will not be affected in any way on account of this new admission.
17. We are sure to do better under his expert guidance.

Circular Regarding Conversion of Partnership into a Private Ltd. Company

Change in constitution of business:

1. We take great pleasure in informing you that our company has become a Private Limited Company w.e.f. July 1, 2000.

2. We are pleased to inform you that we have decided to convert our firm into a Private Limited Company with a view to raise the necessary capital for the proposed expansion and diversification of our business.

3. It is our pleasure to inform you that we are converting our business into a private company so that we could serve you still better.

Advice about new name:

4. Additional capital for the expansion of company's activities has necessitated this step.

5. The new company has been registered with limited liability under the name of "Patel & Desai Pvt. Ltd."

6. Our company, thus, has been renamed as "Fashion Wear Co. (P) Ltd".

Assurance for good future dealings:

7. Although the constitution of the company has changed, we assure all our customers the same co-operation and attention.

8. The nature of business will remain exactly as before and there will be no change in business policy.

9. It goes without saying that this will not, in any way, affect our healthy relationship with our customers.

10. We shall constantly endeavour to meet our business commitments with complete customer satisfaction.

11. We assure that our customers' interests will remain quite safe in our hands.

12. We take this opportunity to assure you that you will receive the same care and attention as in the past in the execution of your orders.

13. We hope the new arrangements will not affect our business relationship in any way but will continue to grow.

Sample Letters

(Circular Announcing Opening of New Business)

Dear Sirs,

We take great pleasure in announcing the opening of a T.V repair shop in your colony's market (Shop No.617) on the auspicious day of Janmashtami.[2] As technical supervisor for Fairview Television company I have competently handled and repaired all kinds of T.V. sets.[8] The opening ceremony of the centre will take place in the morning at 10 o' clock on 4th September, 2000. You are cordially invited.[18]

Thanking you,

Yours faithfully,

(Circular Regarding New Branch)

Dear Sirs,

We take great pleasure in announcing that on 1st of Jan., 2001, we are opening a new branch of ready-made garments at 15 Nehru Place, New Delhi.[1] Although we have so far served you efficiently, you deserve still better services that await you.[6] Mr. Sunil Kumar, our Manager, for the last 20 years, will be in charge of the new branch.[8] We welcome a visit by you to our new branch.[14]

With thanks,

Yours faithfully,

(Circular Regarding Acquisition of a Firm)

Dear Sirs,

We have recently purchased the sole interests in the silk sari business of M/s Mysore Sari Emporium, 15 Main Road, Shahdara.[2] Our long experience in this line and substantial investment place us in a position to offer better goods to the customers.[7] We shall not only continue to trade under the old name but also make every effort to adhere to our predecessor's policy of sound service on which the goodwill of the firm has been built.[11] We propose to offer the old stock in a bargain sale next week on very attractive terms.[17] We hope you will be kind enough to extend your usual co-operation.[19]

Thanking you,

Yours faithfully,

(Notice of Change of Address)

Dear Sirs,

We take great pleasure in informing you that we have shifted to larger premises at Nav Niwas Colony from 1st August, 2000.[1] The shift is due to the fact that the new site is in the heart of the city and within easy reach by rail and road.[9] We are sure of serving you better from this place.[13]

With thanks,

Yours faithfully,

(Announcement Regarding Clearance Sale)

Dear Sirs,

We take great pleasure in informing you that we are holding a clearance sale from February 14 to 19.[2] Attractive discount is being offered on all articles, ranging from 10% to 40%. In case you are unable to visit we shall be happy to reserve for you any goods that you order from the catalogue, to be despatched on February 1.[14]

With thanks,

Yours faithfully,

(Circular Regarding Retirement of a Partner)

Dear Sirs,

We are sorry to announce the retirement of our valued partner Mr. Man Mohan from this firm.[3] He has sought this retirement on account of ill-health.[6] We assure you of the same care and prompt attention to your orders as in the past.[21]

With thanks,

Yours faithfully,

(Circular re. Admission of a New Partner)

Dear Sirs,

We take pleasure in announcing the induction of Mr. Bharat Bhushan as a partner in our firm.[1] This was, in fact, necessitated following the death of our friend and partner Mr. Dhan Raj.[6] A specimen of Mr. Bharat Bhushan's signature is given below.[15]

With thanks,

Yours faithfully,

(Circular re. Conversion of Partnership to a Private Ltd. Co.)

Dear Sirs,

We take great pleasure in informing you that our company has become a Private Limited Company w.e.f. July 1, 2000.[1] Our company thus, has been renamed as "Fashion Wear Co. (P) Ltd.[6] The nature of business will remain exactly as before and there will be no change in business policy.[8]

With thanks,

Yours faithfully,

Agency Correspondence

Any growing business calls for wider markets. And, it is not possible for every company to open branches at all the places where it has markets. Thus, it has to rely on agents – a practice widely accepted all over the world. An agency can be set up on the initiative of the principal or the agent himself. In such an arrangement both parties have to be extremely cautious because the reputation and goodwill of both affect each other's business.

While having such an arrangement, both parties keep an number of factors in mind. The agent has to see whether a potential market for the particular product exists or not and whether it can be easily developed. On the other hand the manufacturer/principal must make sure about the financial soundness of the agent, technical skill to handle the product, his market connections, effectiveness of sales organisation, and the nature and extent of the other agencies he might hold. The supplier/principal can negotiate terms of business/agency commission keeping in view all these matters. He, of course, has to take into account the market possibilities, his own production capacity, interest and policies for promoting the business in a particular area. Now, whether such an arrangement finally comes through or not depends mainly on the requirements or preferences of the principal or the agent.

General Application for an Agency

Beginning:

1. We shall be glad if you would consider our application to act as agents for the sale of your footwear/spark plugs.

2. We are the agents of a number of Bombay based publishers and wish to procure agency for your books also.

3. We take this opportunity to offer our services as agents for the sale of your glassware in our city.

4. We understand from M/s Vohra and Sons that you are looking for agents in Bulandshahr.

5. Given a chance, we shall feel privileged to work for and on behalf of your company.

6. We take this opportunity to offer ourselves as your representatives in the city.

7. Being in this field for a long time we have extremely good connections in the city.

8. Till recently we had been acting as agents of M/s. New Star Publications. But as they have now opened their own office in the city they don't need our services. We are, therefore, free to offer our services to any other firm.

9. Our reputation in the auto industry is well known and we are already dealers for Suzuki and LML scooters.

10. We have a well furnished showroom on the prestigious Mahatma Gandhi Road.

11. On account of our prompt and excellent service, our clientele has grown steadily ever since we established our firm.

12. We hope to hear favourably from you and feel sure that we will have no difficulty in reaching agreeable business terms.

13. If desired, we can give you several first rate references.

14. We anticipate no problem in settling the terms and conditions for such business

Appointment of Local Agent

Inform about granting the agency:

1. We thank you for your letter of 5th October and are pleased to inform you that we have decided to appoint you our agent for Delhi.

2. We take pleasure in informing you that following your discussions with our representative, Mr. I.K. Mundra, who visited you last week, we have appointed you our agent for Bangalore from the 1st of next month.

3. Having carefully taken into consideration the agency terms you have offered and the references you have provided, we are pleased to appoint you our agent for Mathura for a trial period of one year.

4. We are pleased to inform you that our Directors have approved your application for agency with effect from 1st January 2001.

Terms and conditions of agency:

5. We have decided to put you on a trial period of three months initially. During this period we shall pay 7% commission on all the sales.

6. If the terms of the said agreement meet your approval, we request you to return us the duplicate copy duly signed by you.

7. We shall be sending our representative, Mr. B.J. Kapoor, next week with a formal agreement of terms and conditions, to be signed by you.

8. Kindly go through the terms and conditions sent separately and return them duly signed.

9. Your appointment as our agent is, of course, subject to your approval of our terms and conditions, a copy of which is enclosed.

Close of the letter:

10. We hope the enclosed agreement will receive your consent and quote our present prices which are as follows.

11. We have already had business relations with a couple of firms in your city whom we are now intimating about your appointment as our agent.

12. If you agree to these terms, we shall send a formal agreement to be signed by you.

13. Now, will you please let us have your plans and program to organize sales in your district during the first six months.

14. As soon as we hear from you, we shall arrange to despatch the goods for the first three months.

Acceptance of Agency

Convey acceptance:

1. We thank you for your letter of 9th March along with copies of your standard form of agency agreement and are happy to convey our acceptance of your agency.

2. We have received your form of agency agreement and are happy to return it duly signed by our Managing Director, Mr. M.R. Aggarwal.

3. We have gone through your terms of agreement and are pleased to intimate you that we accept your offer.

4. Thank you for your letter of 3rd October, offering us the sole agency for your milk products in Haryana.

5. We thank you for offering us the agency for your sarees in Bangalore and appreciate the confidence you have reposed in us.

Other important things:

6. We have also received your catalogue which covers an extensive range of interesting titles.

7. Your publications are in big demand because they are ideally suited to the High School and under graduate courses.

8. We are prepared to incur an initial expenditure of Rs.50,000/- on advertising and will back it up with active campaign through our sales-staff.

9. We are now sending a circular to prospective customers in this region informing them of our appointment as your agents.

Closure:

10. Thank you for giving us the first opportunity to take your agency here.

11. As desired by you, we enclose a copy of the contract duly signed by our Managing Director, Mr. K.P. Gulati.

12. We now look forward to a mutually beneficial business relationship with you.

13. We already represent several other manufacturers and assure you of our best services.

14. We accept your terms and conditions as set out in the draft agreement and look forward to a happy and successful working relationship with you.

Inquiry for Sole Agency

Begin with your offer:

1. We have recently read with interest your advertisement in 'The Times of India' offering the sole agency of your brassware.

2. We have seen your machine tools in the International Trade Fair at Delhi this year and have found them of high quality.

3. We have been impressed with the high quality and reasonable prices of your photographic material demonstrated in the International Exhibition in Bombay.

4. Having had a discussion with your partner, we have become interested in representing you in Chandigarh.

5. Having had an opportunity to visit your hardware stall in the 'Trade Fair 99', we are inclined to have a sole agency for the same.

Give your credentials:

6. As a leading distributor of high fashion garments with more than ten years' standing in the market, we are well acquainted with the market conditions in the region.

7. Through an active sales organisation, we have established good contacts with leading retailers.

8. Although we handle several other agencies, they are in non-competing lines.
9. You would, of course, be interested in knowing about us. And for this, we would refer you to Bharat Sales Emporium, Delhi and Bank of India, Connaught Place, New Delhi.
10. We are well-known distributors with over fifteen years' standing and branches in most of the principal towns of Gujarat. You can refer to Punjab National Bank, Main street, Ahmedabad, to know more about us.
11. We are well acquainted with the local market conditions and have a wide experience in the trade.

Express expectations of good business:

12. We have seen your catalogue and are convinced that there is a promising market for these products in Karnataka.
13. We are sure your products will have good sales in these areas.
14. We are sure that we will be able to give a boost to the sales of your products.
15. We are confident that with the high quality of your products and our selling experience, we can make a grand success of achieving the sales target for this year.
16. Since we are experts in the field, we are sure of bringing you a good margin of profit.
17. We are confident of bringing you huge profits because of our wide-ranging contacts in the field.

Close the letter on a bright note:

18. We firmly believe that such an arrangement will be of mutual benefit to both of us.
19. We assure you that our handling of your products, as sole agents for the territory of Maharashtra, will be of advantage to both of us.
20. We look forward to your acceptance.
21. We are sure of getting you unexpected profit if we become your sole agent here in Poona.

Reply to Inquiry for the Sole Agency

Convey thanks on receiving inquiry:

1. We thank you for your letter of 22nd November and are pleased to learn that you are interested in promoting the sales of our products.
2. We are happy to learn that, in your opinion, there are good prospects for the sale of our products in your State.
3. Thank you for your letter dt. 8th April and we are pleased to learn that you like our kitchen appliances.
4. We thank you for your letter of 25th November, expressing your interest in our hand-tools.
5. We feel pleased to acknowledge your interest in our electronic products advertisements which you have notice in the national press.

Ask details about terms and prospects regarding the sole agency:

6. We have not yet decided about giving agency for Maharashtra but if your representative calls on us when he is in Delhi next we would be glad to discuss with him the possibility of coming to some agreement with you.

7. Although we have not taken any decision regarding the agency, we have advised our representative Mr. Jugal Kishore to visit you next week.

8. A rough estimate of the amount of stock you could hold, at a given time, would be welcome.

9. We are a growing company and wish to develop trade in your region.

10. We would certainly like to get in touch with your representative, when he is in town, to discuss the prospects in detail regarding the Sole Agency which you have asked for.

11. Meanwhile, we take pleasure in sending you our catalogue and price-lists giving details of discount.

Tell about your immediate programme:

12. In the meantime, your representative can visit us whenever he is in town. He can see for himself the excellent quality of raw material and the manufacturing technology at our factory.

13. Meanwhile, we would be pleased to supply you with an initial order at the prices quoted against a sight draft at 30 days, after booking of the order.

14. Meanwhile, could you please send us the detailed record of your sales performance for the past two years.

15. In the mean time, we are ready to supply you the initial order at the maximum discount and f.o.r.

Agent's Request for More Commission

Ask for more Commission:

1. We would be glad if you consider some upward revision, in your present rate of commission to the wholesale dealers.

2. We write this letter to request you to increase our commission.

3. We trust you will agree with us that the present condition of the sale justifies an increase in the percentage of commission we receive from you.

4. In view of the prevailing competitive condition in the market., we have to request you to increase our rate of commission.

5. Since we have recently brought huge orders and incurred heavy expenses, we have to request you to increase our rate of commission.

Express why it is necessary to increase commission:

6. In fact, because of the latest trends in the market, it has become more difficult to market your goods.

7. Ever since we have taken your agency many competitors have entered the market and established themselves.

8. As a result of increased competition we have been able to hold our sales only by driving our salesmen hard and increasing our publicity budget.

9. And this, of course, calls for compensation from the manufacturer.

10. In order to compete effectively, we would request you to increase the rate of commission.

11. Although your garments are modern and stylish, in view of the fact that many other competitors are already established firmly in the line, it is providing difficult to make a dent on the market.

12. As my sales efforts for your products will now mean additional expenditure on advertisement, I must request you to bear part of the increased costs.

Close with expectation of more Commission:

13. We feel the compensation from your side could be in the form of an increase in commission, say by 10%.

14. We suggest this figure after carefully calculating the increase in our advertising budget/ selling costs.

15. Under the circumstances we sincerely hope you will revise the commission.

16. As is evident from the present scenario, we are left with no option but to ask for a raise of 2 ½% in the rate of commission.

17. I shall be pleased to hear what you have to suggest as regards the increase in commission.

18. Considering our old established relations, we hope you would take a favourable decision on our request.

19. We hope you would consider our present request with understanding and sympathy.

20. We trust you will take a favourable view of the circumstances and allow an increase in the rate of commission.

Manufacturer's Reply to Agent's Request for More Commission

First acknowledge the letter:

1. Thank you for your letter of 21st July.

2. We are in receipt of your letter dated February 2, 2000.

3. Thank you for your letter dt. 8th July on.....

4. We confirm receipt of your letter dated 2nd July, 2000.

5. We thank you for your letter dated 5th August, 2000.

Agree to the agent's proposal:

6. We have noted with utmost concern the problems presented by our competitors in your city.

7. We are pleased to learn the extra efforts you have put to meet the new challenge.

8. Although we are sure that our products, in long run, will stand the test of time, we realise that the growing competition must be met by more active advertising.

9. We agree that it would not be reasonable to expect you to bear the full cost.

10. We realise your difficulty in meeting the challenging situation in the market.

Give information for future programme:

11. However, to increase the commission at this stage would be difficult, as our prices leave us with a very small margin.

12. Instead, we propose to allow you an advertising credit of Rs.1,000/- in the current year towards your additional costs.

13. However, in view of the very small margin of our profit, we can increase your commission by 1 ½% only.

14. Thus, we have accepted your proposal but can allow only 2% increase as a short term measure for 6 months, on account of the current market situation.

15. We hope you will be happy with the alternative arrangement we have suggested.

16. With due appreciation of your efforts to maintain the sales of our products, we regret we will not be in a position to increase your commission for another six months.

Sample Letters
(General Application for Agency)

Dear Sirs,

We shall be glad if you would consider our application to act as agents for the sale of your spark plugs.[1] Our reputation in the auto industry is well known and we are already dealers for Suzuki and LML scooters.[9] We anticipate no problem in settling the terms and conditions for such business.[14]

Thanking you,

Yours faithfully,

(Appointment of Local Agent)

Dear Sirs,

We are pleased to inform you that our Directors have approved your application for agency with effect from 1st January, 2001.[4] Kindly go through the terms and conditions sent separately and return them duly signed.[8] We hope the enclosed agreement will receive your consent and quote our present prices, which are as follows.[10]

With thanks,

Yours faithfully,

(Acceptance of Agency)

Dear Sirs,

We thank you for your letter of 9th March, along with copies of your standard form of agency agreement and are happy to convey our acceptance of your agency.[1] We have also received your catalogue which covers an extensive range of interesting titles.[6] Thank you for giving us the first opportunity to take up your agency here.[10]

With thanks,

Sincerely yours,

(Inquiry for Sole Agency)

Dear Sirs,

We have recently read with interest your advertisement in 'The Times of India' offering the sole agency of your brassware.[1] We are well known distributors with over fifteen years' standing and branches in most of the principal towns of Gujarat. You can refer to Punjab National Bank, Main Street, Ahmedabad, to know more about us.[10] We are sure your products will have good sales in these areas.[13]

Thanking you,

Yours faithfully,

(Reply to Inquiry for the Sole Agency)

Dear Sirs,

We thank you for your letter of 22nd November, and are pleased to learn that your are interested in promoting the sales of our products.[1] Meanwhile could your please send us the detailed records of your sales performance for the past two years.[14] Although we have not taken any decision regarding the agency, we have advised our representative Mr. Jugal Kishore to visit your city next week.[7]

With best wishes,

Sincerely yours,

(Agent's Request for More Commission)

Dear Sirs,

We trust you will agree with us that the present condition of the sale justifies an increase in the percentage of commission we receive from you.[3] Ever since, we have taken your agency many competitors have entered the market and established themselves.[7] Under the circumstances we sincerely hope you will revise the commission.[15]

Thanking you,

Yours faithfully,

(Manufacturer's Reply to Agent's Request for More Commission)

Dear Sirs,

Thank you for your letter of 21st July.[1] We have noted with utmost concern the problems presented by our competitors in your city.[6] We realise your difficulty in meeting the challenging situation in the market.[10] Thus, we have accepted your proposal but can allow only 2% increase as a short term measure for 6 months, on account of the current market situation.[14]

Yours faithfully,

Trade Reference and Status Inquiry

When the goods are sold for cash, there is no need for the seller to inquire into the financial standing of the buyer. But when they are sold on credit, as is the common business practice nowadays, the seller has to make sure about the financial credit-worthiness of the buyer. He must know whether the customer can make the payment in time or not. He can obtain this information from various sources, namely (i) trade references supplied by the buyer himself (ii) the buyer's banker or (iii) various trade associations.

However, the credit through bank is taken against Hundi. The 'Hundi' can be of any duration varying from 30 days to 180 days. This credit is safe since Hundi has legal validity and is accepted as a sure evidence in the civil court.

Supplier's Request for References

Ask for trade references:

1. We shall be glad to take in hand your order dt. 3rd February, for immediate delivery if you send us the customary trade references.

2. We thank you for your order No.L503 for the supply of 100 'medium' hockey sticks.

3. We are pleased to receive your order of 15th May. But since it is your first order we shall be glad to consider credit terms if you kindly provide us with the usual trade references.

4. We are happy to receive your order of 2nd November for 100 Banarasi silk saris. We could, of course, extend the required credit, if you kindly send us the name and address of your bankers.

5. Thank you for your order of 10th June for 100 'Deluxe' dining-tables. However, we would like to inform you that since it is your first dealing with us we require references.

6. We thank you for your order of 4th November, but since this is your first order with us, and as it is customary in our business, we would appreciate your giving us trade reference of a party with whom you have had dealings for the last few years.

7. Will you, therefore, please send us the names and addresses of two other suppliers with whom you have dealings ?

Give assurance of business cooperation:

8. As soon as we hear from the reference we shall despatch the goods. Your order is under processing.

9. You will appreciate that this is a normal practice and trust you won't mind our insisting on it.

10. When opening new accounts it is customary to ask for trade references.Therefore, will you please send names and addresses of the referees.

11. So, to enable us to take up the execution of orders we would be glad if you furnish the names of two firms with whom you have had regular dealings.

12. Please send us the name and address of your bankers for the usual trade references.

References Supplied by the Dealer

Begin the letter in this way:

1. Thank you for your letter of 5ᵗʰ April. As we hope to place further orders with you, we would like to avail of your credit facilities.

2. As requested in your letter of 7ᵗʰ August we are furnishing below the names of two dealers to whom you may refer.

3. In response to your letter dt. 4ᵗʰ January we suggest you to refer to our bankers.........

4. We thank you for your letter of 8ᵗʰ July and quite understand the need for references. We have completed and are now returning you credit application in which we have listed the names and addresses of our bankers and also of two well known firms with whom we have had dealings for many years.

5. In response to your inquiry of 18ᵗʰ November, we would like to say that you may take up references with the following firms with whom we have had dealings for many years.

6. We thank you for your letter of 5ᵗʰ June, 2000 and give the names of the following firms as references for you to inquire into our financial standing.

7. We thank you for your letter of 5ᵗʰ October and are happy to inform you that we have been dealing with M/s Modern Utilities Company of your town for the last five years. Our bankers, Central Bank of India, Parliament Street, New Delhi can also be referred to this purpose.

Write about other important matters:

8. We now have pleasure in sending you our first order for five "Madhur" pocket transistors at your listed price of Rs.570/- less 25% on your usual monthly terms.

9. We note that we may expect delivery of the goods ordered last month and look forward to receiving them in time.

10. We now look forward to get into a large volume of business with you on a regular basis.

11. Now, we hope to get a prompt delivery of the goods ordered by us.

12. Now that the formalities are over, we hope to receive our ordered goods at the earliest.

13. Now we hope this will lead to a long and fruitful business relationship.

14. Here we give the names and addresses of two firms who are our regular suppliers for more than 10 years.

15. For information on our financial standing, we refer you to our bankers.........

16. Should you wish to take up references, the following firms will be pleased to answer your inquiries.

Supplier Takes up References

Starting the letter:

1. M/s. Fancy Footwear of Baroda wish to open an account with us and have given us your name as reference.

2. We have today received an order for Rs.50,000/- for stainless steel utensils from Cookwell Kitchen Stores, Faridabad, who have given us your name as reference.

3. Mr. Anil Kumar of 13, Nehru Road, Agra, has referred us to you for information concerning his credit standing.

4. We have received a large order from M/s. Welcome Garments Stores, New Delhi, and shall be grateful to you for any information you could give us concerning their reliability.

5. M/s. Modern Cosmetics Company, New Delhi, have referred us to you for information regarding their credit standing, as they wish to open an account with us.

6. M/s. Tyre-Tube Traders of Ghaziabad have requested us to supply them 100 truck tubes. Since they wish us to supply the goods on credit they have given us your name as reference.

Asking for reference:

7. We would be grateful if you could provide us with reliable information concerning his firm's credit-worthiness.

8. We would be grateful if you give us the information you can about the firm's general standing.

9. Please confirm whether, in your opinion, this company is reliable for credit upto Rs.50000/- and whether they settle their accounts promptly.

10. We wish to know about the general standing of the firm and if they are likely to be reliable for credit upto Rs.1,00,000/-.

11. We shall be grateful for any information you could give us about this firm.

12. We shall take it as a favour if you could kindly tell us whether you have found this company reliable in dealings and prompt in settling their accounts.

13. We gather that the credit requirements of this firm may go up to R.50000/- per month. We will be grateful for your opinion about their ability to meet commitments of this size.

14. We shall also welcome any other information you could supply us about the firm.

Keeping the information confidential:

15. We assure you that any information supplied by you will be treated in strict confidence.

16. We shall, of course, treat any advice you give us in this regard as strictly confidential.

17. Your reply will naturally be treated in strict confidence.

18. Needless to say that any information you supply us, shall be treated in strict confidence.

19. We shall be equally glad to render you a similar service, should the need arise.

20. We would perform a similar service to you, if an opportunity ever arises.

21. We shall be equally pleased to perform a similar service to you, if ever you require of us.

Expressing thanks:

22. We shall indeed be grateful for your co-operation.

23. Please accept in advance our thanks for any assistance you can give us.

24. Any information you could give us will be greatly appreciated.

25. We shall feel obliged to receive any information in this regard from you.

26. This is something which we need to have business and we will feel thankful for the same.

Enclosing reply envelope:

27. We enclose a self-addressed stamped envelope for your reply.

28. Please find enclosed a self-addressed stamped envelope for your kind reply.

29. Please find herewith a stamped, self-addressed envelope for an early reply.

30. Just to save your time, we are enclosing a stamped and self-addressed envelope.

Replies to References

Express your opinion:

1. We are pleased to state that though the firm referred to in your letter of 3rd June is a small one, it is well known and has been established in this town for more than 25 years.

2. The company M/s.. Greatway Footwear, Model Town, which you have referred to us, is a well-established firm and is very fair in its dealings.

3. We must express surprise that the company you have named has given our name for reference.

4. As far as we know it is a reputed firm, but we have no definite knowledge of its financial standing.

5. Although they have often placed orders with us, they have been of very small amounts.

6. In response to your letter of 5th March, we are glad to report favourably on M/s. Gorgeous Garment Company, Delhi.

7. In reply to your letter of 17th September, we regret to say that we are unable to express a definite opinion about M/s. Gopinath & Co., Churiwalan, Delhi.

8. We regret that the firm about which you enquired in your letter of 15th July is not well known to us.

9. Concerning the firm mentioned in your letter of 28th February, we recommend a policy of caution.

10. We must regret our inability to extend any assistance regarding the information you desired about M/s. Ashok Brothers, New Delhi.

Give details of your opinion:

11. We ourselves have been doing business with this firm for more than five years on credit terms and they have always been regular and timely in settling their accounts.

12. The company you have referred to has been dealing with us for more than 15 years.

13. The account of this firm with us is on quarterly settlement terms, but we have never allowed it to reach the sum you mentioned in your letter.

14. We have had only occasional and small dealings with this firm and even then accounts were not always settled in time.

15. And so, we feel, caution is necessary in this case.

Request for keeping the matter confidential:

16. We hope this information will be helpful and that you will treat it as confidential.

17. We accept your assurance that this information will be treated in strict confidence and regret that we cannot be more helpful in this regard.

18. This information is given to you in confidence and without any legal responsibility on our part.

19. We regret we do not know this firm so closely as to express an opinion about it and that we cannot be of any help to you in this respect.

Sample Letters
(Supplier's Request for References)

Dear Sirs,

We are pleased to receive your order of 15th May. But since, it is your first order we shall be glad to consider credit terms if you kindly provide us with the usual trade references.[3] As soon as we hear from the referees we shall despatch the goods. Your order is under processing.[8]

With best wishes,

Yours faithfully,

(References Supplied by the Dealer)

Dear Sirs,

We thank you for your letter of 5th October and are happy to inform you that we have been dealing with M/s. Modern Utilities Company of your town for the last five years. Our bankers, Central Bank of India, Parliament Street, New Delhi, can also be referred to for this purpose.[7]

With best wishes,

Yours faithfully,

(Supplier Takes up References)

Dear Sirs,

Mr. Anil Kumar of 13, Nehru Road, Agra, has referred us to you for information concerning his credit standing.[3] We would be grateful if you could provide us with reliable information concerning his firm's credit-worthiness.[7] We assure you that any information supplied by you will be treated in strict confidence.[15] We shall, indeed, be grateful for your co-operation.[22]

With thanks,

Yours faithfully,

(Replies to References)

Dear Sirs,

We are pleased to state that though the firm referred to in you letter of 3rd June is a small one, it is well known and has been established in this town for more than 25 years.[1] We ourselves have been doing business with this firm for more than five years on credit terms and they have always been regular and timely in settling their accounts.[11] We hope this information will be helpful and you will treat it as confidential.[16]

With thanks,

Yours faithfully,

Trade Letter with Foreign Buyers

Export and import trade involves complex procedures and documents. There are certain international traditions and conventions accepted all over the world, in this regard. International trade letters are, in many respects, similar to the inland trade letters. Enquiries are made, orders placed, goods received are acknowledged and paid for. Generally foreign trade is carried on the basis of agency system but direct trade relations can also develop.

An exporter normally prefers to send the goods to a known importer in a foreign country. He may appoint his own agent or conduct business through a recognised exporting agent whose function is to collect different goods from different manufacturers. The agents may also look after the packing, and forward, insure and ship the goods. In this, he may be carrying out the instructions of his principal or acting on his own. On the other hand, the importing agent takes care of unloading, customs, warehousing etc. These formalities being over, he also sells the product through familiar trade channels. Strict government control is exercised in each country on all import/export trade. An order sent by an importer to an exporter is called an indent. It contains all necessary details of the articles required, important instructions for packing, marking, numbering and collection of payments, etc. Packing of overseas goods is carefully and methodically done. It is more or less standardised these days. The marking and numbering help the clearing agent to identify parcels/packets and arrange for distribution or delivery to the concerned.

Sample Letter

M/s. Small Business Publications,

Roop Nagar,

DELHI-110 007.

Dear Sirs,

Your Technology books are becoming extremely popular in our country. Of late, there has been a growing demand for them. So, please despatch us 5 dozen sets at the earliest. The books should be securely packed in wooden boxes of 50 kg each and shipped by

S.S. Kumargiri. The packages should be marked B-S-P and numbered. Please also arrange for the insurance. Invoice value of the books should not be more than $500.00.

We are willing to honour drafts through the Indian Overseas Bank, Singapore. We shall be placing more orders if the books are accepted by the Technical Institutions and industrial houses.

Thanking you,

Yours faithfully,

Bill of Exchange

In a bid to advance its economy, every country is keen to promote its foreign trade. In India, there are may corporations like State Trading Corporation, Food Corporation, Export Promotion Council, etc., to promote export business. However, in addition to these, there are many companies with sound financial backing which are recognised by the Government as exporting houses.

When goods are exported, the buyer is informed of the shipment by the exporter. This letter is called Advice Note. It contains details of goods sent, their prices, name of the ship, its probable date of arrival, etc. Generally, the shipping documents are handed over to the Bank for collection of the bill, but sometimes they are directly forwarded to the buyer if the relations are old and well established.

Bill of lading:

A port/ports in each country may have outlets to different parts of the globe. When goods are received on the ship, the commander issues a receipt called Mate's Receipt. In turn, the owner of the ship gives a Bill of Lading on getting the Mate's Receipt and freight charges of the cargo. The B.L. contains details of exporter's name, number of packages, identity marks, importer's name and the country to which they are shipped. This document is sent to the importer through the bank and authorises the importer to take delivery of the goods after clearing customs and other dues.

Original Invoice:

The first copy of the invoice is called original invoice. It is sent by the exporter to the importer and contains value and description of the goods including markings on packages, etc.

Bill of Exchange:

This is an instrument for transfer of money from the buyer to the supplier. The importer of goods pays the stated amount at sight or after sight as agreed upon in business terms.

All the concerned documents are sent to the bank by the exporter in his own town. The bank sends them to the importer's bank in his country. The payment is made forthwith (at sight) or by signing an acceptance (after sight).

From Seller to Buyer Abroad

Inform about the invoice value:

1. In confirmation of our letter of 2nd March, we are pleased to inform you that we verified your account for the consignment of shoes by S.S. Jal Vihar and advise you that we have drawn on you toady for $200 at two month's sight.

2. We are pleased to inform you that with reference to your letter of 2nd March, we have verified your account for the consignment of ready-made garments and have today drawn on you for $200 at two month's sight, as agreed.

3. Confirming our letter of 2nd March, we are glad to say that having verified your account for the Rice consignment by S.S. Jal Seva, we have drawn on you for $200 at two month's sight, as agreed.

4. We confirm having drawn on you a Bill of Exchange for US $500.00 against goods despatched to you by AWB No..... and under our invoice No.....dt...... (AWB-Air Way Bill).

Request for acceptance of draft:

5. We hope the draft will be honoured on presentation and our account credited accordingly.

6. Kindly honour the draft when presented and debit our account accordingly.

7. We hope you will accept the draft to the debit of our accounts on presentation.

8. Kindly honour the draft as and when presented and debit it to our accounts.

Letter Accepting Draft

Acknowledge honouring the draft:

1. With reference to your letter of 15th April, we are pleased to inform you that we have accepted your draft for $200.

2. We are pleased to inform you that in reply to your letter of 21st March we have accepted your draft of $200 at 20 days' sight, as agreed.

3. In response to your letter of 18th December we are glad to inform you that we have accepted your draft of $125.

4. Please refer to your letter of 1st August 2000 regarding the draft for Rs.25,550/- which we have accepted.

5. We are glad to inform you that your draft for Rs.20,225/- has been accepted by us as per your letter dated 12th July, 2000.

6. We have duly presented the draft and honoured it, debiting the same to your account.

7. Draft has been presented and honoured by us and recorded in your accounts.

8. We have received your draft No. SL 58208 and are pleased to inform that we have duly presented and debited to your account as per your instructions.

Letter Regarding Draft from Buyer to Seller

Inform about the goods sold:

1. We are pleased to inform you that, as indicated in our sales account, we have been able to dispose of your ready-made garments for Rs.25,550/-. After allowing for expenses and commission there remains a balance of Rs.20,400/- in your favour.

2. We are pleased to report as per Sales Account enclosed that we could dispose of your supply of hardware for Rs.20,500/-.. Out of this sale, a balance of Rs.15000/- remains in your favour after deducting expenses and commission.

3. As you will observe from the accompanying Sales Account, we have been able to dispose of your plastic buckets for Rs.10,000/-. Out of this sale a balance of Rs.7,750/- remains in your favour after allowing for expenses and commission.

4. So you could kindly draw on us at 30 days' sight , as agreed.

5. So, kindly draw on us for this amount at thirty days, under advice to us, when we shall be happy to honour your draft.

6. You are, therefore, requested to draw on us under advice for this sum.

Reply to Letter Regarding Draft

Express thanks for getting details of sales:

1. We thank you for your letter of 3rd April containing details of Sales Account.

2. Thank you for the Sales Account, that you have sent with your letter of 13th August.

3. We are pleased to acknowledge your letter of 5th May along with the Sales Account.

4. We have received your letter dated 6th August containing details of Sales Account.

5. It has been examined properly and found it in order.

6. We have examined it and found it in order.

7. On examination, the documents have been found in order.

8. The details of Sales Account were found correct.

9. We have accordingly drawn on you through Dena Bank, Arya Samaj Road, New Delhi for Rs.5,500/- at thirty days' sight, as suggested by you.

10. Accordingly we have drawn on you for an amount of Rs.7,750/- through the Central Bank of India, at 30 days, as agreed earlier.

11. So, please be advised that we have drawn on you through Bank of India, G Block, Connaught Place, New Delhi, for the sum of Rs.10,900/- at 30 days' sight.

Letter Regarding Bill for Collection

Give details of draft:

1. We are pleased to enclose the following drafts for favour of collection:

   Rs.5,550/- at sight on Rao & Co.

   Rs.3,300/- for 25th May on Shastri Brothers.

   Rs.7,700/- for 6th August on Soni & Sons.

   Rs.11,500/- payable in Bombay.

2. Kindly find enclosed the following drafts for favour of collection.

3. We are sending herewith the drafts as per details given below for favour of collection:

4. We shall be obliged if you would credit the proceeds to our accounts and advise us of the receipt in due course.

5. Kindly credit the proceeds to our account and intimate receipt by return post.

6. Kindly credit the proceeds to our accounts and inform accordingly.

Sample Letters

(Bill of Exchange : From Seller to Buyer Abroad)

Dear Sirs,

In confirmation of our letter of 2nd March, we are pleased to inform you that we have verified your account for the consignment of shoes by S.S. Jal Vihar and advise you that we have drawn on you today for $200 at two months's sight.[1] We hope the draft will be honoured on presentation and our account credited accordingly.[5]

With thanks,

Yours faithfully,

(Letter Accepting Draft)

Dear Sirs,

We are pleased to inform you that in reply to your letter of 21st March, we have accepted your draft of $200 at 20 days sight, as agreed.[2]

With thanks,

Yours faithfully,

(Letter Regarding Draft from Buyer to Seller)

Dear Sirs,

As you will observe from the accompanying Account Sales, we have been able to dispose of your plastic buckets for Rs.10,000/-. Out of this sale a balance of Rs.7,750/- remains in your favour after allowing for expenses and commission.[3] You are, therefore, requested to draw on us under advice for this sum.[6]

With thanks,

Yours faithfully,

(Reply to Letter Regarding Draft)

Dear Sirs,

Thank you for the Sales Account that you have sent with your letter of 13th August.[2] The documents have been found in order.[7] So, please be advised that we have drawn on you through Bank of India, G Block, Connaught Place, New Delhi for the sum of Rs.10,900/- at 30 days' sight.[11]

Thanking you,

Yours faithfully,

(Letter Regarding Bill for Collection)

Dear Sirs,

We are pleased to enclose the following drafts for favour of collection: Rs.5,550/- at sight on Rao & Co. We shall be obliged if you would credit the proceeds to our account and advise us of the receipt in due course.[4]

Thanking you,

Yours faithfully,

Export-Import Correspondence

George Bernard Shaw, the famous British dramatist of 20th century, had once remarked, "The universal regard for money is the one hopeful fact in our civilization." It is, of course, true that money is a very important aspect of our life. In the modern times, due to the quick modes of communication and transportation the world is becoming shorter and people of different places are coming closer. As a result, foreign trade is becoming the most important of all trades. It is, therefore, necessary to have sufficient knowledge of correspondence dealing with foreign trade, foreign exchange regulations and foreign banking.

Because of the involvement a second country in this case, correspondence has more facets and intricacies to it than that of the internal trade correspondence. Different kinds of letters and performas are used for handling this correspondence. The main features of this correspondence are clarity, courtesy and completeness. This correspondence must be assigned to a person who is fully capable of conveying the business policies of the firm within the framework of foreign exchange rules and regulations. His understanding of the clients on the other side, his own thinking and interest of the foreign trade must synchronize.

Exporter's Inquiry from Manufacturer

Apprise the manufacturer of foreign demand of goods:

1. We are pleased to inform you that one of our clients in Europe is interested in large scale purchase of silk shirts.

2. You will be pleased to learn that one of our clients in Italy wishes to make large scale purchase of Indian handicraft goods.

3. It will be of interest to you to learn that a reputed foreign dealer in imitation jewellery wishes to introduce Indian fashions in his market.

4. We are glad to inform you that a foreign firm is interested in making huge purchases of Indian silk saris.

5. It may be of interest to you to note that a foreign firm is very keen in making purchase of 'Televista' television sets for supply to Kenya.

Now ask the manufacturer about his supply position:

6. Therefore, we wish to know if you are in a position to supply us adequate quantity of high quality shirts of the material.

7. Consequently, we are interested in knowing if you can undertake to supply such goods of export quality.

8. So could you please send us details and specifications of articles available with you which you can supply in bulk at short notice.

9. We are specially interested in small carved pieces of rosewood and ivory.

10. We are basically interested in fabrics printed essentially with Indian motifs.

11. Our client is particularly interested in sandalwood articles.

Suggest competitive price:

12. This is a competitive quotation and likely to open up a very good avenue for your products in the western Europe.

13. We need not tell you that a really competitive quotation can mean excellent future prospects to you.

14. This is with the assumption that our price would be within certain definite limits which our customer has in mind.

Close your letter with a note about making the best of the opportunity:

15. Our trial order will convince you of the promising prospects of this deal.

16. It will be clear to you that supplying a genuine product could bring you huge profits in the form of regular orders.

17. We hardly need to mention that this is an excellent opportunity for you to enter the export market in a big way, provided, the quality of your products meets the high western standards.

Manufacturer's Reply to Exporter

Express thanks for inquiry:

1. We are obliged for your inquiry of 4th August.
2. Thank you for your letter of inquiry dated 4th August, 2000.
3. We are thankful to you for your kind inquiry vide your letter of 4th August, 2000.
4. Thank you for your letter of inquiry dt. 5th April.

Reply to the points of inquiry:

5. We are prepared to supply you the required goods at the quoted prices less 10% discount with free delivery at destination.
6. We hope you will agree with us that our prices are quite competitive. Catalogue is enclosed.
7. We are offering a special reduction of 10% in the prices of your items in view of the size of your order.
8. We assure you that our quotations for both large and small orders will be extremely competitive.
9. We are quite confident of meeting your delivery schedule.
10. We have a large production unit and can meet your order for any reasonable delivery date.

Write about the supply position of your products:

11. Our imitation jewellery is widely exported and has good demand throughout Europe.
12. Our products have been becoming more and more popular in western Europe and have, recently, been introduced into the USA too.
13. We are sending herewith a few samples of the same.
14. Under separate cover, we are sending you some samples for your inspection.
15. You will be pleased to know that we are already a pioneer in this trade.

Express hope for good future business:

16. We now look forward to receiving further instructions from you.
17. Looking forward to receiving your order...
18. We trust you find our terms attractive enough for placing an immediate order.
19. We hope now you will place an early order with us.

An Indent

Give information about sending the indent:

1. We are enclosing indent No.345 for 150 pairs of nylon socks of different colours and designs.
2. Please find herewith our indent No.123 for 50 Kanchipuram silk saris of various shades and colours.

3. With this letter we are sending you our indent No.689 for 200 handwoven scarves of three colours, namely purple, orange and blue.

Give information regarding quality etc. of goods:

4. Please see to it that the sarees are of high quality with attractive prints.
5. Please make sure that the goods are of high standard in order to make a dent in the sophisticated markets of the West.
6. Kindly ensure that all pieces are of high export quality.
7. While executing this order please see to it \that only colours going with the spring seasons are used.
8. Please note that only autumn colours are to be used for this lot.
9. Please make sure that the goods meet the high standards of quality laid down by the Textile Committee.

Also give instructions regarding transactions:

10. We shall be thankful to you if you could attend to the insurance formalities at your end.
11. You may draw on us through our bankers, the Mercantile Bank, at 60 days' sight.
12. We would like you to get the necessary insurance coverage yourself.
13. Please send the consignment with the freight prepaid.

Reply to Indent

Acknowledge the indent:

1. We thank you for your letter of 5th June, 2000 and your indent No.432.
2. This is to acknowledge with thanks receipt of your letter of 5th June along with your indent No.432.
3. We have received your indent No.432 along with your letter dated June 5, 2000.

Write about the progress of execution of indent:

4. We have booked this indent and have forwarded it to your friend in Singapore.
5. The said indent has been booked and forwarded to your party in Tokyo.
6. We have been very prompt in completing the formalities of booking the indent and have forwarded it to your party in London.

Close the letter like this:

7. We shall shortly be informing you of its acceptance after hearing from him.
8. We shall get in touch with you on hearing about the party's acceptance.
9. We shall, soon, be in a position to advise you on hearing from the party about it's acceptance.
10. Immediately on getting a communication from the party, we shall contact you.

Intimation Regarding Execution of Export Order

Advise about export-despatch:

1. We are pleased to inform you of the despatch of 1000 Madras check cotton shirts shipped today by S.S. Jal Bharat.

2. We are glad to advise you that 1000 kg of Tajmahal tea as per your order No. Ex.P/401 of July 21, 2000 have been despatched by S.S. Jal Vihar which left Bombay for London today.

3. We are pleased to inform you of the despatch of your goods by S.S. Neel Sagar leaving Calcutta today for Singapore.

4. We trust that the goods will reach you in good condition and in time.

5. We hope the consignment reaches you safely.

6. We are pleased to inform you that we have today shipped all the goods as per your order No.421 dated..... under AWB No...... dated....... and our invoice No..... dated.......

Give information about documents:

7. We have surrendered, as agreed, the shipping documents to the Bombay Bank at 60 days sight.

8. We trust you will accept on presentation and take delivery of the shipping documents, viz., Bill of Lading, Invoice and Certificate of Origin.

9. We hope you will find all the documents in order.

10. We enclose the bill of lading and shipping documents and hope you will have no difficulty in disposing of the goods.

11. A copy of our invoice No.... the original of the GSP Form A and packing list are enclosed to your reference.

Close the letter in this way:

12. We look forward to hearing that you have been able to obtain satisfactory prices.

13. We hope to have more opportunities to serve you.

14. We hope this is the beginning of a long fruitful relationship between us.

15. We are sure our efficient service will fetch further business.

16. We look forward to further enquiries and orders from you.

Some more common sentences:

17. We are sending you a consignment of Kashmir shawls by S.S. Delhi Darbar, for sale on our account.

18. We regret that we cannot handle your goods on our own account, but would be willing to take them on a consignment basis.

19. We have, today, sent to you a consignment of 100 bags of Dehra Dun rice by S.S. Jal Bahart for which we enclose bill of lading and our invoice.

20. We are delighted to learn that the consignment of 100 Banarasi silk sarees by S.S. Ratnagiri, has fetched you good price.

21. We enclose the bill of lading for goods which will shortly reach you by S.S. Jal Jawahar that left Bombay on 15th October, 2000.

22. Thank you for your letter of 13th February notifying shipment of 200 boxes of nylon shirts by S.S. White Queen.

23. Thank you for your advice of despatch and the bill of lading for the consignment shipped by S.S. Europa.

24. Thank you for your consignment of 200 high quality ivory pieces which have fetched very good price.

25. We are delighted to learn that the consignment of brown leather shoes sent by S.S. Jal Sagar has brought good profits.

Closing sentences:

26. We enclose the bill of lading alongwith shipping documents and hope you will have no difficulty in the collection of the goods.

27. You will, of course, credit our account with the amount due.

28. We look forward to hearing that you have been able to obtain satisfactory profits.

29. We shall send you the proceeds as soon as the goods are sold.

30. We hope the sales will fetch you good profits and we shall have more business with you.

31. We note your instructions concerning the proceeds of the sale and will credit your account with the net amount due.

32. We enclose our account of sales and shall be glad if you draw on us at two months for the amount due.

33. We hope you will be satisfied with the profit of the present consignment and that you will give us further opportunities to handle your consignments.

Exporter Informing Foreign Customer about Executing Order

Thanking and advising about despatching goods:

1. We thank you for your order of 3rd April and would like to inform you that we lost no time in approaching the manufacturers for immediate supply of your goods.

2. Thank you for your order of 100 Kashmiri paper-mache table lamps. We are pleased to inform you that as a result of our prompt contact with the manufacturer, we have been able to arrange for the shipment of consignment by S.S. Neel Sagar, due to leave Bombay on 8th August, 2000.

3. We are grateful to you for your order No. PL-390 of 2nd March, 2000. As soon as we received it, we got in touch with the manufacturers.

4. We are thankful to you for your order No.345 of July 15, 2000 and have pleasure in informing you that we have contacted the manufacturers for supply of goods required by you.

5. We have been able to ship your goods in time by S.S. Jal Seva, as desired by you.

Give detailed information:

6. The goods despatched are exactly as per your specifications and we are confident that they are upto your satisfaction.

7. We are confident of having provided you with exactly what your customers require.

8. There is, of course, no compromise as far as the quality is concerned. And so, we are sure the goods will become popular with your customers.

Instructions for transactions:

9. We have instructed our bankers, the Llyods Bank, Connaught Place, New Delhi, to surrender the goods against payment of our draft of Rs.75,000/- for which an invoice is enclosed.

10. This is, of course, the standard procedure with us for the new customers.

11. We could relax our payment procedure on receiving satisfactory references.

Expectation for more business:

12. We are confident that our handling of your first order will place our relationship on a firm footing.

13. Now we look forward to obtaining a permanent agency for the supply of brassware.

14. We look forward to many repeat orders, to our mutual benefit.

15. We look forward to establishing a lasting and fruitful relationship with you.

Importer Informing Broker About Imported Goods

Inform the broker about receipt of imported goods:

1. We have just received from a leading British house a consignment of 50 boxes of woollen sweaters to which we request you to devote your very best attention.

2. We have very recently received 100 high quality tape-recorder-cum-transistor sets, from a reputed West German firm and invite your attention to these goods.

3. We have recently received fifty world class, complete cosmetic sets from the famous Gala of London, and we would like to bring this to your notice.

Make arrangements for the sale of goods:

4. The commission offered in this case represents an excellent opportunity for working up a most desirable connection with this firm which is a big exporter of sweaters.

5. If this arrangement works out well, we shall be entrusting you with future orders also.

6. Most likely the initial commission of 5% would be maintained.

7. In our view this is an excellent opportunity for establishing a profitable business connection with this firm which is a large exporter of many makes of blades.

Close the letter in this way:

8. We shall be glad if you avail yourselves of the sampling order immediately.

9. Considering the quality of the goods, we are sure you will avail of the golden opportunity by immediately placing a sample order for these products.

10. We expect you will like to order these quality products for your own market.

11. We are confident of getting your order for these rare items of durable quality.

Importer's Letter Re : Receipt of Imported Goods

Acknowledging the documents:

1. We thank you for your Advice Note and the B.L (Bill of Lading) covering machine tools despatched by S.S. Blue Queen, on August 8, 2000.

2. We are pleased to acknowledge the receipts of your Advice as well as Bill of Lading, covering the woollen garments despatched by S.S. Thames Trader.

3. We are glad to intimate that we have received your Advice and also the B.L. regarding the sports goods that you desired by S.S. Jal Bharat.

Write about goods:

4. The packing of the goods was perfect and they have arrived in sound condition.

5. We are pleased to inform that the consignment of tea packets has reached us in good condition.

6. It is a pleasure for us to report that the 200 pieces of handicraft goods despatched by you on 8th August, 2000, have reached us.

7. We hope to market these goods at the best profitable price.

8. We assure you that all efforts will be made to place the consignment at the best possible price.

Instructions for remitting proceeds:

9. The proceeds will, of course, be forwarded to you without delay.

10. We shall, of course, forward to you the proceeds at the earliest.

11. We shall remit the proceeds at our earliest.

12. We have a reputation for being prompt in clearing the proceeds of the goods.

13. We are prompt in clearing the proceeds of the goods.

Broker's Letter to Importer Re: Sale of Imported Goods

Information about sales:

1. We are pleased to state that the 100 boxes of nylon socks entrusted to us have realised a very attractive sum of Rs.60,000/-.

2. We are happy to inform you that the 50 boxes of imported blades supplied by you on April 8, 2000, have all been sold for a total price of Rs.20,000/-.

3. We are pleased to report that your consignment of tape-recorder-cum-transistor sets has been readily disposed of for Rs.25,000/-.

4. On account of painstaking efforts of our salesmen we have been able to sell off your consignment of woollen garments within a fortnight.

5. Our contacts with the business magnates here have enabled us to dispose of the goods fast at a profit of 30%.

Instructions regarding payment:

6. We enclose for this sum our cheque No.234/B on the Bank of Baroda, Parliament Street, New Delhi.

7. You are, therefore, requested to credit our account with Rs.3000/- due to us as commission.

8. Enclosed please find a cheque for this amount drawn on Bank of Bombay, Church Gate, Bombay.

9. A sum of Rs.5,550/- may kindly be credited to our account as commission.

10. We request you to remit the payment of our commission on this account which works out to Rs.5,050/-.

Prospects for more business:

11. We look forward to receiving further orders from you.
12. We trust your suppliers will be satisfied with the profits of this consignment.
13. We hope this will be the beginning of a long and fruitful relationship between us.

Importer's Letter to Foreign Supplier Re. Payment Procedure

Beginning:

1. We have received your invoice No.LP-340 and agree to accept your draft at 60 days for the amount due.
2. Thank you for your letter of 17th November. We should be glad if you agree to draw on us at 30 days' documents against acceptance.
3. As requested in your letter of 3rd June, 2000, we have instructed our bankers, the Bank of Baroda, Parliament Street, New Delhi, to give a credit of Rs.1,00,000/- in your favour.
4. We regret to inform you that because of certain constraints we have to ask for an extension of one month on the term of your bill dated July 25, 2000
5. I regret that at the moment I cannot meet my commitment in full which is due for payment on 23rd December.

Close:

6. Please let us know whether it will be possible for you to give us the credit terms.
7. Please draw on us for the amount due and attach the shipping documents to your draft.
8. We would like to pay by bill of exchange 60 days after sight and shall appreciate if you agree to this.
9. As requested, we shall arrange to open an irrevocable letter of credit in your favour.
10. Our acknowledgement will be given upon acceptance of the bill at Bank of Baroda's London branch at Strand.

Exporter's Letter to Foreign Buyer Re. Payment Procedure

Beginning:

1. We have favourably considered your letter of 25th May and are pleased to grant the credit terms asked for.
2. As requested in your letter of 5th August, we have drawn on you for the amount of our April account at three months from today.
3. As agreed earlier we have drawn on you for the amount of the invoice enclosed.
4. We enclose our invoice No.385 and, as requested, have drawn on you at 60 days for the amount due.
5. As per our agreement, we have drawn on you at 30 day's sight for the amount of the invoice enclosed.

Close:

6. Kindly accept the draft and return it as soon as you can.

7. Kindly honour our draft when presented by your bankers.

8. As desired by you we can put your account on a documents against acceptance basis.

9. We have asked our bank to part with the shipping documents against payment of our draft.

10. Shipping documents and our draft for acceptance have been passed on to the Punjab National Bank, Parliament Street, New Delhi-110 001.

11. As agreed earlier, we have instructed our bank to surrender the documents against payment of our draft.

12. As soon as the credit is confirmed, we shall ship the consignment.

13. Your terms of payment on D.P. basis are acceptable to us and we have instructed our bankers, accordingly.

Sample Letters
(Exporter's Inquiry from Manufacturer)

Dear Sirs,

We are pleased to inform you that one of our clients in Europe is interested in large-scale purchase of silk skirts.[1] Therefore, we wish to know if you are in a position to supply us adequate quantity of high quality shirts of this material.[6] We are basically interested in fabrics printed with essentially Indian motifs.[10] We need not tell you that a really competitive quotation can mean excellent future prospects to you.[13] Our trial order will convince you of the promising prospects of this deal.[15]

Thanking you,

Yours faithfully,

(Manufacturer's Reply to Exporter)

Dear Sirs,

Thank you for your letter of inquiry dated 4th August, 2000.[2] We have a large production unit and can meet your order for any reasonable delivery date.[10] We are sending herewith a few samples of the same.[13] We hope now you will place an early order with us.[19]

Thanking you,

Yours faithfully,

(An Indent by Exporter to Manufacturer)

Dear Sirs,

We are enclosing Indent No.345 for 150 pairs of nylon socks of different colours and designs.[1] Kindly ensure that the goods are of high standard in order to make a dent in the sophisticated markets of the West.[5] Please send the consignment with the freight prepaid.[13]

With thanks,

Sincerely yours,

(Reply of Manufacturer to Exporter reg. Indent)

Dear Sirs,

We thank you for your letter of 5th June, 2000 and your Indent No.432.[1] We have booked this indent and have forwarded it to your friend in Singapore. We shall shortly be informing you of its acceptance after hearing from him.[7]

With thanks,

Yours faithfully,

(Intimation reg. Execution of Export Order)

Dear Sirs,

We are pleased to inform you of the despatch of 1000 Madras check cotton shirts shipped today by S.S. Jal Bharat.[1] We have surrendered, as agreed, the shipping documents to the Bombay Bank at 60 days' sight.[7] We hope to have more opportunities to serve you.[13]

Thanking you,

Yours faithfully,

(Exporter Informing Foreign Customer about Executing Order)

Dear Sirs,

We thank you for your order of 3rd April and would like to inform you that we lost no time in approaching the manufacturers for immediate supply of your goods. The goods despatched are exactly as per your specifications and we are confident that they are upto your satisfaction.[6] We have instructed our bankers, the Llyods Bank, Connaught Place, New Delhi, to surrender the goods against payment of our draft of Rs.75000/- for which an invoice is enclosed.[9] We are confident that our handling of your first order will place our relationship on a firm footing.[12]

Thanking you,

Yours faithfully,

(Importer Informing Broker about Imported Goods)

Dear Sirs,

We have very recently received 100 high quality tape-recorder-cum-transistor sets from a reputed West German firm and invite your attention to these goods.[2] We expect you will like to order these high quality products for your own market.[10] If this arrangement works out well, we shall be entrusting you with future orders also.[5]

Thanking you,

Yours faithfully,

(Importer's Letter reg. Receipt of Imported Goods)

Dear Sirs,

We thank you for your Advice Note and B.L. covering machine tools despatched by S.S. Blue Queen on August 8, 2000.[1] The packing of the goods was perfect and they have arrived in sound condition.[4] The proceeds will, of course, be forwarded to you without delay.[9]

Thanking you,

Yours faithfully,

(Broker's Letter to Importer reg. Sale of Imported Goods)

Dear Sirs,

We are pleased to state that the 100 boxes of nylon socks entrusted to us have realised a very attractive sum of Rs.60000/-.[1] We enclose for this sum our cheque No.234/B on the Bank of Baroda, Parliament Street, New Delhi.[6] We hope this will be the beginning of a long and fruitful relationship between us.[13]

Thanking you,

Sincerely yours,

(Importer's Letter to Foreign Supplier
reg. Payment Procedure)

Dear Sirs,

As requested in your letter of 3rd June, 2000, we have instructed our bankers the Bank of Baroda, Parliament Street, New Delhi., to give a credit of Rs.100,000/- in your favour.[3] Our acknowledgement will be given upon acceptance of the bill at the Bank of Baroda's London branch at Strand.[10]

With thanks,

Yours faithfully,

(Exporter's Letter to Foreign Buyer
reg. Payment Procedure)

Dear Sirs,

We have favourably considered your letter of 25th May, and are pleased to grant the credit terms asked for.[1] As desired by you, we can put your account on a documents against acceptance basis.[8]

With thanks,

Yours faithfully,

Correspondence with Banks

Nothing moves without money. And in the modern civilization, on account of the growing commercialisation, it has come to acquire paramount importance. The banking industry controls this power in almost every part of the world-backward or modern. Disturbance in this industry throws the economy out of gear. Banking correspondence and its techniques, therefore, occupy a pivotal position in modern business and industry. And so, banking procedures and practices have become a full-time subject in modern education.

Such correspondence should be complete, correct and elegant. Every letter has monetary significance as it gives momentum to financial machinery in one direction or the other. So one cannot afford to be careless in this regard. The letters also call for careful drafting and proper despatching.

Patience, care and a proper grasp of the fundamentals of the subject would enable a correspondent to handle this ticklish part of business activity. Proper educational background coupled with experience goes a long way in making one a good letter writer.

Request to Bank for Overdraft

Seek Permission and give details of required overdraft:

1. We thank you for permitting us to overdraw our account up to Rs.50,000/- in the period from October 15 to December 15, 2000, as discussed yesterday and agreed in the meeting between our Branch Manager, Mr, Bhism Narain Gupta, and your Deputy Manager, Mr. R.K. Gulati,.

2. With reference to our discussion with you on 15th May, we request you to permit us an overdraft on our account to the tune of Rs.75000/- during the period from October 15 to December 15, 2000.

3. As I explained to you earlier, I would be grateful if you could allow me to overdraw my account up to a limit of Rs.73,000/- only between October 15 and December 15, 2000.

4. As per our discussions yesterday, we request you to kindly allow us to overdraw our account (No.12346) up to Rs.75,000/- during the period between 1st July,1999 and 6th October, 1999.

5. Certain financial constraints have compelled us to approach you for a concession to overdraw on our account up to the sum of Rs.1,00,000/- from 3rd January to 4th March, 2000.

Give reasons for requesting overdraft:

6. As already explained we need this facility to meet certain immediate financial requirements on account for our expansion programmes.

7. As explained in the meetings, during this period we have to meet certain heavy expenses for augmenting and updating our stocks.

8. As I have already explained to you I require the additional funds to conduct a publicity campaign immediately.

9. In the event of the special sale campaign, unexpected expenditure may have to be incurred during this period.

10. As we plan to disburse bonus to our employees during this month we require additional funds.

Give assurance for meeting the overdraft:

11. Once the festival season starts I hope to receive considerable amount of funds from my customers.

12. The impact of our expansion will certainly be felt by the end of this period, as large payments are falling due from our clients abroad.

13. By the end of this period we hope to get high returns on our publicity campaign.

14. This facility will enable us to invest the money in the campaigns. We are sure to get the returns in the latter half of aforesaid period.

15. We have good reasons to expect heavy returns within the stipulated period.

Ask if a security is required:

16. As desired by you we can deposit savings certificates worth Rs.50,000/- as security.

17. I have an insurance policy of Rs.50,000/- which I am prepared to deposit as security.

18. We have debentures worth Rs.75,000/- and an insurance policy of an equal amount, which we shall deposit as security.

19. Our past commitments regarding overdraft have always been honoured and hence there is nothing for you to negate our proposal.

20. Ever since the inception of our business we have been depending on our bankers for finance and have a good record in this regard.

Express hope for favourable response:

21. We hope it will not be difficult for you to accede to our request.

22. Hoping for a favourable response.......

23. We shall very much appreciate your sympathetic consideration of this request.

24. Expecting a favourable consideration,

25. We hope for an early sanction of the same.

Providing a Guarantor for Overdraft

Beginning:

1. I note with regret from your letter of 8th June that you are not prepared to allow me an advance against personal surety.

2. I regret to learn from your letter of yesterday that you cannot allow me an overdraft of Rs.50,000/- against personal guarantee as requested by me in our meeting on 8th July, 2000.

3. I have received your letter of 2nd January and am sorry to learn that you are unable to allow me any overdraft against personal guarantee.

4. I regret to learn from your letter of 8th July about your inability to allow me an overdraft of Rs.80,000/- against personal surety.

5. I am sorry to learn from your letter of yesterday that my personal guarantee would not get me the facility of overdraft.

Citing some other guarantee:

6. However, I appreciate your position and as desired by you enclose a letter of guarantee duly signed and stamped from M/s. Suraj Kumar & Sons.

7. As a result, I have now obtained a letter of guarantee from Shri Prem Prakash, duly signed and stamped and submit herewith the same.

8. Therefore, please find enclosed a letter of guarantee from M/s. M.L. Rao, duly signed and stamped.

9. Therefore, I am furnishing a guarantee letter from M/s. Kumar & Sons (P) Ltd., 6, Darayganj, New Delhi.

10. Hence we are enclosing a guarantee letter from M/s. Shiv Kumar & Brothers, 6 Shakti Nagar, New Delhi.

Acceptance of the guarantors:

11. I understand that the guarantors are well known to you.

12. I understand that you know them well and their guarantee is acceptable to you.

13. I am told that the party providing guarantee is your old client.

14. The party proposed as the guarantor is of good repute and must be well known to you.

15. The guarantor is an old firm and must be in your good books.

Requesting for the overdraft:

16. I trust that now you will be prepared to accept the surety offered and finance me to the extent of Rs.50,000 /-.

17. I hope this guarantee is acceptable to you and now you can allow me the overdraft facilities upto Rs.75,000/-.

18. I hope you will find this guarantee acceptable and can allow me the advance I require for this period on your usual terms.

19. Now I hope to get the overdraft to the tune of Rs.1,00,000/- for the said period.

20. Having fulfilled your terms and conditions, we now expect the facility for overdraft to the required amount of Rs.80,000/-.

Request to Bank for Opening Current Account

Request for opening a current account:

1. I have recently moved to Chandigarh and opened a drug store by the above name.

2. This is to request you to open a current account in the name of our firm.

3. Recently we have registered our Garments Export Company in the name 'Ashok Impex (Pvt) Ltd,.

4. Please allow us to open a current account with you in the name of our firm.

5. So, we wish to open a current account with you in the company's name.

Send initial deposit:

6. Enclosed please find the specimen signatures of our Managing Director, who alone is authorised to sign cheques on behalf of the concern.

7. The account will be operated by our Managing Director, Shri Ganga Prasad only, and his specimen signatures are enclosed.

8. As both the partners will sign cheques on behalf of the firm, their specimen signatures are enclosed.

9. A cheque for the amount of Rs.50,000/- drawn on the Canara Bank, Connaught Place, New Delhi is sent herewith to be deposited with the opening of our account.

10. We also send herewith a sum of Rs.50,000/- as our initial deposit.

11. Also, please find enclosed a cheque for Rs.50,000/- with which we wish to open our account.

Request to Bank for Credit

Tell why the credit is required:

1. On account of our steel pipes heavy demand in Iraq our export is increasing at a fast pace and we are not able to finance this trade which has been hitherto depending solely on our capital investment.

2. As we have gone in for an expansion of our glassware business it has put a heavy burden on our resources.

3. A considerable increase in our turnover recently encourages us to install new facilities at our steel rolling plant but we cannot do so within our present means.

4. Having booked heavy orders beyond our expectations, we are finding it difficult to execute and finance them on our account.

5. To meet the increasing demand of plastic goods in the market, we have planned to enlarge our sales network.

6. Therefore, we request you to grant us credit upto 50% of the value of our overseas order of 10th August, on production of the Invoice and Bill of Lading.

7. The new facilities are expected to cost Rs. 5 lakh.

8. So, could you please extend us a loan to the extent of 50% of their expected cost, for a period of six months ?

9. I shall be most grateful if you could grant the credit asked for.

10. I hope the foregoing explanation will enable you to grant the credit requested.

11. I shall be glad if you could see your way to grant me a loan of Rs.75,000/- for a period of nine months.

12. Please let us know your charges for rendering us this services.

13. We would request you to intimate us your charges for performing this service.

Sending Sight Draft to Bank

Send sight draft and related documents:

1. We enclose our sight draft on M/s. India Handicrafts Ltd. of London and attach the Bill of Lading as evidence of our shipment and other documents as listed below:

2. Please find herewith our sight draft on M/s. India Emporium, New York, as well as other documents listed below, including the Bill of Lading supporting its shipment.

3. We are sending herewith our sight draft on M/s. India Sari Centre, Singapore and also the Bill of Lading as evidence of our shipping . Also enclosed are the following documents related to the said transaction.

Instruct to give documents after payment for the draft:

4. Kindly deliver these documents to the party named above against payment of the draft.

5. The payment received from the party may be credited to our account after deducting your commission.

6. The documents may be handed over to the party named above on the payment of the enclosed draft.

7. Please credit our account with the amount received after deducting your commission.

8. You may, please, hand over the documents to the party after they pay for the draft.

9. The payment received for the draft may be credited to our account after deduction of your commission.

Instructions to Bank Abroad

Give details of goods:

1. Today we have despatched by S.S. Jal Moti to the Singapore office of the Shipping Corporation of India, a consignment of 100 silk saris to be held at your disposal.

2. We have to inform you that 100 pieces of 8' x 10' Kashmiri carpets have been despatched by S.S. Jal Sagar which left Bombay on 7th November, 2000 for Hong Kong. This is in execution of the order from M/s. Govind Ramani & Co., Hong Kong.

3. We have today sent a consignemnt of 200 lamb's wools sweaters to the Hong Kong office of India Shipping Company by S.S. Motihar.

4. Shipped on an order from M/s. Fancy Warmwear of your city, this consignment is to be held at your disposal.

5. Please note that we have yesterday despatched 100 packets of ready-made garments to International Traders, Sydney in execution of an order from M/s. Greatway Garments (Pvt) Ltd.,

Tell the status of the party:

6. However, we have very little knowledge about this party.

7. However, it being a foreign party, we know little about them.

8. But we know little about the ordering party.

Tell the bank what to do under the circumstances:

9. Under the circumstances we think it would be rather unwise to surrender the shipping documents against mere acceptance of the Bill of Exchange.

10. Under the circumstances we would not like to surrender the shipping documents just on the acceptance of the Bill of Exchange.

11. We, accordingly, enclose a sight draft on them, together with the Bill of Lading.

12. We are, therefore, sending you a sight draft on them, as also the Bill of Lading.

13. So, we must ask you to obtain payment of all that is due, before you allow them to take possession of the goods.

14. So, kindly insist on full payment of the dues before you part with the goods.

15. So, these goods are to be transferred to the party concerned only after all the dues are settled.

16. You will, of course, debit our account with all necessary expenses.

17. Kindly debit your expenses in this regard to our account.

18. Please surrender the enclosed documents to M/s. Hayward & Co. of London when they accept the enclosed draft.

19. Kindly release the documents only on payment of our sight draft for Rs. 75,000/-.

20. So, kindly obtain acceptance of this draft before handing over the shipping documents.

21. Please present the bill for acceptance and then discount it for the credit of our account.

22. Please present this bill for acceptance of the payment and credit us with the proceeds.

23. As a result, the letter of consent for clearing of goods may be released only on payment of sight draft.

Importer's Letter to Bank Reg. Imported Goods

Beginning:

1. I enclose the accepted bill, drawn on me by M/s. John & James of London and should now be glad to receive the shipping documents.

2. Please accept the following draft for me, pay them and at maturity debit them to my account.

3. Please arrange with your correspondent in London to open a credit in favour of our firm.

4. Please find herewith a draft in my name and credit the amount to my account later on.

5. Kindly instruct your representative in Kathmandu to open a credit in favour of our firm.

Close:

6. Please accept the amount draft for me and debit your charges to my account.

7. Will you please state the amount of your charges for arranging the necessary credits ?

8. Kindly also let us know about your charges for arranging the required credits.

9. After deducting your commission please credit the amount to my account.

10. Please also let us know about your commission charges at an early date.

General Banking Matters

1. We are surprised to learn from your letter of 15th April that M/s. Comfort Shoe Company have refused to accept our draft which was duly advised.

2. We cannot account for M/s. Good Garments Corporation's refusal to accept our draft despite the fact that it was duly advised.

3. Could you please oblige us by presenting the bill again ?

4. Please present the bill once again.

5. If acceptance is again refused, please return the draft to us.

6. In the event of it's being refused again, the bill may kindly be returned to us.

Payment instructions:

7. Please transfer the Rupee equivalent of $ 2000 to James & Jones, Manchester, in favour of Bonny Baby Good Products, London EC-2.

8. This sum represents payment for costs incurred by that firm on our behalf.

Special Instructions:

9. Thank you for advising us of receipt of $ 1000 from the Indian Overseas Bank, on behalf of M/s. Ready Food Exports of London.

10. Kindly credit this sum to our account No.24348.

11. Please let us know after making the necessary transfer.

12. This is to confirm my telephonic message of this morning requesting you to stop payment of cheque No.SB 508352 of 3rd March, 2000 for Rs.1,00,000/-.

13. Please arrange to buy for me the following securities within the price range given below.

14. Should you require a guarantor, Mr. Sunil Kumar of Kumar Enterprises, New Delhi, has kindly consented to act in this capacity.

On dishonouring the cheque:

15. We are surprised to learn that you have dishonoured our cheque No.82453 of the 2nd April for Rs.73,400/- in favour of M/s. Pretty Plastic Products with the remarks 'Funds not sufficient'.

16. And this is despite the fact that we had submitted a local cheque for Rs. 84,000/- for collection nearly two weeks back and there was ample time to credit this sum to our account.

17. So, kindly inform us of your reasons for dishonouring the cheque as it would affect our reputation.

18. We regret to learn that you have dishonoured our cheque No.W 23507 for an amount of Rs. 50,000/-. Since we have good amount in the bank, we fail to understand the reason for this.

19. On our cheque being dishonoured we lose our image in the market. Kindly furnish the reasons at the earliest.

Sample Letters
(Request to Bank for Overdraft)

Dear Sirs,

As I explained to you earlier, I would be grateful if you could allow me to overdraw my account upto a limit of Rs.73,000/- only between October 15 and December 15, 2000.[3] As I have already explained to you I require the additional funds to conduct a publicity campaign immediately.[8] Once the festival season starts, I shall receive considerable amount of funds from my customers.[11] As desired by you we can deposit savings certificates worth Rs.50,00/- as security.[16] We hope it will not be difficult for you to accede to our request.[21]

Thanking you,

Yours faithfully,

(Providing a Guarantor for Overdraft)

Dear Sirs,

I note with regret from your letter of 8th June that you are not prepared to allow me an advance against personal surety.[1] However, I appreciate your position and as desired by you enclose a letter of guarantee from M/s. Suraj Kumar & Sons, duly signed and stamped.[6] I understand that the guarantors are well known to you. I trust that now you will be prepared to accept the surety offered and finance me to the extent of Rs.50,000/-.[16]

With thanks,

Yours faithfully,

(Request to Bank for Opening Current Account)

Dear Sirs,

I have recently moved to Chandigarh and opened a drug store by the above name.[1] Please allow us to open a current account with you in the name of our firm.[4] Also, please find enclosed a cheque for Rs.50000/- with which we wish to open our account.[11]

With thanks,

Yours faithfully,

(Request to Bank for Credit)

Dear Sirs,

On account of our steel pipes heavy demand in Iraq our export is increasing at a fast pace and we are not able to finance this trade which has been hitherto depending solely on our capital investment.[1] Therefore, we request you to grant us credit upto 50% of the value of our overseas order of 10th August on production of the invoice and Bill of Lading.[6] Please let us know your charges for rendering us this service.[12]

Thanking you,

Yours faithfully,

(Sending Sight Draft to Bank)

Dear Sirs,

Please find herewith our sight draft on M/s. India Emporium, New York, as well as other documents listed below including the Bill of Lading supporting its shipment. Please credit our account with the amount received after deducting your commission.[7]

Thanking you,

Yours faithfully,

(Instruction to Bank Abroad)

Dear Sirs,

Today we have despatched by S.S. Jal Moti to the Singapore office of the Shipping Corporation of India, a consignment of 100 silk saris to be held at your disposal.[1] However, we have very little knowledge about this party.[6] We, accordingly, enclose a sight draft on them together with the Bill of Lading.[11]

With thanks,

Yours faithfully,

(Importer's Letter to Bank reg. Imported Goods)

Dear Sirs,

Please arrange with your correspondents in London to open a credit in favour of our firm.[3] Kindly also let us know about your charges for arranging the required credits.[8]

With thanks,

Yours faithfully,

(General Banking Matters)

Dear Sirs,

We are surprised to learn from your letter of 15th April that M/s. Comfort Shoe Company have refused to accept our draft which was duly advised.[1] Could you please oblige us by presenting the bill again.[3]

With thanks,

Yours faithfully,

(On Transferring the Amount)

Dear Sirs,

Please transfer the Rupee equivalent of $2000 to James & Jones, Manchester in favour of Bonny Baby Food Products, London EC-2.[7] This sum represents payment for costs incurred by that firm on our behalf.[8] Please let us know after making the necessary transfer.[11]

Thanking you,

Yours faithfully,

(On Dishonouring the Cheque)

Dear Sirs,

We are surprised to learn that you have dishonoured our cheque No.82453 of the 2nd April for Rs.73,400/- in favour of M/s. Pretty Plastic Products with the remarks "Funds not sufficient".[15] And this is despite the fact that we had submitted a local cheque for Rs.84,000/- for collection nearly two weeks back and there was ample time to credit this sum to our account.[16] So kindly inform us of your reasons for dishonouring the cheque as it would affect our reputation.[17]

Thanking you,

Yours faithfully,

Correspondence with Insurance Companies

In the modern times there are different kinds of Insurance companies which cover a variety of risks. Personal life is covered against accidents and death and businesses are covered against damage, fire, loss, theft etc. In India today there are two different types of Insurance companies-Life Insurance and General Insurance. Under the Life Insurance scheme a person can get himself insured for 20-25 years for a certain amount. During this period he has to pay the Insurance Company a regular instalment which is called premium. At the end of the period he gets the full amount for which he was insured plus some other benefits. In case he dies during this period his nominee gets the full amount before the maturity of the Insurance Policy. However, in the case of General Insurance, goods are covered under various schemes. In case of loss, damage, fire etc., the Insurance Company pays the client the amount for which a particular article was insured. Therefore, practice prevails in all big businesses to take an insurance cover for goods despatched and even for goods stored in godowns and warehouses. At a nominal expenditure, the risk of loss is covered and the trader can rest assured on this account.

However, here we are generally concerned with insurance coverage of articles and goods during their transit from one place to another whether by post office, rail or road, air or sea. Let us examine some such cases.

Request for Insurance of Goods in Transit

Beginning:

1. Please quote your lowest All-Risk rates for shipment of 100 cases of hand-tools to Singapore from Bombay. The invoice value of the consignment is Rs.1,00,000/-.

2. Please hold us covered under insurance for the cosignment referred to below.

3. We shall be glad if you provide cover for 100 boxes of shoes valued at Rs.50,000/- in transit from Bombay to Singapore.

4. We wish to renew the above policy for the same amount and on the same terms as before to cover our assets at our office at No.4, Shastri Road.

5. Will you please arrange to take out an all-risk insurance for us on the following consignment of woollen garments from our factory at the above address to Colombo-100 bags of woollen garments by S.S. Ratnagiri due to leave Madras on 8th August. The invoice value of the consignment is Rs.1,00,000/-.

6. Please let us know at the earliest on what terms and conditions this insurance can be arranged.

7. Please send us the necessary proposal form.

8. We leave the details to you, but wish to have the consignment covered against all risks.

9. The consignment is covered by our open policy No.NB-675554 and we shall be glad to receive your certificate of insurance.

10. We request you to send us the charges from Madras to Colombo for the said insurance

Intimation to Insurance Co. reg. Damage by Fire

Give Information about fire:

1. We regret to inform you that a fire broke out in our godown last night at 11.30 p.m.
2. We are sorry to inform you that last night around 10 o'clock, a large part of our bookshop was gutted by fire.
3. We are sorry to inform you that yesterday afternoon a fire broke out in our godwon at 4 Nehru Road and caused extensive damage to the stocks.
4. We regret to inform you that a fire broke out in our factory premises at Ballabgarh last night at 11.30 p.m. and as the fire brigade reached late nothing could be saved.
5. It seems to have occurred of short circuit in power supply.

Then send the details of the loss estimate:

6. In our rough estimation, the damage is to the extent of Rs.50,000/-.
7. We assess the damage caused by this fire at around Rs.50,000/-.
8. According to our calculations the extent of the damage is about Rs.50,000/-.
9. Having gone through the details, we estimated the demages roughly at Rs. 5,00,000/-

Give further instructions:

10. However, please send your representatives as early as possible to survey the loss.
11. So, please send your assessors at the earliest.
12. Kindly let us know what are the particulars to be furnished for making a claim for the loss.
13. We shall be grateful to you for letting us know the procedure we have to follow for making our claim for compensation.
14. We are ready to produce evidence to enable your agent to estimate the loss.
15. Kindly send your representative to estimate the loss and complete formalities.

Insurance Claim

Inform the loss first:

1. Yesterday night a burglary took place at our house and a number of jewellery articles were stolen.
2. This morning my car No.XYZ 1234 was stolen from the parking lot opposite Regal Cinema, Connaught Circus, New Delhi.
3. This is to report that some time during last night the boot of my car, parked opposite my residence was forced open and certain new spare parts of the car were stolen.
4. I regret to report the theft of my car No.DHC 583 insured with you under the above policy.
5. I regret to report that a fire broke out in my house at the above address last night and extensively damaged one of my bedrooms.

Now give details:

6. The jewellery consisted of a pearl necklace, four gold bangles and a diamond ring. So, the estimate of total loss is around Rs.2,50,000/-.

7. The car, as mentioned in insurance papers, is a sky-blue Maruti 800, of 1995 model. Its registration number is............

8. It is a 1995 model Fiat of blue colour.

9. Our rough estimate of the total damage is around Rs.1,05,000/-.

10. The car is brown 1994 model bearing No............

11. A complaint to this effect has also been lodged with the nearest police station, at Gokhale Marg.

12. We have, of course, immediately informed the police about the burglary.

13. A report of the theft has also been lodged at the nearest police station at Tilak Marg.

14. We have lodged F.I.R with the nearest police station at Sarojini Nagar.

15. An F.I.R. of the theft was immediately lodged with the nearest police station at Bangalow Road.

Write about the claim:

16. Would you please send me a Claim-Form so that I can make a formal claim under the policy.

17. Please let me know how I should proceed for making a claim under my insurance policy.

18. Kindly advise me the claim procedure.

19. Please let us know at the earliest how we should go about making the claim.

20. Please find enclosed the form of claim for the loss of my car............

Request for Reduction in Insurance Rates

Non-acceptance of rates:

1. We regret to state that we are not satisfied with your rate of 15 paise per cent quoted for the insurance of our premises at the above address against fire.

2. We regret to say that your rate of 15 paise per cent for fire insurance of our premises at the address given above is not acceptable to us.

3. We regret to inform you that the rate of 15 paise per cent that you have quoted for insurance of our premises at the address given above against the risk of fire, is on the higher side.

4. We are sorry to state that your insurance charges are not acceptable to us as they are quite high.

5. We are surprised to see your high rates for insurance coverage of my workshop.

Reasons for non-acceptance:

6. There appears to be no justification for this rate as other companies are prepared to cover on identical conditions at 10 paise per cent.

7. We do not think this rate is justified as other companies charge 10 paise per cent for providing insurance cover under the same terms and conditions.

8. This high rate seems to be unjustified because other companies have been charging 10 paise per cent to provide such insurance.

9. As a matter of fact, we still hold policies at 10 paise per cent and it is only our desire to distribute the risk over many companies that prompted us to accept your quotations.

10. We actually have insurance cover at the lower rate, but wish to distribute the risk.

11. We, therefore, request you to cover us to the extent of Rs.1,00,000/- only.

12. In view of your high rates we request you to cover us to the extent of Rs.85,000/- only.

13. However, please note that at this stage we could considerably increase this amount if your rates are reduced to 10 paise per cent.

Tell that reduced rates may fetch more cash amount:

14. Still we would like to point out to you that a reduction in your rate could increase the risk amount to a considerable extent.

15. We shall highly appreciate your final reply to our proposal at your earliest convenience.

16. We would be happy to have your response to our proposal by return of post.

General Insurance Matters

Insurance of goods sent by railway:

1. We shall be despatching 50 bicycles from Faridabad to Bombay by passenger train on 6th March, 2001.

2. The total value of these bicycles is Rs.40,000/-.

3. We wish this consignment to be covered from our godown at the above address to our client's godown in Bombay.

4. Please let us know the total amount of premium payable for insuring the above goods against all risks.

Insurance of goods shipped:

5. Please take out an all-risk policy for five cases of superior cotton shirts valued at Rs.50,000/- and to be shipped to Singapore by S.S. Jal Vihar, sailing from Bombay on 8th February.

6. The shipment is for M/s. Indian Fashion Centre, Singapore.

7. We wish to take out an all-risk policy for 10 cases of woollen garments valued at Rs.1,00,000/-. The consignment is to leave Bombay for Singapore by S.S. Neel Sagar on 10th August.

Information about damaged goods:

8. Please find herewith a copy of the report of the customs authorities regarding medicine bottles worth Rs.5,000/- which we received in a damaged condition.

9. This consignment was sent by our agent in Tokyo, by S.S. Jal Sagar.

10. As the consignment was fully insured against all risks, we request you to please assess our loss and make an early payment.

Renewal of Policy;

11. With reference to policy No.234, which expires on 14th May., 2001 we are enclosing a cheque for Rs.8,810/- for renewing the same for a further period of one year.

12. The value of stock and assets being the same, we have sent the amount as per last year's premium.

13. Please confirm the renewal and send your official receipt by return post.

Sample Letters

(Request for insurance of goods in transit)

Dear Sirs,

Please quote your lowest all-risk rates for shipment of 100 cases of hand tools for Singapore from Bombay. The invoice value of the consignment is Rs.1,00,000/-.[1] Please let us know at the earliest on what terms and conditions this insurance can be arranged.[6]

Thanking you,

Yours faithfully,

(Intimation to Insurance co. reg. Damage by Fire)

Dear Sirs,

We regret to inform you that a fire broke out in our godown last night at 11.30 p.m.[1] In our rough estimation the damage is to the extent of Rs.50,000/-.[6] However, please send your representative as early as possible to survey the loss.[10]

Thanking you,

Yours faithfully,

(Insurance Claim)

Dear Sirs,

This morning my car No.XYZ 1234 was stolen from the parking lot opposite Regal Cinema, Connaught Circus, New Delhi.[2] It is a 1995 model Fiat of blue colour.[8] A complaint to this effect has also been lodged with the nearest police station, at Gokhale Marg.[11] Would you please send me a Claim Form so that I can make claim under the policy.[16]

Thanking you,

Yours faithfully,

(Request for Reduction in Insurance Rates)

Dear Sirs,

We regret to state that we are not satisfied with your rate of 15 paise per cent quoted for the insurance of our premises at the above address against fire.[1] There appears to be no justification for this rate, as other companies are prepared to cover on identical conditions at 10 paise percent.[6] We, therefore, request you to cover us to the extent of Rs.1,00,000/- only.[11] Still we would like to point out to you that as reduction in your rate could increase the risk amount to a considerable extent.[14]

Thanking you,

Yours faithfully,

```
                 (Goods  sent  by  Railway)
Dear Sirs,

We shall be despatching 50 bicylces from Faridabad to Bombay by
passenger train on 6th March, 2001. The total value of these bicycles is
Rs.40,000/-.² We wish this consignment to be covered from our godown at
the above address to our client's godown in Bombay.³ Please let us know
the total amount of premium payable for insuring the above goods against
all risk.⁴

Thanking you,

Yours faithfully,
```

```
                  (Goods  sent  by  Ship)
Dear Sirs,

Please take out an all-risk policy for five cases of superior cotton
shirts valued at Rs.50,000/- to be shipped to Singapore by S.S. Jal Vihar,
sailing from Bombay on 8th February.⁵ The shipment is for M/s. Indian
Fashion Centre, Singapore.⁶

Thanking you,

Yours faithfully,
```

```
                  (Renewal  of  Policy)
Dear Sirs,

With reference to policy No.234 which expires on 14th May, 2001, we are
enclosing a cheque for Rs.8,810/- for renewing the same for a further
period of one year.¹ The value of stock and assets being the same, we have
sent the amount as per last year's premium.¹² Please confirm the renewal
and send your official receipt per return.¹³

Thanking you,

Yours faithfully,
```

Correspondence with the Post Office

Postal network is an important means of communication throughout the world today. While for the common man it means ordinary delivery of letters and parcels, for the bigger establishment its role is much more significant. On account of its efficient delivery system, business establishments have come to depend heavily on it. Normally correspondence with the post office is done on the printed stationery provided by the post office. But at times, there are occasions when general letters have to be written. In such letters necessary details about dates and reference numbers must be mentioned. Here are a few sample letters.

Applying to Post office for V.P.P. Journal

Beginning of the letter:

1. Please note that our daily average of V.P.P. articles has gone up to 50 from 15th November.

2. We take this opportunity to inform you that the number of V.P.P. articles sent by us daily on an average has now reached fifty.

3. This is to inform you that the daily average of our V.P.P. despatches has now reached 50.

Closing of the letter:

4. So, we would request you to issue a special V.P.P. Journal in our name.

5. Kindly, therefore, issue us a special V.P.P. Journal.

6. Therefore, please issue us a special V.P.P. Journal.

7. As our daily average of V.P.P. has now reached 50, we hereby request you to please give us a special V.P.P. Journal.

Applying to Post Office for Business Reply Permit

Reasons for application:

1. In order to expand our business further, we wish to send Reply-Paid envelops to our clients.

2. We wish to extend the facility of Reply-Paid envelopes to our customers in the interest of expanding our business.

3. In the interest of our expanding business we wish to extend the Reply-Paid card facility to our customers.

4. We wish to provide the facility of Reply-Paid envelopes to our customers.

Close of this letter is similar to the above letter of the V.P.P Journal

Complaint reg. Non-receipt of V.P.P. Money/Article

Details of articles/V.P.P. M.O.:

1. We had sent a V.P.P dated 5th May, 2000, for Rs.250/- through your post office to M/s. K.L. Rao and Sons, 14, Mylapore, Madras.

2. On 14th March, 2000, we had sent V.P.P. No.245 for Rs.175/- through your post office to M/s. Book House, Gohkale Road, Dadar, Bombay.

3. We wish to inform you that V.P.P. No.0821 dated 11th January, 2000 for an amount of Rs.410/- had been sent through your post office to M/s. Shastri & Sons, Shivaji Road, Baroda.

Further information;

4. Although more than two months have passed since then we have neither received the payment nor the V.P.P back.

5. Although more than one month has passed, we don't have any information about it. We have neither received the payment nor the article back.

6. It has been more than two months since the V.P.P. was sent, but we have received neither the payment for it nor the article back.

7. It is surprising that we don't have any intimation about it nor did we receive back the amount for the said V.P.P even after a lapse of two months.

8. Could you please let us know the reasons for this at the earliest.

Request for tracing out the goods:

9. We shall appreciate your looking into the matter immediately.

10. So, please find out without any further delay what happened to it.

11. Please, therefore, make immediate inquiries and let us know the position.

Sample Letters

(Applying to post office for V.P.P. Journal)

Dear Sirs,

This is to inform you that the daily average of our V.P.P. despatches has now reached 50.[3] So, we would request you to issue a special V.P.P Journal in our name.[4]

With thanks,

Yours faithfully,

(Applying to post office for business reply permit)

Dear Sir,

We wish to extend the facility of Reply-Paid envelopes to our customers in the interest of expanding our business.[2] Kindly, therefore, issue us a permit for Reply-Paid envelopes.

Thanking you,

Yours faithfully,

(Complaint reg. Non-receipt of V.P.P. Money/Article)

Dear Sir,

We had sent a V.P.P dated 5th May, 2000, for Rs.250/- through your post office to M/s. K.L. Rao, 14 Mylapore, Madras.[1] It is surprising that we don't have any information about it nor did we receive back the amount for the said V.P.P. even after a lapse of two months.[7]

We shall appreciate your looking into the matter immediately.[10]

With thanks,

Yours faithfully,

Personnel Correspondence

The letters dealing with interviews, appointments, termination of services, resignations, requests for testimonials and references etc, are handled by the personnel department of an office. These are, thus, called personnel letters. Like other commercial letters, these are also specialised letters with a definite style and format.

Call for interview

When a post is advertised a number of applications are received in response. A prospective employer cannot call all the applicants. He has to be selective, keeping in view the educational qualifications and experience of the applicants.

However, while inviting the applicants for the interview various important points have to be kept in mind. Normally, certificates and testimonials are asked for. But in certain interview, it becomes desirable to personally study the specimens of the candidate's professional work. So, one may also ask for them in the interview letter.

If more than one candidate is to be invited not all of them should be called at the same time. Keeping in view the average time one would take with a candidate, one can give different times to the candidates. Sometimes the candidates are called on different days. If required, the candidate can also be asked to confirm whether he would attend the interview or not.

It is also desirable to adopt a personal and friendly tone to put the applicant at ease.

Appointment Letters

Normally, in companies two types of appointment letters are issued-provisional and confirmatory. The provisional letters put the candidate on a probation for a certain period. Only after satisfactory completion of the probationary period the employee is confirmed in the job.

Sometimes the terms and conditions of appointment are mentioned in the letter itself and at times separately. Whatever be the case, it should state clearly the salary and other conditions of appointment and also a reference to the duties to be carried out. If the appointment is made verbally at the time of interview, it is desirable that it is confirmed by a letter afterwards.

References and Testimonials

It is advisable that testimonials are obtained directly from the referees, because when they are handed over to the candidates, they normally do not certify unfavourably. However, open testimonials for further use should be issued only in very special cases concerning persons of proven ability over a long period of time. Courtesy demands that before giving any names, prior permission should be obtained from the referees.

If you are writing to obtain a testimonials you should give your particulars in detail. These would enable the referee to identify you and know about the job you are applying for.

It is not legally binding on anyone to give testimonial. But if it is written one should be careful to give authentic information. Otherwise the writer may find himself legally liable either to the applicant, or to the employer if the information is 'optimistically misleading'. As a precaution, such envelopes should be sealed and marked as 'private' or 'confidential'.

Terminating the services

At the time of appointment, an employee is recruited on certain terms and conditions. And so his services can be terminated in accordance with the original agreement. On the other hand he himself can leave the job, fulfilling the conditions initially agreed upon.

Call for Interview

Acknowledge the application and mention the date of interview:

1. Please refer to your application for the post of Sales Engineer. You are requested to call at our office at 11.30 a.m. on 8th October. When you call please ask for the Marketing Manager, Mr. Praveen Kumar.

2. With reference to your application for the post of Private Secretary to our General Manager, please call on the undersigned on Monday, the 24th January, between 10.00 a.m. and 4.00 p.m.

3. In response to your application for the post of Marketing Manager, you are requested to call on our General Manager, Mr. Virendra Walia, on 10th August at 11.00 a.m.

4. In response to your application for the post of an Executive Secretary in our company, you are requested to come for an interview and test on July 5, at 3.00 p.m.

Mention, if testimonials etc. are required:

5. Our Resident Editor, Mr. Gopal Bhandari, has asked me to acknowledge your application dated October 8, 2000 for the post of sub-editor. You are requested to contact his P.A. Mr. Subhash Saxena anytime between 10.00 a.m. and 4.00 p.m. and ask for an appointment with Mr. Bhandari.

6. Please refer to your application dated September, 5 for the post of Store-keeper in our organisation. You are requested to call on our Personal Manager, Mr. Debu Chaudhary at 3.30 p.m. on 10th September.

7. Please bring with you the testimonials and some specimens of your work.

8. Kindly also bring copies of relevant certificates with you.

9. Please bring with you attested copies of your testimonials and a character certificate.

10. Along with your certificates, please also bring at least two testimonials from your former employers.

11. Please confirm either by telephone or through a letter whether you will be able to come.

12. Please note that you will not be entitled to any T.A. or D.A. for attending the aforesaid interview.

13. As per company rules, you will be entitled to one-side second class fare from your town.

Sample Letter

Dear Sir,

Our Resident Editor, Mr. Gopal Bhandari has asked me to acknowledge your application dated October 8, 2000, for the post of sub-editor. You are requested to contact his P.A. Mr. Subhash Saxena anytime between 10.00 a.m. and 4.00 p.m. and ask for an appointment with Mr. Bhandari.[5] Please bring with you the testimonials and some specimens of your work.[7] Please note that you will not be entitled to any T.A or D. A for attending the aforesaid interview.[12]

Thanking you,

Yours faithfully,

Appointment Letters

Starting the letter:

1. Further to your interview with our General Manager, Mr. Kanti Ghosh, I am pleased to appoint you on the post of Sales Engineer in our firm.

2. With reference to your interview held on last Tuesday with our Managing Director, I am pleased to offer you the position of Publicity Officer in our Company.

3. I am pleased to offer you the post of Personal Assistant to our Legal Adviser, Mr. Man Mohan Gupta.

4. This is to confirm the offer we made to you when you called on us on Monday.

5. I am pleased to inform you of your selection for the post of Assistant Manager in our Organisation.

Close:

6. I am writing to confirm the offer we made to you when you called yesterday.

Terms and Conditions:

7. Your duties will be as explained to you at the time of interview, but more particularly you will be directly answerable to the Divisional Manager.

8. Your appointment carries a salary of Rs.7500/- p.m. during the probation period. After the satisfactory completion of this period, we may consider a further raise in the salary.

9. The office hours are 9. 30 a.m. to 6.00 p.m. The atmosphere is pleasant and it offers better prospects for the right candidate.

10. You will be entitled to four week's leave every year.

11. The appointment may be terminated at any time by either side giving two months' notice.

12. The engagement is for one year initially which can be renewed by mutual arrangement for further periods subject to three month's notice on either side.

13. Please confirm immediately your acceptance of this appointment on the terms enclosed and let us know if you can join your duties from the 1st of the next month.

14. Should you decide to accept the appointment, please attend the office at 10.00 a.m on Monday and report to Mr. Prem Kumar.

15. Kindly confirm your acceptance of this offer immediately.

16. Please acknowledge and confirm your acceptance to our offer.

Sample Letter

Dear Sir,

I am pleased to inform you of your selection for the post of Assistant Manager in our organisation.[5] Your duties will be as explained at the time of interview, but more particularly you will be directly answerable to the Divisional Manager.[7] Your appointment carries a salary of Rs.7500/- p.m. during the probation period. After the satisfactory completion of this period, we may consider a further raise in the salary.[8]

You will be entitled to four week's leave every year.[10]

Kindly confirm your acceptance to this offer immediately.[15]

Thanking you,

Yours faithfully,

Provisional Appointment Letter

Dear Sir/Madam,

The management is pleased to appoint you a Steno-Secretary in our company on the following terms and conditions:

1. You will be on probation for a period of three months on the expiry of which your services shall automatically stand terminated unless you are specifically confirmed in writing on or before the date mentioned.

2. Your services can also be terminated at any time during the probationary period without notice.

3. You will be paid a sum of Rs.4,700 p.m. as consolidated salary.

4. You will abide by all the standing orders/rules & regulations of the company as may be in force from time to time which inter-alia provide that:

    (i) You will accept transfer anywhere in India and also to any concern/concerns in any section/plant/deptt./unit under the same ownership/management.

    (ii) You will not engage yourself in any outside work over and above your legitimate work in the company while you are on duty, on holidays or leave.

    (iii) After confirmation, you will retire from services on completion of 55 years of age or after 30 years of service whichever occur earlier, unless the management in its discretion for special reason permit you to continue thereafter.

5. i) In case you absent yourself from duty without prior permission or proper leave, you shall be deemed to have voluntarily abandoned your service.

    ii) If and when the information furnished by you in your application regarding your qualifications, experience, employment and last salary drawn etc. are found incorrect or untrue, you will be terminated from service without any notice or compensation.

6. Your services shall be terminated without notice and without assigning any reason due to loss of confidence, gross negligence, inefficiency of work or any other wilful misconduct on your part.

7. In case you leave/abandon your service during the aforesaid period, fifteen days' salary shall be deducted from your salary or Management reserves the right to recover the same.

If you accept and agree to the above terms and conditions of your appointment, please sign the duplicate copy of this letter of appointment as token of your acceptance.

Thanking you,

Yours faithfully,

Confirmation Letter

Dear Sir/Madam,

The management is pleased to confirm your appointment as Steno-Secretary in our company on the following terms and conditions:

1. You will be paid a sum of Rs.5,800/- (Five Thousand Eight Hundred Only) per month as salary from October 1, 2001.

2. Your services can be terminated by giving one month notice by either side, without assigning any reason whatsoever.

3. You will abide by all the standing orders/rules & regulations of the company as may be in force from time to time.

4. Your services can be transferred to anywhere in India and also to any concern/concerns in any shift/section/plant/deptt./unit under the same ownership/management or on deputation to any other firm.

5. While in the employment of the company you will not engage yourself in any other business, occupation or profession whether part time or full time without the written permission of the company.

6. Your services can be terminated without notice and without assigning any reason due to loss of confidence, gross negligence, inefficiency in work or any other wilful misconduct on your part.

7. You will retire from service in the Company on completion of 58 years of age or after 30 years of service, whichever occurs earlier.

8. In case you absent yourself from duty without prior permission or proper leave, you shall be deemed to have voluntarily abandoned your service.

9. The rights in any order, contracts or jobs secured by you or in any process/discovery/invention or copyright of writings/exposures/recordings etc. made during the course of employment with us shall belong to the Company.

If you accept and agree to the above terms and conditions of your appointment please sign the duplicate copy of this letter of appointment as taken of your acceptance.

Thanking you,

Yours faithfully,

Letters Taking up References

Starting of the letter:

1. Mr. Kamal Kishore has applied to us for the post of Office Superintendent and we would be grateful if you could furnish us with details about his character and abilities.

2. Mr. Nand Lal of your office has applied for a peon's job in our office. He has given your name as referee in this regard.

3. Mr. Kamalakar Shastri has applied for the post of Steno-Secretary in this office and has referred us to you for any information regarding his character and abilities.

4. Mr. Ram Lal, presently employed by you as a sub-editor has applied for a similar job in our paper.

5. Mr. Kamal Kishore, an artist in your organisation has applied for the post of an illustrator in our agency.

6. Mr. Shyam Bihari Aggarwal, a translator in your organisation, has applied for the post of a Senior Translator (from Hindi to English) in our company.

Ask for specific information:

7. We shall be grateful if you could let us know whether you found his work satisfactory.

8. We shall feel obliged if could say how good and fast he is at illustration.

9. In our impression he is a good translator, but we are not sure whether he is capable of taking the full charge of the translation department.

10. He appears to be fluent in both the languages. But we want to be sure if he is the right candidate for this job.

11. We shall be grateful if you would answer the following questions about his character and abilities:

    i. Is he conscientious, intelligent and trustworthy ?

    ii. Is his health satisfactory ?

    iii. Does he get on well with his colleagues ?

    iv. Are his shorthand and typewriting speeds satisfactory ?

    v. Is he efficient in tabulating and statistical work?

    vi. Is his output satisfactory ?

    vii. Is he capable of producing good letters from dictated notes ?

Close:

12. I shall be most grateful for any information you could give me in this regard.

13. We shall, of course, regard as strictly confidential any information you give us.

14. We shall treat as strictly confidential any information you are kind enough to give us.

15. We shall very much appreciate any information you give us. It will, of course, be treated as strictly confidential.

Sample Letter

Dear Sir,

Mr. Shyam Bihari Aggsarwal, a Translator in your organistion has applied for the post of Senior Translator (from Hindi to English) in our company.[6] In our impression he is a good translator, but we are not sure whether he is capable of taking the full charge of the translation department.[9] We shall very much appreciate any information you could give us. It will of course be treated as strictly confidential.[15]

Thanking you,

Yours faithfully,

Replies to Reference Inquiries

Starting of the letter:

1. Please refer to your letter of 8th August inquiring about Mr. Sushil Chandra who has applied in your firm for the post of Assistant.

2. In reply to your inquiry regarding Mr. Arun Mehta, I am pleased to say that he has been employed with me for the past three years and I have found him an intelligent and industrious young man.

3. In response to your inquiry about Mr. Madan Mohan, we are pleased to state that we have always found him trustworthy and reliable.

4. This is in response to your inquiry concerning Mr. Krishna Chandra who has applied for the post of Store Keeper in your office.

5. In response to your inquiry of 9th November, I wish to state that Mr. Anil Kumar is a man of high morals and integrity.

6. I am pleased to be able to reply favourably in response to your inquiry regarding Mr. Kamlakar Shastri.

7. I am replying to your inquiries of 8th April regarding Mr. Ram Lal.

8. Mr. Kishore Bhimani about whom you inquire has been employed by my company for the past 10 years.

9. He came to us from Creative Advertising where he had been employed as a junior artist.

10. This young man was a member of our proof reading department from November 1, 1995 to July 31, 2000.

Refer to Specific Qualities:

11. He is an excellent translator and can translate from Hindi to English and vice versa competently. He is a reliable and steady worker and bears an excellent character.

12. Apart from subbing he has also been doing reporting assisgnments and I am happy to say that he has always had a nose for news.

13. With us he has been mainly doing pasting jobs as we don't have any illustration work. However, I gather that he is a very fine illustrator and the right candidate for the job in your agency.

14. We released him because his work fell below the standards that we normally required. It is, however, possible that he may do well in a different set-up.

15. He was always unpunctual and had a disturbing influence on other members of the staff. With a little self-discipline he might do well but from my own personal experience I cannot recommend him to you.

Close:

16. We feel that he would be an asset to any organisation and wish him all the best.

17. I shall be very sorry to lose his services, but realise that his abilities demand wider scope than I can proivde.

18. I can recommend him to you with every confidence knowing that if you appointed him he would serve you well.

19. So, I am sorry I cannot conscientiously recommend her.

Letters Instituting Domestic Enquiry

Start the letter in this way:

1. It has been reported to the management that you misbehaved with the head clerk Shri Ram Niwas on 3.00 p.m. on 12th October, 2000.

2. Shri R.N. Sharma has made a complaint in writing that on 15.11.00 you refused to obey his orders and threatened him with violence in the presence of other staff.

3. It has been observed that you have been late in coming to office at least eight to ten days every month and also absent yourself many times without proper leave or information.

4. We understand that the file of our client M/s. Indo-Arab trading Co. has been misplaced by you and is not traceable so far.

5. Inspite of many verbal warnings given to you from time to time, you have been grossly negligent and inefficient in your work.

Inform about the time, place and name of the enquiry officer:

6. The management has decided to hold a domestic enquiry into this incident.

7. Shri. Vimal Ahuja, our Personnel Manager, will hold the enquiry on 25.11.2000 in his room on the complaint of Mr. R.N. Sharma.

8. Please note an enquiry into your conduct will be held on 15th March, 2001 in the Committee Room. Shri V.N. Das shall be the Enquiry Officer.

9. You are requested to appear before the Enquiry Officer at the place and time mentioned above.

10. Please note that you should come with all oral and documentary evidence on which you wish to rely for your defence.

11. You will remain suspended pending the completion of enquiry against you.

Impress about the need to attend the Enquiry:

12. It is in your own interest to attend the enquiry at the place and time given.

13. In case you willingly absent yourself from the enquiry, it shall proceed in your absence.

```
┌─────────────────────────────────────────────────────────────┐
│                    Sample Letter                            │
│  Dear Sir,                                                  │
│                                                             │
│  Shri R.N. Sharma has made a complaint in writing that on 15.11.2000 you │
│  refused to obey his orders and threatened him with violence in the │
│  presence of other staff.²                                 │
│                                                             │
│  The management has decided to hold a domestic enquiry into this incident.⁶ │
│  Shri Vimal Ahuja, our Personnel Manager will hold the inquiry on 25.11.2000 │
│  in his room on the complaint of Mr. R.N. Sharma.⁷         │
│                                                             │
│  You are requested to appear before the Enquiry Officer at the place and │
│  time mentioned above.⁹ Please note that you should come with all oral and │
│  documentary evidence on which you wish to rely for your defence.¹⁰ │
│                                                             │
│  You will remain suspended pending the completion of enquiry against you.¹¹ │
│                                                             │
│  Thanking you,                                              │
│                                                             │
│  Yours faithfully,                                         │
└─────────────────────────────────────────────────────────────┘
```

Letter Informing Result of Enquiry

Introduction:

1. Shri R.N. Sharma had complained in writing that you refused to obey his orders and also threatened him with violence in the presence of other staff.

2. An important file of our client M/s. Indo-Arab Trading Co. had been misplaced by you resulting in loss to the firm.

3. You had been verbally warned many times regarding gross negligence and inefficiency in your work.

Mention about the inquiry instituted:

4. The management had decided to institute a domestic enquiry into this incident.

5. It was decided to hold an enquiry into your conduct.

6. Shri Vimal Ahuja, our Personnel Manager was appointed the Enquiry Officer to hold an enquiry on 25.11.2000 in his room.

7. You attended the enquiry at the stipulated time and place and produced oral and documentary evidence in your defence.

8. The Enquiry Officer has held you guilty of the charges levelled against you.

9. In his report the Enquiry Officer has held you guilty of gross misconduct and recommended your dismissal.

10. You have been exonerated of all charges against you.

Now state the action proposed:

11. The management has agreed with the findings of the Enquiry Officer and have decided to terminate your services.

12. However, the management has decided to take a lenient view of your misconduct in view of your excellent past record, and has decided to withhold your annual increment for the next two years.

13. You are hereby warned to be more efficient and careful in your work.

Letters Terminating Employment

Start by giving reasons:

1. As you are aware the re-organisation of our office has become a subject of investigation by a firm of management consultants.

2. I regret to inform you that on account of heavy recession in the business, we have to resort to retrenchment of the staff.

3. Further to the talk you had with Mr. Vijay Vohra yesterday, I regret to inform you that your services will not be required by the company after the end of this month.

4. As you are aware we are compelled to close this branch office on account of unhealthy competition in the market.

5. And so, we shall not be requiring your services anymore.

6. As you know Mr. Vohra had to speak to you on a number of occasions about the unsatisfactory nature of your work and this was coupled with your persistent unpunctuality inspite of several warnings.

7. I regret to inform you that as a result of their recommendations your post as an accounts clerk will shortly become redundant.

Middle part of the letter:

8. I hope you will soon settle down well somewhere else and I extend my best wishes.

9. We have been quite satisfied with your services and hope you will soon find another suitable position.

10. We are sorry that circumstances make it necessary for us to ask you to leave us.

11. You will, of course, be entitled to six months' salary as the retrenchment allowance and the gratuity.

12. You will, of course, be entitled to a redundancy payment. In your case this will account to 1 ½ weeks' pay at the rate prevailing when your services end for each of the five years of your service calculated as follows : 1 ½ x 1000 x 5 namely Rs.7500/-.

Close;

13. We wish you all success for the future.

14. You can collect your dues from the office at any time and can have a relieving certificate also.

15. This letter may also be treated as one month's notice prior to the termination of the services. After the expiry of this notice period, you will automatically cease to be our employee.

Sample Letter

Dear Sir,

As you are aware the re-organisation of our office has become a subject of investigation by a firm of management consultants.[1] I regret to inform you that as a result of their recommendations your post as an accounts clerk will shortly become redundant.[7] You will of course be entitled to a redundancy payment. In your case this will account to 1 ½ weeks' pay at the rate prevailing when your services end for each of the five years of services calculated as follows : 1 ½ x 1000 x 5 namely Rs.7500/-.[12] We wish you all success for the future.[13]

Thanking you,

Yours faithfully,

Vocabulary

A

a.a.r	against all risks
absorb	to take in or cancel out
absorb higher costs	to accept without raising prices
academic	relating to scholarly learning
acceptance of the draft	a bill signed to indicate agreement with its terms
acquainted with	aware of
acquire	gain, get, obtain
adapted	altered to suit, made to fit
adjustment	alteration
adversely affected	made worse
advertising media	forms of publicity
after sight	after acceptance, from date bill is accepted
ahead of schedule	before the appointed time
alive	keen
all essential facts	all the information necessary
all round	general, applying to all goods
alternative	a choice of something different
amalgamate	join together
appreciated	highly valued
appreciative	showing gratitude
approach	method
appropriate	suited to the occasion, suitable
appropriate quarter	concerned people
approval	agreement, consent
arbitration	settlement of disputes by independent persons
assurance	a firm promise, word of honour
assured	satisfied, confident
at maturity	when payment becomes due
at our disposal	for our use
automatic	self-regulating

B

background	upbringing, training
banish	drive away
bankruptcy	inability to pay one's debts

bank transfer	a direct transfer of funds by one bank to another
been let down	been treated badly
bond	a binding agreement
bonded store	warehouse for goods liable to customs duty
brochure	a small book or pamphlet
bulk cargoes	those not packed but loaded loose
buying motive	reason for buying
by instalments	in separate lots
by separate post	by another post

c

car-ferry	transportation of cars over narrow water
cargo capacity	maximum amount that can be carried
carriage paid	sender pays for transport
cash against documents	payment made upon delivery of shipping documents
celebration offer	an offer to mark the occasion
certificate of origin	a document entitling importer to preferential customs duties
check our standing	enquire as to our position in business
c i f Calcutta	price covers charges for insurance and transport to the port named
c i f values	values covering cost, insurance and freight
clearing agent	one who deals with the goods when they arrive
clear your account	to pay the balance owing
come to light	been discovered
commission house	a commission agency organised as a firm or company
commitment	engagement to carry out certain duties, obligation
	accepted or undertaken
compensate	to make some allowance in return
compensation	an amount that makes good the loss
complimentary reference	a few words of praise
compliment slip	a short printed greetings
comply with	carry out, observe
comprehension	the power to understand
concession	a privilege or favour granted, a benefit of some kind

concisely	in a few words
conclusive	final
condolence	sympathy with another's sorrow
confine	restrict
confirm	to state or verify as correct
conform to	to be modelled on
conscientious	careful to do the right thing
consecutive	unbroken, running together
consequently	as a result
consideration	legal term for "something given"
consignee	the one to whom the goods are sent
consignor	the one who sends the goods
constitution	structure
consultant	a professional adviser
conventional	according to custom
conviction	a strong belief
countermanded	cancelled
counter offer	an alternative to another person's offer
counter proposal	an alternative to someone's proposal
couriers	travelling attendants
courteous	polite, considerate
cover	the protection provided by insurance
covering letter	a letter enclosing documents
covenant	a clause in a deed (a sealed contract)
cover note	a document giving temporary insurance cover pending issue of policy
craftsmanship	expert skill in making things
credit standing	financial position
credit-worthy	believed to be financially sound
crockery	earthenware vessels, plates etc.,
current demand	demand at the present time
currently	at the present time
currently advertised	announced at the present time
cut losses	to reduce losses

D

D/A terms	documents against acceptance
deadline	the final date for payment

debenture	a bond bearing interest
defer	delay, postpone
defer payment	to pay later
deferred	delayed
deferred rebate	a discount to be allowed later
deliberately incurred	done intentionally
demolition	breaking up, destruction
demonstrate	to show how the machines work
devaluation	reduction in value
diminished	lessened, reduced
disclaiming	refusing to be responsible for
discount bills	to obtain payment on bills of exchange before the due date at a figure below face value
discretion	freedom of action
dispel any suspicion	to remove doubt
dispense with	to do without
dispose of the consignment	sell the goods
dispute	to contest, oppose
distasteful	unpleasant
domiciled in London	marked as payable in London
D/P terms	documents against payment
draft	a bill of exchange before (or requiring) acceptance
drawee	the person on whom a bill of exchange is drawn
drawer (of a cheque)	the party making the payment
draw on us	send a draft bill of exchange for acceptance
duplicate	an exact copy
durable	long lasting

E

effectively	successfully, with good results
elaborate	complicated
endorse	sign on the back
en route for	on the way to
ensures	secures, makes certain
entail	make necessary
enterprise	activities
establish	set up

esteem	good opinion
exaggerate	overstate
exchange control	official controls in the foreign exchange market
executives	management staff
express consent	permission clearly stated
extensive	wide ranging, considerable
extinguisher	an appliance for putting out fires

F

Factor	one of a number of causes, an agent who deals in his own name & has possession of the goods he is required to sell
favourable comment	a few words of praise
firm conditions	a condition that cannot be varied
firm order	a definite order
first priority	attention before all else
flexible	capable of adjustment
f o r values	values cover cost of placing goods on board.
f o r Kanpur	price covers all charges to Kanpur including loading on to train
formalities	usual or established practices of transacting business
forthcoming	available, ready for collection, about to be held
forwarding agents	agents who arrange for transportation of goods
fragile	easily broken
freight	the charge made for transporting goods
freight rates	transport charges

G

generous	unselfish
gone astray	been lost in transit
gratified	pleased
grossly	very much, considerably
gross proceeds	taking before deduction of expenses
grudge	ill will
guaranteed fast colour	guaranteed note to fade
guarantor	on who agrees to answer for another's debts

H

habitual	customary
hardware	articles of iron, copper etc.,
hold our own	maintain our position in the market
honour cheques	to accept and pay out on cheques
honoured	paid when due
household effects	furniture, etc.,

I

identical	the very same
immaterial	of no importance
inadequate	insufficient
incur	to be responsible for
indent	to order goods (especially from abroad); an order especially from abroad
indispensable	absolutely necessary
individual items	items of one kind only
individually examined	each inspected separately
inducement to buy	reason for buying
inflation	a rise in the general level of prices
in full settlement	in complete discharge of the debt
initial cover	the value insured at the beginning
initially	at the beginning
initial publicity	advertising in the early stages
in proportion to	according to
insertions	separate inclusions
inspire	to bring influence to bear
inspire customer confidence	encourage a feeling of security
installation	act of putting apparatus in position
insulation	covering used to retain heat
insurance cover	protection from loss
in the field	as an outside representative
in the long run	in the end, eventually
intimate	close
in triplicate	three copies required
intrusion	an unwelcome act
investigation	a detailed enquiry
irrespective of their	apart from their total worth aggregate value

irrevocable	cannot be altered or cancelled
irrevocable credit	a credit that cannot be cancelled without the exporter's consent
irritable	easily annoyed

J

Justify	prove to be right

L

lag behind	to follow slowly
laid professionally	laid by an expert
let them down	failed in our duty
level headed	having sound common sense
liberal	generous, plentiful
limp	not stiff
lines	items
linguist	a person skilled in foreign languages
liquidator	an official appointed to conduct the proceedings for closing down a business
load factor	the number of seats occupied

M

maintenance	upkeep, support
manuscript	a document written by hand
maritime	relating to sea
mass produced	made in large quantities
may not materialize	may not be fulfilled
media	methods of advertising
merchandise	articles of commerce
merchandising	trading
minimum	smallest amount
modify	alter, reorganize
moisture	dampness
more competitive	less expensive
mutual arrangement	both parties in agreement

N

negotiable security	a document representing money, which transfers a secure title to a person who takes it honestly
nominal	small, inconsiderable
normally	usually
notary public	usually a solicitor specially authorized to witness deeds and other important documents
notify	inform, to make known

O

obsolescent	becoming out of date
obsolete	no longer used, out of date
on account	in part payment
on approval	for inspection and return if not wanted
on a sliding scale	varying with the quantity bought
on consignment	for sale on exporter's behalf
on time	punctually
open account terms	credit terms with periodic settlements
opportunity	a good chance
option	the right to accept or refuse
oral notification	a verbal message
outstanding	remaining unpaid
outstanding balance	the amount still owing
overall cost	total cost
overdraft	an amount withdrawn in excess of balance held
overdrawn	withdrawn in excess of balance available
overdue	remaining unpaid, in arrears
overhead	the general expenses of a business
oversight	mistake, omission
over trading	trading especially buying on credit, beyond one's means

P

passing away	death
passing phase	a temporary state of affairs
payment on account	part payment
payments on invoice	payment due as invoices are presented
periodical	issued at regular intervals

Ph. D. degree	the degree of Doctorate of Philosophy
pilferage	small thefts
post retirement	after retirement
precaution	a protective step taken in advance
preface	introductory statement placed in a book
preliminary	introductory
preliminary examination	a general first examination
preliminary negotiations	earlier discussions as to terms
premium	the payment made for insurance
prestige	influence, reputation
prior to	before
proceedings	going out, going ahead
proforma invoice	an invoice sent for information only
prolonged	lasting a long time
promissory note	a signed promise to pay stated sum of money on a certain date
promote	help to increase
prompted	encouraged, persuaded
properties	houses or other buildings
property	premises
proposal form	a written request for insurance cover
prospect	expectation
prospective	expected, hoped for
prospective customer	person who may be expected to buy
prospective employer	the possible future employer
prospects	chances of success
provision	a term or condition in an agreement
provisionally	temporarily, liable to be revised
provisional reservation	subject to confirmation
push your business	engage in energetic selling
push your products	use active selling methods

Q

Quickly spotted	promptly noticed

R

range	representative collection
rash statement	a statement made recklessly

read between the lines	to gather the true meaning
ready sale	a quick sale
real property	land and buildings
reassuring	creating confidence
rebate	a refund, an allowance
reciprocate	to return a similar service or favour
recur	occur again, are repeated
rediscounting	to discount a bill is to obtain payment for it before the due date, at a figure below face value
redundant	surplus to requirements
references	names of persons who may be referred to
reference sample	a piece taken from the cloth supplied
reflected	included, covered by
reject	refuse
rejection	refusal to accept
relative importance	importance in relation to one another
relocated	transferred to other positions
reluctantly	with regret
reluctantly compelled	forced unwillingly
remit	to send money
remittance	a payment (or sum of money) sent
remunerative	profitable
repeat order	successive order for similar goods
representative selection	a selection covering all types
reputable	of good standing or reputation
requisites	things needed
resent	take offence at
reservation fee	the charge for booking a seat
resort to	to turn to, to engage in
resources	financial position or means
respectively	relating to each in turn
restraint	reserve, free from exaggeration, careful control
revealed	showed, disclosed
revocable	can be altered or cancelled
rid yourself	free yourself
round off	finish off neatly
routine request	requests of an everyday kind

S

sales promotion programmes	schemes for increasing sales
sales talk	complimentary references to the goods
salvage	items that can be recovered
scheduled	listed
searching enquiries	a thorough investigation
security	bonds, certificates or other property pledged to cover a debt
selling point	a benefit claimed for a product
serge	a strong twilled (i.e., diagonally lined) cloth
settlement	payment, completion by payment
sight draft	a bill of exchange payable at a fixed time from acceptance or immediately upon acceptance
sixty days' sight	for payment within sixty days of acceptance
sliding scale	varying with quantity
smallest of margins	a very small profit
sole	exclusive, the one and only
sole charge	in complete control
sole representatives	the only agents
special concession	special discounts or other advantages
specialist	a person devoted to one branch of an occupation
specification	a detailed description of material used
standard goods	goods not made especially to order
standardized	made to the same size and pattern
standing	status, established reputation
standing credit	a credit of fixed amount
standing order	an order to make certain payments at stated times
statistician	a person skilled in statistics or the study of facts
stenciling	typing on special paper to produce a master for duplicating
stereo	three dimensional
subject to	reduced by
substantial	considerable in amount
substitutes	goods that take the place of others
supersede	take the place of something else

supplementary	additional
syndicates	groups formed for a common purpose

T

tabulate	arrange in a list
tampered with	improperly interfered with
tapped	used for drawing water
tariff	a list of charges
tenor of a draft	the period for which a bill of exchange is drawn
territory	region or country
testimony	evidence
30 d/s	30 days after sight i.e. after acceptance of the bill
3% one month	subject to a deduction of 3% if paid within one month
time basis	charged according to time taken
to have recourse	to take legal
to law	action
to realize on our assets	to sell assets in order to raise cash
to the point	relating to the matter dealt with
trade reference	names of traders who may be referred to
transit	conveyance
transact	conduct, carry on
transit shed	a shed through which goods pass
trends	general tendencies
tribute	expression of regard or appreciation
turnover	total sales
typing pool	a centralized typing system

U

ultimately	finally
undertaking	a promise
universally acknowledged	accepted by everyone
unrivalled	without equal, second to none
unsolicited	not asked for
unqualified	clear, complete

V

valid	hold good, legally binding or in order
velveteens	imitation velvet fabrics
venture	an undertaking to which risk is attached, the voyage and its risks
verify the claims	to prove the truth of statements made
vital	essential
voluntarily	of one's own free will
vulgarize	make common or coarse

W

waive	forego, go without
well found	based on sound reasons
without notice	no previous advice is necessary
without question	without raising any objection
with restraint	without exaggeration
working capital	the capital needed to keep a business running
worn threadbare	become dull and wearisome

The Funny Side of ENGLISH

—*O. Abooty*

A read-n-laugh manual to the English language

The **Funny Side of English** takes you on a pleasure trip through the English language. Besides being an international language, English is also a funny and crazy tongue—which this book on recreational English amply proves.

Interesting aspects about the language are unravelled across every chapter. The alphabetical chapters—from *ABC Language to Words Worth Reviving*—will open a world of amazing and amusing English. An absolute engrosser, you will find this a hard-to-put-down book, finishing it at one sitting.

Discover:

❖ Amusing words U'll trip over pronouncing! ❖ Queer words that read the same—both ways! ❖ Hilarious words U can use (or misuse) both ways! ❖ Comic words that are pregnant—with other words! ❖ Quixotic words that mean what they do—and also the opposite! ❖ The crazy world of Irish Bulls, malapropism and Spoonerism! ❖ How to abuse friends—without using swear words! ❖ How punctuation marks can kill (or save) people! ❖ Limericks (including DIRTY ones)! ❖ Fun with puns and much more...

Demy size, Pages: 232
Price: Rs. 80/- • Postage: Rs. 10/-

2000 English Phrases & Sentences
for all situations

—*Colonel Rajeev Mongia*

Improve your written & spoken English

The 2,000 phrases and sentences in this book highlight the rich tapestry of expressions in the English language. Many words and phrases have intriguing meanings that may not be apparent or register at first glance. Some words have contrasting meanings in different situations. Yet others are just the opposite of what the word or sentence seems to suggest!

The book is categorised into 12 segments that classify sentences into various types. This facilitates the reader's search for the correct sentence in specific scenarios and the book can be used as a reference guide to find the right sentence, much like a dictionary used for words.

2000 English Phrases and Sentences will enhance the written and spoken English of the readers. Besides, the book will be of immense help to almost everyone from all walks of life, including schoolchildren, college students, parents, teachers and various other professionals.

Big Size • Pages: 128
Price: Rs. 80/- • Postage: Rs. 15/-

Official Notings & Draftings (टिप्पणियां एवं प्रारूप-लेखन)

—*Dr. Shiv Narayan Chaturvedi*

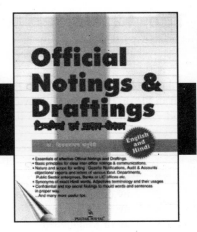

This authoritative book has been a sincere effort of the author who worked for 23 years in the Hindi Department of the Lal Bahadur Shastri Administrative Academy, Mussoorie. Hindi is both the National and the official language of India since independence. Hindi is the mother tongue of the majority—approximately, 450 million Indians. Ever since Hindi gained the status of the official language, the moral responsibility of making the language acceptable in perfect administrative form has gradually increased. For the growth, development and expansion of Hindi, this book—'*Official Notings and Draftings*' is a positive endeavour.

For official purposes, Governmental officials and employees are deeply enamoured of English in official transactions and failed to accept Hindi seriously. It is because of a lack of confidence to use proper words or sentences in Hindi.

This book would enlighten the readers about the fact that each official English expression has an Hindi equivalent to it. It would be a genuine effort to promote the status of Hindi as the official language of the country.

Official Notings and Draftings are meant for those (particularly for English speaking individuals) who are in the central or state government offices, industrial houses, private establishments, banks or railways or in L.I.C., etc.

Being an administrator, or a Section officer/Supervisor, or a Clerk or an Assistant, one must keep in mind that the skill in official procedure, especially in noting, drafting or in communication is an art—that one must master.

And this book gives the reader an insight into those valuable techniques to structure the official language.

Salient features: • *Gazette Notifications* • *Administrative Notings* • *Accounts & Audit Notings* • *Audit Objections* • *Draft Telegrams* • *Synonyms of Secret Reports* • *Adjective Terminology*

Big Size • Pages: 240
Price: Rs. 150/- • Postage: Rs. 15/-

The 12 Universal Laws of Success

—Herbert Harris
Time Magazine Columnist

THE
12
UNIVERSAL
LAWS OF
SUCCESS

Herbert Harris
Time Magazine columnist

This book is a valuable guide to the young persons who are just starting out in life on their own. It provides valuable techniques, knowledge and understanding which will help them avoid pitfalls that always confront novices.

The 12 Universal Laws of Success are:—

1. Law of Thought
2. Law of Change
3. Law of Vision
4. Law of Command
5. Law of Magnetism
6. Law of Focus
7. Law of Action
8. Law of Value
9. Law of Relationships
10. Law of Supply
11. Law of Persistence
12. Law of Truth

Follow them and become successful.

Demy Size • Pages: 192
Price: Rs. 195/-
Postage: Rs. 15/-

Boost Your Brain-Power

—Dr G Francis Xavier, PhD

Powerful techniques to develop super brainpower
for successful living

Do you have an irresistible desire to accomplish something great and outstanding in life? Do you have a passion to develop Extraordinary Memory, Increased IQ, Imagination, Creativity and Visualisation? Do you wish to lead a happy, stress-free life with vibrant health? To achieve all this, you need to enhance the power of your brain, which is the master organ in the body.

Boost your Brainpower shows you the way by offering a variety of time-tested and proven techniques based on the ancient wisdom of the East, combined with practical modern research findings of the West, which include:

❖ Proper food, nutrition and supplements
❖ Exercises, both physical and mental
❖ Yoga, pranayama and meditation
❖ Boosting brainpower via puzzles, riddles and magic squares.

This is an invaluable book for all those who wish to lead a happy, enriched and successful life.

Demy Size • Pages: 144
Price: Rs. 96/-
Postage: Rs. 15/-

Analytical Writing & Essays for Admission to Foreign Universities

—*M.J. Ashok*

PASSPORT TO PROGRESS...

One of the most important criteria for being successful in securing admission to top ranking and reputed Universities abroad, especially in the United States, is the high level of scores obtained in international tests such as GMAT®, GRE®, TOEFL®, etc.

These tests include the all-important component of analytical writing tasks on given issues. These apart, prospective students are also required to pen excellent essays on specific topics chosen by the Universities concerned. It is through a critical appraisal of these essays that the selection committee of the concerned College or University is able to effectively gauge the applicants and gain valuable insight into their academic standing and intellectual prowess.

This book attempts to deeply familiarise the student with the art and skills involved in penning excellent essays by exposing him to a wide variety of Model Essays on diverse topics, apart from Model Responses to a wide spectrum of Analytical Issues with special reference to the requirements of the International Tests mentioned above.

Each section begins with an 'Introduction' which outlines the precise writing strategies to be adopted for that particular task, followed by a collection of Model Responses.

Big Size • Pages: 169
Price: Rs. 125/- • Postage: Rs. 15/-

Winning Résumé

—Jayant Neogy

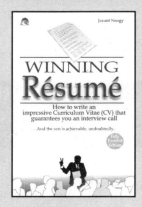

How to write an impressive Curriculum Vitae (CV) that guarantees you an interview call ...And the rest is achievable, undoubtedly.

Your résumé is your first introduction to the employer who has never seen you before. You need to give it the best shot to make the first winning move. The book 'Winning Résumé' fulfils this long-felt need for a contemporary guide on résumé writing that is in line with the expectations of global employers in this Information Technology driven age. The book breaks away from the traditional world of sequential cataloguing of degrees and job histories. Instead, it provides candidates seeking new jobs or job changes with contemporary techniques to fulfil a difficult task, to produce polished, subtle and refined advertisement-copy about their own selves.

This book is the result of an extensive research, practical experience and deep insight. There are practical guidelines for crafting a winning résumé that will stand out amongst a thousand others. Key points are highlighted throughout the book by using bold text on the left side of paragraphs; useful 'tips' are identified by figures of a wise owl. To point out errors and grave mistakes in résumés 'traps' are identified by figures of skull and crossbones. After going through the book the readers will get a thorough understanding of the changes in philosophy and techniques that have revolutionised presentation of curriculum vitae. It is a sure-shot for success in one's pursuit of an illustrious career.

Demy Size • Pages: 136
Price: Rs. 96/-
Postage: Rs. 15/-

Sure Success in Interviews

—Jayant Neogy

The most comprehensive one-source guide for succeeding in interviews.

This book's contents are far richer and deeper than other books on the subject. No contemporary book in the Indian market covers topics such as SWOT analysis, portfolio preparation, wardrobe tips, body language and interview preparation techniques that use question-and-answer sessions with analysis of top answers.

An exhaustive data bank of frequently asked questions and model answers ensures you hold an advantage over other candidates. Finally, there's a bonus section containing tips on good résumé writing practices.

Sure Success in Interviews is a truly comprehensive, one-source guide that will turn you into a professional performer at any interview.

This book enables you to: • How to write a winning résumé • Practical hints to overcome nervousness & boost confidence • SWOT (Strengths, Weaknesses, Opportunities & Threats) analysis • Portfolio preparation • Tips on wardrobe & self-grooming • Understanding body language • Interview preparation techniques through Q&A sessions • The art of successful follow-up.

Demy Size • Pages: 156
Price: Rs. 96/-
Postage: Rs. 15/-

Words & Phrases that carry Uncommon Meanings

—Dr. A.P. Sharma

The book aims to display uncommon expressions that look common but are uncommon in usage and meaning. The uncommon expressions are interwoven within the conversations fitted into suitable situations. Dialogues containing common and uncommon expressions, phrases and idioms are developed in a most fascinating style displaying a rich vocabulary and appropriate language that provides a modern touch. In this respect, the reader will have a face to face chance to experience varied and trying situations during different sets of conversations.

The book not only provides new vistas of vision as regards learning how to converse with the people, but also extends before the reader new sets of situations knitted in dialogues enabling one to enrich his/her linguistic capabilities.

Pages: 136
Price: Rs. 50/-
Postage: Rs. 15/-

Improve Your WORD POWER
A concise way to increase your word power

—Clifford Sawhney

English is a unique language which has innumerable great poets and authors from the past as well as the present, who have contributed profusely to its rich heritage. Nonetheless, we cannot ignore the complexities of the English language which sometimes perplex a reader or even a scholar of this language.

Improve Your Word Power by Clifford Sawhney simplifies all these complexities of the language by providing answers to the many nagging grammatical queries, syntax, style, choice of words, spellings, etc. This book serves as a complete guide and elaborately explains the different usages of nouns, adjectives, adverbs, phrases, proverbs and so on. Hence, it will undoubtedly serve as a bible for both the lovers and wizards of English language.

Pages: 232
Price: Rs. 80/-
Postage: Rs. 15/-

Talk the way Americans do!

—Joseph Melillo and
Edward M. Melillo, J.D.

Over 5000 entries of American Slang
terms, words & phrases to enrich
your colloquial word power

Here are over 5,000 American slang terms at your fingertips. A book that is geared for everyone, whether young or old, foreign or domestic. It's fun to read and the simplest to understand. Your curiosity will have you flipping through the pages. You may not want to put it down. In the end, you will know a lot more, and understand much better, what in carnation is read or said.

Demy Size • Pages: 384
Price: Rs. 196/- • Postage: Rs. 15/-

Dictionary of Modern Phrases with Meanings & Usage

—Joel Lyall

Arranged in Alphabetical Order

The beauty of any language lies in the appropriate usage of a word or phrase. English, too, has its norms and nuances, and one should know the exact meaning and implication of each word. Many words and phrases have intriguing meanings that may not be apparent at first glance.

This is a unique book of its kind, making its appearance in India for the first time. It is a diligent compilation of modern phrases currently in use the world over. The illustrative examples make understanding easy.

This book of modern phrases will help you hone up your grasp and command over the language and pack a punch in your speech and writing.

A must for all those who wish to improve their English and communication skill.

Pages: 208
Price: Rs. 80/-
Postage: Rs. 15/-

Sentence Correction for admission to Foreign Universities

—A.P. Sharma

GMAT, GRE & TOEFL

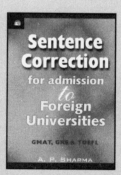

- ✓ This booklet is intended to teach how to reduce the errors that occur in the Sentence Correction Test for Admission to Foreign Universities.

- ✓ It also teaches us how to locate the various types of errors in sentences.

- ✓ The basic rules of Grammar have been explained briefly and systematically.

- ✓ The examples and exercises given in this booklet will make you familiar with the different types of questions and provide you with sufficient practice to use the different techniques for answering each type of question.

- ✓ There is also a practice test to evaluate your progress and make you perfect.

Pages: 168
Price: Rs. 60/-
Postage: Rs. 15/-